The South in the
History of the Nation

The South in the History of the Nation

A Reader

VOLUME TWO: FROM RECONSTRUCTION

Edited by

William A. Link
University of North Carolina at Greensboro

and

Marjorie Spruill Wheeler
University of Southern Mississippi

BEDFORD/ST. MARTIN'S   BOSTON ❧ NEW YORK

For Bedford/St. Martin's

History Editor: Katherine E. Kurzman
Developmental Editor: Ellen Kuhl
Production Editor: Lori Chong Roncka
Production Supervisor: Catherine Hetmansky
Marketing Manager: Charles Cavaliere
Editorial Assistant: Molly Kalkstein
Production Assistant: Helaine Denenberg
Copyeditor: Ara Salibian
Text Design: Geri Davis, The Davis Group Inc.
Cover Design: Diana Coe
Cover Art: Marion Post Wolcott, *Negro Man Climbing Stairs of Movie Theater, Belzoni, Mississippi,* 1939. Courtesy of Linda Wolcott-Moore Fine Art Photography.
Composition: ComCom, an RR Donnelley & Sons Company
Printing and Binding: Haddon Craftsmen, Inc.

President: Charles H. Christensen
Editorial Director: Joan E. Feinberg
Director of Editing, Design, and Production: Marcia Cohen
Managing Editor: Elizabeth M. Schaaf

Library of Congress Catalog Card Number: 98–87545

For information, write: Bedford/St. Martin's, 75 Arlington Street, Boston, MA 02116 (617-426-7440)

ISBN: 0–312–13357–X (Volume One)
      0–312–15787–8 (Volume Two)

PREFACE

This book is intended for use in the U.S. history survey course, but a quick perusal of its contents will reveal that it is not a typical reader. Like most of the available survey readers, *The South in the History of the Nation* is organized by topics that most instructors cover, from early encounters between Europeans and Native Americans to social changes in our own time. The readings are split between two volumes, which overlap at the Civil War and Reconstruction.

In many respects, though, this is a very different book. To help students become engaged more fully with the study of American history, we have tried to place it into a more familiar, accessible context. In every chapter, readings relate local and regional developments to themes of national importance, showing that the historical forces that propelled events such as colonial development, Jacksonian democracy, Progressivism, and the New Deal had unique manifestations in the South. Yet these developments, and others, were part of a larger national picture, affecting all Americans in one way or another.

While these two volumes can easily be used in courses about the South, we have designed them primarily for American history survey courses. The reader will be especially interesting to students and instructors in the South, as it "brings home" national themes and issues, but it is intended to be helpful to students and teachers in any part of the nation who are interested in regionalism in American history. Each of the two volumes contains fifteen chapters, organized around topics that are standard fare in American history courses all across the country. Brief chapter introductions provide context for the regional documents and connect the chapter topic to larger themes in American history. Exercises (under the heading *As you read*) at the end of the introductions prepare students to read the documents actively. Each document is preceded by a headnote that provides background on the source and its relevance to the chapter topic. And each chapter concludes with a brief list of secondary sources in which students can find further information.

The primary source materials in *The South in the History of the Nation* are, we believe, unique in other respects. We have aimed for balance and ease of use by instructors and students throughout both volumes. The readings include social and political history, and they reflect diverse voices—black and white, Native and European, male and female, rich and poor—that mirror our diverse national history. Finally, we believe these documents are eminently readable and should prove exciting as well as informative to students, providing the basis for meaningful and spirited class discussions.

Intentionally, we have used a broad conception of "the South." We include the eleven states that seceded from the Union in 1860–61 and formed the Confederacy: Virginia, North Carolina, South Carolina, Georgia, Florida, Alabama, Mississippi, Louisiana, Tennessee, Arkansas, and Texas. Although Texas was as much western as southern, we believe that it offers a rich study of the blending of regional characteristics. We also include border states that could be considered "southern" but did not secede, such as Maryland and Kentucky. Documents from these thirteen states together represent the diversity of the region, illustrating the different experiences encountered within the South while collectively reflecting the broader national experience.

Founded on the novel concept that regional materials can aid the teaching of a national history, *The South in the History of the Nation* required an unusual amount of planning and careful organization. As editors, we quickly became conscious of creating a new kind of reader. We restructured the book several times and tried out materials on our own students, receiving useful feedback. We conferred extensively with the editors at Bedford/St. Martin's on many different occasions, and only after considerable discussion did we settle on a format for presenting these regional materials that, we believe, will be very helpful in the teaching of American history.

Acknowledgments

The successful completion of this book depended on the support and advice of a large number of people. We thank graduate student assistants Jason Dawsey of the University of Southern Mississippi (USM), and Chris Patterson and Brett Rumble of the University of North Carolina at Greensboro (UNCG), who assisted in locating the documents for the book and shared our enthusiasm about the project. Lori Wright and Christine R. Flood of UNCG and Sheila Smith of USM were unfailingly helpful through several years. While Scott Spruill Wheeler contributed as a research assistant, Josie M. Link helped with last-minute copyediting.

Historians Ed Ayers, William A. Blair, Emily Clark, Karen Cox, Leesha Faulkner, Glenda Gilmore, Steve Hochman, Karen Leatham, Jon Sensbach, James "Pat" Smith, and Lisa Tolbert all contributed ideas. UNCG archivist Betty Carter and USM's Yvonne Arnold provided materials on short notice. We would also like to thank the University of Southern Mississippi and the University of North Carolina at Greensboro for various forms of institutional support for the project. We are particularly grateful to USM history department chair Orazio Ciccarelli; former UNCG history department head Steven F. Lawson; UNCG dean Walter H. Beale; former USM vice president for academic affairs Karen Yarbrough; UNCG provost Ed Uprichard; USM president Horace Fleming; and UNCG chancellor Pat Sullivan.

Without the patience, prodding, and constant support of Bedford/St. Martin's and its very talented editorial and production staff, this project would never have reached fruition. The original conception of this book came from conversations with Chuck Christensen and Joan Feinberg, and their continuing enthusiasm sustained us over the course of several years. Niels Aaboe and Katherine Kurzman also helped in the development and completion of the book. Ellen Kuhl contributed unflagging support, dogged persistence, and frequent editorial interventions that were instrumental in the project's completion. We are also very grateful to Lori Chong Roncka for overseeing the production of the final book copy and to Elizabeth Schaaf, the managing editor; we are indebted to Ara Salibian for his expert copyediting. Others at B/SM who helped include Fred Courtright, Helaine Denenberg, Molly Kalkstein, Ed Tonderys, Elizabeth Marcus, Jennifer Rush, and Jo Swanson. We also greatly appreciate the aid of historians around the country who provided input while the book was being designed: Ed Ayers, Anne Bailey, Robert Becker, Kathleen Berkeley, William A. Blair, W. Fitzhugh Brundage, Robert Calvert, Valerie Jean Conner, John Daly, Charles Eagles, Sarah Gardner, Glenda Gilmore, William Harris, Mark Hill, Susan Hult, Wallace Hutcheon, Mary Carroll Johansen, Stephen Kneeshaw, Jessica Kross, Janice Leone, Carl Moneyhon, James Tice Moore, Fred Roach, Dennis Rousey, Jon Sensbach, Bryant Simon, Sheila Skemp, Marcia Synnott, Lisa Toland, and Harold Wilson. Finally, as always, we have depended on the love and support of our spouses, Susannah Link and David Wheeler, and our children, Percy, Maggie, and Josie Link and Scott and Jesse Wheeler.

William A. Link, Greensboro, N.C.

Marjorie Spruill Wheeler, Hattiesburg, Miss.

CONTENTS

Preface   v

CHAPTER ONE
RECONSTRUCTION
Black Freedom and the Ku Klux Klan   1

1. The Rise of the Klan
   *Alexander K. Davis and Lydia Anderson, Testimony for the
   Joint Select Committee in Macon, Mississippi, 1871*   4

2. A Northern View
   Harper's Weekly, "The Ku-Klux Conspiracy," 1872   13

3. Missionary Women and Black Education
   Maria Waterbury, From Seven Years among
   the Freedmen, *1890*   17

4. The Legacy of the Klan
   *Albion W. Tourgée, "The Causes, Character, and Consequences
   of the Ku-Klux Organization," 1880*   20

CHAPTER TWO
WESTWARD EXPANSION
The Texas Border Wars   26

5. Horse Thieves on the Mexican Border
   *Mexican Commission, Report on the Northern Frontier
   Question, 1875*   28

6. "In the Country of the Bad Man"
    *Luvenia Conway Roberts, On Living with the Texas
    Rangers, 1928*   33

7. Buffalo Soldiers on the Border
    *Major J. F. Wade, Colonel Edward Hatch, Edwards Pierrepont,
    and Stephen Powers, Reports on the Solis Affair, 1875*   39

CHAPTER THREE
THE GILDED AGE
The Farmers' Alliance and Populism   **45**

8. What Did Farmers Want?
    *"Little Jennie" Scott Wilson and Ben Terrell, Addresses to the
    Texas and Georgia Farmers' Alliances, 1888 and 1889*   47

9. An Economic Proposal
    Committee on the Monetary System, Report, 1889   51

10. The St. Louis Demands
    *The Farmers' Alliance and Industrial Union,
    Manifesto, 1889*   55

11. The Alliance and Southern Politics
    The National Economist, *the* Richmond Exchange Reporter,
    and the Virginia Sun, *Newspaper Articles, 1890–1892*   56

12. The Populist Program
    The People's Party of America, Omaha Platform, 1892   62

CHAPTER FOUR
THE 1890s
Race Crisis in the New South   **68**

13. The "Atlanta Compromise"
    Booker T. Washington, Atlanta Exposition Address, 1895   70

14. Voices of Protest
    *Ida B. Wells and Alexander L. Manly, On Lynching, 1892
    and 1898*   74

15. An Explosion of Violence
    *Gunner Jesse Blake and Anonymous, On Racial Violence in
    Wilmington, North Carolina, 1898*   79

16. A Plea for Justice
    *George H. White, Address to the United States House of
    Representatives, 1901*   85

CHAPTER FIVE
THE AGE OF INDUSTRIALISM
From Farm to Mill   92

17. Rural Life in Tennessee and Virginia
    *Lizzie (Sallie Newman) Gibson, Robert Barnett, Catherine
    Fitch Stout, and Hattie Murphey McDade, Oral History
    Interviews, 1939*   94

18. Moving to the Mills
    August Kohn, "Why They Go to the Mills," 1907   99

19. The Making of the Mill Community
    *Mary Frederickson and Brent Glass, Interview with Flossie
    Moore Durham, 1976*   105

CHAPTER SIX
THE PROGRESSIVE ERA
Woman Suffrage and Progressivism in the South   111

20. A Woman's Place Is In Politics
    *Madeline McDowell Breckenridge, Adella Hunt Logan,
    and S. P. Brooks, Arguments for Woman Suffrage, 1912
    and 1914*   113

21. Southern Arguments against Suffrage
    Antisuffrage Leaflets, 1915 and c. 1919   121

22. "The Pulse of the South"
    *The Southern Review, "How the South Really Feels about
    Woman Suffrage," 1920*   125

CHAPTER SEVEN
WORLD WAR I
The Debate about Intervention   132

23. Public Opinion
    Literary Digest, "American Sympathies in the War," 1914   134

24. The Case for Preparedness
    *Lilian Pike Roome and John Sharp Williams, Arguments for
    Intervention, 1915 and 1916*   138

25. An Opponent of War
    Claude Kitchin, Speech before Congress, 1917   141

CHAPTER EIGHT

THE 1920s
Fundamentalism and the Scopes Trial   146

26. The Fundamentalist Case
     T. T. Martin, From Hell and the High Schools, 1923   149
27. The Scopes Trial
     Outlook, "Evolution in Tennessee," 1925   153
28. Surveying the Scene
     John Porter Fort, "Behind the Scenes in Tennessee," 1925   156
29. Fundamentalism's Legacy
     H. L. Mencken, Editorial, 1925   161

CHAPTER NINE

THE GREAT DEPRESSION
The New Deal and the New South   166

30. The Appeal of the Communist Party
     Angelo Herndon, From You Cannot Kill the Working Class,
     c. 1934   168
31. Sharing the Wealth
     Huey P. Long, From "Every Man a King," 1934   181
32. The Tennessee Valley Authority and Grass-Roots Democracy
     Odette Keun, From A Foreigner Looks at the TVA, 1937   187

CHAPTER TEN

WORLD WAR II
The War That Brought Old Dixie Down   195

33. Serving in a Jim Crow Army
     Charlie Mabrey Jr. and Clarence E. Adams, Letters to the
     Editor, 1943 and 1944   198
34. A Liberating Experience for African Americans
     Myrlie Evers, On How the War Affected Medgar
     Evers, 1967   201
35. The Impact on Women
     Marion Stegman, Polly Crow, Ernestine Slade, Peggy Terry,
     and Audrey Ward Norman, Recollections of War Jobs,
     1943–on   203
36. Structural Changes in the South
     John Dos Passos, "Gold Rush Down South," 1943   213

CHAPTER ELEVEN
The McCarthy Era
Frank Porter Graham and the Ordeal of Southern Liberalism 218

37. Dr. Frank Attacked
    A. W. Black, "Looking at Dr. Frank Graham's Record," 1948 220
38. Frank Graham Defended
    Wayne Morse, "In Fairness to a Great American," 1948 222
39. The Fulton Lewis Broadcast
    Fulton Lewis Jr. and Frank Porter Graham, Accusation and Response, 1949 225
40. HUAC and Southern Liberalism
    House Un-American Activities Committee, Report on Frank Graham, 1949 228

CHAPTER TWELVE
The Civil Rights Movement
Murder in Mississippi 233

41. Opening the "Closed Society"
    Bob Moses, Hollis Watkins, Tom Hayden, Sandra Cason (Casey Hayden), Peter Orris, and Unita Blackwell, Interviews, 1970s 236
42. "Big Ambitions"
    Rita Schwerner, Letter to Anne Braden, 1964 241
43. The Sovereignty Commission Investigates
    A. L. Hopkins, Reports, 1964 243
44. The Response of the White Community
    Florence Mars, From Witness in Philadelphia, *1977* 248
45. "Be Sick and Tired with Me"
    Dave Dennis, Eulogy for James Chaney, 1964 256

CHAPTER THIRTEEN
The Vietnam War
The South Divided 259

46. The War and Public Opinion
    William C. Westmoreland, Oral History, 1990 262
47. Civil Rights and Foreign Policy
    Martin Luther King Jr., "A Time to Break Silence," 1967 264

48. Race Relations in the Armed Services
     *Douglas Anderson, Donald L. Whitfield, Don F. Browne, and
     Reginald Edwards, Oral Histories, 1981 and 1984*   268

49. Criticism of Protesters
     Spiro T. Agnew, Speeches in Louisiana and Alabama, 1969   275

50. Student Protest and Community Response
     *"Concerned Students for Peace" and Washington, North Carolina,
     Residents, Letters to the Editor, 1970*   279

CHAPTER FOURTEEN
THE 1970s
The ERA and the Rise of the Pro-Family Movement   285

51. Presidential Support
     Jimmy Carter, Remarks on Signing Proclamation 4515, 1977   288

52. ERA Supporters Speak Out
     *Maria Bliss, Katie Morgan, Jessie Rae Scott, Marse Grant,
     and Elizabeth Koontz, Statements in Favor of
     Ratification, 1977*   290

53. Southern Conservatives Fight the ERA
     *Sam Ervin Jr., STOP ERA, and Jerry Falwell, Statements
     against Ratification, 1971, 1975, and 1980*   296

54. Failures and Successes
     *Rosalynn Carter, Reflections on the Carter Administration's
     Record on Women's Rights, 1984*   302

CHAPTER FIFTEEN
CONTEMPORARY AMERICA
The New Immigration in South Florida   308

55. The Cuban Experience
     *Business Week, "How the Immigrants Made It in Miami"
     and "South Florida's Melting Pot Is About to Boil," 1971
     and 1985*   310

56. Haitian Boat People
     *Alex Stepick and Jake C. Miller, Accounts of Haitian Refugees,
     1982 and 1984*   317

57. Assimilation and Conflict
     *Mireya Navarro, "Black and Cuban American: Bias in Two Worlds,"
     1997*   323

The South in the
History of the Nation

CHAPTER ONE

RECONSTRUCTION

Black Freedom and the Ku Klux Klan

The end of the Civil War raised basic questions about African American civil and political rights. What would be the position of newly freed slaves in national life? What rights would they possess? Who would define these rights? What would the role of the national government be in assuring civil and political rights for freed people? Should African Americans participate fully in the political dialogue about the South's future? If so, what should their role be? Beyond the mandates of the Fourteenth and Fifteenth Amendments — which declared that freed slaves were citizens and enfranchised all male citizens over the age of twenty-one — there was considerable room for disagreement among whites and blacks, Northerners and Southerners, Democrats and Republicans. After 1865, these clashing expectations manifested themselves violently in the Ku Klux Klan.

Historians, too, have disagreed about the role African Americans played in Reconstruction. Many of those writing near the turn of the twentieth century were sharply critical of a "tragic era" during which, they believed, southern blacks plunged headlong and disastrously into politics; implicit in this interpretation was a racist assumption that African Americans were ill-prepared and unsuited for political participation and leadership. Describing Reconstruction's successes, later historians contested this view. Even more recent scholars, emphasizing the centrality of the freed slaves' quest for freedom, have been less charitable about the results of Reconstruction — much of which they have portrayed as a failure.

Although historians have disagreed in these interpretations, they have agreed that African Americans were at the core of the issues of the day. A central thread of Reconstruction lies in the attempt of black people to secure their freedom from slavery — and the ways in which southern and northern whites responded to these

1

attempts. The war had been a liberating experience; thousands of black soldiers served in it and participated in the invasion of the South. Thousands more remained under slavery, to be sure, but they too witnessed the erosion of slavery as a system. Emancipation was a joyous experience, but black leaders were determined to secure their freedom by seeking out a full measure of civil and political equality. African Americans became politically mobilized almost immediately: soon after the war, many black leaders, convinced that the destruction of slavery was not fully possible without political empowerment, fought to obtain the vote for African Americans. They believed that their new status as freed people depended on it.

Many southern whites, in contrast, greeted the new, postemancipation turmoil in race relations with disbelief. Northern whites expressed responses ranging from indifference, fear of black emigration out of the South, or sympathy for African Americans. But southern whites had lived under a system of slavery in which the assumed inferiority of African Americans, free and slave, was embedded in law, custom, politics, and economic life. Most resented black political participation and opposed efforts by blacks to obtain other dimensions of freedom in working conditions, schools, and churches. Despite emancipation, the status of black people remained unclear, and many southern white leaders sought to reestablish — without reestablishing slavery — the old system of white supremacy. These clashing expectations set the stage for violent conflict. In many states of the South, anti-Reconstruction "conservative" parties came into existence during the late 1860s. And a secret terrorist organization, the Ku Klux Klan, formed to intimidate African Americans and white Republicans as part of a concerted effort to end Reconstruction.

The Klan first appeared in eastern Tennessee during the spring or summer of 1866, and white paramilitary organizations began to spring up elsewhere in the South within a year. By 1868, the Klan was fully organized in most of the South and operated campaigns of terror across the region. With the peak of Klan violence in the late 1860s and early 1870s, scores of African Americans became victims of organized terror. The intent of the violence was to upend Reconstruction and unseat Republicans spearheading it. As part of this objective, the Klan sought to limit black civil and political freedom. In a number of states, white opponents of Reconstruction used the KKK and terrorism — beatings, whippings, lynchings — as tools to overturn Republican rule, capitalizing on white fears and unease about civil and political equality for African Americans, in the process exposing divisions among black and white Republicans. Although its actions had specific political ends, the Klan struck at the basic definition of freedom.

For the most part, Klan violence elicited ineffective — or even counterproductive — responses from southern Republican regimes. The federal government did little to intervene before the early 1870s; what was necessary was armed protection in areas of Klan activity. But by then the damage to African American groups and Republican Party infrastructure had already been done. By April 1871, Klan outrages were so common that Congress organized a special Joint Select Committee to investigate the situation. Meanwhile, new federal anti-Klan legislation empowered prosecutions during 1871–72, and that put a temporary end to the reign of terror, although not to the Klan. In February 1872, the Joint Select Committee concluded its investigation and issued reports. The minority report — written by the Democrats on the committee — denied the existence of an organized uprising and maintained that the Klan represented the reaction of liberty-loving people to their repression.

But the majority report, written by the committee's Republicans, described a widespread Klan conspiracy that connected terror with a broader political effort to upend Reconstruction and Republican influence. Based on vast documentation, it ultimately convinced the northern public and provided a basis for an expanded federal prosecution effort. With strong backing from Congress and President Ulysses S. Grant, federal officials began a concerted effort to uproot the Klan. But the federal intervention was largely too little and too late, for a pattern of political oppression and intimidation of black voters and their white Republican allies had been well established.

The documents in this chapter examine the impact of the Klan on African American aspirations to freedom during Reconstruction. Testimony from two Mississippi blacks illustrates the ways in which their efforts to define the boundaries of freedom met determined and violent resistance from local whites. The extent to which the Klan spread throughout the South is indisputable; its effects on northern public opinion are shown in an excerpt from *Harper's Weekly*. Efforts to educate freed people, largely spearheaded by northern women such as Maria Waterbury, also became targets for terrorist violence. And as Albion W. Tourgée suggests in an excerpt from *The Invisible Empire*, the rise of the Klan was broad-ranging and extensive in scope, rooted in fundamentally different expectations between whites and blacks about the meaning of freedom.

As you read, keep in mind the differing backgrounds and perspectives of the authors of these documents. According to the sources, what did black people want from freedom? How did white people (northern and southern) differ in their expectations? In what ways do the sources agree or disagree about the causes and consequences of Klan activity?

1. The Rise of the Klan

ALEXANDER K. DAVIS AND LYDIA ANDERSON
Testimony for the Joint Select Committee in Macon, Mississippi
1871

In Mississippi, tensions between whites and blacks were particularly acute because that state possessed an African American majority, many of whom actively participated in politics. Violence and terror against blacks were rampant across the state in the spring of 1871. Because these outrages seemed to take place with impunity in Mississippi and elsewhere, Congress acted and in April 1871 organized a Joint Select Committee composed of seven senators and fourteen representatives to conduct an investigation of the Klan. It dispatched subcommittees to southern states "lately in insurrection" to interview scores of black and white witnesses to Klan violence. The following two excerpts from this testimony are from Noxubee County, a center of Mississippi's white terror. As these African American witnesses suggest, white intimidation tactics targeted the diverse ways in which blacks sought out freedom.

Macon, Mississippi, *November* 6, 1871

ALEXANDER K. DAVIS (colored) sworn and examined.
By the Chairman:
Question: State your place of residence.
Answer: Macon, Noxubee County, Mississippi.
Question: State your occupation.
Answer: I am, you might say, a law-student. I have been admitted to the bar; I claim that for my occupation.
Question: Are you a candidate for the legislature at this time?
Answer: Yes, sir.
Question: Have you ever been a member of the legislature?
Answer: Yes, sir; I represented this county in the last legislature.
Question: How long have you lived in Noxubee County?
Answer: I have lived here since June, 1869.
Question: Where did you live previous to that time?
Answer: I lived in Shelby County, Tennessee, sir.
Question: What opportunities have you enjoyed of knowing the condition of affairs in this county as to peace and good order, and the observance of the laws?

Alexander K. Davis and Lydia Anderson, "Report of the Joint Select Committee to Inquire into the Condition of Affairs in the Late Insurrectionary States," 42d Cong., 2d sess., 1871, H. Rept. 22, 13 vols., 11:469–79, 510–12.

Answer: Well, sir, I can only say that the only opportunities I have had to know them was as a grand juror of the United States court, of the district court for the northern district of Mississippi.

Question: Are you pretty generally acquainted with the colored people of this county?

Answer: In all the counties in the eastern tier of counties I am pretty well acquainted — Kemper, Lowndes, Monroe, and Chickasaw; and I am pretty well known, and know a great many prominent colored men through these counties.

Question: Are you pretty well acquainted through the different townships of this county?

Answer: I am pretty thoroughly acquainted in the county, but I do not know that I know a great deal of the township and section lines.

Question: I mean the different neighborhoods in the county?

Answer: O, yes; I am as thoroughly acquainted, probably, as any man in the county.

Question: You may state whether you know, or have been informed, of any outrages committed upon colored people of this county by combinations of disguised men.

Answer: I could not state that I know of any of my own knowledge. I have seen parties who have been whipped, with scars on their backs, and they stated that it had been done by disguised parties.

Question: You may give to the committee such cases as have been reported to you, with the particulars so far as you are informed.

Answer: I will have to refresh my memory a little, in order to state dates and names, there are so many of them. Probably I could better furnish you a list of the different parties themselves, and you could examine them.

Question: Have you any such list prepared?

Answer: I can prepare one, sir, through the course of the day, and furnish it to the committee.

Question: For the present you may give such cases as occur to you, and when you have opportunity you may prepare the list you speak of.

Answer: The first case that came to my knowledge was a woman by the name of Betsey Lucas, who lives here in Macon now. She then lived at a Mr. Robert Jackson's, in the northern portion of this county, near the Lowndes County line, about eight miles north of this place.

Question: What were the particulars of her case?

Answer: She was living with Mr. Jackson, and a party of men came there. It was in the month of March, 1870, I think, or maybe a little later. It may have been as late as — it was between the months of March and May; I don't remember just when it was, but I think I can find that out at home, as I took a note of it at the time. They took her out and put a rope around her neck, a bridle-rein, and whipped her, and gave her a certain number of days to get away. That I learned from her; that was her sworn testimony, too.

Question: Did you learn from her whether the men were disguised?

Answer: All disguised. She said she recognized some of the parties by — some of them had only their faces disguised, but their clothing, their pants and coats, she recognized, and their voices. She recognized some of them. . . .

Question: What did Betsey tell you she was whipped for, or what did she say the men who inflicted the whipping said was the cause?

Answer: She said she could not account for the whipping at all. One white man, who was along with the party when she was whipped, and was a member of the klan, stated that she was whipped for messing with this man, Jackson, she lived with, or was hired to. That was his story about it. . . .

Question: If you have finished all you have to say about the case of Betsey Lucas, you may pass on to the next case which occurs to you.

Answer: The next case occurred about the same time, I think on the same night. It was the ordering off of some colored families that had been settled upon what was called the bottom place, here in this county, of Mr. William May. Mr. May settled a lot of colored people on a place of his there, and gave them lands for a term of years, to clear them up, and, I believe, gave them some assistance in building and improving, and they were all run off on that night — at least ordered off and notified that if they were there at a certain stated night or day, what would be the consequence, and they moved off.

Question: Was that done by the same party that whipped Betsey Lucas?

Answer: The same party. All the men were there, I believe, with one exception; that one exception was the captain; he was not present that night — the captain of the squad.

Question: What was his name?

Answer: He was said to be the captain, and was a man by the name of C. M. Doss.

Question: How many families were driven off from that bottom place?

Answer: I think there were five — I can't be positive as to the number.

Question: Is Mr. Doss living still in the county?

Answer: Yes, sir.

Question: Did these families leave pursuant to this warning?

Answer: Yes, sir.

Question: Go on.

Answer: The same night — or the next raid they made. I merely give this as evidence I have had, and from reports of the parties who were along and know.

Question: Do you regard the information you have of these transactions as reliable?

Answer: I do; there isn't any of it of my own knowledge. I never saw one of these parties.

Question: That is proper evidence. You may proceed.

Answer: They went to — I have forgotten whose plantation it was, now — but they were there to look up some parties, and there was a colored man killed by the name of Coger. It seems that this man, Sam, they had nothing against him, or didn't want him, but he talked to them a little plain, and they just fired into him and killed him. It was all the same raid. . . .

Question: Do you recollect any other cases of whipping or murder or other outrages in this county?

Answer: Yes, sir; about the latter part of March or 1st of April, 1871, there was a half a dozen cases of whipping down here about Mushulaville, in this county. The most noted of them was the whipping of Aleck Hughes. Aleck had rented a place down near Mushulaville. He was a very industrious young fellow, and made a crop there last year. This year he bought some stock and they whipped him and run him off. They whipped him nearly to death, or so he was not able to go. They left him for dead. They hung him up, and I saw his back two months afterwards, and it was a perfect scab then. He said that after they hung him up he begged them not to kill him, and they gave him his choice to take five hundred lashes or be shot or hung. He consented to take five hundred lashes, and he said he guessed they gave them to him. They whipped him, and he didn't know when they quit — didn't know anything about it. That is his own story. He is in the county now. He was a witness, and was a very prominent witness, and thought it was not safe for him to come back, and he is over at Holly Springs now; but his team and everything is out here. He had a crop in; eighteen or twenty acres in cotton, about thirty acres in corn; I believe he has instituted a suit in the United States court for damages against the parties. He recognized two or three of the parties. One of the parties that he recognized on account of a little horse that he rode, that he (Aleck) had owned himself, and had sold him. He claims that he hadn't paid him for it, and he thought that may be was one of the reasons for his whipping, because he had asked him for the money. He had owned a little horse, and sold it to a man in the neighborhood; and he got after him for the money, and he abused him and struck him, and a few nights afterward told him he had got a little too saucy and impudent, and they had come down to correct him.

Question: Who told him?

Answer: He named the party that told him this. I think it was the same man that rode his horse. I don't remember which one now; there was so many. There were only five though that whipped him. They went to his house and took his gun and pistol after they had whipped him. They didn't catch him at his house at all. He was looking for them — expecting them. He had heard they were coming for him, and he went off that night. He was staying over at another colored man's house in the neighborhood.

Question: And they took his gun that night?

Answer: Yes, sir; after they whipped him; and they went to his house and got his gun and pistol. He told them where it was, and they went and got it. I am just giving the outlines. I do not know the particulars. . . .

Question: What is the sentiment of the whites in this county as to the colored schools?

Answer: Well, sir, in a portion of the county the majority of the whites, I think, are favorable; in all the northeast portion of the county, and Macon beat here, and probably Shuqualak and that district down there, the majority of the whites, I think, are favorable to the free schools; but in the southeast corner, and southwest corner, and the northwest corner of the county, and all the west part of the county, the most of the whites are opposed to free schools for anybody, white or black. I have met a great many persons and talked with them. I met a leading man in the northwest corner of the county who keeps a store up there, a wealthy man, and he told me he thought it an outrage. He thought the principle was wrong that he should be taxed to educate other people's children; he said he had to educate his own, and he did not think it was right. It is generally said that what he says is the sentiment of his whole community. He is a very quiet man, though, and I have never heard of his participating in the disturbances. That is pretty generally the feeling.

Question: Is that the sole objection made to the free schools, the expense it entails in the shape of taxes?

Answer: That is the only public objection they make. What their private views are I do not pretend to say at all. The only objection I have heard of their making to any of the friends of the system is that they did not think they ought to be taxed to support them.

Question: Do you hear any opposition to colored suffrage?

Answer: Well, no, sir; there is no open opposition in this county, scarcely; our paper here opposes it; it has at its head a motto, "All the time in opposition to negro suffrage"; that is, it raised it after the election of 1869, and pulled it down a few weeks ago. I presume they will raise it again after this election is over; everybody that is a candidate now for every party claims to be a friend to universal suffrage. We have three or four tickets in the field, all claiming to be friends to negro suffrage.

Question: That was the motto of the democratic paper published here from 1869 until within a few weeks past, I understand you?

Answer: Yes, sir; they raised it right after the election in 1869; I think the motto was, "Uncompromising opposition to negro suffrage"; that is the substance, but not the exact language.

Question: Have you heard any considerable number of democrats denounce that motto as not representing the sentiments of the democratic party in this county?

Answer: No, sir; I have heard some few. I have heard it myself, that motto, and I have heard one or two say that it did not represent the sentiments of their party. The most prominent democrats here now claim that there is no opposition to universal suffrage or free schools, and that they are not opposed to radicalism.

Question: Do you believe them to be sincere in the sentiments they express?

Answer: No, sir; I don't believe them.

Question: Have there been any cases in which any white men, implicated in the various outrages you have detailed, have ever been brought to justice and punished?

Answer: None; I never have heard of one yet being punished. I have heard of several attempts to investigate, but they have never succeeded. I have had witnesses tell me that they have gone before grand juries here — I know witnesses that told me they were going before grand juries to report certain parties that they recognized that had committed outrages, and they went before the grand juries and have seen parties on that grand jury that they knew were connected with the Klan, or were members of the bands that had committed these outrages; and they then and there stated that they didn't know anything about it — just heard of it. They said they didn't think it was safe to do so, and I know it was so. There are white men in this town; I know a man that has lived here always, and probably has at stake as much as anybody in this county; he told me this morning that he wouldn't testify what he knew before this committee, because, he said, it would be published; he said he didn't intend to be slaughtered. There are plenty of men here, sir, that will not do it. They don't believe that there will be any effort made — that their testimony before this committee will simply amount to informing the outside world as to these outrages, and that is about all; and that they will not lend any aid at all to bring these parties to justice, and it will only place them in the position of being more obnoxious to these men and more liable to be killed.

Macon, Mississippi, *November* 6, 1871

LYDIA ANDERSON (colored) sworn and examined.
By the Chairman:
Question: Where do you live?
Answer: I live here now. I have been living between Winston and Noxubee, in the edge of Noxubee, about three miles above Mushulaville.
Question: What induced you to come here?
Answer: Well, I don't know whether they threatened my life or not, but I was told I had better go to Macon, and I did so.
Question: Had you been threatened?
Answer: No, sir; only in this way.
Question: Had you ever been whipped?
Answer: Yes, sir.
Question: When were you whipped?
Answer: It has been about five months, as well as I can recollect.
Question: Where were you living when you were whipped?
Answer: At Massa Anderson's; Killes (Achilles) Anderson.
Question: Who whipped you?
Answer: It is what they call the Ku-Klux.
Question: At night?
Answer: Yes, sir.
Question: Was it in your own house?
Answer: They took me out of my bed — out of my house.
Question: How many men were concerned in it?
Answer: There was four.
Question: Had they disguises on?
Answer: Yes, sir; they all wore dresses.
Question: Had gowns on?
Answer: Yes, sir; all had gowns on, and one of them had a sheet over him.
Question: Was there anything over their faces?

Answer: Yes, sir; they had horns here and here, at the corners of the head, [illustrating].

Question: So you could not see the faces at all?

Answer: No, sir; I couldn't see the faces.

Question: Did they come to your house on foot or on horseback?

Answer: On horses.

Question: Did they have any pistols or guns?

Answer: Yes, sir; they had pistols.

Question: Was anybody in the house with you at the time?

Answer: No, sir; not then. My daughter was staying at the house, and she was at the washing-place washing, and she spied them, but she didn't tell me. She thought she would go and wake up sister. She brought her the news and went back to her — and went back after her soap. She saw them coming and went into her sister's house. She says, "I believe them nasty things is about here. Where's mother?" She said, "Mother is asleep," so she goes into her sister's house. She wasn't there no time before they came tearing through the yard as hard as they could stave, right up to my son-in-law's house door.

Question: Were you living with your son-in-law?

Answer: Yes, sir. He jumped up in his sleep and says, "What's the matter?" She says, "There's the Ku-Klux." As she said that he opened the door, and Fuller — that's my son-in-law's name — said he, "Yes, sir." He said, "Is Aunt Liddy here?" Fuller says, "Yes, sir." He said, "Where is she?" Fuller said, "In her own house." Said he, "Is she asleep?" "Yes, I expect she has gone to bed." "Tell her to come out; we want to see her; we just want to ask her some questions; we are not going to hurt a hair of her head." As quick as I stepped out, as soon as I put my foot on the step, he says, "March to them woods there, or I'll blow your God damned brains out." That scared my son-in-law, and he run to the house and waked up my young master, and he asked him what was the matter, and he told him the Ku-Klux was there. He said, "Fuller, did you know them?" He says, "No, I didn't." "Well," says he, "I can't do nothing."

Question: That was what your young master said?

Answer: Yes, sir. He couldn't do nothing; if the boy could he would. I raised him; I nursed him and fed him, and he thought as much of me almost as he did of his mother; but they took me out there and whipped me.

Question: How long did they whip you?

Answer: They didn't whip me very long. It has been about five months since they whipped me. I stayed there two weeks, and it has been four months and two weeks since I have been here; that makes five months. I was living at the factory last Christmas. My son-in-law said, "Mother, you have worked and hired long enough without pay, and I am able to take you in my own house and take care of you." After I went there — old Mr. Richards is about a mile below — and I went to work with Mrs. Richards; I hired to her. Mrs. Richards says, "Why not stay with me?" I said I would just as quick as any other. She says, "I just want such an old woman as you to help me about cooking and milking"; and I said I would stay with the old lady. She said it would not be hard, and I was there a week. She wanted to go up to Choctaw to see her children, and she said, "Now, if I go away, will you take care of my things good?" I said, "Yes, I would." My old master had recommended me for a good hand; he had raised me from a little thing. She said, "I want to go to see my children, I have been gone so long, and if you will stay here and take care of my things I will give you a good present when I get back." The old creature started Monday morning, and then Monday night and Tuesday morning her husband commenced some of his talk. I didn't understand him. He says, "The witches rode me last night." I says, "I have heard of witches riding folks, but they never have rode me." I didn't know what he meant. He says, "You ought to come in and keep me company." Says I, "I am not afraid of staying around there." He says, "The old lady told you to take good care of me." I says, "I am going to cook your victuals and make your bed and take care of you." He kept talking that way, and finally I found out what he was talking about, and I said, "No, sir; my old master raised me like his own child; that's one thing that they never accused me of, and never shall, and that's not my disposition." In that week my daughter came there; she wanted to live there; the foolish child wants always to stay with me. I says, "Child, you may stay if they hire you," and says I, "Mrs. Richards, my daughter is come, and if you would like a house-girl she will stay with you." She says, "If she will stay on the same terms as you do I will take her." I had a baby girl about so high, [illustrating], and when she came he dropped off with me and flies to this young girl, young woman grown. She is the one I was telling you of was there, and this little girl told me what her sister said this old man said to her. I never let on; I said if he became too free she will tell me after a while. I made no fuss. On Friday morning he was coming down here, last court, and they thought I was gone out milking, but I stopped behind the chimney, and I heard him say, "What do you want me to fetch you from Macon?" She said, "Nothing; I don't want nothing you have got." She says, "If I did such a thing as that that you want, she would beat me nearly to death." Says he, "O, your mother won't know it." She says, "Yes, she will; my mother don't allow no such bother, nor any of the other girls to do it, and I am right to mind my mother." He went off and he told me then he wanted me to make the children do it, and I made them do it, and Friday evening my young master came up. My old master was to have a dinner with the neighbors, and he sent his son to ask, "Where is old Mr. Richards?" and I says, "He went to Macon to-day." He says, "Tell him to come up to dinner, and ma wants you to come, for you have always been ma's cook." I said I would come, and when night come I told him about it; when he came home. He never said nothing, and so my daughter, Saturday morning, says, "Ma, are you going to the dinner?" I says, "I don't know; I promised the old lady I would stay and take care of her things until she comes back. If you want to go I will stay here." She says, "I want to go." I says, "Now don't you think because you are free you can go off. You go and ask the old man, no odds if you are free; you ask him if you can go." She went and done it. He said, "No; you were gone to dinner last Saturday, and I hired you to work." She says, "Mr. Richards, I have done all you told me." He says, "You go to work." Well, there was not a thing to do. Says I, "Martha, you sweep these weeds around here." She says after a while to him, "I know the reason you want to keep me from going; I won't let you keep me." He says, "You hush." I was in the kitchen and heard it. I says, "You tell me right here what that was, or I'll knock you down," and she told me and I went and set down on the doorstep, and he jumped up and went off and came back with a great hickory stick, as big as your thumb. She was at the gate sweeping, and he came in and drawed down on Martha three times. She run back, and I stepped up and asked, "What's the matter?" She said, "Mr. Richards is whipping me." I says, "Mr. Richards, what's the matter? Didn't I tell you when them children come here, if they didn't mind you, all you had to do was to tell me and I would make them mind you? What are you whipping her for?" He says, "I'll whip her again." Says I to her, "Martha, get your things and go." He says, "She had better go." Says I, "She is a woman, and I'm going too. I told you that if my children didn't mind you, you should come to me and tell me, and I would make them mind, and now what are you whipping that girl for? You think I don't know, but I do know. She shan't stay and I shan't stay." There was a black man living on the plantation; he moved down on that same place. I went back up to the owner of the factory; his wife had never wanted me to leave; I cooked until I tired myself down; I said I would rest myself awhile; she asked me to come there again awhile; the woman sent her husband after me and I went up next day. This black man told my son-in-law, and told me, that they had been trying to catch me ever since I had been going back and forward; that's what made me know who they were, and I could tell them by the voices, because it was nobody else but them.

    Question: You say there were four who were concerned in whipping you?

    Answer: Yes, sir; but only one whipped, but he whipped me enough for all.

    Question: How many licks did they strike you?

    Answer: Nine licks and cut my skin, and the marks is on my back.

    Question: What did they say it was for?

    Answer: They said I talked of the Ku-Klux.

    Question: Did you know that man?

    Answer: No, sir; he said I did; he jabbed a pistol at me and said, "God damn you, do you know me?"

    Question: Who do you think these men were?

    Answer: Old master's sons.

    Question: The sons of old man Richards?

    Answer: Yes, sir; I will say it until I die; they were his sons; they were the ones the black man told my son-in-law were trying to catch me ever since I was gone to the factory.

    Question: Has anybody ever been taken up for this whipping?

    Answer: No, sir; not that I know of.

    Question: Did you ever make any complaint to a justice of the peace?

    Answer: No, sir; I was afraid to speak a word.

    Question: Did they warn you not to tell of it?

    Answer: No, sir; they told me, "Go on now, and I'll see you again in a few days, and I'll give you five hundred lashes the next time I see you."

    Question: Did they tell you to leave the county?

Answer: No, sir; the water was up then and I couldn't cross, and that kept me as long as I did stay there; then I came away. . . .

2. A Northern View

HARPER'S WEEKLY
"The Ku-Klux Conspiracy"
1872

The majority report of the Joint Select Committee appointed by Congress in 1871 determined that the Klan engaged in a widespread effort to turn back Reconstruction in the South. This view, which came to dominate northern perceptions, has in fact been borne out by recent historians, who conclude that the chief implication of Klan violence was the erosion of political support for the Republicans. The following excerpt from a Harper's Weekly *article on the Klan reflects that view. Yet, in some respects, the emphasis here — how political factors weighed heavily in the Klan — stands in contrast to the concerns of many of the Joint Select Committee's witnesses, who stressed the social impact of white terror.*

. . . The Congressional reports on the Ku-Klux conspiracy show the real causes of the decline in the value of every kind of property in the Southern States, and the dangers that threaten the future of their industry and trade. The Democratic party has fallen under the control of a murderous faction: its more intelligent and prudent members have not sufficient courage to free themselves from the tyranny of robbers and assassins; the colored population and the white Republicans, the industrious and the honest, in many parts of the South are disfranchised by intimidation and open violence; the governments of several States are plain usurpations; a minority of lawless men rule over the powerless majority, and once more threaten rebellion, defy the national government, and bring ruin upon their fellow-citizens. The Ku-Klux conspiracy has extended its mysterious links through

Harper's Weekly, 19 October 1872. Reprinted in *African American History in the Press, 1851–1899: From the Coming of the Civil War to the Rise of Jim Crow as Reported and Illustrated in Selected Newspapers of the Time,* vol. 2, 1870–1899, ed. Robert L. Harris Jr., David Dennard, Cynthia Neverdon-Morton, and Jacqueline Rose, The Schneider Collection (Detroit: Gale, 1996), 705–8.

every Southern State: it has usually flourished before and after every election with a sudden vigor, and has then sunk into obscurity until the hour for new efforts arrived; its measures are always the same, whether in Texas or Missouri; its members ride around at night in strange disguises; their victims are white and colored Republicans, their wives and children, honest working-men, teachers, and active Baptist or Methodist ministers; sometimes United States officials or State judges and Senators have fallen before their rifles; sometimes the clergyman has been shot in his pulpit or the lawyer in his court-house; but oftener they are content to rob and burn the negro cabin, to seam the backs of its unlucky tenants with pitiless lashes, or leave the husband and the father bleeding and dying in the midst of his horror-stricken family. The pitiless cruelty of these Southern Democrats — for the chief object of the Ku-Klux assassins is always to insure the election of the Democratic officials — surpasses the barbarity of the savage. . . .

In several of the counties of South Carolina the Ku-Klux ruled for a long period unchecked; hundreds of persons suffered from their unparalelled malignity; the sick, the aged, and the feeble were torn from their beds at night, whipped, tortured, or shot; women were often the express objects of their cruelty. Scarcely a year ago, disguised with masks, horns upon their heads, long dresses, and fantastic ornaments, these representatives of the fallen chivalry dashed along the roads of South Carolina in the depth of night, committed their atrocities upon the harmless and the innocent, and tormented the helpless and the weak. They openly declared to their bleeding victims that they must promise to vote for the Democratic party, or they would return and kill them. Many, after severe whippings, yielded to their dreadful argument. The newspapers were filled with the recantations of white and black Republicans, who had been converted to Democratic principles by stripes and wounds. One aged victim, beaten and bruised, crawled to the court-house steps, and there pronounced in faltering words his abjuration of Republican heresy. And if for a moment the murderous association seems suppressed in South Carolina, there can be no doubt that it would at once renew its outrages should the national government fall into the hands of its friends.

In Alabama the rage of the Democratic politicians seems chiefly turned against school-teachers, Methodist and Baptist preachers, and white Republicans who strive to elevate the colored race. The Ku-Klux labors have proved successful: a Democratic Governor has been elected (Lindsay), who denies the existence of any Ku-Klux conspiracy, and will see nothing of the brutal system of intimidation by which he has won an office; the State is ominously quiet. Governor Lindsay boasts of his power over the colored voters; the Democratic politicians assert that they are fast winning the negroes to their side — by what means who can fail to see? and that it can not be by any known train of argument is shown from the open assertion of leading Democrats that, had they the power, they would take from the colored population the right to vote at all.

The measures employed by the Democrats to recruit their party from the Republican side is best shown in the testimony of the Rev. Mr. Lakin, and his narrative of the fearful deeds of the Ku-Klux in Alabama is sustained and made probable by the long series of their similar crimes in every Southern State. Mr. Lakin was sent to Alabama by Bishop Clark, of Ohio, to renew the Methodist Episcopal Church in that State. He seems to have been unusually successful. He traveled over nearly all the counties of the State. He numbered seventy ministers or teachers among his assistants; he was presiding elder of his district, and was gladly welcomed in many humble cottages on the mountains, and in every negro cabin. He was chosen president of the State university. But in 1868 the Ku-Klux were awakened by the approaching election, and by the cheering words of their friends in the North, of Seymour, Buckalew, Kernan, and Wood;[1] they drove the Rev. Mr. Lakin from the university; they threatened death to every Republican student. In the *Independent Monitor,* of Tuscaloosa, Alabama, appeared a leading article warning the new president to leave the State at once, and a cut was given, in which the Rev. Mr. Lakin was represented as hanging from the limb of a tree. It was also suggested that the end of "negroism" was near, and that there was room on the same limb for every "Grant negro." The Ku-Klux now renewed their terrible career, nor have we space even to allude to the details of their frightful deeds. Judge Thurlow was shot at Huntsville, where the disguised assassins had ridden in openly and in "line of battle"; Judge Charlton, another active Republican, was pursued and shot; a band of Ku-Klux rode into the town of Eutaw, in irresistible strength, seized a Mr. Boyd in his room at the hotel, and murdered him. The Rev. Mr. Lakin was threatened, shot at, and finally driven to take refuge in the mountains. The fate of many of his assistant preachers revives the image of the persecutions of Decius or Diocletian.[2] A Mr. Sullivan was barbarously whipped; the Rev. J. A. M'Cutchen, a presiding elder, was driven from Demopolis; the Rev. James Buchanan, and the Rev. John W. Tailly, another presiding elder, were expelled by force; the Rev. Jesse Kingston was shot in his pulpit; the Rev. James Dorman whipped; Dean Reynolds whipped and left nearly dead, with both arms broken; a colored preacher and his son were murdered on the public road; the Rev. Mr. Taylor severely beaten; six churches were burned in one district; schoolhouses were every where destroyed, and the teachers, male or female, driven away or infamously ill treated; while in many a negro cabin disguised assassins murdered the unoffending inmates, and spread terror beyond conception in all the colored population of Alabama. Such were the means by which Alabama was converted to Democracy, and by which Mr. Greeley[3] and his associates must hope to gain the Southern vote.

The Ku-Klux sprang up almost at the same moment through all the Southern States. It terrified and subdued Louisiana; it swept over Texas; mounted and disguised ruffians rode through Mississippi in 1871, breaking up the colored schools, and driving away preachers and teachers; they covered Western Tennessee; they murdered, whipped, and tormented in North Carolina. In Georgia,

---

[1] **Seymour . . . Wood:** northern Democratic leaders Horatio Seymour, Charles R. Buckalew, Francis Kernan, and Fernando Wood.
[2] **Decius . . . Diocletian:** Roman emperors who persecuted Christians.
[3] **Mr. Greeley:** Horace Greeley, New York newspaper editor and, in 1872, Democratic presidential nominee.

we are told by Mr. Stearnes,[4] whole counties of colored voters are disfranchised by the terrors of their fearful orgies. Not even the Congressional Committee has been able to pierce the depths of this widespread conspiracy. The Democratic leaders of the South, who profit by its secret influence, endeavor to hide in doubt and obscurity the means by which they forced Republican States to vote for Seymour and Blair,[5] and by which they hope again to drive them to vote for Greeley and the Democracy. They pretend that the period of license is past; that a year of the rigid intervention of the national government has suffered to dissolve forever the wide spread conspiracy which in 1871 was active in its enormities in every Southern State; that every colored citizen may vote safely in Alabama, and every white Republican till his plantation in Georgia in peace. He may; but it is on the condition that he will support the Democratic candidates and the Democratic policy. Whatever be the opinion of Northern or Southern politicians, the colored and the white Republicans of the South know that the Ku-Klux conspiracy is not dissolved; that the men who rode last year in masks and grotesque disguises over Georgia and Mississippi are more ready now than they were then to murder an aged Fowler almost in the arms of his wife ("He was so old a gentleman," she said, "that she did not think they could do it"); to shoot Methodist ministers in their pulpits; to whip Republican voters until they profess Democracy, and drive them to proclaim their shame, in faltering accents, on the steps of a court-house, or in the public papers; to disfranchise counties and States. And he can scarcely deserve the confidence of honest men who professes to believe that because the Ku-Klux has hidden from justice, it is not yet firmly united, pledged to rebellion, resolute to effect its aim; that it has not its allies at the North as cruel and as barbarous as in its own section; that an organized conspiracy does not still exist in every Southern State, laboring to provoke civil war and to destroy the Union. We might learn in every negro family, and in the home of every true Republican at the South, the universal terror of the midnight assassins by which the Democracy has risen to power. . . .

It is certain that a large majority of the Southern people would rejoice to see these "pests of society" swept away forever by the rigorous hand of the government. The merchant and the mechanic, the farmer and the laborer, had they dared, would long ago have suppressed the infamous association. But they are terrified into silence. It is not improbable that most of the honest Democrats have no sympathy with their murderous allies. And the whole colored population awaits, in prayerful silence, the result of the approaching election. . . .[6] What freeman is there but will give his vote against that faction whose only hope of success lies in ruling the Southern States by violence and fraud? What honest man but will

---

[4] **Mr. Stearnes:** Eben Sperry Stearns, Massachusetts educator who later headed the State Normal School in Nashville, Tennessee.
[5] **Seymour and Blair:** Horace Seymour and Francis Preston Blair Jr., the Democratic nominees for president and vice president in 1868.
[6] **the approaching election:** the presidential election of 1872, in which incumbent Ulysses S. Grant would be reelected by an overwhelming majority.

labor with ceaseless energy to set free the South from these enemies of industry, knowledge, liberty, and Union? . . .

3. Missionary Women and Black Education

MARIA WATERBURY
From *Seven Years among the Freedmen*
1890

An important part of African Americans' search for freedom focused on education. During and after the Civil War, schools were founded to teach slaves who had been liberated by the Union army. Some of these schools were operated by the Freedmen's Bureau, a federal agency established in 1865 to supervise the transition from slavery to freedom; northern church groups — as well as interdenominational organizations such as the American Missionary Association — ran many other schools. Scores of missionary teachers, many of them northern white women, arrived in the South. They received an enthusiastic greeting from African Americans, but their reception from southern whites was more qualified. In a number of states, the efforts of northern teachers were seen as meddling; they became the subject of political attacks and, sometimes, even violence.

In this memoir, Maria Waterbury, a missionary teacher from Illinois who arrived in the South sometime in the 1870s, describes her experiences in rural Mississippi, where missionary schools became the targets of Klan terror.

Journal — 1877
Ku-Klux Outrages

A well-educated man from South Carolina, who had taught all the white school in the place for fourteen years; his wife not able to read a word; five children, three of whom are women in size. The mother, though not book learned,

Maria Waterbury, *Seven Years among the Freedmen* (1890), 2d ed., rev. and enl., The Black Heritage Library Collection (Freeport, N.Y.: Books for Libraries Press, 1971), 129–31, 133–34, 136–38.

teaches her daughters to do all kinds of work. In a small cook-house, in the rear of the dwelling, each of the daughters take turns in cooking. Here we saw rice used as a vegetable, eaten with meat, as in Carolina, where it grows so abundantly. The bread and coffee were excellent, and the kindness of this family drew every one to them.

Here, for want of a county poor-house, were boarded the poor, who were a county charge, and here the northern teachers found a boarding place.

The family is large, and Mr. Sandsby, the father, having returned from the town, twenty-five miles away, is standing with his back to the great fire-place, telling the home circle of the doings in the county.

"The Ku-Klux have whipped the colonel, madam," addressing the teacher, "and have sent me word they will call on you. Of course I will defend you and my family, with my gun and dogs, as well as I can," said the tall South Carolina gentleman; "but they'll burn the house immediately, and what now is our wisest course, that's the question! There are many colored people here, and very much attached to the school they are; but it isn't safe to trust them in an emergency. They are not well armed, and they haven't dogs at their command; and the Ku-Klux have both arms and dogs, and they know if they are half of them killed, there is no jury in this state that will give them justice.

"It's never thought much of a sin to kill a colored man in a southern state, and one of the proverbs of the secret society known as the Ku-Klux, is, that '*Dead men tell no tales.*' The other proverb, that mostly governs them, is, '*This is a white man's government*'; and so, with some whisky on board, they manage to intimidate the blacks, and make them vote mostly their own way.

"There's an election close at hand, and this raid is to scare them to vote the ticket they give them. So much for freedom in old Mississippi, madam; and you'll find, too, they are bent on so scaring the blacks, that the children will be afraid to attend the school.

"They've killed the colored man who ferried them over the Tombigbee, and now, what's best to be done? We must act promptly; they'll be here by to-morrow night."

All night the blacks had a prayer-meeting, and at sunrise, sent Uncle Billy to see the teacher, and try to persuade her to stay.

Morning exercises in the school-room; Scripture lesson: "Let not your heart be troubled; ye believe in God, believe also in me. In my Father's house are many mansions: I go to prepare a place for you." "In the world ye shall have tribulation: but be of good cheer; I have overcome the world." "The angel of the Lord encampeth round about them that fear him, and delivereth them."

Singing, prayer, and calling the roll. The teacher tells the scholars she is going to take a vacation, and will send them word when the school is to begin again; gives each pupil a beautiful Scotch Bible, donated by the Y. M. C. A. of Scotland, which she has been saving to give at the end of the term. . . .

We had slept but little all night, as the blacks had an all-night prayer-meeting, and we could hear their shouts, songs, and prayers, sounding on the still night air; but we made the journey without much inconvenience, save that we crossed over a dozen streams, some of them so swollen we had to jump up on the saddle, and let the horse nearly swim through. A colored boy rode a mule, and went with the teacher, to show the way.

Arriving at the town, which was the county seat of a large county, we found the colonel, superintendent of schools, also government officer, had been badly whipped by a hundred masked men. They detailed ten of their number to do the whipping, which was done with a leather strap. The colonel had gone a dozen miles from town, taking with him two northern teachers; had located them in their school, and stopped at a house three miles on his homeward journey, to stay all night. The house was surrounded by a hundred masked men on horseback. A few of these *brave ones* entered the house, took the colonel, tied him to a tree, and mercilessly whipped him, he telling them if they killed him, it would bring more war to their homes, as he was a government officer, and the government was bound to punish the offense. The colonel, more dead than alive, was left at the house, while the riders returned to their homes. A driver was found to drive for the school officer, and ere morning he reached home, and soon his neighbors filled the house with their calls, proffering their sympathy, and loud in denouncing such work in their state. Here were members of the same church the colonel had joined, on going South to live; here was the grocery man who supplied the colonel's family with eatables; here were many living close around the dwelling of this man, who, though a government officer, was devoting his hours, when not on duty for the government, to benefiting both white and colored, in the capacity of head officer of the free-school system they were trying to establish in this state; all these, and some others, who had come to proffer their condolence, *were found to be the very Ku-Klux who whipped their neighbor.*

The case was brought before the civil courts, but the lawyers adjourned it from time to time for *three years,* then a southern jury *acquitted the Ku-Klux,* and when they returned from the trial, a company of ladies met them at the depot, with a flag, and band of music. . . .

Another Raid

Miss Ada was a devoted Christian girl, the daughter of a first-class lawyer in Illinois. The missionary spirit had fired her soul, and filled with desires to benefit the ex-slaves, she left a home of luxury to come South and be a despised teacher of the colored race. She lived in one room of an old house. Aunt Melinda, a colored woman occupied a part of the house, cooked the food of the teacher, and carried it to her room. The school taught by the lady was a short distance away, in an uncomfortable shed-like building. The scholars were learning fast, and greatly attached to the teacher. A night school for adults was taught, and good progress was being made by all the pupils.

The school had gone on not yet two months, when at two o'clock in the morning, the sound of many horsemen was heard, and soon a rap at the door announced the presence of the Ku-Klux. They ordered the door opened immediately, speaking in a guttural tone, behind a mask, saying they were in haste, as they had a long ways to go.

"Yes, yes," said Miss Ada, who had sprung from her bed at the first rap, and thrown on a wrapper, "as soon as I light a lamp," taking the precaution to secrete her gold watch and chain, which lay on the table.

"Open the door or we'll break it open," came from the hasty night riders, and with a prayer for help, the teacher opened the door, to be greeted by a dozen masked and armed men. Masks of white, trimmed with black, and their pistols at half cock, they entered the room. The lady invited them to sit down, and said she felt such a sense of the presence of God with her, that a thought of fear never entered her mind. With pistol in hand the captain of the band gave his orders for her to leave in three days saying, "This is a white man's government," also inquiring if she had a home, and why she should leave it to engage in so mean a calling.

"We will not have white people mixed up with niggers," said the Captain, and after inquiring the time of her, thinking to get sight of her watch, said they must go. As they went out, one said to another, "She wa'n't scared a bit."

Miss Ada in relating it, said, "I shed tears when they were gone, to think I was worthy to feel the mighty presence of God so much." "The angel of the Lord encampeth round about them that fear him, and delivereth them."

4. The Legacy of the Klan

ALBION W. TOURGÉE
"The Causes, Character, and Consequences of the Ku-Klux Organization"
1880

Thousands of Northerners migrated to the South during Reconstruction. They were tarred with the derogatory title of carpetbagger *because they supposedly arrived with all their possessions in a carpetbag, with the intention of enriching themselves at the expense of the local citizenry. In fact, many moved South for humanitarian reasons or because their war experience exposed them to the region, although others came because of economic opportunity. Albion W. Tourgée, a carpetbagger from Ohio, served in the Union army and moved to North Carolina in 1865. He almost immediately became deeply involved in Republican politics, and between 1869 and*

Albion Winegar Tourgée, *The Invisible Empire*, introduction and notes by Otto H. Olsen (Baton Rouge: Louisiana State University Press, 1989), 131–33, 136–40, 144–45.

1871, as a state judge, mounted a heroic effort to prosecute Klan activity. Although the Klan disappeared in North Carolina after 1871, Tourgée eventually became so frustrated that he left in disgust in 1879.

Soon after his departure, Tourgée wrote the best-selling novel A Fool's Errand, which described fictionally his experiences in North Carolina. The Invisible Empire, a supplement to the novel, spells out the Klan's impact with startling clarity. In this excerpt, Tourgée summarizes his explanation for its rise and success.

The Causes

The reader who has followed us thus far has obtained some faint idea of the most wonderful combination of armed men for unlawful purposes which the civilized world has ever known. There have been conspiracies and revolutions more desperate and daring, but none so widespread, secret, universal among so great a people, and above all so successful. It may be well to review briefly in conclusion the causes, character, purpose, and effect of this remarkable organization.

The cause — or to speak more accurately, the occasion — of its rise and sudden growth is, no doubt, somewhat complex. Its objective point was the overthrow of what is known as the reconstructionary legislation, including the abrogation or nullification of the thirteenth, fourteenth, and fifteenth amendments to the Federal Constitution; and the cause of its sudden spread was the almost universal hostility, on the part of the whites of the South, to this legislation and its *anticipated* results. For it should be kept constantly in mind that this organization was instituted and *in active operation in at least four States before a single one of the reconstructed State governments had been organized.*

Effects of the War

The reason of this hostility is not difficult to assign, though its elements are almost as various as the classes of mind and temperament which were affected by it. With some it was probably exasperation and chagrin at the results of the war. No doubt this was the chief incentive acting upon the minds of those who originally instituted in Tennessee this famous scheme of secret resistance to the policy of the government. Not only the sting of defeat but the shame of punishment without its terror combined to induce those who had cast all their hopes of honor and success upon the Confederate cause to lend themselves to any thing that would tend to humiliate the power which, in addition to the fact of conquest, had endeavored to impose upon them the stigma of treason. There is no doubt that the disfranchisement of those who had engaged in rebellion — or a "war for secession," as they prefer that it should be termed — was almost universally deemed an insult and an outrage only second in infamy to the enfranchisement of the colored man, which was contemporaneous with it. It is a matter of the utmost difficulty for a Northern man to realize the strength and character of this sentiment at the South. . . .

The "Carpet-Bagger" and "Caste"

This feeling was of course intensified by that pride of caste and prejudice of race, as well as the accustomed intolerance of diverse opinions which have already been considered as characteristic of the South. The antipathy to Northern men became laughable in its absurdity. The cry of "Carpet-bag" governments has been bandied about until it has become a synonym for oppression and infamy. That the reconstructionary governments were failures goes without denial; that incompetency and extravagance characterized them is a most natural result of their organization; but that any one of them was controlled by men of Northern birth is an idea of the sheerest folly and absurdity. In hardly one of them were there a score of officers, great and small, who were of Northern birth. . . .

The Fear of Servile Insurrection

There was another cause for the sudden spread of the Klan throughout the South which it is hard for the Northern mind to appreciate. Despite the marvelous peacefulness and long-suffering of the colored race, the people of the South had come to entertain an instinctive horror of servile or negro insurrections. Under the old slave *régime* this feeling was no doubt, in a measure, the product of that conscience which "doth make cowards of us all"; for it is unlikely that one could practice that "sum of all villainies," as Wesley[1] vigorously phrased the description of Slavery, without doing violence to that moral mentor. It was, however, much more the result of that demagogic clamor which had for fifty years or more dwelt with inexhaustible clamor upon the inherent and ineradicable savageness of the gentle and docile race that was held in such carefully guarded subjection. This feeling was manifested and deepened in those days by the terrible enactments in which the "Black Codes" of the South abounded, all designed to check disobedience of any kind, and especially that which might lead to organized resistance. The constant repetition of this bugbear of a servile insurrection as a defensive argument for the institution of Slavery had impressed every man, woman, and child at the South with a vague and unutterable horror of the ever-anticipated day when the docile African should be transformed into a demon too black for hell's own purlieus.[2] Year after year, for more than one generation, the Southern heart had been fired by the depiction of these horrors. In every political campaign the opposing orators upon the stump had striven to outdo each other in portraying the terrors of San Domingo and the Nat Turner insurrection, until they became words used to frighten children into good behavior. It came to be the chronic nightmare of the Southern mind. Every wayside bush hid an insurrection.

---

[1] **Wesley:** John Wesley, English Methodist and antislavery reformer.
[2] **purlieus:** environs.

Men were seized with a frenzy of unutterable rage at the thought, and women became delirious with apprehension at its mere mention. It was the root of much of that wild-eyed lunacy which bursts forth among the Southern people at the utterance of the magic slogan of to-day, "a war of races." There is no doubt but very many otherwise intelligent men and women are confirmed lunatics upon this subject. It has become a sort of holy horror with them. No greater offence can be given in a Southern household than to laugh at its absurdity. The race prejudice has been fostered and encouraged for political effect, until it has become a part of the mental and moral fiber of the people. There is no doubt but this feeling, taken in connection with the enfranchisement of the blacks, induced thousands of good citizens to ally themselves with the Klan upon the idea that they were acting in self-defence in so doing, and especially that they were securing the safety of their wives and children thereby.

Need of a Patrol

The old "patrol" system of the ante-bellum days and a devout belief in its necessity was also one of the active causes of the rapid spread of the Klan. This system was established by legislative enactment in all the Southern States. It varied somewhat in its details and in the powers conferred upon the patrolmen, or "patrollers" as they were popularly called. The purpose of the system, however, was declared to be "the preservation of order, and proper subordination among the colored population." The patrol generally consisted of a certain number of men, appointed for each captain's district or other local subdivision of the county, whose duty it was to patrol the public highway at night; to arrest and whip all negroes found beyond the limits of their masters' plantations after dark without a pass from the owner or overseer; to visit the "nigger quarters" on the plantations and see that no meetings or assemblies were held without the presence of a white man; and, in general, to exercise the severest scrutiny of the private life and demeanor of the subject-race. This system of espionage and the enforcement of the code designed for the control of the blacks without form of trial, had a great influence upon the mental status of both races. It deprived the person, house, and property of the freedmen of all that sanctity which the law throws around the person, home, and possessions of the white man, in the minds of both the Caucasian and the African. The former came to believe that he had the right to trespass, and the latter that he must submit to this claim. As the spirit of the new era did not admit of such statutory espionage and summary correction of the black as had been admitted by all to be necessary in the days of Slavery, and as it was undeniable that emancipation had not changed the nature of the inferior race nor removed all grounds for disaffection on his part, it was but natural that there should be a general sentiment that some volunteer substitute was necessary. As the power to whip and chastise for any infraction of the code of slave-etiquette was conferred upon the patrol, it was equally natural that they should regard the exercise of such authority by the Klan as not only necessary but quite a fit and proper thing to be done by them.

The Brutality of Slavery

The chief ground of doubt at the North in regard to the atrocities of the Klan, the Bull-dozers, and the Rifle Clubs,[3] is that it seems altogether incredible that the being so long and loudly self-vaunted as the very incarnation of all that is noble, generous, brave, and Christianlike — the ideal "Southern gentleman" — should assent to or engage in such atrocities. The trouble about this reasoning is that the "Southern gentleman," according to the Northern conception of him, is an almost mythical personage. The North has mistaken the terms used in self-description by the Southern aristocrat, who was at no time economical of adjectives. The perfect gentleman of the South is very apt, along with many splendid qualities and noble impulses, to possess others which at the North would be accounted very reprehensible. He is simply like other men, good according to the style and measure of his era and surroundings. In the old days a man might be a perfect gentleman and yet a cruel master, a keen speculator in human flesh, the sire of his own slaves, — and literally a dealer in his own flesh and blood. The Northern mind was horrified at such a combination. Yet it should not have been. The greatest evil of slavery was that it brutified the feelings of the master-race and lowered and degraded their estimate of humanity. . . .

It should be remembered that the institution of Slavery so warped and marred the common-law that grave and reverend — yea, conscientious, learned, and Christian men announced from the bench, with all the solemn sanction of the judicial ermine, doctrines with regard to the master's power over the person of the slave which are now considered barbarous and unlawful when applied to his brute possessions. In some States it was held that slavery vested the master with absolute power over the life of the slave; and, in all, that he might kill him to enforce obedience or to punish insolence. It is true that the slave was protected to a certain extent from the violence and passion of those not entitled to exercise mastery over him, but that was merely or chiefly for the sake of the master whose property he was. . . .

The Controlling Powers

The idea which has prevailed that the Ku-Klux were simply rough, lawless, irresponsible young rowdies is a singularly absurd reflection on the "best" classes — their power and inherited authority over their poorer neighbors. The minority which forced an overwhelming majority into what the victims themselves termed "the rich man's war and the poor man's fight," is still omnipotent in the domain of Southern public opinion. If they had disapproved of the doings of these men, the Klan would have shrivelled before the first breath of denunciation. But that breath never came with any earnestness or sincerity of tone until the object of the organization, the *destruction of the negro's political power*, had been fully ac-

---

[3] **Bull-dozers . . . Rifle Clubs:** along with the Klan, these were white paramilitary groups seeking to intimidate African Americans and Republicans.

complished. It is a reflection on the power of the best citizens to indulge the idea that the rabble could do any thing in opposition to their wishes. Professedly, they feebly "deplored" what was done, but in fact they either directly encouraged or were discreetly silent. That thousands of them loaned their horses for poor men to ride upon raids is just as certain as that they should put substitutes into the army under "the twenty-nigger law."[4]

Another thing which shows that the claim made in extenuation — that it was merely the work of rough spirits of the lower classes — is a libel on the common people of the South, is the fact that the best classes never prosecuted nor denounced these acts, but were always their apologists and defenders. Besides that, they kept the secrets of the Klan better than the Masons have ever kept the mysteries of their craft. It was an open secret in families and neighborhoods. Ladies met together in sewing-circles to make the disguises. Churches were used as places of assembly. Children were intrusted with secrets which will make them shudder in old age. Yet the freemasonry of a common impulse kept them as true as steel. As a rule, the only ones who flinched were a few of the more unfortunate or more cowardly of its members. Not a woman or a child lisped a syllable that might betray the fatal secret. It was a holy trust which the Southern cause had cast upon them, and they would have died rather than betray it. . . .

There is no sort of doubt that it originated with the best classes of the South, was managed and controlled by them, and was at all times under their direction. It was their creature and their agent to work out their purposes and ends. . . .

---

[4] **"the twenty-nigger law"**: refers to the exemption from the draft that the Confederate government granted to owners of twenty or more slaves.

Suggestions for Further Reading

Du Bois, W. E. B. *Black Reconstruction*. New York: Harcourt and Brace, 1935.

Edwards, Laura F. *Gendered Strife and Confusion: The Political Culture of Reconstruction*. Urbana: University of Illinois Press, 1997.

Foner, Eric. *Reconstruction: America's Unfinished Revolution, 1863–1877*. New York: Harper & Row, 1988.

Litwack, Leon F. *Been in the Storm So Long: The Aftermath of Slavery*. New York: Alfred A. Knopf, 1979.

Trelease, Allen W. *White Terror: The Ku Klux Klan Conspiracy and Southern Reconstruction*. New York: Harper & Row, 1971. Reprint, Westport, Conn.: Greenwood Press, 1979.

CHAPTER TWO

WESTWARD EXPANSION

The Texas Border Wars

In the generation after Reconstruction, expanded railroads, increased mobility, and growth in agriculture remade the West and the South. Both regions became societies of great contrasts between wealth and poverty, cities and dusty villages, honor and continuing violence, and the rhetoric of chivalry and the reality of racial oppression. Texas provides a unique window into these developments, for its inhabitants — perhaps more than any other state's — experienced intense cultural and racial conflict as what historians have called the "New West" and the "New South" converged. Along an open border with Mexico, Texas coalesced into a society in which the newly dominant Anglo culture clashed with the preexisting Mexican and Native American social systems. On the rim of the southern and western plains, these three cultures waged an intense and often violent struggle.

The 1870s and 1880s were decades of rapid economic development and social change. The spreading rail network opened Texas to penetration by the market economy: the miles of railroad track more than trebled. Massive immigration followed, elevating the state's population from around 800,000 people in 1870 to more than 2.2 million only twenty years later. People moved to Texas because of its economic opportunities, and the majority of newcomers were black and white Southerners. Large numbers of immigrants moved to the booming cotton belt of East Texas; others poured onto the central and western plains, where many farmed the arid lands or joined the growing cattle industry. Free-ranging herds of horses and cattle, descended from livestock brought by the Spanish, grazed throughout Texas. After the Civil War, enterprising herders began to round up the animals and move them north to rail connections in Kansas for shipment to stockyards in Chicago and, from there, to markets in eastern urban centers.

The large majority of Anglos in Texas quickly became engaged in a profound struggle with the strong cultures of Native Americans and Mexicans. This struggle, dating to the founding of the Texas Republic, became a central aspect of the state's settlement and development: the 1836 victory over Mexican president Antonio Lopez de Santa Anna at the battle of San Jacinto had established American dominance over the Mexicans in Texas, but protracted warfare along the 265-mile border continued for many decades, always simmering, sometimes exploding. The Mexican government exerted only loose control over its northern frontier, where local warlords prevailed and bandits frequently moved across the border to raid American ranches.

The lucrative American cattle industry was particularly appealing to Mexican raiders. In response to continuing depredations, the Anglos formed the Texas Rangers, a state police unit that applied summary force along the frontier. Organized in the 1830s and 1840s as "ranging companies" of often loosely organized militia, the Rangers established law and order among the unruly immigrants arriving in the state; they did not hesitate to shoot outlaws or high-spirited cowboys in Texas towns. Because of their reputation for violence and brutality, the Rangers were temporarily disbanded during Reconstruction, only to be reconstituted in 1874 as a weapon in what amounted to a continuing war against Mexicans and Native Americans. Although many of the Texas Rangers were little more than ruthless killers, a powerful mystique about their exploits emerged.

Simultaneously, Texans fought ferociously with the state's Native Americans. In the antebellum years, Anglos had battled the nomadic Comanches near San Antonio and the more agricultural Cherokees of eastern Texas, pushing the Comanches and Kiowas north and expelling all Native Americans from East Texas. Expansion of the white population and its spread westward led to continuing conflict in the years after the Civil War. At the same time, white hunters armed with high-powered rifles descended upon the plains and, with the tacit approval of the U.S. Army, killed millions of bison. The great buffalo herds that had extended throughout the plains were virtually wiped out by the 1870s.

The buffalo killing applied one kind of pressure to Plains Indians; the arrival of thousands of ranchers and farmers, another. Indian attacks on settlers began to occur more frequently, and the U.S. Army responded with a concerted effort to limit Indians to reservations. In 1872, army forces under the command of William T. Sherman and Philip Sheridan authorized the capture of marauding Indians; over the next three years American troops rounded up and exterminated Native Americans not on the reservations. By 1875, the Kiowas and Comanches were no longer threats to white settlements.

A significant participant in the border wars of the 1870s was a contingent of black Union soldiers who continued to serve in the U.S. Army. Some 180,000 African Americans had served in the Union army, which rapidly demobilized at the end of the Civil War; by 1866 it had shrunk to an authorized force of less than

55,000 men. Of this small regular army, Congress authorized the organization of six regiments of black troops — four of them infantry, two cavalry. They were among those sent to protect white settlers in the West and to subdue the lawless border area of Texas. Indians called them "buffalo soldiers," according to one account, and the black soldiers eagerly embraced the term as part of their tradition.

The readings in this chapter provide a glimpse of various dimensions of the border wars in post–Civil War Texas. The Mexican commission's report on the frontier examines the problems of the border from a Mexican point of view and suggests the extent of the warfare that was waged there. Luvenia Conway Roberts recounts the activities of the Texas Rangers from the point of view of a frontier woman. Finally, letters between officers of the 9th Cavalry and government officials discuss armed conflict between the "buffalo soldiers" and Mexicans on the Rio Grande border.

As you read, ascertain the cultural and racial perspectives of the authors of these documents. How did they regard other groups? How did cultural conflict between Anglos and Mexicans manifest itself? What attitudes did Anglos, Native Americans, Mexicans, and African American "buffalo soldiers" have toward each other?

5. Horse Thieves on the Mexican Border

MEXICAN COMMISSION
Report on the Northern Frontier Question
1875

In the period between the independence of Texas in 1836 and the Mexican-American War a decade later, a low-level war raged in the form of banditry by Mexicans and reprisals by Anglos; the border remained unstable for most of the nineteenth century. Differing interpretations of the origins of the conflict reflect pronounced differences in cultural perspective. From the Anglo point of view, the dif-

Report of the Investigating Commission of the Northern Frontier Question. Reprinted in *The Mexican Experience in Texas*, ed. Carlos E. Cortés (New York: Arno Press, 1976), 11–18.

*ficulties arose from Mexican duplicity and thievery. Mexicans saw the matter dif-
ferently. The turbulence on its northern frontier prompted Mexico to create a border
investigating commission, which published a comprehensive report in May 1873.
The report, challenging the Anglos' assumptions, was sharply critical of weak Texas
law enforcement and called for a new era of peaceful relations between the two
countries.*

———————————

... In the examination of the relations between the frontiers since 1848, the
first striking point is the system of cattle thieves. During the Texan war and afterwards, in fact up to 1848, horse and cattle stealing increased to so great an extent,
in the district north of Rio Bravo to Nueces, as to almost depopulate the country
by ridding the inhabitants of their stock.

Bands of Americans, Texans, Mexicans, and Indians, in a few years, exhausted
the wealth of that region. The settlers were few in number, and lacked the vigi-
lance of either the Mexican or Texan authorities, so that they not only lost their
wealth, but gave scope to a degree of license and immorality of itself dangerous
and degrading. The early emigrants to that part of Texas did nothing towards correcting this state of things, but, on the contrary, aggravated the evil, for they were
not themselves noted for rectitude or sobriety. It was the refuge for criminals flying from justice in Mexico; adventurers from the United States, who sought a fortune, unscrupulous of the means of procuring it; and vagrants from all parts of the
State of Texas, hoping, in the shadow of existing disorganization and lawlessness,
to escape punishment for their crimes. Under this head the Commission does not
class all the early emigrants to Southwestern Texas since 1848. Far from this; it acknowledges in many of them the highest moral standard, but, compared with the
mass, they constituted but a small proportion, too small to give tone to that class
of people, and check the characteristic lawlessness of the district.

The thirst for wealth had become such a strong passion, that any means of
procuring it seemed fair and legal. The district from Rio Bravo to Nueces had
been cleared of its live stock; only the land remained; and rapacity knowing no
bounds, the lands were seized, by many through force of arms, but generally by
persons clothed with feigned legal power. This frontier district, extending along
the Rio Bravo, abounded in droves of horses: the horse thieves of Mexico commenced operations here, which assumed from the onset alarming proportions,
and the traffic in Texas of horses stolen from Mexico became a matter of commonplace merchandise. The facility which the horse thieves enjoyed, since 1848,
of disposing of the stolen animals on the Texan shore of the Rio Bravo, increased
the evil to an alarming extent. This pernicious influence has injured the industrial
impulses of the Mexican frontier, since the results of horse stealing, and the evil
influence of the thieves, have proven more fatal to the country than the revolutions.

Horse stealing in Mexico may be classed under two different heads: one, the
appropriation of roving droves, taken a few leagues from the banks of the Rio

Bravo, within Mexican territory, transported across the river into Texas, and driven in lots into the interior of the State; the other is the seizure of horses in the interior of the Mexican frontier wherever horses can be found.

Although testimonial evidence on all these points has been most useful and important, yet circumstantial proofs culled from the archives have in all cases been more conclusive. In those examined by the Commission are a series of regulations framed by the municipal and police authorities for the suppression of horse thieves in the towns lying on the bank of the river. Very few of these measures looked to the prevention of the traffic in stolen cattle from Texas, from which it would seem that this evil did not exist to the same extent; whilst on the contrary, the laws had in view the damages resulting from horse stealing in Mexico, and the transportation of the horses into Texas, proving that this was the greater traffic, and the one that needed greater legislation. Measures for the prevention of this crime have been issued in every town along the river, from which it may be deduced that like injuries were experienced in every village on the Mexican line; and as these preventive measures were constant and frequently repeated, it would seem that the injuries were constant and frequently recurring.

It is useless for the Commission to go into a detailed account of the various measures adopted by Mexican authorities to suppress this evil, but, considering these documents of intrinsic value as bearing on the characteristic relations of both frontiers, the Commission took especial care in the selection of extracts from all of these regulations, arranging them in chronological order, and at times copying them entirely, when they offered any particular interest.

The great weight of these proofs cannot be estimated from a few isolated measures of this kind, but must be judged as a whole; for whilst instituting a repressive system of horse stealing on the Mexican frontier for the Texan market, since 1848, they also indicate the robberies organized on the Texan shore of the Rio Bravo, in injury to Mexican proprietors.

The judicial record is another element for illustrating the frontier question, since 1848, as regards horse stealing in Mexico. In the majority of criminal prosecutions against the cattle thieves, the evidence produced went to show that the stolen animals had been conducted by the thieves to the United States frontier, and then sold to dealers. The Commission has made chronological extracts from all criminal cases relative to cattle thieves tried before the judicial court of each of the towns they visited, and the entire number of these different extracts corroborates the deductions made from the preventive measures adopted by the executive authorities. The number of horses stolen in Mexico for the Texan market may be judged by the following:

1st. From the testimony of those whose horses were stolen, and who had proofs of their having been carried into Texas. The horses, having on several occasions been pursued, were found by their masters, who instituted criminal proceedings against the thieves, the result of which sometimes proved favorable, but generally the costs were so heavy that they often amounted to as much, and at times to more, than the value of the property recovered.

2d. From that of persons who were eye-witnesses to the acts of the robbers, some of them men who had charge of the horses, others who had seen the horses driven across the river to the Texan border, and still others who had aided in the pursuit from the bank of the river into the interior of Texas.

3d. By testimony of members of the police force who, in pursuit of the thieves, noticed that their depredations extended to Jimenez, Marina, and Tamaulipas, sixty leagues south of the Rio Bravo, after the continued robberies had exhausted the horses of the districts of Matamoros and San Fernando, thirty leagues south of the river.

4th. From evidence of those competent to judge of horseflesh, and familiar with their pasturage since 1848, who have remarked the diminution or total disappearance of them in certain districts where horses had previously abounded, from robberies and entirely independent of their destruction from revolutions.

5th. From that of merchants who, having driven horses into Texas, found difficulty in disposing of them, by reason of the low prices at which stolen horses could be bought, and which was far below their market value. Stolen horses are generally sold in Texas at prices below what the proprietors charge for them in Mexico. Competition is constant when it is remembered that robberies are continued. The nearer you approach the Rio Bravo the greater the competition, and for this reason the dealers in horses honestly procured drive them into the northern part of Texas when possible, so as to secure better sales, and escape the competition with dealers of stolen horses who assemble in the neighborhood of the Rio Bravo.

Notwithstanding all these convincing and varied proofs, which the minutest scrutiny only served to corroborate, and despite the previous testimony given by persons, the majority of whom bear the most unimpeachable reputations, the Commission, in its research for the true facts of the case through the medium of official documents, did not fail to make use of the slightest written proof that could be made of avail.

The repeated measures taken by the administrative authorities doubtless indicate the increase of horse stealing in Mexico for the Texan market, for it is not natural that regulations of such a stringent nature could, through a long series of years, have been enacted by different persons and in different districts, and so tenaciously adhered to, had not the interest at stake been one of great importance; on the contrary, all the data collected from this source point to the general evil, but the Commission needed something still more definite than legal enactments, pointing only to generalities. Statistics are in their infancy in this country, and unable to furnish the Commission with the exact figures, and they were in consequence compelled to be satisfied with the best information they could procure, from scarce and isolated sources.

The robberies at length assumed such proportions that the Town Council of Reynosa, on the 11th of March, 1852, addressed the Mexican consul at Brownsville, informing him of the injuries suffered by the proprietors; and also stating that a band of Americans under Frederick Mathews had established themselves in Las Salinas, and collected a drove of horses amounting to four hundred, stolen from the pasturage on the bank of the river; the corporation also added that this was not the first time that Mathews had engaged in such traffic, and asked the consul to inform the authorities of Brownsville, and request that something be done to stay the evil.

The consul replied that he had conferred with the collector of customs, and that that officer had ordered the horses so introduced by Mathews to be seized as contraband; that the last heard of Mathews he was near Nueces on his way to San Patricio, and that they hoped to overtake him. The consul added that he had induced the collector of customs, to publish a notice threatening the importers of horses with the penalty of the law, if any were found guilty of making contraband importations.

This notice was accordingly published in the "Bandera Americana," a periodical issued in Brownsville, a copy of which dated April 17th, 1853, has been filed with the *"expediente."*[1] In this notice, John S. Rhea, collector of customs at Point Isabel, declares that having received information that a large number of horses had been stolen from Mexican citizens of Reynosa, and had been illegally introduced into the States, and taken to the interior of Texas to be sold, the inhabitants are warned of the penalties of law incurred by any who knowingly and willingly take part in these fraudulent proceedings.

They were not successful in recovering all the horses stolen by Mathews; a part only were taken on their way to San Antonio de Bejar, of which seizure the consul gave notice to the authorities of that town; but such was the insecure and disorganized condition of affairs in Texas, that the owners of the stolen animals were attacked by bands of American highwaymen, attempting to regain the stolen property by main force.

Not only do these various documents exhibit the exactness of the judgment formed by the Commission, but they also show how the illicit traffic had increased, mentioning one lot of stolen horses amounting to over four hundred in number. The gravity of the question is revealed by the steps taken by the town council in the appeal to the Mexican consul at Brownsville, and in the prompt measures taken by the custom-house officials, especially those at Point Isabel, who not only took the matter up, but sought through the application of the laws, the remedy of the ills complained of and endured on the Mexican frontier, probably because they were well aware of the extent of the injuries done to the inhabitants along the whole length of the Mexican line.

Horse stealing on so vast a scale from the pastures along the river has greatly diminished in the last few years. The Commission is of opinion that this diminution may be attributed to the scarcity of animals, owing to robberies and revolutions; but although horse stealing lessened in the river pasturage, it continued with some energy in the districts somewhat distant from the river, where the interests of the country were greater.

Laying aside all the corroborative evidence by the various witnesses on this point, there is one document well worthy of special attention. Don Trinidad Garza

---

[1]*expediente:* a court case, or literally, "file."

y Melo, a lawyer, made some notes for the criminal statistics of Nuevo Leon, on the 4th of February, 1870, and these were published long before any one dreamed that they would serve as an index for these investigations. Señor Garza Melo was Judge of the Supreme Court of the State in the years 1868 and 1869, and he affirms that the data from which his work was compiled were selected from *"expedientes"* issued by him. Out of three hundred and eighty-six cases tried before him in those two years, one hundred and thirty-three, that is, the third part, were for horse stealing. He attributes the frequency of this crime to the three following causes: the disorders growing out of a common pasturage; the extent and loneliness of the plains; and finally, the proximity of the Rio Bravo, to the left shore of which the stolen animals could be so easily and quickly transported, with the certainty of disposing of them without delay in foreign territory, and with the still more positive certainty of not being pursued or molested.

By the frequency of the crime the number of animals stolen may be fairly estimated; by the number of cases tried we can judge of the evil; by the condemnation of the delinquents in some cases, and by the accusations, even where there was no evidence to point to the true criminal, it will be conclusive that a wrong exists, and that its destructive results may still be perceived; that it has only changed its vantage ground; that as soon as the animals in one district had been captured and the interests of the country damaged, it had passed to another, where its evil influence was experienced by not only the proprietors, but also the laboring classes of society. . . .

6. "In the Country of the Bad Man"

LUVENIA CONWAY ROBERTS
On Living with the Texas Rangers
1928

Born in 1849, Luvenia Conway met and married Daniel Webster Roberts, a thirty-three-year-old Ranger, in Columbus, Texas, in 1875. A determined woman, she decided that marriage would not separate her from her husband; she followed him and

Luvenia Conway Roberts, A Woman's Reminiscences of Six Years in Camp with the Texas Rangers (Austin: Von Boeckmann-Jones Company, 1928). Reprinted in Texas Tears and Texas Sunshine: Voices of Frontier Women, ed. Jo Ella Powell Exley (College Station: Texas A&M Press, 1985), 194, 199, 201–2, 204–7.

*was a witness to his career. In her memoir, published after her death, she describes
how the Texas Rangers became active participants in the border wars of the 1870s.*

Married September 13, 1875, Captain D. W. Roberts and Miss Lou Conway, the
Rev. Dr. Archer officiating. The gallant groom and his accomplished bride departed on the train immediately after the ceremony. The best wishes of all attend
them.

This brief notice appeared in the *Columbus (Texas) Times.* The clergyman
had preached the day before, Sunday, at Osage, some distance from Columbus.
He returned by train; there was only one train a day; as we were to leave on this
same train the conductor obligingly held it while the minister came to the house
and pronounced the words "until death do us part."

Captain Roberts commanded a company of Rangers stationed in Menard
County, which was on the extreme frontier. His home was in Blanco County. He
had been engaged in buying and selling cattle. At that time Columbus was the ter-
minus of the railroad, and a good shipping point. It was during his visits to Columbus on business that we became acquainted.

My friends thought that I was courageous; in fact, quite nervy to leave civilization and go into an Indian country. But it did not require either; I was much
in love with my gallant captain and willing to share his fate wherever and whatever it might be. Besides the romantic side of it appealed to me strongly. I was
thrilled with the idea of going to the frontier, the home of the pioneer.

We came direct to the beautiful city of Austin. I had made trips to Houston,
Galveston, and San Antonio — all located in a level country. The hills of Austin
were beautiful, and, now since I have visited other States, I still believe that the
scenic beauty of Austin and surrounding country cannot be excelled. . . .

The Rangers supplied me with various pets. Among them were squirrels,
prairie dogs, a cub bear, a dog, and a canary bird. I enjoyed the bear while he was
little, but he got cross as he grew up and I turned him loose. We were never dull
in camp. Several of the Rangers were musical, and had their instruments with
them. Captain Roberts was a fine violinist. A race track was laid out, and there was
horse racing. Card playing was not allowed, and it was not done openly. Betting
on horse races was permitted, but the Rangers ran their races for amusement. We
had a croquet set, and that game was enjoyed.

After we had been in camp a few months it was decided to go up the river
about thirty miles, which meant that far from any settlement. Going into that
wild country exposed us to encounters with Indians. A strong guard — ten men —
was taken along. That number had been victorious in their last fight with Indians,
so we felt well protected. After we had made our new camp, and before we commenced to fish, it was agreed that we would not scatter and that everyone would
keep his gun by him. Such sport as we enjoyed! As fast as a hook could be cast it
would be caught up by a fish. I have often wondered whether a white man had
ever fished there before us. We spent two pleasant days. No live Indians were

seen, but we found the skeleton of a dead one where he had been buried in a crevice of rock. When we returned to camp, I felt that I had been on a scout, and I have always had a suspicion that it was so reported to headquarters, but this I do not know to be a fact. . . .

We received orders to move. We were sorry to leave the camp where we had spent such a delightful time. But the company had orders to proceed to Laredo on account of some trouble with Mexicans. I was not allowed to go. It was a great disappointment. I accompanied the command as far as San Antonio, and was left there. I boarded at the Adams House on Flores Street. I realize now that I was exposed to great danger. The house was filled with tuberculars. We would sit in the living room, then called parlor, filled with tuberculars, and supplied with cuspidors. Two died in the house from that disease while I was there. How ignorant we were in "the good old days"!

After spending two months in San Antonio, I was delighted to receive a message from my husband telling me to join him at Sabinal. I took the first stagecoach out. Captain Roberts had come on in advance of the company, and we boarded in Sabinal until the Rangers arrived and established camp twelve miles below the town. Three families resided at Sabinal, so we were fortunate in finding a place to board. I was glad to get back to camp.

We found that a very different country from Menard. Game was not so abundant. Fishing was good, but not as good as at Menard. It was not the frontier that we loved so well.

Our camp was in a beautiful live oak grove, and there we spent the winter of 1877–78. The Indians made no raids while we were there, but the Rangers had plenty to do running down outlaws. Many arrests were made. The wives of some of the married prisoners camped near us in order to be near their husbands. They were permitted to talk to their husbands only in the presence of a guard. The innocent suffered with the guilty. They may have been good women. It must have been heartrending to them to see their husbands in shackles. I pitied them. But nature is cruel, and they were victims of that law. In "the good old days" marriage was binding. . . . I believe in divorces, and am glad to see the change, but regret that they have become so numerous. . . .

Captain Roberts was ordered to take his company to Menard County and to establish his camp on the San Saba River five miles below Fort McKavett. Fort McKavett was located on the San Saba River twenty miles above our former camp. The trip from Austin to Menard was uneventful. On arriving at our destination, we pitched our tents under some beautiful oaks.

Up to this time we had had only one tent and a kitchen, but at Camp San Saba we were supplied a second tent, which because of its size the Rangers named the "elephant." We felt that our household was growing. The "elephant" I furnished as my guest chamber, and equipped it with army cot, washstand, a small table, and a mirror hung on the tent pole. Our kitchen was built of logs, with a tent for a roof. Both our tents were floored; we had outgrown gunny-sack floor covering. The two tents and kitchen were surrounded by a brush fence, with a whitewashed gate that looked quite imposing. The State furnished us a cook. The rations issued to the Rangers included only the substantials, but were of such generous quantity that we had a surplus to exchange for butter, milk, eggs, etc. Honey was obtained from bee trees. Game and fish were abundant.

The Rangers and the Yankee soldiers were now neighbors. The soldiers at Fort McKavett had never furnished protection against Indian depredations. Had they afforded such protection, Company D would not have been sent there. The soldiers did not go after the Indians the way the Rangers did. Their movements were military, regulated by a lot of red tape, and they couldn't catch them. The Rangers used no ceremony; they mounted their horses, ran down the Indians and killed them. The soldiers received thirteen dollars a month; the Rangers received forty dollars. When a soldier wished to quit the service before his enlistment expired the only way out was to desert; when a Ranger wanted to quit, his commander would readily give him a discharge on the ground that a dissatisfied Ranger was not efficient. Rangers had their hearts in the service; they were protecting the frontier of their home State. Soldiers and officers had no social intercourse; Rangers visited at captain's headquarters, and were frequently invited to a meal.

The officers at the fort were friendly, and one of them said to Captain Roberts, "Your fights here in the shadow of this post are so humiliating that I feel like resigning." On my visit to the post I met my first house guest, Miss Cora Ogden of San Antonio. She was visiting her brother, who was sutler.[1] She was a charming young lady. I entertained her by taking her hunting and fishing. There was always a Ranger who would volunteer to go with us, get the bait, and bait the hooks. We took a good many rides behind mules, and regretted very much that we could not ride horseback. Unfortunately there was but one sidesaddle and one habit available; it would have been impossible to have ridden a man's saddle without exposing an ankle. Some evenings we visited the main camp to listen to the string band.

The Rangers and the military exchanged courtesies in the following manner: The officers and their wives would drive down to our camp to listen to our string band, and we would go up and hear their brass band. . . .

The Rangers were kept quite busy during the summer, scouting for Indians. However, they found time to stage a minstrel performance at Menard. The citizens of that place were planning to build a church; the Rangers gave the play for their benefit. They cleared sixty dollars, which was the first cash contribution to the church building fund. My guest chamber was frequently occupied, for I enjoyed the company of young ladies. It was fun to visit the big camp and watch the rehearsals. The manager of the play was able to select some good talent. Sometimes the boys would attend a dance at Menard; on such occasions there was "rustling" for clothes. The Captain would sometimes lend a suit, and the others would invariably tell the girls about it. Practical jokes varied camp life. Even I caught the spirit. The Rangers were always on the anxious seat when the Legislature assembled to make the biennial appropriations. Would the appropriations for the Rangers be continued? Would they all be continued in the service? The mail

[1]**sutler:** a civilian provisioner.

was looked forward to with great eagerness at such times. Captain Roberts was away one day when the mail was brought. There was a letter to him from the Adjutant General. The Rangers came to me to know what the letter contained. I read it to them correctly that the appropriation had been made, but I added, "Discharge every man under five feet ten." Then there was some measuring. When Captain Roberts returned and read the letter to them, they knew I had manufactured that last statement, but they did not hold it against me.

Each quarter Captain Roberts made the trip to Austin for the Rangers' pay, and I accompanied him. Most of these trips were uneventful, but they afforded enjoyable visits to our friends. But the trip I am going to tell about now was different. It rained all day between Mason and Fredericksburg. We found it impossible to reach the Nimitz Hotel by night. As we knew of no place where we could find shelter for the night we were worried. Fortunately, we met a man who told us that at the end of the next mile we would find a trail which would lead us to a house. It was dark when we reached the house. A woman met us, and kindly consented to give us lodging. She at once began by apologizing to me, or rather explaining why they were so poor. She said, "All my children are gals. We might get along better if 'he' would stay at home and work, but 'he' has to be gone away all the time preaching." The house was one long room. It was occupied by two families. Each had a separate fireplace, and each had several children. Our hostess prepared our supper by cooking some corndodgers in a skillet, and by frying some bacon in the same skillet — the only cooking vessel she had. She gave us some black coffee. The table seated four, which was our number. After supper our hostess pointed out the bed we were to occupy, which was in a row with several others. There were no partitions and no curtains. Undressing was a public affair. If the present style of dress had been in vogue then, undressing would have been a simple thing, but in those days we wore clothes.[2] I managed the best I could. Soon after we retired "he" came home. While "he" was partaking of the evening meal "he" said, "I hear a lot about hard times when I'm gone, but I never see it until I come home." It was with great difficulty that I restrained myself from getting up and choking him. I wanted to say, "You lazy, trifling thing; running around, eating hot biscuit and fried chicken; and your family starving." I know our hostess served us with the best she had. The condition of that poor family made a lasting impression on my mind. . . .

Our camp was located in a beautiful live oak grove on the Llano River. The country is hilly. It was at that time on the extreme frontier. There were few settlements. There was not a fence in Kimble County. The first house to be built of lumber was on Farmer's Ranch, twenty miles above Junction. The lumber was hauled from Round Rock by ox teams.

The day before we reached our new camp four men were killed in Junction. I was very strongly impressed that we were in a bad man's country. My inclination to hunt and fish suddenly vanished. Camp appeared to me the safest place to

---

[2]**we wore clothes:** Roberts is referring to the corsets and bulky garments worn by white women in the 1870s.

stay. With Ranger protection I did venture to carry my laundry to Junction. I found it comprised a few log cabins, so frequently described as the home of the pioneer. On our way back to camp the boys told me that they had heard at the post office that the women washed on the banks of the river and that they had had several fights. It made me very uncomfortable to know that we were in a country where women fought. I renewed my determination to stay close in camp and to take up my embroidery to pass the time. A few days later I accompanied the Rangers, who were going after the mail, to bring back my laundry. I got out at the house where I had left the clothes; the Rangers went on to the post office. I walked boldly to the door, I might say fearlessly, without any premonition of the danger to which I was exposed. There were three women present, and as soon as I looked at them I saw their belligerent attitude. I was so taken by surprise that my voice may have trembled when I asked for my clothes. They said the clothes were washed, but that they would never wash for me again. Then they began to tell me their opinion of people who thought themselves better than other folks. They told me that they had been well raised, had always kept the best company, and continued for some time to pour forth a tirade of abuse, mixed with swear words, about stuck-up people. Money, they said, doesn't make anyone better. During all this time I had not said a word; I could think of nothing to say that would save me. But when they spoke of money, I said, "Surely, you are not mistaking us for rich people. Rangers are all poor." On hearing my reply they were mollified. There was a great change in their manner. They assumed a friendly attitude, and one of them asked me to have a "chaw." That placed me in an awkward if not dangerous dilemma. I was afraid to refuse for fear of giving offense. At that moment the Rangers drove up. I declined with thanks. I was glad to get back to camp. Later I learned that I had offended these women by not inviting them to visit me when I took the laundry down.

For nearly two weeks I stuck to my resolution to stay in camp, but the monotony of camp and the tempting attractiveness of the Llano River caused me to waver. I took my gun and went back to hunting and fishing, which were fine. Company could not be had; girls were scarce, and my acquaintance was limited.

Life was not monotonous for the Rangers. While the Indians had ceased to raid in Menard, they continued to depredate in Kimble. Besides hunting Indians, there was much police duty. We were not only in an Indian country, but also in the country of the bad man. The Rangers were continually making arrests, and invariably they would be "cussed out" by the wives. When the Rangers planned to make an arrest, they took station near the suspect's house the night before, and rushed upon it about daylight next morning before the culprit would have time to escape. The Rangers told the following joke on Captain Roberts. The Captain opened a door just as day was breaking; he didn't knock, and entered without ceremony. When he opened the door the wife confronted him. He said, "Good morning, Madam." She said, "Good morning, the devil," and began cursing him and his Rangers. It was not a pleasant business. There was no jail in Kimble County; prisoners were taken to Mason. . . .

7. Buffalo Soldiers on the Border

Major J. F. Wade, Colonel Edward Hatch, Edwards Pierrepont, and Stephen Powers
Reports on the Solis Affair
1875

For two years, in 1874 and 1875, under the command of white officer and Civil War veteran Edward Hatch, the all-black 9th Cavalry, based at Fort Ringgold, conducted regular patrols along the border in search of cattle thieves and bandits. Their presence was largely unappreciated, partly because much of the citizenry of the lower Rio Grande Valley was involved with cattle thievery and partly because of local residents' intense racism. Consequently, the 9th suffered from frequent harassment by local officials. In December 1874, after Hatch banned gamblers from the fort, a local jury indicted him for "false imprisonment."

In January 1875, an attempt by the 9th Cavalry to patrol the border led to a shootout between black soldiers and Mexicans at the Solis ranch. Two troopers and at least one Mexican were killed, and a local jury indicted some members of the 9th for murder. As these letters suggest, American officials were convinced that tensions between Mexicans and Texans made a fair trial impossible.

Major J. F. Wade's Report to the Assistant Adjutant General.

Headquarters Ringgold Barracks. Texas
May 12th 1875

Assistant Adjutant General:
Department of Texas.
San Antonio Texas.

Sir:

I have the honor to forward herewith vouchers for one hundred dollars ($100.00) for services rendered by John C. Sullivan, Attorney at Law, in the cases of Sergeant Edward Troutman and Privates Charley Blackstone, and John Fredericks, Company "G," 9th Cavalry. The services were rendered under the following circumstances: On the 26th of January 1875, these men and, two others (Jerry Owsley and Moses Turner, Company "G," 9th Cavalry) were on patrol along the

Blacks in the United States Armed Forces: Basic Documents, vol. 3, Freedom and Jim Crow, 1865–1917, ed. Morris J. MacGregor and Bernard C. Nalty (Wilmington, Del.: Scholarly Resources, 1977), 101–13. (Some spelling and punctuation has been modernized.)

river under orders from the commanding Officer of this Post, looking for the illegal crossing of cattle, and on the afternoon of that day arrived at the Solesis [*sic*] ranch, went into camp and remained there until between 8 and 9 O'clock P.M. when they were suddenly fired upon from the ranch. No one was hurt and they at once saddled up and moved in the direction of this Post: but had moved less than one mile when they were met by a large party of Mexicans who at once fired upon them and Owsley and Turner were killed, the others escaped and returned to this Post, being pursued and fired upon by mounted men. On the 27 Colonel Hatch 9th Cavalry went to the ranch with a detachment of his regiment and arrested all Mexicans to be found there. He also found one Mexican had been killed and two others wounded, the night before. The Deputy Sheriff, Justice of the Peace and a Coroners Jury arrived during the day and an inquest was held. The Coroners Jury found that the soldiers had been quiet and orderly during their stay at the ranch; that they were fired upon without provocation and that the killing of the Mexican and wounding of one of the others was done by the party who fired on the camp, that the other Mexican was wounded by the Soldiers at the time they were fired upon the second time. They also found nine Mexicans among those arrested and several others who had escaped across the river, guilty of the killing of the Soldiers. The nine men were brought to Rio Grande City and committed for trial, and *in a day or two released on bail* by the Justice of the Peace. Nothing more was done in the case until the last term of the District Court (in April last) when the Grand Jury found an indictment for murder against the nine Mexicans — one of them was tried and acquitted and the *others turned loose.*

The Grand Jury also found an indictment against Sergeant Troutman and Privates Blackstone and Fredericks, for the killing of the Mexican at the ranch. These men were at the time before the court as witnesses and were immediately arrested and lodged in jail. They then employed Mr. Sullivan as Counsel and were brought before the District Judge on a writ of Habeas Corpus,[1] with a view to being released on bail. The Judge decided that the evidence was not sufficient to hold them without bail and directed that they should be released upon giving five hundred dollars ($500.00) bail each. This they have not yet been able to do and are still in jail. The witnesses against these soldiers are *the men who did the firing* as found by the Coroners Jury, and the principal witness on the part of the state when brought before the District Judge to give evidence *against the soldiers, admitted that he had given evidence twice before; once before the Coroners Jury and once before the Justice of the Peace, and on both occasions had sworn to a lie:* but insisted that his *last evidence was true.*

These soldiers aided by Mr. W. G. Tachau Post Trader, have paid the amount mentioned in the vouchers and I would earnestly recommend that, if it can be done, the amount be refunded by the Government. I would also invite the attention of the Commanding General to the fact that able Counsel should be provided

---

[1]**Habeas Corpus:** under English common law, the requirement that those accused of crimes must be charged and tried, or released.

for these men. They will undoubtedly be tried on the charge of murder at the next term of the District Court in July next. There is no evidence against them, except that of the Mexicans *who killed two of their detachment,* still should they be tried in this County before a Mexican Jury and with no one to defend them, I fear they would be convicted. I do not think it would be possible to give them a fair and impartial trial in this County, therefore whoever is to defend them should be here in time to thoroughly look up the case, and if possible get the venue changed.

From my knowledge of the case I am fully convinced that these Soldiers did no more than they were ordered, and that the attack upon them was utterly unprovoked, and for the purpose of getting them out of the way in order to cross cattle, and evidence can be obtained that cattle were crossed the same night and sold in Camarga the next day.

At the same term of Court the cases of Colonel Edward Hatch and Second Lieutenant J. W. French, 9th Cavalry indicted by the Grand jury for burglary will be brought up and from what I know of the feeling of people in this County and the fact that most of the Juries here are composed of Mexicans, I think they as well as the Soldiers charged with murder will require the best Counsel that can be provided for them.

Very respectfully
Your obedt Servant
J. F. Wade
Major 9th Cavalry
Commanding

Two enclosures

Colonel Edward Hatch's Report
to the Assistant Adjutant General

San Antonio, Texas
May 17, 1875.

A. A. General
Dep't of Texas,
San Antonio, Texas

Sir:

I have the honor to Enclose the following letters from Major James F. Wade, 9th U.S. Cavalry, and Lieutenant John S. Loud, Adjutant 9th U.S. Cavalry, dated Ringgold Barracks, April 28, 1875.

Though these letters are not written officially, they present information of such a character, that I deem it important to lay them before you.

They state that three soldiers of "G" Company, 9th Cavalry, are now in jail, awaiting trial for murder, that they were taken, when summoned as witnesses, before the District Court at Rio Grande City, and that it is impossible to obtain bail for them from any person living in the Country.

For the murder of which the Soldiers are arrested, a Coroners Jury has already acquitted them. The Mexican murdered, was undoubtedly killed by their own people in the ambuscade of the patrol, when two soldiers were killed.

The soldiers were on duty at the time, on their nightly patrol, for the purpose of preventing running of stock over the Rio Grande.

In addition to the above I am informed, Lieutenant French, 9th U.S. Cavalry, and myself are under inditements [*sic*] for burglary. It is presumed in the absence of official information, the inditements are based on an order given [to] Lieutenant French to recover the arms and blankets stolen from the soldiers, stolen on January 26, 1875, at the Solice Ranche [*sic*], Texas. . . .

The cabins entered, some twenty miles from the Ranche, were not inhabited at the time, whether the people had left, fearing that the missing property would be looked for, I am not prepared to say, the cabins had not been occupied for some days.

I believe there is no actual foundation for these inditements under the laws of Texas, or any other State, that it is a part of the policy of the Mexican Element, when they can secure the assistance of a few Americans to harass both Officers and Soldiers, and therefore ask that the Government furnish such counsel as may be necessary to conduct the cases before the Courts.

These letters also show, that murder of Americans, who are not in sympathy with the Mexican marauders and their adherents, continues; that the condition of affairs cannot remain much longer as they now are, undoubtedly the followers of Cortina[1] occupy both banks of the river and there seems to be at present a system of terror being inaugurated to control the Country in their interest with the civil authorities and to use the State Laws whenever convenient to harass the military.

> I am Sir, very respectfully
> Your obdt Servant
> (Sgd.) Edward Hatch
> Colonel 9th Cavalry.

---

[1]**Cortina:** Juan Nepomuceno Cortina, an heir to a large ranch in Texas, led Mexican resistance to Anglo rule on both sides of the Rio Grande.

Attorney General Pierrepont's Response
to the Secretary of War

Department of Justice
Washington, *May 25, 1875.*

Hon. W. W. Belknap,
Secretary of War.

Sir,

I have the honor to acknowledge the receipt of your letter of the 22nd instant[1] enclosing a copy of a report made on the 14th instant by Inspector General Davis in regard to affairs along the Rio Grande, and inviting my attention to so much of said report as relates to the confinement of United States soldiers, and requesting that their cases be transferred to the United States courts and counsel furnished for their defence.

In reply I have to inform you that I have transmitted a copy of the report of Inspector General Davis to the District Attorney for the Eastern District of Texas, with instructions to take such measures as may be necessary for the release of these soldiers, to have their cases transferred to the United States courts, and to defend the same. I have further directed him to give this matter his prompt and personal attention, and to advise me, from time to time, of his action in the premises.

When he shall have reported his action to the Department, I will advise you of it.

Very respectfully
Your ob't serv't.
Edwards Pierrepont
Attorney General

[1]**instant:** the current month.

Stephen Powers's Report to Major J. G. Boyle

Brownsville, Texas.
Nov. 27th, 1875.

Major J. G. Boyle.
U. S. Dist. Atty.
Galveston, Texas.

Sir:

In the cases of Fredericks and others, under indictment in Starr Co., I beg to report; that I proceeded to Starr Co., and by proper showing, had the venue in their cases changed to this County, where I believe we caught a fair jury.

General Hatch, also under indictment for false imprisonment and burglary, growing out of the same matter as involved in the above cases, I regret to say did not reach Starr Co., during the late term of the district Court there, but has arrived by last Steamer.

I venture the suggestion, that if the War Department was justly impressed of the great malice involved in the prosecution of this gallant Officer, for the gratification of purely local prejudice, there would be no hesitation in ordering him to assigned duty in New Mexico.

There is no pretense that evidence is available to convict either him or the other defendants: — but the prosecution is kept alive from motives of personal greed by certain interested parties.

Your ob't Servant
Signed, Stephen Powers.

Suggestions for Further Reading

Garcia, Mario T. *Desert Immigrants: The Mexicans of El Paso, 1880–1920.* New Haven, Conn.: Yale University Press, 1981.

Leckie, William H. *The Buffalo Soldiers: A Narrative of the Negro Cavalry in the West.* Norman: University of Oklahoma Press, 1967.

Limerick, Patricia Nelson. *The Legacy of Conquest: The Unbroken Past of the American West.* New York: Norton, 1987.

Samora, Julian. *Gunpowder Justice: A Reassessment of the Texas Rangers.* Notre Dame, Ind.: University of Notre Dame Press, 1979.

White, Richard. *"It's Your Misfortune and None of My Own": A History of the American West.* Norman: University of Oklahoma Press, 1991.

CHAPTER THREE

THE GILDED AGE

The Farmers' Alliance and Populism

The sweeping economic changes of the nineteenth century affected all Americans, but none more profoundly than farmers. The expansion of the railroad network between 1870 and 1900 revolutionized agriculture, linking it to a national, even international, market economy in which goods could be transported to distant markets. But it also subjected farmers to the whims of the market. By the 1880s and 1890s, the effects of these changes were becoming evident to farmers, and many of them were deeply disturbed. It was out of this context that the largest mass movement in American history — Populism — came into existence.

The heart of Populism was in the rural South. In the mid-1880s, farmers in eastern Texas organized and instituted a program of cooperative purchasing and marketing. Their new organization, the Farmers' Alliance, sought to obtain better prices for cotton and more favorable terms for credit. Initially founded as a state organization, the alliance soon grew beyond the confines of Texas. In 1887, organizers spread throughout the South, finding a receptive audience among which to recruit new members.

The appeal of the new group was a collective outrage over the Gilded Age's new economic universe: southern farmers felt deprived of their traditional independence and autonomy, at the mercy of external, impersonal forces. Although more successful in some states than in others, the organization undeniably enjoyed broad appeal. For the most part, it drew farmers of different classes and even different races; along with the white Farmers' Alliance, there were also all-black groups known as the Colored Farmers' Alliance. The initial appeal of both was their promise to alter the direction of change through an exchange system that sought to restructure relationships with outside market forces — in particular, the agents of capitalism: railroads and merchants.

The alliance described itself as a nonpolitical organization, but early on many of its activities were very political; in some states it even became an active lobbying organization. In congressional elections in 1890, for example, local alliances applied a "yardstick" by which to measure candidates' faithfulness to their principles. At the state level, that often meant supporting new laws to regulate railroads. At the national level, the main objective was the creation of a national subtreasury to establish a federal system of credit to farmers. The alliance thus far had failed to obtain either of these objectives.

Although most southern members were Democrats, many of them became frustrated with the seeming unresponsiveness of the party. At successive national conventions in St. Louis (1889), Ocala, Florida (1890), and Cincinnati (1891), the Farmers' Alliance advocated fundamental changes, many of which went beyond the mainstream approach to political economy. It not only endorsed the increased regulation of railroads — including the ability to set rates — but ultimately many members began to favor public ownership of the nation's transportation system. The subtreasury plan, endorsed at St. Louis, envisioned unprecedented federal involvement in insuring that farmers had access to credit by providing low-cost federal loans secured by the promise of future crops. By 1891, an active wing of the Farmers' Alliance favored a "mid-road" approach, in which they would secede from the Democratic Party and form a separate People's Party. Their experiences in the organization had, for many, created a powerful sense of association; they held a common view of the displacement of rural America, and they shared a faith in Jacksonian republicanism, in small-scale enterprise, and in a cooperative commonwealth that rejected the avaricious capitalism of the Gilded Age.

The alliance's increased politicization, however, created tremendous strains in an organization that encompassed Democrats and Republicans, Northerners and Southerners, blacks and whites. At the Cincinnati meeting in May 1891, about thirteen hundred delegates, disillusioned with Democrats' failure to support alliance measures at either the state or national level, organized the People's Party — thus giving rise to the Populist movement.

Over the next four years, Populism became a potent force in American social and political life. In the presidential election of 1892, Populist candidate James B. Weaver received twenty-two electoral votes — the first serious third-party candidate since the Civil War. Moreover, Populists either were elected or shared power in a number of states, including Colorado and North Carolina. But they failed in other states of the South, the original home of the alliance, where Weaver attracted no majorities and earned no electoral votes. In 1896, the party "fused" with the Democrats under presidential candidate William Jennings Bryan, and what had been the largest protest movement in American history dissipated into an isolated, internally divided movement.

Populism nonetheless imparted a powerful legacy for the twentieth century. In place of the concepts prevailing in Gilded Age America, it offered the vision of a future in which government would police the actions of corporations and help to maintain a humane society. It advanced a notion of local-level, grass-roots participation in and control of social, economic, and political life, and it offered a critique of the way politics and policy making were practiced in the late nineteenth century.

The documents in this chapter reflect how the Farmers' Alliance perceived the changes brought by the Gilded Age. "Little Jennie" Wilson and Ben Terrell attempt to explain these changes — and how alliance people understood them. Key to the alliance analysis was the monetary system, as shown in a December 1889 issue of the leading newspaper of the organization, the *National Economist*. As the alliance steadily moved into the political realm, this analysis found its way into several political platforms, including the St. Louis Demands of December 1889. The organization's profound unhappiness with the two political parties by the early 1890s is evident in articles from the *National Economist* and the *Richmond Exchange Reporter*. The final two documents — a call to arms from a Virginia Populist newspaper and the political platform adopted by the Populist Party at Omaha — illustrate the factors leading to the emergence of third-party politics.

As you read, pay attention to the way men and women in the alliance perceived economic change. How did this affect their view of the political system and, in particular, party politics? What proposals did they offer to change the economic and political systems? To what extent were these changes radical, and to what extent were they conservative?

8. What Did Farmers Want?

"LITTLE JENNIE" SCOTT WILSON AND BEN TERRELL
Addresses to the Texas and Georgia Farmers' Alliances
1888 and 1889

The men and women attracted to the Southern Farmers' Alliance expressed a basic unease about the social and political conditions of Gilded Age America. Most of them believed that impersonal economic forces were reshaping their lives, but that the political system was doing little to protect them and what they called the "producer" classes — independent farmers and artisans. As early as 1887, alliance organizer-lecturers fanned out through the South to spread a new message to farmers. As Texan "Little Jennie" Wilson suggests, many women took an active part in alliance affairs; they had little compunction about this form of public involvement. Wilson delivered to a Texas audience the message that farmers could reshape the political environment. So did Ben Terrell, one of the better alliance recruiters, who spoke to a group in Fulton County, Georgia. Both Wilson and Terrell appealed to traditional political values of the farmers they addressed, but they suggested a program of activism.

"Little Jennie" Scott Wilson's Address to the Texas Farmers' Alliance

August 28, 1888

Ladies and gentlemen: Thousands of friends and enemies to the Alliance have prophesied that the Alliance would [commit] suicide. One fearing that it would; the other, hoping and confidently believing that it would. But today the mists have cleared away and every intelligent Alliance man recognizes that it is founded upon a solid careful basis, and that it has taken such a hold upon, and has been so implanted in the minds of the sturdy farmers of our sunny Southland, that it will live, spread and prosper despite opposition or political scheming. It is true that the leaders in this mammoth and overshadowing move now being upheld and supported by the honest yeomenry of the land, may make some unintentional mistakes but there is a deep and abiding determination among the great masses of farmers to no longer submit to the present monstrous system of . . . misrule and open-daylight legalized robbery and oppression. . . . Some of the wide awake enemies of the Alliance tell us this movement will result in war, that it reminds them of secession days when the South was going to whip the North and gain her independence. Is there any comparison? The Southern states seceded from the Union but the Farmers' Alliance has not seceded from anything. We are only claiming our rights and fighting for them under the same old national stars and stripes. The war between the states was fought with cannon and musketry while this war is being waged with pen and thought. In the war between the states, there was blood stain all over the land while in this war the only stain is ink upon paper. The Alliance is fast assuming gigantic proportions whose influence is felt all over our country and the great monopolies of the land are trembling when viewing its increasing power. The Texas Alliance headquarters at Dallas already

Women in the Texas Populist Movement: Letters to the "Southern Mercury," ed. Marion K. Barthelme (College Station: Texas A&M University Press, 1997), 164–65.

do a monthly business, I believe, of over $200,000 in filling cooperative orders. The order is now running large flouring mills and ginneries and expects to establish many more local ones throughout Texas. There are over 200,000 members in Texas today and the membership is experiencing a healthy growth.

Some say that women have no business in the order. When Columbus braved the perils of unknown seas to add America to the world, whose hand was it that fitted him for the voyage? A woman, Queen Isabella. Every effectual man who has left his mark in the world is but another Columbus for whom some Isabella in the form of a mother has laid down her comforts, yes, her chance, her jewels. I would suggest to all those who think ladies are out of their place in the Alliance and have no discretion and are given to telling all they know or hear, that they had better read up a little and be less explosive themselves in the lobbies of convention halls. . . .

Ben Terrell's Address to the Georgia Farmers' Alliance

March 1889

Ladies, gentlemen, brethren of the Farmers' Alliance, I am always pleased to speak to farmers, and I only wish that what I am going to say to-day may be of some service to you.

If, while in your State, I am able by my addresses, by my advice, by any means within my power to place you in a better position, get you to become more hopeful, to be better Alliance men, better organized and more in unison, then I shall have accomplished the purpose for which I have visited you.

No Ax to Grind.   I am not a citizen of your State, and can gain nothing personally by my labors in Georgia. I have no ax to grind. I have no stock in any newspaper in the State, and in nothing can I reap a personal reward for my work with you. In my speeches I have never spoken, and will never speak, a word that is not for your benefit as a citizen of Georgia, not only as farmers but as citizens. If I thought the principles of the Alliance injurious or hurtful, I should hesitate to embrace them. If the principles taught by our order were hurtful, morally or mentally, I would quit the order at once. If I thought it would engender class prejudices, and cause one class of citizens to array itself against another, I would never make another Alliance speech. I say to you that whoever believes that the Alliance was organized to make war against any citizen, or class of citizens, of Georgia has totally misunderstood the aims of the order. We can not do that. We may, and must, in a manly way, protect our own business, and my purpose in coming to you is to point out, as clearly as may be in my power, what that business and what those interests are.

National Economist, 30 March 1889.

The Objects of the Alliance.   The Alliance wishes to devise some plan by which you will better your condition. You will thus better the condition of every man in Georgia.

Upon the producer rests the burden of the support of all other classes. Do not understand me to say that other classes are not necessary; but they exist and are supported by the producers of wealth. Not alone the man who plants and tills the ground, but all the men who labor, who dig the iron ore from our hills, who crush it, who manufacture iron from it, and from iron steel, and they who increase the value of that steel by beating it into knife blades — these are the wealth producers. These wealth producers bear the burden of all the rest of the human family. If men become millionaires it is because they have taken from the producer more than their due amount. No man can amass a million dollars unless he obtains a larger percentage of the product of the labor of the country than is his due. Wealth distributed is a great blessing. Wealth concentrated is a great curse. There could be no worse condition of society than to have it divided into the very rich and the very poor. There will always be trouble when such conditions exist.

The Palsey of Riches.   Wherever wealth is concentrated, grasped in the hands of a few, men are dwarfed, mentally, morally, and socially, and in lands where such conditions exist, as in Mexico, Germany, Ireland, Russia, and other countries — in fact wherever there are the very poor and the very rich, you will see the same unfortunate results. We, fellow citizens, have not yet reached this condition, and in the United States we have the grandest and most independent yeomanry on earth, but if the present tendency continues, we, too, will reach the same unhappy position. We are tending toward the concentration of capital. Thirty years ago the farmers owned more than one half the wealth in this country. To-day they own less than one-quarter. Your State has made a great advance in wealth, yet the men who produce that wealth are decreasing in power, influence, and comfort day by day. They are falling into ignorance. Their curse is a want of education and refinement and the desire for a higher life. If it be war to try to change these conditions, to help you become wealthy and refined, then I am at war. I contend that these conditions are hurtful to my country, therefore my patriotism and manhood force me to make war against them. In this course I shall use my influence and give my whole life, if necessary, to the task of uniting the farmers of this country. [Applause.]

Union the Only Hope.   With me nothing is too sacred, too high, or too low to attack, if I believe it hurtful to our organization. I believe that in organization alone there is hope for us. We can not hope for success outside of union. I would not be just to you nor honest to myself if I did not attack everything hurtful and favor everything I think beneficial to the success of the Alliance.

I want you to bear in mind that you must avoid personalities. I contend that a newspaper has the right to take any position it chooses, but when it takes a position adverse to the cause we are fighting for I will say that it is not worthy of your support. The press is the greatest power in the land. The greatest power, because it makes the laws you are governed by. It is also the most responsible power because it creates the public sentiment which demands certain laws.

9. An Economic Proposal

COMMITTEE ON THE MONETARY SYSTEM
Report
1889

After the Civil War, the United States, like all of the Western industrial world, embraced the gold standard as the medium of international exchange and the basis of the value of national currencies. Although this helped stabilize international exchange, the United States ran a trade deficit throughout the Gilded Age, resulting in a relatively small supply of gold and a decline in prices. Acutely aware of the price decline — and of the adverse consequences for farmers — leaders of the Farmers' Alliance were profoundly concerned about the currency issue. Farmers, many of whom were in debt, were particularly hard-hit by deflation. Accordingly, they embraced two measures identified in this report published in the National Economist: *first, the use of silver as a source of currency and, second, the extension of government-supported "subtreasuries" as a way to extend credit to cash-poor farmers. Both "free silver" and the subtreasury plan became cardinal features of the alliance's political goals.*

The financial policy of the general Government seems to-day to be peculiarly adapted to further the interests of the speculating class, at the expense and to the manifest detriment of the productive class, and while there are many forms of relief offered, there has up to the present time been no true remedy presented which has secured a support universal enough to render its adoption probable. Neither

National Economist, 28 December 1889.

of the political parties offer a remedy adequate to our necessities, and the two parties that have been in power since the war have pursued practically the same financial policy. The situation is this: The most desirable and necessary reform is one that will adjust the financial system of the general Government so that its provisions cannot be utilized by a class, which thereby becomes privileged and is in consequence contrary to the genius of our Government, and which is to-day the principal cause of the depressed condition of agriculture. Regardless of all this political parties bitterly ignore these great evils and refuse to remove their cause, and the importunities of the privileged class have no doubt often led the executive and legislative branches of the Government to believe that the masses were passive and reconciled to the existence of this system whereby a privileged class can, by means of the power of money to oppress, exact from labor all that it produces except a bare subsistence. Since then it is the most necessary of all reforms, and receives no attention from any of the prominent political parties, it is highly appropriate and important that our efforts be concentrated to secure the needed reform in this direction, provided all can agree upon such measures. Such action will no wise connect this movement to any partisan effort, as it can be applied to the party to which each member belongs.

In seeking a true and practical remedy for the evils that now flow from the imperfections in our financial system, let us first consider what is the greatest evil, and on what it depends. The greatest evil, the one that outstrips all others so far that it is instantly recognized as the chief, and known with certainty to be more oppressive to the productive interests of the country than any other influence, is that which delegates to a certain class the power to fix the price of all kinds of produce and of all commodities. This power is not delegated directly, but it is delegated indirectly by allowing such class to issue a large percent of the money used as the circulating medium of the country, and having the balance of such circulating medium, which is issued by the Government, a fixed quantity that is not augmented to correspond with the necessities of the times. In consequence of this the money issued by the privileged class, which they are at liberty to withdraw at pleasure, can be, and is, so manipulated as to control the volume of circulating medium in the country sufficiently to produce fluctuations in general prices at their pleasure. It may be likened unto a simple illustration in philosophy: The inflexible volume of the Government issue is the fulcrum, the volume of the bank issue is the lever power, and price is the point at which power is applied, and it is either raised or lowered with great certainty to correspond with the volume of bank issue. Any mechanic will instantly recognize the fact that the quickest and surest way of destroying the power of the lever to raise or lower price is to remove the resistance offered by the fulcrum — the inflexible volume of Government issue. The power to regulate the volume of money so as to control price is so manipulated as to develop and apply a potent force, for which we have in the English language no name; but it is the power of money to oppress, and is demonstrated as follows: In the last four months of the year the agricultural products of the whole year having been harvested, they are placed on the market to buy money. The amount of money necessary to supply this demand is equal to many times the actual amount in circulation. Nevertheless the class that controls the volume of the circulating medium desire to purchase these agricultural products for speculative purposes, so they reduce the volume of money by hoarding, in the face of the augmented demand, and thereby advance the exchangeable value of the then inadequate volume of money, which is equivalent to reducing the price of the agricultural products. True agriculturists should hold their products and not sell at these ruinously low prices. And no doubt they would if they could; but to prevent that, practically all debts, taxes, and interest are made to mature at that time, and they being forced to have money at a certain season when they have the product of their labor to sell, the power of money to oppress by its scarcity is applied until it makes them turn loose their products so low that their labor expended does not average them fifty cents per day. This illustrates the power of money to oppress; the remedy, as before, lies in removing the power of the fulcrum — the inflexible Government issue — and supplying a Government issue, the volume of which shall be increased to correspond with the actual addition to the wealth of the Nation presented by agriculture at harvest time, and diminished as such agricultural products are consumed. Such a flexibility of volume would guarantee a stability of price based on cost of production which would be compelled to reckon the pay for agricultural labor at the same rates as other employment. Such flexibility would rob money of its most potent power — the power to oppress — and place a premium on productive effort. But how may so desirable a result be secured? Let us see. By applying the same principles now in force in the monetary system of the United States with only slight modification in the detail of their execution. The Government and the people of this country realize that the amount of gold and silver, and the certificates based on these metals, do not comprise a volume of money sufficient to supply the wants of the country, and in order to increase the volume, the Government allows individuals to associate themselves into a body corporate, and deposit with the Government bonds which represent National indebtedness, which the Government holds in trust and issues to such corporation paper money equal to ninety percent of the value of the bonds, and charges said corporation interest at the rate of one percent per annum for the use of said paper money. This allows the issue of paper money to increase the volume of the circulating medium on a perfectly safe basis, because the margin is a guarantee that the banks will redeem the bonds before they mature. But now we find that the circulation secured by this method is still not adequate; or to take a very conservative position, if we admit that it is adequate on the average, we know that the fact of its being entirely inadequate for half the year makes its inflexibility an engine of oppression, because a season in which it is inadequate must be followed by one of superabundance in order to bring about the average, and such a range in volume means great fluctuations in prices which cut against the producer, both in buying and selling, because he must sell at a season when produce is low, and buy when commodities are high. This system, now in vogue by the United States government of supplementing its circulating medium by a safe and redeemable paper money, should be pushed a little further and conducted in such a manner as to secure a certain augmentation of supply at the season of the year in which the agricultural additions to the wealth of the Nation demand money, and a diminution in such supply of money as said agricultural products are consumed. It is not an average adequate amount that is needed, because under it the greatest abuses may prevail, but a certain adequate amount that adjusts itself to the wants of the country at all seasons. For this purpose let us demand that the United States government modify its present financial system:

1. So as to allow the free and unlimited coinage of silver or the issue of silver certificates against an unlimited deposit of bullion.

2. That the system of using certain banks as United States depositories be abolished, and in place of said system, establish in every county in each of the States that offers for sale during the one year five hundred thousand dollars worth of farm products; including wheat, corn, oats, barley, rye, rice, tobacco, cotton, wool, and sugar, all together; a sub-treasury office, which shall have in connection with it such warehouses or elevators as are necessary for carefully storing and preserving such agricultural products as are offered it for storage, and it should be the duty of such sub-treasury department to receive such agricultural products as are offered for storage and make a careful examination of such products and class same as to quality and give a certificate of the deposit showing the amount and quality, and that United States legal-tender paper money equal to eighty percent of the local current value of the products deposited has been advanced on same on interest at the rate of one percent per annum, on the condition that the owner or such other person as he may authorize will redeem the agricultural product within twelve months from date of the certificate or the trustee will sell same at public auction to the highest bidder for the purpose of satisfying the debt. Besides the one percent interest the sub-treasurer should be allowed to charge a trifle for handling and storage, and a reasonable amount for insurance, but the premises necessary for conducting this business should be secured by the various counties donating to the general government the land and the government building the very best modern buildings, fire-proof and substantial. With this method in vogue the farmer, when his produce was harvested, would place it in storage where it would be perfectly safe and he would secure four-fifths of its value to supply his pressing necessity for money at one percent per annum. He would negotiate and sell his warehouse or elevator certificates whenever the current price suited him, receiving from the person to whom he sold, only the difference between the price agreed upon and the amount already paid by the sub-treasurer. When, however, these storage certificates reached the hand of the miller or factory, or other consumer, he to get the product would have to return to the sub-treasurer the sum of money advanced, together with the interest on same and the storage and insurance charges on the product. This is no new or untried scheme; it is safe and conservative; it harmonizes and carries out the system already in vogue on a really safer plan because the products of the country that must be consumed every year are really the very best security in the world, and with more justice to society at large.

10. The St. Louis Demands

THE FARMERS' ALLIANCE AND INDUSTRIAL UNION
Manifesto
1889

In December 1889, the Northern and Southern Farmers' Alliances, along with representatives of labor groups, convened in St. Louis with the goal of creating a new, national organization of farmers and laborers. The St. Louis meeting was rife with tension between the more numerous Southerners (they outnumbered their northern counterparts by nearly three to one) and northern agrarians. With Civil War veterans on both sides in attendance, conditions did not favor a new, cross-sectional group, and the St. Louis convention failed to reach a consensus. Although delegates also refused to endorse a common statement, the Southern Alliance — now calling itself the Farmers' Alliance and Industrial Union — drafted a manifesto articulating the movement's objectives. The St. Louis Demands were a major step toward deeper political involvement, for the manifesto's goals required a strong alliance presence in both state and national government.

Agreement made this day by and between the undersigned committee representing the National Farmers' Alliance and Industrial Union on the one part, and the undersigned committee representing the Knights of Labor on the other part, Witnesseth: The undersigned committee representing the Knights of Labor having read the demands of the National Farmers' Alliance and Industrial Union which are embodied in this agreement hereby endorse the same on behalf of the Knights of Labor, and for the purpose of giving practical effect to the demands herein set forth, the legislative committees of both organizations will act in concert before Congress for the purpose of securing the enactment of laws in harmony with the demands mutually agreed.

And it is further agreed, in order to carry out these objects, we will support for office only such men as can be depended upon to enact these principles in statute law uninfluenced by party caucus.

The demands hereinbefore referred to are as follows:

1. That we demand the abolition of national banks and the substitution of legal tender treasury notes in lieu of national bank notes, issued in sufficient volume to do the business of the country on a cash system; regulating the amount needed, on a per capita basis as the business interests of the country expand; and

The St. Louis Demands, 21 December 1889. Reprinted in *The Populist Revolt: A History of the Farmers' Alliance and the People's Party,* by John D. Hicks (Minneapolis: University of Minnesota Press, 1931), 427–28.

that all money issued by the Government shall be legal tender in payment of all debts, both public and private.

2. That we demand that Congress shall pass such laws as shall effectually prevent the dealing in futures of all agricultural and mechanical productions, preserving a stringent system of procedure in trials as shall secure the prompt conviction, and imposing such penalties as shall secure the most perfect compliance with the law.

3. That we demand the free and unlimited coinage of silver.

4. That we demand the passage of laws prohibiting the alien ownership of land, and that Congress take early steps to devise some plan to obtain all lands now owned by aliens and foreign syndicates; and that all lands now held by railroad and other corporations in excess of such as is actually used and needed by them, be reclaimed by the Government and held for actual settlers only.

5. Believing in the doctrine of "equal rights to all, and special privileges to none," we demand that taxation, National or State, shall not be used to build up one interest or class at the expense of another.

We believe that the money of the country should be kept as much as possible in the hands of the people, and hence we demand that all revenues, National, State, or county, shall be limited to the necessary expenses of the Government economically and honestly administered.

6. That Congress issue a sufficient amount of fractional paper currency to facilitate exchange through the medium of the United States mail.

7. We demand that the means of communication and transportation shall be owned by and operated in the interest of the people as is the United States postal system.

11. The Alliance and Southern Politics

THE NATIONAL ECONOMIST, THE RICHMOND EXCHANGE REPORTER, AND THE VIRGINIA SUN
Newspaper Articles
1890–1892

Alliance leaders were fundamentally suspicious of the political system, which they believed to be corrupted. Their loss of faith in its ability to accommodate itself to their demands — which became, over time, a sort of self-fulfilling prophecy — drove alliance leaders toward other political solutions. If the two-party system would not pro-

vide answers, many members believed, the time was ripe for the organization of an independent third party. The political agenda of the alliance figured prominently in these articles appearing in January 1890 in the National Economist, *almost two years later in a state alliance newspaper, the* Richmond Exchange Reporter, *and in June 1892 in the populist* Virginia Sun.

THE NATIONAL ECONOMIST

"Shall the Caucus Reign?" January 18, 1890

The press of this country has lately been pleased to note the dethronement of the last representative of monarchy in the Americas, and it is the boast that from the frozen circle of the North to the ice-bound Horn of the South the continents know no man to whom accident of birth gives a privilege to tax or to exact homage. But in this great republic, set as an example to the other republics laid fair to receive Nature's sunshine over the vast continents, there is a creature of custom. . . . Laws are passed, reforms are defeated, and those recreant to the instruction of constituents maintained in power by a device which has grown as a parasite upon the system of representative government. In view of this condition it would seem that one of the strongest, best directed, and most practical steps at the St. Louis meeting was the declaration contained in the agreement with the committee of Knights of Labor,[1] whereby the two great orders united upon the declaration that —

> We will support for office only such men as can be depended upon to enact these principles into statute law uninfluenced by party caucus.

Under the prevalent system of party discipline the most dangerous enemy reforms have to encounter is the caucus. Reforms always begin with the minority, and it is an axiom that reformers are always a minority. The caucus is intended to, and effectually does, prevent minorities of the respective parties from consorting together and agitating for reforms to which each may be pledged. By its influence the minority of one party is made to oppose a minority in another party, though both minorities may be pledged to a given measure. It is the disciplinary means by which the legislator is held to duty to party, regardless of duty to constituency; just as the subject is held to service of the war-making king, despite the natural claims of family, morality, or religion.

Were the inquiry into the power of caucus directed to the origin of the scheme, disappointment might be expressed that it originated in a free country, among the representatives of a free people. That it might, if not abused, be a means of strength by rallying to the support of any given measure all who favor its passage, or by joining into opposition all who oppose, is a reasonable proposition.

---

[1] **Knights of Labor:** a powerful labor union in the 1880s.

National Economist, 18 January 1890.

But the province of the caucus which is here criticised, and which is the actual caucus seen in the party politics today, is to prevent most effectually the very thing suggested. By it friends of a given reform are separated into hostile camps, each prohibited from receiving or giving aid to the others, and each forced to battle in detachment by the hostile interests; indeed, each in conflict with the others by virtue of the power of party discipline. Men who feel their duty to the people who delegated them stronger than that to party must bear the ban of recalcitrance to party, and must expect that everything which counts as a reward for party service will be withheld from them, and that the antagonism of every party henchman will be aroused, so that their re-election to office will be not only without the aid of their parties, but despite the opposition of the party machine.

In this declaration of party independence the producers have taken the first step, which costs, and which counts, in the march toward industrial freedom. The caucus is the hot-bed in which has been propagated the entire brood of bad laws under which the people are making their brave fight against monopolies, trusts, and combines. In their secret councils were devised the many forms in which the excessive taxation is made to oppress the people. No scheme is too unjust, no burden too unequal, for a caucus to espouse, if it only bring to the party success in its great aim at control of the country.

Caucus is the last of the American kings. He is a monarch of more finesse and power than any who have preceded him. The effort of the workers to be rid of him is commendable. Their declaration of independence is patriotic. The fight, to be effective, must be a long and persistent one. But for the fact that the farmers of America have never failed in any fight in which prerogative was the antagonist, grave doubt of the issue might be entertained. The farmers of this country are slow to anger, but they fight to win. They will fight the evils of the caucus system, as the caucus is now managed, and, if need be, the rule of the caucus, with its dark records, will have to go.

What Does the Alliance Mean?   The Alliance makes its own declaration of purposes, clear, distinct, and unequivocal. One of its purposes is not to break up the Democratic party on the one hand, or the Republican party on the other. Why then do political editors insist that they mean to do first one, then the other, and sometimes both, and to set up in their room an oath-bound, secret, political organization? We have denied this until we are tired [of] denying it. Once more, the thing is not true. The Alliance does not aim at the destruction of the political parties, but the reform and control of them. No purpose is entertained by the organization of setting men by the ears, nor of indulging in the asperities which have so long disgraced political debate. Our purpose is, if we can, to take the political parties out of the hands of the petty bosses, including those of every kind and degree. We intend to assert the power of numbers in the primaries, and thereby, if we can, take the party nominations out of the hands of people who have controlled them, and to nominate and elect better men. This we have a clear right to do, and we can not be driven from our purpose by the idle denunciations and "noisy breath" of self-constituted censors, editors, or others. If they have a fancy to fill the air with this sort of "inarticulate howls," no man will hinder them. Neither will any sensible man any more regard them than does he the howling of the idle wind. Such people have been giving us advice gratis and unsolicited, and by wholesale. We are not in that line of business, but in order to make them a fair return we desire to say that if such people think such howlings are in the smallest degree going to influence any person's conduct, we are of the opinion that they are mistaken. Men who are in earnest are open to the influence of reason, and they are at all times ready to listen to appeals from responsible and reasonable sources, but they are not to be cowed or coerced by the frothings of irresponsible and empty-headed bosses. We believe certain great reforms in the financial system of the Government are necessary, and at the same time that they are just and right, and that they will benefit all classes of the people. If we insist upon these reforms while the bosses oppose them, and we, by controlling the primaries, nominate men pledged to them, is that breaking up the party? What are they going to do, these bosses and the editors they control? Are they going to break up the party because they can no longer run it for the personal ends and ambitions of their set? When it comes to this it is a question whether a "secret, oath-bound political organization" is better or worse than such a political banditti. These men take the position that they will smash the party unless they can rule it for their own purposes or in furtherance of their own views. If the Alliance, a majority of the party, will not submit to hold by them, a very small minority, and to vote as directed by them, and nominate and elect candidates set up by them, then the Alliance is chargeable with breaking up the party. Was ever such nonsense heard before? It is high time we had heard the last of it. It would be an easy and cheap way to break up the Alliance, and reduce its voting strength to subjugation to the political boss, the professional politician, the party caucus, if it could be made effectual. Nothing is so cheap as this kind of wrath, which, if it cost anything to manufacture, would not be so lavishly poured out. It is a species of natural gas which explodes spontaneously and makes a great splutter, and emits a bad smell, but illuminates nothing. Doubtless these persons are giving us their best counsel, and if they knew how valueless we hold it, they would take the only brief piece of gratuitous advice we have for them and shut up. The situation of American agriculture is far too serious, the depressed and degraded condition of those who man all the great productive industries of this great country is far too grievous, for the Alliance to turn aside from its great mission to bandy words in idle dissension with these party henchmen. If parties can not discover a *modus vivendi*[2] with the Alliance we are afraid they must go. We desire a few closing words with those earnestly patriotic leaders of both parties whose abilities, whose experience, and whose services entitle them to the respect of the people. That there are such men in both parties we freely concede; we believe a greater number of them than is generally admitted. We say to them that they are in duty bound to give due diligence to the study of the true meaning of this Alliance movement on the part of those who, impelled by necessity, have concerted

---

[2]*modus vivendi:* a temporary arrangement, or working solution.

together to take measures for their common safety. We ask them to give to the solution of the great economic questions which must be solved, and speedily solved, on a non-partizan basis, the benefit of your talents, and experience, and influence. And we tell them plainly we will not consent to give indefinite support to men who are known to us to be at heart hostile to us, and unfriendly to our interests. We can not be relied upon to continue to give voting strength to parties which despise our necessities, and leaders who deliberately insult our intelligence. If this be party treason, make the most of it!

THE RICHMOND EXCHANGE REPORTER

"The Two Parties," December 12, 1891

Take a good look at them, and you will see that they are but one. They are both down on the Alliance. Why? Because we spoil their game. The Alliance has an uncomfortable habit of calling a spade a spade, as befits the farmers' organization, but the two parties are agreed that "things are not what they seem." There is nothing real about party politics but the offices and their prostitution to the money power. It is a game expressly designed to keep the people out of their rights, and at the same time not to let them know it.

One party is on one side, and the other party on the other side, and the people in the middle. Both parties are striving to secure control of the government for what there is in it, and for nothing else, and that party will win which can induce the most people over to its side. How to induce the people to come over to its side is the great party question, and as money is the greatest of all inducers, that party will win which can control the most money. And now is the opportunity of the money power. They shall have all the campaign funds they want, so they fool the people to wrangle over dead issues instead of rising in their might and demanding that the power of money to oppress shall forever be abolished.

The money power says, "We are well satisfied with the present arrangement. By being allowed to control currency, we can put prices down when we buy, and we can put them up when we sell. We can make all the money we want. What better government than ours? Never since the world was made could men with money make money faster. And the people, poor fools, know nothing about it. Trust the two parties for managing them. They both want our money, and can't get along without it. Never fear that they will give us away. They will worry over the tariff — a difference of a percent won't hurt us — they will keep sectionalism alive with their force bills and 'stinking Confederate rags' while 'the nigger in the wood-pile' guarantees a solid South against a solid North. Isn't it a pretty game, and haven't we got it all our own way? It costs like the mischief in campaign funds, but it is the best paying investment we can make."

All right, ye cold-blood traitors. Fiddle on, but know that Rome is burning.

Richmond Exchange Reporter, 12 December 1891.

The *Virginia Sun*

June 1, 1892

To the People of Virginia, Irrespective of Past or Present Party Affiliation:

A crisis in the history of our State and country is upon us. How will you meet it? The question, in a nut shell, which every man must answer, is — Shall the dollar rule the people, or shall the people rule the dollar? What answer have you to this question from the Republican party and from the Democratic party? The verdict of the Republican party for twenty seven years has been that the dollar shall rule the people. The Democratic party has for years promised that the people should govern the dollar, but how have they voted? Always, the other way. Can you and will you longer imperil your liberty, and even your right to exist as freemen, upon their future promises? The people in their innocence and ignorance always thought that a majority ruled in the lower House of Congress, but they find now that it is controlled absolutely by a small minority. On that great and vital question of money, both parties have proved to the country by their own acts that there is no difference between Democrat and Republican. Come then and unite with us on that strong and broad declaration of our principles as embodied in the St. Louis platform. This means action for the good of all and injury to no one. This destroys the combination now existing among the money kings and monopolists. This gives to each person in this broad land an equal and even chance in the battle of life. If you love your homes and your country, if you would save for your children the pleasant heritage won by your fathers, then you will join the grand army of patriots which is everywhere enrolling for the redemption of our people from the heel of the oppressor.

Now is no time to stand idly by. Duty calls every man who has the spirit of a man, and manhood will triumph. Let us join hearts and hands in this glorious cause, and the God of mercy and justice will smile upon our efforts.

THE STATE CONVENTION will be held in the city of Richmond, on Thursday, the 23d day of June, at the hour of noon, and each county and city in the State is invited to be represented, when each will be entitled to one vote. There is no restriction as to the number of delegates, and each county or city may decide the number of its delegation in its own wisdom. In the case of a larger delegation than one, the majority of the delegation will cast its one vote.

The object of the Convention is to elect delegates to the National Convention of the People's Party at Omaha, July 4th, to nominate a State electoral ticket, and to permanently organize the People's Party of Virginia.

Every county and city should be represented, and if no steps have been taken to that end, the friends of the cause should at once take action. Your county or city must meet in mass meeting of sympathizers, and elect your delegation to Richmond. Posters for the purpose of calling local mass meetings may be had on application to the CENTRAL COMMITTEE, Box 48, Richmond, Va.

Everything must have a beginning, and all's well that ends well.
Let the good work go bravely on.

STATE CENTRAL COMMITTEE.

12. The Populist Program

The People's Party of America
Omaha Platform
1892

Although the Farmers' Alliance began as a nonpolitical and nonpartisan organization, almost from the outset it involved itself in politics. It expected results from the election of political leaders between 1890 and 1892; for the most part, the experience was disheartening. Leaders of the Democratic Party were unreceptive — and often hostile — to their demands: southern Democrats were instrumental in killing congressional efforts to create a subtreasury, and they beat back alliance efforts to push through legislation regulating railroads.

A substantial portion of the Southern Alliance had long believed that a move toward an independent third party was inevitable. The formal organization of the People's Party of America was marked by a convention held in Omaha, Nebraska. The platform of that convention, reproduced below, embodied ideas that had long been present among members of the Farmers' Alliance, labor leaders, and other Gilded Age reformers.

———————

Assembled upon the 116th anniversary of the Declaration of Independence, the People's Party of America, in their first national convention, invoking upon their action the blessing of Almighty God, puts forth, in the name and on behalf of the people of this country, the following preamble and declaration of principles: —

The conditions which surround us best justify our cooperation: we meet in the midst of a nation brought to the verge of moral, political, and material ruin.

The Omaha Platform, 4 July 1892. Reprinted in *The Populist Revolt: A History of the Farmers' Alliance and the People's Party*, by John D. Hicks (Minneapolis: University of Minnesota Press, 1931), 439–44.

Corruption dominates the ballot-box, the legislatures, the Congress, and touches even the ermine of the bench. The people are demoralized; most of the States have been compelled to isolate the voters at the polling-places to prevent universal intimidation or bribery. The newspapers are largely subsidized or muzzled; public opinion silenced; business prostrated; our homes covered with mortgages; labor impoverished; and the land concentrating in the hands of the capitalists. The urban workmen are denied the right of organization for self-protection; imported pauperized labor beats down their wages; a hireling standing army, unrecognized by our laws, is established to shoot them down, and they are rapidly degenerating into European conditions. The fruits of the toil of millions are boldly stolen to build up colossal fortunes for a few, unprecedented in the history of mankind; and the possessors of these, in turn, despise the republic and endanger liberty. From the same prolific womb of governmental injustice we breed the two great classes — tramps and millionaires.

The national power to create money is appropriated to enrich bondholders; a vast public debt, payable in legal tender currency, has been funded into gold-bearing bonds, thereby adding millions to the burdens of the people. Silver, which has been accepted as coin since the dawn of history, has been demonetized to add to the purchasing power of gold by decreasing the value of all forms of property as well as human labor; and the supply of currency is purposely abridged to fatten usurers, bankrupt enterprise, and enslave industry. A vast conspiracy against mankind has been organized on two continents, and it is rapidly taking possession of the world. If not met and overthrown at once, it forebodes terrible social convulsions, the destruction of civilization, or the establishment of an absolute despotism.

We have witnessed for more than a quarter of a century the struggles of the two great political parties for power and plunder, while grievous wrongs have been inflicted upon the suffering people. We charge that the controlling influences dominating both these parties have permitted the existing dreadful conditions to develop without serious effort to prevent or restrain them. Neither do they now promise us any substantial reform. They have agreed together to ignore in the coming campaign every issue but one. They propose to drown the outcries of a plundered people with the uproar of a sham battle over the tariff, so that capitalists, corporations, national banks, rings, trusts, watered stock, the demonetization of silver, and the oppressions of the usurers may all be lost sight of. They propose to sacrifice our homes, lives, and children on the altar of mammon;[1] to destroy the multitude in order to secure corruption funds from the millionaires.

Assembled on the anniversary of the birthday of the nation, and filled with the spirit of the grand general and chieftain who established our independence, we seek to restore the government of the Republic to the hands of "the plain people," with whose class it originated. We assert our purposes to be identical with the purposes of the National Constitution, "to form a more perfect union and establish

---

[1]**mammon:** material riches, generally regarded as having an evil influence.

justice, insure domestic tranquillity, provide for the common defence, promote the general welfare, and secure the blessings of liberty for ourselves and our posterity." We declare that this republic can only endure as a free government while built upon the love of the whole people for each other and for the nation; that it cannot be pinned together by bayonets; that the civil war is over, and that every passion and resentment which grew out of it must die with it; and that we must be in fact, as we are in name, one united brotherhood of freemen.

Our country finds itself confronted by conditions for which there is no precedent in the history of the world; our annual agricultural productions amount to billions of dollars in value, which must, within a few weeks or months, be exchanged for billions of dollars of commodities consumed in their production; the existing currency supply is wholly inadequate to make this exchange; the results are falling prices, the formation of combines and rings, the impoverishment of the producing class. We pledge ourselves, if given power, we will labor to correct these evils by wise and reasonable legislation, in accordance with the terms of our platform. We believe that the powers of government — in other words, of the people — should be expanded (as in the case of the postal service) as rapidly and as far as the good sense of an intelligent people and the teachings of experience shall justify, to the end that oppression, injustice, and poverty shall eventually cease in the land.

While our sympathies as a party of reform are naturally upon the side of every proposition which will tend to make men intelligent, virtuous, and temperate, we nevertheless regard these questions — important as they are — as secondary to the great issues now pressing for solution, and upon which not only our individual prosperity but the very existence of free institutions depends; and we ask all men to first help us to determine whether we are to have a republic to administer before we differ as to the conditions upon which it is to be administered; believing that the forces of reform this day organized will never cease to move forward until every wrong is remedied, and equal rights and equal privileges securely established for all the men and women of this country.

We declare, therefore, —

First.　That the union of the labor forces of the United States this day consummated shall be permanent and perpetual; may its spirit enter all hearts for the salvation of the republic and the uplifting of mankind!

Second.　Wealth belongs to him who creates it, and every dollar taken from industry without an equivalent is robbery. "If any will not work, neither shall he eat." The interests of rural and civic labor are the same; their enemies are identical.

Third.　We believe that the time has come when the railroad corporations will either own the people or the people must own the railroads; and, should the government enter upon the work of owning and managing all railroads, we should favor an amendment to the Constitution by which all persons engaged in the government service shall be placed under a civil service regulation of the most rigid character, so as to prevent the increase of the power of the national administration by the use of such additional government employees.

First, *Money*. We demand a national currency, safe, sound, and flexible, issued by the general government only, a full legal tender for all debts, public and private, and that, without the use of banking corporations, a just, equitable, and efficient means of distribution direct to the people, at a tax not to exceed two percent per annum, to be provided as set forth in the sub-treasury plan of the Farmers' Alliance, or a better system; also, by payments in discharge of its obligations for public improvements.

(a) We demand free and unlimited coinage of silver and gold at the present legal ratio of sixteen to one.

(b) We demand that the amount of circulating medium be speedily increased to not less than fifty dollars per capita.

(c) We demand a graduated income tax.

(d) We believe that the money of the country should be kept as much as possible in the hands of the people, and hence we demand that all state and national revenues shall be limited to the necessary expenses of the government economically and honestly administered.

(e) We demand that postal savings banks be established by the government for the safe deposit of the earnings of the people and to facilitate exchange.

Second, *Transportation*. Transportation being a means of exchange and a public necessity, the government should own and operate the railroads in the interest of the people.

(a) The telegraph and telephone, like the post-office system, being a necessity for the transmission of news, should be owned and operated by the government in the interest of the people.

Third, *Land*. The land, including all the natural sources of wealth, is the heritage of the people, and should not be monopolized for speculative purposes, and alien ownership of land should be prohibited. All land now held by railroads and other corporations in excess of their actual needs, and all lands now owned by aliens, should be reclaimed by the government and held for actual settlers only.

Resolutions

Whereas, Other questions have been presented for our consideration, we hereby submit the following, not as a part of the platform of the People's party, but as resolutions expressive of the sentiment of this convention.

1. *Resolved,* That we demand a free ballot and a fair count in all elections, and pledge ourselves to secure it to every legal voter without federal intervention, through the adoption by the States of the unperverted Australian or secret ballot system.

2. *Resolved,* That the revenue derived from a graduated income tax should be applied to the reduction of the burden of taxation now resting upon the domestic industries of this country.

3. *Resolved,* That we pledge our support to fair and liberal pensions to ex-Union soldiers and sailors.

4. *Resolved,* that we condemn the fallacy of protecting American labor under the present system, which opens our ports to the pauper and criminal classes of the world, and crowds out our wage-earners; and we denounce the present ineffective laws against contract labor, and demand the further restriction of undesirable immigration.

5. *Resolved,* That we cordially sympathize with the efforts of organized workingmen to shorten the hours of labor, and demand a rigid enforcement of the existing eight-hour law on government work, and ask that a penalty clause be added to the said law.

6. *Resolved,* That we regard the maintenance of a large standing army of mercenaries, known as the Pinkerton system, as a menace to our liberties, and we demand its abolition; and we condemn the recent invasion of the Territory of Wyoming by the hired assassins of plutocracy, assisted by federal officials.

7. *Resolved,* That we commend to the favorable consideration of the people and the reform press the legislative system known as the initiative and referendum.

8. *Resolved,* That we favor a constitutional provision limiting the office of President and Vice-President to one term, and providing for the election of senators of the United States by a direct vote of the people.

9. *Resolved,* That we oppose any subsidy or national aid to any private corporation for any purpose.

10. *Resolved,* That this convention sympathizes with the Knights of Labor and their righteous contest with the tyrannical combine of clothing manufacturers of Rochester, and declares it to be the duty of all who hate tyranny and oppression to refuse to purchase the goods made by said manufacturers, or to patronize any merchants who sell such goods.

Suggestions for Further Reading

Goldberg, Michael L. *An Army of Women: Gender and Politics in Gilded Age Kansas.* Baltimore: Johns Hopkins University Press, 1997.

Goodwyn, Lawrence. *Democratic Promise: The Populist Moment in America.* New York: Oxford University Press, 1976.

McMath, Robert C. *Populist Vanguard: A History of the Southern Farmers' Alliance.* Chapel Hill: University of North Carolina Press, 1975.

Mitchell, Theodore R. *Political Education in the Southern Farmers' Alliance, 1887–1900.* Madison: University of Wisconsin Press, 1987.

Schwartz, Michael. *Radical Protest and Social Structure: The Southern Farmers' Alliance and Cotton Tenancy, 1880–1890.* New York: Academic Press, 1976.

CHAPTER FOUR

THE 1890s

Race Crisis in the New South

In the late nineteenth century, in what historian Rayford Logan has called the nadir in American race relations, New South leaders with old ideas about racial inequality forced African Americans out of politics and adopted pervasive "Jim Crow" laws that segregated the South. The Republican Party and the federal government failed to intervene, essentially abandoning southern blacks to their fate.

The restoration of white supremacy in politics and the segregation of society took place gradually and unevenly across the South. In the 1870s and 1880s, the "Redeemer" coalition of planters, merchants, and industrialists who dominated the New South used violence and intimidation to keep blacks from the polls or ensured Democratic victories by committing election fraud or coercing blacks into voting for white conservatives. Nevertheless, African Americans continued to vote and to hold office in many parts of the South into the 1890s, cooperating with white Republicans and at times forming coalitions with Independents and Populists.

Alarmed by alliances or potential alliances of blacks and disaffected whites, the Redeemers also worried that Congress would require federal supervision of elections or enforce the Fourteenth Amendment, which stipulated that states that deprived eligible voters of their rights would have their number of congressmen reduced. Thus, in the 1890s, conservative leaders took steps to reestablish white supremacy in politics "legally" and permanently by adopting voter registration requirements — such as literacy tests and poll taxes — intended to enfranchise the "best qualified" citizens only. These restrictions, they insisted, were constitutional and even "progressive" because they did not explicitly discriminate on the basis of race and eliminated the "need" for fraud or violence by removing undesirables from the electorate. Though some white illiterates were disfranchised along with blacks, whites were protected by "grandfather clauses" (exempting men whose ancestors had voted before the Civil War) and by discriminatory application of the registration laws. Beginning with Mississippi in 1890, every southern state restricted suffrage through legislation or changes in their state constitutions. By 1906, the South had essentially disfranchised its African American population.

To secure white support for disfranchisement, Democratic leaders mounted white supremacy campaigns in which orators and editors demanded that *all* whites rally around the Democratic Party — the party of their Confederate forebears and defender of state's rights. They spoke of the enfranchisement of former slaves as a horrible mistake that had led to "negro domination" and encouraged insolence and assaults on white women. From the stump and in the press, Democratic spokesmen regaled their audiences with lurid tales of alleged rapes by "raving black beasts" and called upon white men of all classes to support disfranchisement in the name of the "White Goddess of Democracy," the white womanhood of the South. Lower-class whites — many of them farmers who were suffering economically and resented the success of the South's growing black middle class — responded enthusiastically, and the level of violence against blacks rose dramatically. Approximately one hundred blacks were lynched every year during this period.

Despite white Southerners' fears of northern intervention, neither the Supreme Court nor Congress moved to protect the rights of African Americans. In 1883 the Supreme Court declared unconstitutional the Civil Rights Act of 1875, which had outlawed racial segregation in transportation and public accommodations and prevented the exclusion of blacks from jury duty; and in 1896, *Plessy v. Ferguson* upheld a Louisiana segregation statute and stamped the Court's approval on "separate but equal" public facilities. Congress refused to consider the adoption of antilynching bills that would have provided federal protection against the systematic terrorism prevalent in the 1890s.

Ironically, the Republican Party's overwhelming success at the national level in the wake of the Populist revolt decreased its need for southern Republican support and undermined the party's already wavering commitment to black suffrage. In addition, many Reconstruction-era Republican leaders who had been firm advocates of voting rights for the freedmen had died or retired. For a number of reasons, including the presence in the North of large numbers of immigrants deemed undesirable as voters, support for universal suffrage was waning all over America. Increasingly, northern whites agreed with southern whites that the South should be allowed to solve its own "Negro problem."

Among black Southerners there were various responses to these reactionary steps taken by white Southerners and the wholesale retreat of the federal government from its Reconstruction-era policies. Booker T. Washington, head of Tuskegee Institute in Alabama, proposed a passive acceptance of the status quo and simply to make the best of it. His remarks were accepted erroneously by many whites of the 1890s (and even some Americans today) as *the* response of southern blacks. However, other African American leaders, in the South as well as in the North, vigorously protested these major reversals in their status. They resisted the imposition of racial segregation, which was not only degrading but also undermined black progress in education and economic enterprises. Southern blacks fought disfranchisement and continued to participate in politics; but fraud, violence, and the legal maneuvering of the 1890s finally made this virtually impossible and forced many into exile from the South.

In this chapter, Booker T. Washington's famous "Atlanta Compromise" address articulates his accommodationist policies. Next, two defiant African American newspaper editors, Ida B. Wells and Alexander Manly, vigorously protest the treatment of African Americans in the 1890s. Gunner Jesse Blake and an anonymous black woman offer conflicting accounts of white violence in Wilmington, North Carolina. And in an address to Congress, George White, the only black congressman remaining in 1901, protests the many injustices suffered by his race and the powerlessness of a disfranchised people to protect themselves.

As you read, consider these questions: What were the various reactions of southern African American leaders to the reverses suffered by the black community in the late nineteenth century? What actions did they urge blacks and whites to take in response to disfranchisement, the increase in segregation, and the epidemic of lynchings in the 1890s? What role did interracial sex and violence play in southern politics during this era?

13. The "Atlanta Compromise"

BOOKER T. WASHINGTON
Atlanta Exposition Address
1895

Booker T. Washington, a former slave, was head of Tuskegee Institute in Alabama. He was elevated to a position of national leadership as a result of this address, given at the opening ceremonies at the Cotton States and International Exposition in Atlanta in 1895. Whites saw him as a peacemaker offering a solution to the

Booker T. Washington, *Up From Slavery* (Boston, 1901). Reprinted in *Afro-American History: Primary Sources*, ed. Thomas R. Frazier (New York: Harcourt, Brace and World, 1970), 216–20.

"Negro problem"; letters of congratulation poured in — even from President Grover Cleveland, who said, "If our coloured fellow-citizens do not from your utterances gather new hope and form new determination to gain every valuable advantage offered them by the citizenship, it will be strange indeed." Many blacks were alarmed, however, by Washington's address. W. E. B. Du Bois, a Harvard-educated professor at Atlanta University, derisively labeled the proposal the "Atlanta compromise" and insisted that Washington's policies would contribute to a permanently disfranchised, servile status for African Americans. Washington's defenders insisted that he was quietly working against segregation, lynching, and educational discrimination.

Mr. President and Gentlemen of the Board of Directors and Citizens:

One-third of the population of the South is of the Negro race. No enterprise seeking the material, civil, or moral welfare of this section can disregard this element of our population and reach the highest success. I but convey to you, Mr. President and Directors, the sentiment of the masses of my race when I say that in no way have the value and manhood of the American Negro been more fittingly and generously recognized than by the managers of this magnificent Exposition at every stage of its progress. It is a recognition that will do more to cement the friendship of the two races than any occurrence since the dawn of our freedom.

Not only this, but the opportunity here afforded will awaken among us a new era of industrial progress. Ignorant and inexperienced, it is not strange that in the first years of our new life we began at the top instead of at the bottom; that a seat in Congress or the state legislature was more sought than real estate or industrial skill; that the political convention of stump speaking had more attractions than starting a dairy farm or truck garden.

A ship lost at sea for many days suddenly sighted a friendly vessel. From the mast of the unfortunate vessel was seen a signal, "Water, water; we die of thirst!" The answer from the friendly vessel at once came back, "Cast down your bucket where you are." A second time the signal, "Water, water; send us water!" ran up from the distressed vessel, and was answered, "Cast down your bucket where you are." And a third and fourth signal for water was answered, "Cast down your bucket where you are." The captain of the distressed vessel, at last heeding the injunction, cast down his bucket, and it came up full of fresh, sparkling water from the mouth of the Amazon River. To those of my race who depend on bettering their condition in a foreign land or who underestimate the importance of cultivating friendly relations with the Southern white man, who is their next-door neighbour, I would say: "Cast down your bucket where you are" — cast it down in making friends in every manly way of the people of all races by whom we are surrounded.

Cast it down in agriculture, mechanics, in commerce, in domestic service, and in the professions. And in this connection it is well to bear in mind that whatever other sins the South may be called to bear, when it comes to business, pure and simple, it is in the South that the Negro is given a man's chance in the commercial world, and in nothing is this Exposition more eloquent than in emphasizing this chance. Our greatest danger is that in the great leap from slavery to freedom we may overlook the fact that the masses of us are to live by the productions of our hands, and fail to keep in mind that we shall prosper in proportion as we learn to dignify and glorify common labour and put brains and skill into the common occupations of life; shall prosper in proportion as we learn to draw the line between the superficial and the substantial, the ornamental gewgaws of life and the useful. No race can prosper till it learns that there is as much dignity in tilling a field as in writing a poem. It is at the bottom of life we must begin, and not at the top. Nor should we permit our grievances to overshadow our opportunities.

To those of the white race who look to the incoming of those of foreign birth and strange tongue and habits for the prosperity of the South,[1] were I permitted I would repeat what I say to my own race, "Cast down your bucket where you are." Cast it down among the eight millions of Negroes whose habits you know, whose fidelity and love you have tested in days when to have proved treacherous meant the ruin of your firesides. Cast down your bucket among these people who have, without strikes and labour wars, tilled your fields, cleared your forests, builded your railroads and cities, and brought forth treasures from the bowels of the earth, and helped make possible this magnificent representation of the progress of the South. Casting down your bucket among my people, helping and encouraging them as you are doing on these grounds, and to education of head, hand, and heart, you will find that they will buy your surplus land, make blossom the waste places in your fields, and run your factories. While doing this, you can be sure in the future, as in the past, that you and your families will be surrounded by the most patient, faithful, law-abiding, and unresentful people that the world has seen. As we have proved our loyalty to you in the past, in nursing your children, watching by the sickbed of your mothers and fathers, and often following them with tear-dimmed eyes to their graves, so in the future, in our humble way, we shall stand by you with a devotion that no foreigner can approach, ready to lay down our lives, if need be, in defence of yours, interlacing our industrial, commercial, civil, and religious life with yours in a way that shall make the interests of both races one. In all things that are purely social we can be as separate as the fingers, yet one as the hand in all things essential to mutual progress.

There is no defence or security for any of us except in the highest intelligence and development of all. If anywhere there are efforts tending to curtail the fullest growth of the Negro, let these efforts be turned into stimulating, encouraging, and making him the most useful and intelligent citizen. Effort or means so invested will pay a thousand percent interest. These efforts will be twice blessed — "blessing him that gives and him that takes."

There is no escape through law of man or God from the inevitable: —

[1]Washington is referring to the official efforts of southern state governments to attract white European immigrants.

The laws of changeless justice bind
Oppressor with oppressed;
And close as sin and suffering joined
We march to fate abreast.

Nearly sixteen millions of hands will aid you in pulling the load upward, or they will pull against you the load downward. We shall constitute one-third and more of the ignorance and crime of the South, or one-third its intelligence and progress; we shall contribute one-third to the business and industrial prosperity of the South, or we shall prove a veritable body of death, stagnating, depressing, retarding every effort to advance the body politic.

Gentlemen of the Exposition, as we present to you our humble effort at an exhibition of our progress, you must not expect overmuch. Starting thirty years ago with ownership here and there in a few quilts and pumpkins and chickens (gathered from miscellaneous sources), remember the path that has led from these to the inventions and production of agricultural implements, buggies, steam-engines, newspapers, books, statuary, carving, paintings, the management of drug-stores and banks, has not been trodden without contact with thorns and thistles. While we take pride in what we exhibit as a result of our independent efforts, we do not for a moment forget that our part in this exhibition would fall far short of your expectations but for the constant help that has come to our educational life, not only from the Southern states, but especially from Northern philanthropists, who have made their gifts a constant stream of blessing and encouragement.

The wisest among my race understand that the agitation of questions of social equality is the extremest folly, and that progress in the enjoyment of all the privileges that will come to us must be the result of severe and constant struggle rather than an artificial forcing. No race that has anything to contribute to the markets of the world is long in any degree ostracized. It is important and right that all privileges of the law be ours, but it is vastly more important that we be prepared for the exercises of these privileges. The opportunity to earn a dollar in a factory just now is worth infinitely more than the opportunity to spend a dollar in an opera-house.

In conclusion, may I repeat that nothing in thirty years has given us more hope and encouragement, and drawn us so near to you of the white race, as this opportunity offered by the Exposition; and here bending, as it were, over the altar that represents the results of the struggles of your race and mine, both starting practically empty-handed three decades ago, I pledge that in your effort to work out the great and intricate problem which God has laid at the doors of the South, you shall have at all times the patient, sympathetic help of my race; only let this be constantly in mind, that, while from representations in these buildings of the product of field, of forest, of mine, of factory, letters, and art, much good will come, yet far above and beyond material benefits will be that higher good, that, let us pray God, will come, in a blotting out of sectional differences and racial animosities and suspicions, in a determination to administer absolute justice, in a willing obedience among all classes to the mandates of law. This, then, coupled with our material prosperity, will bring into our beloved South a new heaven and a new earth.

14. Voices of Protest

IDA B. WELLS AND ALEXANDER L. MANLY
On Lynching
1892 and 1898

*Born a slave in Mississippi, Ida B. Wells was a teacher in Memphis before she be-
came editor and co-owner of the Memphis newspaper* Free Speech. *Prompted by the
lynchings of three friends, she began to argue in print that lynching was a systematic ritual perpetrated to thwart black progress rather than punishment for assaults
against white women. As a result, her press was destroyed by white men who threatened to torture and kill her if she ever returned to Tennessee. Wells went on to become an internationally known crusader against lynching and other injustices, a
leading suffragist, and a founder of the National Association for the Advancement
of Colored People (NAACP). "Self Help," reprinted here, is a chapter from* Southern Horrors: Lynch Law in All Its Phases, *published in 1892 as the first of several
pamphlets she wrote to "tell the truth" about lynching and suggest ways that African
Americans could take action to stop it.*

*Alexander Manly, the descendant of an antebellum governor of North Carolina
and a slave, was educated at Hampton Institute. His paper, the* Daily Record, *was one
of the few African American daily newspapers in the South. Manly published this editorial on August 18, 1898, in response to a speech by a prominent Georgia Populist,
Rebecca Latimer Felton, who accused white men of being lax in their protection of
white women and once said, "If it needs lynching to protect a woman's dearest possession from the raving human beasts — then I say lynch: a thousand times a week if
necessary." Manly's defiant editorial on interrracial liaisons and lynching played into
the hands of white supremacists eager to stir up racial violence in North Carolina: the
white newspaper in Wilmington reprinted it every day until the November 1898 election in which whites adopted legislation that disfranchised the state's black population.*

IDA B. WELLS

1892

In the creation of this healthier public sentiment,[1] the Afro-American can do
for himself what no one else can do for him. The world looks on with wonder that
we have conceded so much and remain law-abiding under such great outrage and
provocation.

---

[1]**this healthier public sentiment:** refers to public demand for the "strong arm of the law" to be
"brought to bear upon lynchers" through severe punishment.

Ida B. Wells, *Southern Horrors: Lynch Law in All Its Phases* (New York: New York Age Print, 1892).
Reprinted in *Southern Horrors and Other Writings: The Anti-Lynching Campaign of Ida B. Wells,
1892–1900,* ed. Jacqueline Jones Royster (Boston: Bedford/St. Martin's, 1997), 69–72.

To Northern capital and Afro-American labor the South owes its rehabilitation. If labor is withdrawn capital will not remain. The Afro-American is thus the backbone of the South. A thorough knowledge and judicious exercise of this power in lynching localities could many times effect a bloodless revolution. The white man's dollar is his god, and to stop this will be to stop outrages in many localities.

The Afro-Americans of Memphis denounced the lynching of three of their best citizens, and urged and waited for the authorities to act in the matter and bring the lynchers to justice. No attempt was made to do so, and the black men left the city by thousands, bringing about great stagnation in every branch of business. Those who remained so injured the business of the street car company by staying off the cars, that the superintendent, manager, and treasurer called personally on the editor of the "Free Speech," asked them to urge our people to give them their patronage again. Other business men became alarmed over the situation and the "Free Speech" was run away that the colored people might be more easily controlled. A meeting of white citizens in June, three months after the lynching, passed resolutions for the first time, condemning it. *But they did not punish the lynchers.* Every one of them was known by name, because they had been selected to do the dirty work, by some of the very citizens who passed these resolutions. Memphis is fast losing her black population, who proclaim as they go that there is no protection for the life and property of any Afro-American citizen in Memphis who is not a slave.

The Afro-American citizens of Kentucky, whose intellectual and financial improvement has been phenomenal, have never had a separate car law until now. Delegations and petitions poured into the Legislature against it, yet the bill passed and the Jim Crow Car of Kentucky is a legalized institution. Will the great mass of Negroes continue to patronize the railroad? A special from Covington, Ky., says:

Covington, June 13th.—The railroads of the State are beginning to feel very markedly, the effects of the separate coach bill recently passed by the Legislature. No class of people in the State have so many and so largely attended excursions as the blacks. All these have been abandoned, and regular travel is reduced to a minimum. A competent authority says the loss to the various roads will reach $1,000,000 this year.

A call to a State Conference in Lexington, Ky., last June had delegates from every county in the State. Those delegates, the ministers, teachers, heads of secret and other orders, and the head of every family should pass the word around for every member of the race in Kentucky to stay off railroads unless obliged to ride[.] If they did so, and their advice was followed persistently the convention would not need to petition the Legislature to repeal the law or raise money to file a suit. The railroad corporations would be so effected they would in self-defense lobby to have the separate car law repealed. On the other hand, as long as the railroads can get Afro-American excursions they will always have plenty of money to fight all the suits brought against them. They will be aided in so doing by the same partisan public sentiment which passed the law. White men passed the law, and white judges and juries would pass upon the suits against the law, and render judgment in line with their prejudices and in deference to the greater financial power.

The appeal to the white man's pocket has ever been more effectual than all the appeals ever made to his conscience. Nothing, absolutely nothing, is to be gained by a further sacrifice of manhood and self-respect. By the right exercise of his power as the industrial factor of the South, the Afro-American can demand and secure his rights, the punishment of lynchers, and a fair trial for accused rapists.

Of the many inhuman outrages of this present year, the only case where the proposed lynching did *not* occur, was where the men armed themselves in Jacksonville, Fla., and Paducah, Ky., and prevented it. The only times an Afro-American who was assaulted got away has been when he had a gun and used it in self-defense.

The lesson this teaches and which every Afro-American should ponder well, is that a Winchester rifle should have a place of honor in every black home, and it should be used for that protection which the law refuses to give. When the white man who is always the aggressor knows he runs as great risk of biting the dust every time his Afro-American victim does, he will have greater respect for Afro-American life. The more the Afro-American yields and cringes and begs, the more he has to do so, the more he is insulted, outraged and lynched.

The assertion has been substantiated throughout these pages that the press contains unreliable and doctored reports of lynchings, and one of the most necessary things for the race to do is to get these facts before the public. The people must know before they can act, and there is no educator to compare with the press.

The Afro-American papers are the only ones which will print the truth, and they lack means to employ agents and detectives to get at the facts. The race must rally a mighty host to the support of their journals, and thus enable them to do much in the way of investigation.

A lynching occurred at Port Jarvis, N.Y., the first week in June. A white and colored man were implicated in the assault upon a white girl. It was charged that the white man paid the colored boy to make the assault, which he did on the public highway in broad day time, and was lynched. This, too, was done by "parties unknown." The white man in the case still lives. He was imprisoned and promises to fight the case on trial. At the preliminary examination, it developed that he had been a suitor of the girl's. She had repulsed and refused him, yet had given him money, and he had sent threatening letters demanding more.

The day before this examination she was so wrought up, she left home and wandered miles away. When found she said she did so because she was afraid of the man's testimony. Why should she be afraid of the prisoner? Why should she yield to his demands for money if not to prevent him exposing something he knew? It seems explainable only on the hypothesis that a *liaison* existed between the colored boy and the girl, and the white man knew of it. The press is singularly silent. Has it a motive? We owe it to ourselves to find out.

The story comes from Larned, Kansas, Oct. 1st, that a young white lady held at bay until daylight, without alarming any one in the house, "a burly Negro" who entered her room and bed. The "burly Negro" was promptly lynched without investigation or examination of inconsistent stories.

A house was found burned down near Montgomery, Ala., in Monroe County, Oct. 13th, a few weeks ago; also the burned bodies of the owners and melted piles of gold and silver.

These discoveries led to the conclusion that the awful crime was not prompted by motives of robbery. The suggestion of the whites was that "brutal lust was the incentive, and as there are nearly 200 Negroes living within a radius of five miles of the place the conclusion was inevitable that some of them were the perpetrators."

Upon this "suggestion" probably made by the real criminal, the mob acted upon the "conclusion" and arrested ten Afro-Americans, four of whom, they tell the world, confessed to the deed of murdering Richard L. Johnson and outraging his daughter, Jeanette. These four men, Berrell Jones, Moses Johnson, Jim and John Packer, none of them 25 years of age, upon this conclusion, were taken from jail, hanged, shot, and burned while yet alive the night of Oct. 12th. The same report says Mr. Johnson was on the best of terms with his Negro tenants.

The race thus outraged must find out the facts of this awful hurling of men into eternity on supposition, and give them to the indifferent and apathetic country. We feel this to be a garbled report, but how can we prove it?

Near Vicksburg, Miss., a murder was committed by a gang of burglars. Of course it must have been done by Negroes, and Negroes were arrested for it. It is believed that 2 men, Smith Tooley and John Adams belonged to a gang controlled by white men and, fearing exposure, on the night of July 4th, they were hanged in the Court House yard by those interested in silencing them. Robberies since committed in the same vicinity have been known to be by white men who had their faces blackened. We strongly believe in the innocence of these murdered men, but we have no proof. No other news goes out to the world save that which stamps us as a race of cut-throats, robbers and lustful wild beasts. So great is Southern hate and prejudice, they legally (?) hung poor little thirteen year old Mildrey Brown at Columbia, S.C., Oct. 7th, on the circumstantial evidence that she poisoned a white infant. If her guilt had been proven unmistakably, had she been white, Mildrey Brown would never have been hung.

The country would have been aroused and South Carolina disgraced forever for such a crime. The Afro-American himself did not know as he should have known as his journals should be in a position to have him know and act.

Nothing is more definitely settled than he must act for himself. I have shown how he may employ the boycott, emigration and the press, and I feel that by a combination of all these agencies can be effectually stamped out lynch law, that last relic of barbarism and slavery. "The gods help those who help themselves."

Alexander L. Manly

August 18, 1898

A Mrs. Felton, from Georgia, makes a speech before the Agricultural Society at Tybee, Ga., in which she advocates lynching as an extreme measure. This woman makes a strong plea for womanhood, and if the alleged crimes of rape were half so frequent as is oft-times reported, her plea would be worthy of consideration.

Wilmington (N.C.) Daily Record, 18 August 1898. Reprinted in the *Raleigh (N.C.) News and Observer*, 26 August 1898.

Mrs. Felton, like many other so-called Christians, loses sight of the basic principle of the religion of Christ in her plea for one class of people as against another. If a missionary spirit is essential for the uplifting of the poor white girls, why is it? The morals of the poor white people are on a par with their colored neighbors of like conditions, and if any one doubts the statement let him visit among them. The whole lump needs to be leavened by those who profess so much religion and showing them that the preservation of virtue is an essential for the life of any people.

Mrs. Felton begins well for she admits that education will better protect the girls on the farm from the assaulter. This we admit and it should not be confined to the white any more than to the colored girls. The papers are filled often with reports of rapes of white women, and the subsequent lynching of the alleged rapists. The editors pour forth volleys of aspersions against all negroes because of the few who may be guilty. If the papers and speakers of the other race would condemn the commission of crime because it is crime and not try to make it appear that the negroes were the only criminals, they would find their strongest allies in the intelligent negroes themselves, and together the whites and blacks would root the evil out of both races.

We suggest that the whites guard their women more closely, as Mrs. Felton says, thus giving no opportunity for the human fiend, be he white or black. You leave your goods out of doors and then complain because they are taken away. Poor white men are careless in the matter of protecting their women, especially on farms. They are careless of their conduct toward them and our experience among poor white people in the country teaches us that the women of that race are not any more particular in the matter of clandestine meetings with colored men, than are the white men with colored women. Meetings of this kind go on for some time until the woman's infatuation or the man's boldness, bring attention to them and the man is lynched for rape. Every negro lynched is called a "big, burly, black brute," when in fact many of those who have been dealt with have had white men for their fathers, and were not only not "black" and "burly" but were sufficiently attractive for white girls of culture and refinement to fall in love with them as is well known to all.

Mrs. Felton must begin at the fountain head if she wishes to purify the stream.

Teach your men purity. Let virtue be something more than an excuse for them to intimidate and torture a helpless people. Tell your men that it is no worse for a black man to be intimate with a white woman, than for a white man to be intimate with a colored woman.

You set yourselves down as a lot of carping hypocrites; in fact you cry aloud for the virtue of your women while you seek to destroy the morality of ours. Don't think ever that your women will remain pure while you are debauching ours. You sow the seed — the harvest will come in due time.

15. An Explosion of Violence

Gunner Jesse Blake and Anonymous
On Racial Violence in Wilmington, North Carolina
1898

Rigid segregation and disfranchisement were relatively late in coming to North Carolina. In Wilmington, blacks constituted more than half of the population, had a flourishing middle class, and had gained considerable political power prior to 1898 when, determined to regain power, Democrats successfully drove a wedge between white Populists and blacks by exploiting fears of black assaults against white women. Two days after their victory, racial tensions exploded into violence as whites seized control of local politics and drove black incumbents from the city. The following statements present two very different accounts of the violence. The first, given to a sympathetic white writer in the 1930s by Gunner Jesse Blake, a Confederate veteran who participated in what he calls the "Rebellion," celebrates the whites' victory in 1898. The second, written by a clearly terrified black Wilmington woman, just after the riot, is an attempt to get President William McKinley to intervene.

Gunner Jesse Blake

"So, I am going to give you the inside story of this insurrection," he proceeded, "wherein the white people of Wilmington overthrew the constituted municipal authority overnight and substituted a reform rule, doing all this legally and with some needless bloodshed, to be sure, but at the same time they eliminated the Negroes from the political life of the city and the state. This Rebellion was the very beginning of Negro disfranchisement in the South and an important step in the establishment of 'White Supremacy' in the Southland. . . .

"The Rebellion was an organized resistance," Mr. Blake said, "on the part of the white citizens of this community to the established government, which had long irked them because it was dominated by 'Carpet Baggers' and Negroes, and also because the better element here wished to establish 'White Supremacy' in the city, the state and throughout the South, and thereby remove the then stupid and ignorant Negroes from their numerically dominating position in the government. . . .

"The older generation of Southern born men were at their wits' end. They had passed through the rigors of the North-South war and through the tyrannies of Reconstruction when Confiscation . . . of properties without due process of law,

Harry Hayden, *The Wilmington Rebellion* (1936). In *Reading the American Past: Selected Historical Documents*, ed. Michael P. Johnson, vol. 2, *From 1865* (Boston: Bedford/St. Martin's, 1998), 76–81.

was the rule rather than the exception. They had seen 'Forty Acres and a Mule' buy many a Negro's vote.

"Black rapists were attacking Southern girls and women, those pure and lovely creatures who graced the homes in Dixie Land, and the brutes were committing this dastardly crime with more frequency while the majority of them were escaping punishment through the influence of the powers that be.

"These old Southern gentlemen had calculated that time and time only would remove the terrors of Reconstruction, a condition that was imposed upon the conquered Southerners by the victorious Northerners, but they were not willing to sit supinely by and see their girls and women assaulted by beastly brutes.

"The better element among the Northerners in the North could not want them and their little friends to grow up amid such conditions. . . .

"A group of nine citizens met at the home of Mr. Hugh MacRae and there decided that the attitude and actions of the Negroes made it necessary for them to take some steps towards protecting their families and homes in their immediate neighborhood, Seventh and Market Streets. . . .

"This group of citizens, . . . referred to as the 'Secret Nine,' divided the city into sections, placing a responsible citizen as captain in charge of each area. . . .

"The better element planned to gain relief from Negro impudence and domination, from grafting and from immoral conditions; the 'Secret Nine' and the white leaders marked time, hoping something would happen to arouse the citizenry to concerted action.

"But the 'watch-and-wait policy' of the 'Secret Nine' did not obtain for long, as during the latter part of October [1898] there appeared in the columns of [t]he *Wilmington* (Negro) *Daily Record* an editorial, written by the Negro editor, Alex Manly, which aroused a state-wide revulsion to the city and state administrations then in the hands of the Republicans and Fusionists. The editorial attempted to justify the Negro rape fiends at the expense of the virtue of Southern womanhood." . . .

"That editorial," Mr. Blake declared . . . , "is the straw that broke Mister Nigger's political back in the Southland." . . .

"Excitement reigned supreme on election day and the day following," Mr. Blake said, adding that "the tension between the races was at the breaking point, as two Pinkerton detectives, Negroes, had reported to their white employers that the Negro women, servants in the homes of white citizens, had agreed to set fire to the dwellings of their employers, and the Negro men had openly threatened to 'burn the town down' if the 'White Supremacy' issue was carried in the political contest. The very atmosphere was surcharged with tinder, and only a spark, a misstep by individuals of either race, was needed to set the whites and the blacks at each other's throats.

"When Mr. Hugh MacRae was sitting on his porch on Market Street on the afternoon of the election, he saw a band of 'Red Shirts,' fifty in number, with blood in their eyes; mounted upon fiery and well caparisoned steeds and led by Mike Dowling, an Irishman, who had organized this band of vigilantes. The hot headed 'Red Shirts' paused in front of Mr. MacRae's home and the level headed Scotsman walked toward the group to learn what was amiss.

"Dowling told Mr. MacRae that they were headed for 'The Record' building to lynch Editor Manly and burn the structure. Mr. MacRae pleaded with Dowling and his 'Red Shirts' to desist in their plans. Messrs. MacRae, Dowling and other leaders of the 'Red Shirts' repaired across the street to Sasser's Drug store and there he, Mr. MacRae, showed them a 'Declaration of White Independence' that he had drawn up for presentation at a mass meeting of white citizens the next day.

"The 'Red Shirts' were finally persuaded by Mr. MacRae to abandon their plans for the lynching, but only after Mr. MacRae had called up the newspapers on the telephone and dictated a call for a mass meeting of the citizens for the next morning. . . .

"A thousand or more white citizens, representative of all walks of life . . . attended the mass meeting in the New Hanover county court house the next morning, November 10, at 11 o'clock.

"Colonel Alfred Moore Waddell, a mild mannered Southern gentleman, noted for his extremely conservative tendencies, was called upon to preside over the gathering. In addressing this meeting, Colonel Waddell said: . . . 'We will not live under these intolerable conditions. No society can stand it. We intend to change it, if we have to choke the current of Cape Fear River with (Negro) carcasses!' "

"*That* declaration," Mr. Blake said, "brought forth tremendous applause from the large gathering of white men at the mass meeting. . . .

"Colonel Waddell . . . announced that he heartily approved the set of resolutions which had been prepared by Mr. Hugh MacRae and which included the latter's 'Declaration of White Independence.'

"These resolutions were unanimously approved by the meeting, followed by a wonderful demonstration, the assemblage rising to its feet and cheering: 'Right! Right! Right!' and there were cries of 'Fumigate' the city with 'The Record' and 'Lynch Manly.' "

Blake then read the resolutions from the scrap book, as follows:

Believing that the Constitution of the United States contemplated a government to be carried on by an enlightened people; believing that its framers did not anticipate the enfranchisement of an ignorant population of African origin, and believing that those men of the state of North Carolina, who joined in framing the union, did not contemplate for their descendants subjection to an inferior race.

We, the undersigned citizens of the city of Wilmington and county of New Hanover, do hereby declare that we will no longer be ruled and will never again be ruled, by men of African origin.

This condition we have in part endured because we felt that the consequences of the war of secession were such as to deprive us of the fair consideration of many of our countrymen. . . .

"Armed with a Winchester rifle, Colonel Waddell ordered the citizens to form in front of the Armory for an orderly procession out to 'The Record' plant. . . .

"As this band of silent yet determined men marched up Market Street it passed the beautiful colonial columned mansion, the Bellamy home. From the balcony of this mansion, a Chief justice of the United States Supreme Court,

Salmon P. Chase, delivered an address shortly after Lincoln's tragic assassination, advocating Negro suffrage and thereby sowing the seeds that were now blossoming forth into a white rebellion.

"The printing press of 'The Record' was wrecked by the maddened white men, who also destroyed other equipment, and the type that had been used in producing the editorial that had reflected upon the virtue and character of Southern womanhood was scattered to the four winds by these men, who stood four-square for the virtue of their women and for the supremacy of the white race over the African.

"Some lamps that had been hanging from the ceiling of the plant were torn down and thrown upon the floor, which then became saturated with kerosene oil; and then a member of the band struck a match, with the result that the two-story frame building was soon in flames.

"The leaders and most of the citizens had designed only to destroy the press," Mr. Blake averred, adding . . . "all of which proves that a mob, no matter how well disciplined, is no stronger than its weakest link.

"The crowd of armed men, which had destroyed the plant and building of the nefarious *Wilmington* (Negro) *Daily Record,* dispersed, repairing peacefully to their respective homes," Mr. Blake said. . . .

"But in about an hour the tension between the two races broke with the shooting of William H. (Bill) Mayo, a white citizen, who was wounded by the first shot that was fired in the Wilmington Rebellion as he was standing on the sidewalk near his home. . . . Mayo's assailant, Dan Wright, was captured by members of the Wilmington Light Infantry and the Naval Reserves after he had been riddled by 13 bullets. Wright died next day in a hospital.

"Then the 'Red Shirts' began to ride and the Negroes began to run. . . . The Africans, or at least those Negroes who had foolishly believed in the remote possibility of social equality with the former masters of their parents, began to slink before the Caucasians. They, the Negroes, appeared to turn primal, slinking away like tigers at bay, snarling as they retreated before the bristling bayonets, barking guns and flaming 'Red Shirts.'

"Six Negroes were shot down near the corner of Fourth and Brunswick Streets, the Negro casualties for the day — November 11, 1898 — totaling nine. One of these, who had fired at the whites from a Negro dance hall, 'Manhattan,' over in 'Brooklyn,' was shot 15 or 20 times. . . .

"One 'Red Shirt' said he had seen six Negroes shot down near the Cape Fear Lumber Company's plant and that their bodies were buried in a ditch. . . . Another 'Red Shirt' described the killing of nine Negroes by a lone white man, who killed them one at a time with his Winchester rifle as they filed out of a shanty door in 'Brooklyn' and after they had fired on him. . . . Another told of how a Negro had been killed and his body thrown in Cape Fear River after he had approached two white men on the wharf. . . .

"Other military units came to Wilmington to assist the white citizens in establishing 'White Supremacy' here. . . . Military organizations from as far South as New Orleans telegraphed offering to come here if their services were needed in the contest.

"When the Rebellion was in full blast 'The Committee of Twenty-five' appointed . . . a committee to call upon Mayor Silas P. Wright and the Board of Aldermen and demand that these officials resign. The mayor had expressed a willingness to quit, but not during the crisis. He changed his mind, however, when he saw white citizens walking the streets with revolvers in their hands. The Negroes, too, had suddenly turned submissive, they were carrying their hats in their hands. . . .

"African continued to cringe before Caucasian as the troops paraded the streets, as the guns barked and the bayonets flared, for a new municipal administration of the 'White Supremacy' persuasion had been established in a day! The old order of Negro domination over the white citizenry had ended."

ANONYMOUS

Wilmington N.C. Nov. 13, 1898

Wm. McKinley — President of the United States of America

Hon. Sir,

I, a Negro woman of this city, appeal to you from the depths of my heart, to do something in the Negro's behalf. The outside world only knows one side of the trouble here, there is no paper to tell the truth about the Negro here in this or any other Southern state. The Negro in this town had no arms (except pistols perhaps in some instances) with which to defend themselves from the attack of lawless whites. On the 10th Thursday morning between eight and nine o'clock when all Negro men had gone to their places of work, the white men led by Col. A. M. Waddell, Jno [John] D. Bellamy, and S. H. Fishblatt marched from the Light Infantry armory on Market st. up to seventh down seventh to Love & Charity Hall (which is owned by a society of Negroes.) And where the Negro daily press was.) and set it afire & burnt it up. And firing Guns Winchesters they also had a Hotchkiss gun & two Colt rapid fire guns. We the negro expected nothing of the kind as they (the whites) had frightened them from the polls saying they would be there with their shotguns, so the few that did vote did so quietly. And we thought after giving up to them and they carried the state it was settled. But they or Jno D. Bellamy told them — in addition to the guns they already had they could keep back federal interference. And he could have the Soldiers at Ft Caswell to take up arms against the United States. After destroying the building they went over in Brooklyn another Negro settlement mostly, and began searching everyone and if you did not submit would be shot down on the spot. They searched all the Negro Churches. And to day (Sunday) we dare not go to our places of worship. They found no guns or ammunition in any of the places for there was none. And to satisfy their Bloodthirsty appetites would Kill unoffending Negro men to or on their

Anonymous to William McKinley, 13 November 1898. File 17743-1898, RG R660, Department of Justice, National Archives. Reprinted in *Root of Bitterness: Documents of the Social History of American Women*, ed. Nancy F. Cott et al., 2d ed. (Boston: Northeastern University Press, 1996), 420–22.

way from dinner. Some of our most worthy Negro Men have been made to leave the city. Also some whites, G. J. French, Deputy Sheriff, Chief of Police Jno R. Melton, Dr. S. P. Wright Mayor and R. H. Bunting united states commissioner. We don't know where Mr. Chadbourn the post master is, and two or three others white. I call on you the head of the American nation to help these humble subjects. We are loyal, we go when duty calls us. And are we to die like rats in a trap? With no place to seek redress or to go with our Greivances? Can we call on any other nation for help? Why do you forsake the Negro? who is not to blame for being here. This Grand and noble nation who flies to the help of suffering humanity of another nation? and leave the Secessionists and born Rioters to slay us. Oh, that we had never seen the light of the world. When our parents belonged to them, why the negro was all right[;] now, when they work and accumalate property they are all wrong. The Negroes that have been banished are all property owners to considerable extent, had they been worthless negroes, we would not care.

Will you for God sake in your next message to Congress give us some releif. If you send us all to Africa we will be willing or a number of us will gladly go. Is this the land of the free and the home of the brave? How can the Negro sing my country tis of thee? For Humanity sake help us, for Christ sake do. We the Negro can do nothing but pray. There seems to be no help for us. No paper will tell the truth about the Negro. The men of the 1st North Carolina were home on a furlough and they took a high hand in the nefarious work. Also the companies from every little town came in to kill the negro. There was not any Rioting simply the strong slaying the weak. They speak of special police every white man and boy from 12 years up has a gun or pistol, and the negro had nothing, his soul he could not say was his own. Oh, do see how we are Slaughtered, when our husbands go to work we do not look for their return. The Man who promises the Negro protection now as Mayor is the one who in his speech at the Opera house said the Cape Fear should be strewn with carcasses. Some papers I see say it was right to eject the Negro editor. That is all right but why should a whole city full of negroes suffer for Manly when he was hundred of miles away. And the paper had ceased publication. We were glad it was so for our own safety. But they tried to slay us all. To day we are mourners in a strange land with no protection near. God help us. Do something to alleviate our sorrows if you please. I cannot sign my name and live. But every word of this is true. The laws of our state is no good for the negro anyhow. Yours in much distress, Wilmington NC.

[P.S.] Please send releif as soon as possible, or we perish.

16. A Plea for Justice

GEORGE H. WHITE
Address to the United States House of Representatives
1901

A Howard University graduate and a lawyer, George H. White represented North Carolina's Second Congressional District, known as the "Black Second," which was deliberately constructed in 1872 by the state legislature to concentrate black voting strength and keep other districts under white control. He was elected in 1896 and re-elected in 1898, but after the success of the 1898 white supremacy campaign, he did not run again, knowing it would be futile.

Aware of his historic role as the last representative of his race remaining in Congress, and eager to counter the characterizations of black Americans offered on the floor of the House by other southern congressmen, White was determined not to leave office without leaving his side of the story in the Congressional Record. *On January 29, 1901, after trying in vain to get the floor to speak on the subject of disfranchisement, he arose during a discussion of an agricultural appropriations bill and "digressed" to give this passionate address on disfranchisement and the plight of black Americans. After completing his term White announced his plans to move to the North, saying, "I cannot live in North Carolina and be a man and be treated as a man."*

I want to enter a plea for the colored man, the colored woman, the colored boy, and the colored girl of this country. I would not thus digress from the question at issue and detain the House in a discussion of the interests of this particular people at this time but for the constant and the persistent efforts of certain gentlemen[1] upon this floor to mold and rivet public sentiment against us as a people and to lose no opportunity to hold up the unfortunate few who commit crimes and depredations and lead lives of infamy and shame, as other races do, as fair specimens of representatives of the entire colored race. And at no time, perhaps, during the Fifty-sixth Congress were these charges and countercharges, containing, as they do, slanderous statements, more persistently magnified and pressed upon the attention of the nation than during the consideration of the recent reappor-

---

[1]**certain gentlemen:** Oscar Underwood of Alabama, Stanyarne Wilson of South Carolina, and W. W. Kitchin of North Carolina.

George H. White, *Congressional Record*, 56th Cong., 2d sess. (29 January 1901), pp. 1634–38. Reprinted in *Afro-American History: Primary Sources*, ed. Thomas R. Frazier (New York: Harcourt, Brace and World, 1970), 200–7, 209–10.

tionment bill, which is now a law. As stated some days ago on this floor by me, I then sought diligently to obtain an opportunity to answer some of the statements made by gentlemen from different States, but the privilege was denied me; and I therefore must embrace this opportunity to say, out of season, perhaps, that which I was not permitted to say in season.

In the catalogue of members of Congress in this House perhaps none have been more persistent in their determination to bring the black man into disrepute and, with a labored effort, to show that he was unworthy of the right of citizenship than my colleague from North Carolina, Mr. Kitchin. During the first session of this Congress, while the Constitutional amendment was pending in North Carolina, he labored long and hard to show that the white race was at all times and under all circumstances superior to the negro by inheritance if not otherwise, and the excuse for his party supporting that amendment, which has since been adopted, was that an illiterate negro was unfit to participate in making the laws of a sovereign State and the administration and execution of them; but an illiterate white man living by his side, with no more or perhaps not as much property, with no more exalted character, no higher thoughts of civilization, no more knowledge of the handicraft of government, had by birth, because he was white, inherited some peculiar qualification, clear, I presume, only in the mind of the gentleman who endeavored to impress it upon others, that entitled him to vote, though he knew nothing whatever of letters. . . .

I would like to call the gentleman's attention to the fact that the Constitution of the United States forbids the granting of any title of nobility to any citizen thereof, and while it does not in letters forbid the inheritance of this superior caste, I believe in the fertile imagination of the gentleman promulgating it, his position is at least in conflict with the spirit of that organic law of the land. He insists and, I believe, has introduced a resolution in this House for the repeal of the fifteenth amendment to the Constitution. As an excuse for his peculiar notions about the exercise of the right of franchise by citizens of the United States of different nationality, perhaps it would not be amiss to call the attention of this House to a few facts and figures surrounding his birth and rearing. To begin with, he was born in one of the counties in my district, Halifax, a rather significant name.

I might state as a further general fact that the Democrats of North Carolina got possession of the State and local government since my last election in 1898, and that I bid adieu to these historic walls on the 4th day of next March, and that the brother of Mr. Kitchin will succeed me. Comment is unnecessary. In the town where this young gentleman was born, at the general election last August for the adoption of the constitutional amendment, and the general election for State and county officers, Scotland Neck had a registered white vote of 395, most of whom of course were Democrats, and a registered colored vote of 534, virtually if not all of whom were Republicans, and so voted. When the count was announced, however, there were 831 Democrats to 75 Republicans; but in the town of Halifax, same county, the result was much more pronounced.

In that town the registered Republican vote was 345, and the total registered vote of the township was 539, but when the count was announced it stood 990

Democrats to 41 Republicans, or 492 more Democratic votes counted than were registered votes in the township. Comment here is unnecessary, nor do I think it necessary for anyone to wonder at the peculiar notion my colleague has with reference to the manner of voting and the method of counting those votes, nor is it to be a wonder that he is a member of this Congress, having been brought up and educated in such wonderful notions of dealing out fair-handed justice to his fellowman.

It would be unfair, however, for me to leave the inference upon the minds of those who hear me that all of the white people of the State of North Carolina hold views with Mr. Kitchin and think as he does. Thank God there are many noble exceptions to the example he sets, that, too, in the Democratic party; men who have never been afraid that one uneducated, poor, depressed negro could put to flight and chase into degradation two educated, wealthy, thrifty white men. There never has been, nor ever will be, any negro domination in that State, and no one knows it any better than the Democratic party. It is a convenient howl, however, often resorted to in order to consummate a diabolical purpose by scaring the weak and gullible whites into support of measures and men suitable to the demagogue and the ambitious office seeker, whose crave for office overshadows and puts to flight all other considerations, fair or unfair. . . .

It is an undisputed fact that the negro vote in . . . most of the . . . Southern States, [has] been effectively suppressed, either one way or the other — in some instances by constitutional amendment and State legislation, in others by cold-blooded fraud and intimidation, but whatever the method pursued, it is not denied, but frankly admitted in the speeches in this House, that the black vote has been eliminated to a large extent. Then, when some of us insist that the plain letter of the Constitution of the United States, which all of us have sworn to support, should be carried out, as expressed in the second section of the fourteenth amendment thereof, to wit:

> Representatives shall be apportioned among the several States according to their respective numbers, counting the whole number of persons in each State, excluding Indians not taxed. But when the right to vote at any election for the choice of electors for President and Vice-President of the United States, Representatives in Congress, the executive and judicial officers of a State, or the members of a legislature thereof, is denied to any of the male inhabitants of such State, being twenty-one years of age, and citizens of the United States, or in any way abridged, except for participation in rebellion, or other crime, the basis of representation therein shall be reduced in proportion which the number of such male citizens shall bear to the whole number of male citizens twenty-one years of age in such State.

That section makes the duty of every member of Congress plain, and yet the gentleman from Alabama [Mr. Underwood] says that the attempt to enforce this section of the organic law is the throwing down of firebrands, and notifies the world that this attempt to execute the highest law of the land will be retaliated by the South, and the inference is that the negro will be even more severely punished than the horrors through which he has already come.

Let me make it plain: The divine law, as well as most of the State laws, says, in substance: "He that sheddeth man's blood, by man shall his blood be shed." A highwayman commits murder, and when the officers of the law undertake to arrest, try, and punish him commensurate with the enormity of his crime, he straightens himself up to his full height and defiantly says to them: "Let me alone; I will not be arrested, I will not be tried, I'll have none of the execution of your laws, and in the event you attempt to execute your laws upon me, I will see to it that many more men, women, or children are murdered."

Here's the plain letter of the Constitution, the plain, simple, sworn duty of every member of Congress; yet these gentlemen from the South say "Yes, we have violated your Constitution of the nation; we regarded it as a local necessity; and now, if you undertake to punish us as the Constitution prescribes, we will see to it that our former deeds of disloyalty to that instrument, our former acts of disfranchisement and opposition to the highest law of the land will be repeated many fold."

Not content with all that has been done to the black man, not because of any deeds that he has done, Mr. Underwood advances the startling information that these people have been thrust upon the whites of the South, forgetting, perhaps, the horrors of the slave trade, the unspeakable horrors of the transit from the shores of Africa by means of the middle passage to the American clime; the enforced bondage of the blacks and their descendants for two and a half centuries in the United States, now, for the first time perhaps in the history of our lives, the information comes that these poor, helpless, and in the main inoffensive people were thrust upon our Southern brethren.

Individually, and so far as my race is concerned, I care but little about the reduction of Southern representation, except in so far as it becomes my duty to aid in the proper execution of all the laws of the land in whatever sphere in which I may be placed. Such reduction in representation, it is true, would make more secure the installment of the great Republican party in power for many years to come in all of its branches, and at the same time enable that great party to be able to dispense with the further support of the loyal Negro vote; and I might here parenthetically state that there are some members of the Republican party to-day — "lily whites," if you please — who, after receiving the unalloyed support of the negro vote for over thirty years, now feel that they have grown a little too good for association with him politically, and are disposed to dump him overboard. I am glad to observe, however, that this class constitutes a very small percentage of those to whom we have always looked for friendship and protection. . . .

I trust I will be pardoned for making a passing reference to one more gentleman — Mr. Wilson of South Carolina. . . . He insists that they, the Southern whites, are the black man's best friend, and that they are taking him by the hand and trying to lift him up, that they are educating him. For all that he and all Southern people have done in this regard, I wish in behalf of the colored people of the South to extend our thanks. We are not ungrateful to friends, but feel that our toil has made our friends able to contribute the stinty pittance which we have received at their hands.

I read in a Democratic paper a few days ago, the *Washington Times,* an extract taken from a South Carolina paper, which was intended to exhibit the eagerness with which the negro is grasping every opportunity for educating himself. The clipping showed that the money for each white child in the State ranged from three to five times as much per capita as was given to each colored child. This is helping us some, but not to the extent that one would infer from the gentleman's speech.

If the gentleman to whom I have referred will pardon me, I would like to advance the statement that the musty records of 1868, filed away in the archives of Southern capitols, as to what the negro was thirty-two years ago, is not a proper standard by which the negro living on the threshold of the twentieth century should be measured. Since that time we have reduced the illiteracy of the race at least 45 percent. We have written and published near 500 books. We have nearly 300 newspapers, 3 of which are dailies. We have now in practice over 2,000 lawyers and a corresponding number of doctors. We have accumulated over $12,000,000 worth of school property and about $40,000,000 worth of church property. We have about 140,000 farms and homes, valued at in the neighborhood of $750,000,000, and personal property valued at about $170,000,000. We have raised about $11,000,000 for educational purposes, and the property per capita for every colored man, woman, and child in the United States is estimated at $75.

We are operating successfully several banks, commercial enterprises among our people in the Southland, including 1 silk mill and 1 cotton factory. We have 32,000 teachers in the schools of the country; we have built, with the aid of our friends, about 2,000 churches, and support 7 colleges, 17 academies, 50 high schools, 5 law schools, 5 medical schools, and 25 theological seminaries. We have over 600,000 acres of land in the South alone. The cotton produced, mainly by black labor, has increased from 4,669,770 bales in 1860 to 11,235,000 in 1899. All this we have done under the most adverse circumstances. We have done it in the face of lynching, burning at the stake, with the humiliation of "Jim Crow" cars, the disfranchisement of our male citizens, slander and degradation of our women, with the factories closed against us, no negro permitted to be conductor on the railway cars, whether run through the streets of our cities or across the prairies of our great country, no negro permitted to run as engineer on a locomotive, most of the mines closed against us. Labor unions — carpenters, painters, brick masons, machinists, hackmen, and those supplying nearly every conceivable avocation for livelihood have banded themselves together to better their condition, but, with few exceptions, the black face has been left out. The negroes are seldom employed in our mercantile stores. At this we do not wonder. Some day we hope to have them employed in our own stores. With all these odds against us, we are forging our way ahead, slowly, perhaps, but surely. You may tie us and then taunt us for a lack of bravery, but one day we will break the bonds. You may use our labor for two and a half centuries and then taunt us for our poverty, but let me remind you we will not always remain poor. You may withhold even the knowledge of how to read God's word and learn the way from earth to glory and then taunt us for our ignorance, but we would remind you that there is plenty of room at the top, and we are climbing.

After enforced debauchery, with the many kindred horrors incident to slavery, it comes with ill grace from the perpetrators of these deeds to hold up the short-comings of some of our race to ridicule and scorn.

"The new man, the slave who has grown out of the ashes of thirty-five years ago, is inducted into the political and social system, cast into the arena of man-hood, where he constitutes a new element and becomes a competitor for all its emoluments. He is put upon trial to test his ability to be counted worthy of free-dom, worthy of the elective franchise; and after thirty-five years of struggling against almost insurmountable odds, under conditions but little removed from slavery itself, he asks a fair and just judgment, not of those whose prejudice has en-deavored to forestall, to frustrate his every forward movement, rather those who have lent a helping hand, that he might demonstrate the truth of 'the fatherhood of God and the brotherhood of man.' "

Mr. Chairman, permit me to digress for a few moments for the purpose of calling the attention of the House to two bills which I regard as important, intro-duced by me in the early part of the first session of this Congress. The first was to give the United States control and entire jurisdiction over all cases of lynching and death by mob violence. During the last session of this Congress I took occasion to address myself in detail to this particular measure, but with all my efforts the bill still sweetly sleeps in the room of the committee to which it was referred. The necessity of legislation along this line is daily being demonstrated. The arena of the lyncher no longer is confined to Southern climes, but is stretching its hydra head over all parts of the Union. . . .

This evil peculiar to America, yes, to the United States, must be met some-how, some day.

The other bill to which I wish to call attention is one introduced by me to ap-propriate $1,000,000 to reimburse depositors of the late Freedman's Savings and Trust Company. . . .

May I hope that the Committee on Banking and Currency who has charge of this measure will yet see its way clear to do tardy justice, long deferred, to this much wronged and unsuspecting people. If individual sections of the country, in-dividual political parties can afford to commit deeds of wrong against us, cer-tainly a great nation like ours will see to it that a people so loyal to its flag as the black man has shown himself in every war from the birth of the Union to this day, will not permit this obligation to go longer uncanceled.

Now, Mr. Chairman, before concluding my remarks I want to submit a brief recipe for the solution of the so-called American negro problem. He asks no spe-cial favors, but simply demands that he be given the same chance for existence, for earning a livelihood, for raising himself in the scales of manhood and wom-anhood that are accorded to kindred nationalities. Treat him as a man; go into his home and learn of his social conditions; learn of his cares, his troubles, and his hopes for the future; gain his confidence; open the doors of industry to him; let the word "negro," "colored," and "black" be stricken from all the organizations enumerated in the federation of labor.

Help him to overcome his weaknesses, punish the crime-committing class by the courts of the land, measure the standard of the race by its best material, cease to mold prejudicial and unjust public sentiment against him, and my word for it, he will learn to support, hold up the hands of, and join in with that political party, that institution, whether secular or religious, in every community where he lives, which is destined to do the greatest good for the greatest number. Obliterate race hatred, party prejudice, and help us to achieve nobler ends, greater results, and become more satisfactory citizens to our brother in white.

This, Mr. Chairman, is perhaps the negroes' temporary farewell to the American Congress; but let me say, Phœnix-like he will rise up some day and come again. These parting words are in behalf of an outraged, heart-broken, bruised, and bleeding, but God-fearing people, faithful, industrious, loyal people — rising people, full of potential force.

Mr. Chairman, in the trial of Lord Bacon, when the court disturbed the counsel for the defendant, Sir Walter Raleigh raised himself up to his full height and, addressing the court, said:

Sir, I am pleading for the life of a human being.

The only apology that I have to make for the earnestness with which I have spoken is that I am pleading for the life, the liberty, the future happiness, and manhood suffrage for one-eighth of the entire population of the United States. [Loud applause.]

Suggestions for Further Reading

Anderson, Eric. *Race and Politics in North Carolina, 1872–1901: The Black Second.* Baton Rouge: Louisiana State University Press, 1981.

Ayers, Edward L. *The Promise of the New South: Life after Reconstruction.* New York: Oxford University Press, 1992.

Brundage, W. Fitzhugh. *Lynching in the New South: Georgia and Virginia, 1880–1930.* Champaign: University of Illinois Press, 1993.

Cecelski, David S., and Timothy B. Tyson, eds. *Democracy Betrayed: The Wilmington Race Riot of 1898 and Its Legacy.* Chapel Hill: University of North Carolina Press, 1998.

Gilmore, Glenda Elizabeth. *Gender and Jim Crow: Women and the Politics of White Supremacy in North Carolina, 1896–1920.* Chapel Hill: University of North Carolina Press, 1996.

Kousser, J. Morgan. *The Shaping of Southern Politics: Suffrage Restriction and the Establishment of the One-Party South, 1880–1910.* New Haven: Yale University Press, 1974.

Royster, Jacqueline Jones, ed. *Southern Horrors and Other Writings: The Anti-Lynching Campaign of Ida B. Wells, 1892–1900.* Boston: Bedford/St. Martin's, 1997.

Woodward, C. Vann. *The Strange Career of Jim Crow.* 3d rev. ed. New York: Oxford University Press, 1974.

CHAPTER FIVE

THE AGE OF INDUSTRIALISM

From Farm to Mill

By the turn of the twentieth century, Americans lived in a transformed society. The railroad revolution was complete, and the greatly enhanced reach of the market economy had generated new wealth for Americans and appreciably improved the standard of living for many of them. Most notably, U.S. agriculture, manufacturing, and mining dominated world markets. But the new industrial economy was also, in many ways, very unsettling. Farmers found themselves in a completely different environment. Because they now produced crops for distant markets, they were subject to the vagaries of rising and declining prices in those markets. Railroads and industry spurred migration to towns and cities, and by the early 1900s the focus of social, cultural, economic, and political life had shifted to urban America. Rural life became, by comparison, less attractive.

Textile mills thrived in the Piedmont — a region extending from Maryland, through Virginia and the Carolinas, and across central Georgia and Alabama — which, because of the red clay soil and rapidly flowing rivers and streams, had been the most underdeveloped and rural region of the Southeast. Prior to the Civil War, much of the Piedmont South was isolated, populated primarily by semi-independent, nonslaveholding "yeoman" farmers. The advent of the railroad changed all of this. Many new towns — such as Roanoke, Virginia, and Durham, North Carolina — sprang up along new rail lines and became thriving markets and centers of manufacturing. After the 1870s, these urban areas became magnets for further migration and development.

Between the 1880s and World War I, Piedmont towns aggressively sought out new industry. Organizing local support as well as outside investment, boosters pushed the development of a "New South" that would turn from its traditions of slavery and plantation agriculture toward a future of factories and industrialization.

Although tobacco and furniture-making factories appeared in this period, by far the most important new industry was the manufacture of cotton textiles: until the late nineteenth century, most textile mills had been located in New England; by the 1880s, however, the industry began to move south.

The people migrating from farm to mill had to undergo a profound social transition. Southern immigrants came from Piedmont or hill country farms, where social life was distinctive. Plantation agriculture had not made great inroads in the Piedmont and the hills and mountains west of it during the antebellum period. Most farmers still grew small amounts of a "cash crop" — that is, a nonfood crop such as cotton or tobacco — for income. They might also have raised corn and hogs for sale to local consumers, but this did not afford much exposure to the larger market economy.

The arrival of railroads ended rural Southerners' self-sufficiency and independence. In addition to drawing farmers into commercial agriculture, the ensuing access to the market economy also provided opportunities for other capitalist enterprises. Northern investment poured in as mining, lumber, and other extractive industries sprang up throughout the region. Meanwhile, factories appeared, and around them grew new industrial towns.

Workers in the South, like workers across the United States, migrated in large numbers to these towns. Abandoning declining farms and rural communities, they were attracted primarily by the prospect of "public work" — regular employment that brought regular wages. Like Northerners, rural Southerners migrated to industrial areas to flee poverty. But in doing so they faced particular hardships. In place of seasonal and independent labor, they faced an unrelenting industrial routine in cotton textile factories controlled by bosses and managers — and a rigid class system that separated workers and managers in the mill villages. The physical environment of the mill was noisy and hot, and the air was filled with cotton lint that managed to get into literally everything. As mill villages expanded in the years immediately prior to World War I, they typically became even more structured and rigid in their control of workers.

The documents in this chapter focus on the transition that southern workers made in moving from the farm to the mill. In the first group, residents of southern Appalachia describe some of the conditions in their rural communities near the turn of the twentieth century. (These conditions changed, clearly, for many of them left the land.) August Kohn examines some of the reasons people migrated to the mills and some of the social consequences of an industrial lifestyle. And, in the final selection, Flossie Durham recalls her experiences as a young girl working in a cotton textile factory at the turn of the century.

As you read, compare rural life to life in the industrialized mill communities. What did workers do to try to establish a new community in the mill village? How did owners and managers regard workers? How did the attitudes of workers and owner/managers differ?

17. Rural Life in Tennessee and Virginia

Lizzie (Sallie Newman) Gibson, Robert Barnett, Catherine Fitch Stout, and Hattie Murphey McDade
Oral History Interviews
1939

In no region was the contrast between rural and industrial ways of living more apparent than southern Appalachia. For much of the nineteenth century, in the vast region of the Piedmont, thousands of Southerners lived in isolated hill and mountain communities. After the Civil War, the advent of railroads gave rise to mines and lumber and textile mills; these new industries in turn transformed the society and economy of the region.

The following are selected from two sets of oral history interviews: the first is one among the thousands of interviews of white and black Southerners conducted during the 1930s by the Federal Writers Project; the others come from a series of interviews conducted by local historian Roy Edwin Thomas during the 1970s and early 1980s in the Appalachian South. The interviewees describe different aspects of life during their childhoods at the close of the nineteenth century and the beginning of the twentieth.

Lizzie (Sallie Newman) Gibson

Roanoke, Virginia

Tell you the story of my life? Why you sound just like Jo here, beggin' me to tell him about when I was a girl and walked three miles to school in the winter, and always getting my toes and heels frostbit two or three times before the cold weather was over.

Talk about Trouble: A New Deal Portrait of Virginians in the Great Depression, ed. Nancy J. Martin-Perdue and Charles L. Perdue Jr. (Chapel Hill: University of North Carolina Press, 1996), 77–79.

Well, I guess my life's no different from hundreds of the other girls that was raised on the farm, come into town to work in the mills, and ended up by marrying and going to raisin' kids. I was born in Patrick County, right there in the mountains and not so far from Lovers' Leap. That's where they say the Indian sweethearts jumped to their deaths sooner than be parted. The fairy stones come from Patrick, too. But me or my folks never had so much luck there that I'd ever be sorry we all got away.

My father was a hill farmer. We lived on a piece of land he got from his Pa and it was too rough to grow more than enough to feed us all. Nine of us children and we all got out as soon as we could. The two oldest boys went to the West Virginia mines up the North Fork hollow; and one was killed there when they had the big slide. I have one brother in Illinois working on a farm, and it's a sight to hear him tell how many hogs they raise every year for the Chicago slaughter pens.

No, Pa and Ma didn't have much education. Right after the War lots of folks didn't. And Ma never learned to read or write, but she could spin and weave as pretty as ever you saw. Even after I was a big girl — and I was the baby of the family — she used to plant her a patch of flax every year. Did you ever see a flax patch in bloom? Well I do say! You sure have missed a mighty fine sight. It grows about waist-high and when it's waving in the wind, all covered with blue flowers just the color of the sky on a hot summer's day, you'd have to go a far piece to find anything half so pretty. Lots of trouble though, flax is, and I'm glad I can buy my linen over the counter. But I set lots of store by some towels and such that Ma wove and give to me when we first set up housekeeping.

Yes, I left home the week after I was twenty-one and got steady work in the mills right from the start. Noah was already working at the Viscose, and him and me got to courting right away. I wanted to wait awhile to get married, but evenings got mighty lonely and we thought I could keep right on with my job after we got hitched. You know how that was. Pretty soon my first boy was on his way and I had to quit.

He was a pretty little fellow and lived to be three years old. When Jo here was just past his first year he [the oldest child] took pneumonia and died almost overnight, you might say. That most killed Noah, and me too. He was such a cute little tyke and crazy about his mom and pop. The next year I had a stillborn little girl, and the third little boy died with diphtheria the year Sue was born. That one was the spit image of Noah. Just seems like I loved all my babies too good and the good Lord took 'em away.

Yes, everybody says Sue looks like me. A great big girl she is for three years, but I used to be big and strong too. I didn't need no powder or coloring for my face either. And Noah used to tease me about my blushing when he was coming to see me. I've got skinny and sallow in late years and don't feel so good anymore. Ma enjoyed her health until she was past seventy, but seems like I've got sickly and all run to skin and bones.

You want to hear more about my folks? Well, let's see. My granddad Howe fought in the War four years. And when he got home he didn't have anything to plow his land with but one old ox, and no seeds, or nothing else much. He lived to be eighty-nine years old and used to say he was of fightin' stock. He had three boys and divided his land three ways, deeding them all a little piece to farm. I have two sisters in Roanoke, and one here in Vinton. They work in the mills, except Kate, the oldest. She is around fifty now and has two girls and a boy working. And they want she should take a rest, though she is a fast weaver yet.

Not much I can tell you about Noah's folks, except they are country folks same as mine. He was born on a farm in Bedford County, and his Pa is still living out there near Thaxton. He has a right smart bit of land, and the oldest boy stays on there and tends it. The children love to go out there in the summer and wade in the branch and pick blackberries. I like that, too, if the briars wa'n't so mean to stick a body.

Noah got more schooling than I did. I went to a two-room school and didn't get through the seventh grade. But Noah had one year of high school. He's an awful smart boy and always was. And big-hearted, so's we'll never have anything for he'll give it all away faster than he can make it — always helping some of his folks or mine one. But land sakes, it's better, I say, to be too open-handed than tight-fisted any day. And I never could abide a stingy person.

Well, what you know! Talked all this time and never told you what kind of work my man does. He works in the engineering department at Viscose. It's mighty dirty work but he has daylight [day shift], the pay is good, and Viscose is always grand to them as works there. There's not a lazy bone in Noah's body, even if I — as shouldn't — say so. And even after his day's work is done, he is always pottering around here doin' something.

We have a garden on our lot we own in the next square, and he already has that planted. Spaded it up his'self. And did all the planting with Jo here to drop the beans as he put in the corn. For years we have planned to get us a little home on that lot, but seems like something always comes along to get our nest egg. We rent this house, and it's convenient and all we need, I guess. We have a good old Ford, and my washing machine and refrigerator are both good as new. Christmas we got us a new Philco radio and it's a sight how we all enjoy that, even the baby.

You're asking me something now when you ask what we plan for the kids. I do know that I want Jo to get through high school. And then I guess he will want to go with Viscose. Noah and me would both like that. As for Sue, well it don't make much difference about her schooling just so she gets through the grades. Guess she will marry when time comes and we don't aim to let her work if we can help it. Noah always says just so they grow up decent and honest is the main thing.

Amusements, you say? Well, we go to the pictures once in a long time. And I visit some with the neighbors and keep Noah company after the children are asleep. We are still plannin' and hopin' to build us a house someday. And we used to talk about that a heap, you know: how we would set out the bushes, and have some fruit trees, and a whole lot of chickens fenced off from the garden. He used to argue me down about the color to paint — me being all for a dark color that wouldn't show smoke so quick and him all set for a pure white with dark green blinds at all the windows.

Get off my lap, Sue, and let's show the lady the little house that your pop built. Watch the step and don't let the baby put her sticky hands on your coat. There it is. Noah calls it a Dutch Colonial house, if you know what that means. He built it right to a scale and it's a mite over four feet tall. All the little windows are put-tied in like real ones, and the outside blinds and all the doors are on real little hinges. Noah built on it — off and on — for over a year, and the children played with it until they got over liking to open and shut all the dormer windows.

How come I took it for a chicken house? Well, the old hen dragged the little chickens all over the place in the wet, so's Noah just built this little paling fence around the house and put them inside. It's nice and dry in the house, but land [abridged "land's" or "lord's sake"?] it ought to be, with the best tin roofing money could buy and the real little gutters all soldered into place. Yes, the old hen can step over the fence when she feels called to, but not one of the little ones can follow her — without Sue gets to fooling with them, lifting them in and out, or opens the little gate, and forgets to shut it again.

I hated [it] someway, though, when Noah put the old hen in [the house]. Makes me feel like he don't feel like we'll ever get our Dutch house started. He laughs and says it's too good a house to go to waste. But just the same I'd soon he had left it empty. Already the good white paint is getting dirty and the floor inside will never be fit to be seen after them filthy things feed awhile longer. Shoo, you hateful old hen! I know she is the stubbornest old thing in the world, climbing up on Noah's nice little back porch. I always plan to plant me a wisteria vine over the back porch if we ever get the place.

ROBERT BARNETT

Burbank, Tennessee

I never knowed ennybody that dried wild meat, deer ur bear meat. But I've heerd fellers tell about it. I guess it was all right to eat.

But I remember 'at they'd kill a beef an' they'd dry some of it. Jist th' lean meat. I've eat it. It's good.

They ewst to be a man by th' name of Rank Stanley 'at lived just b'low us, up in th' mountain, yander.

An' he got a big oxen — one of his big fat oxen's leg broken. An' they skinned that big oxen — they killed 'im an' skinned 'im. An' they dried a lot a' that beef. They strung it on little 'hogany sticks, an' hung it up. An' hit'uz good an' dry.

An' I'd go down there an' his wife 'ud give me a piece of that dried beef. An' hit'uz good, good an' tender. Course, when it'uz dried, it's a little hard to chew.

Southern Appalachia, 1885–1915: Oral Histories from Residents of the State Corner Area of North Carolina, Tennessee, and Virginia, comp. Roy Edwin Thomas (Jefferson, N.C.: McFarland & Co., 1991), 43–44, 108–9.

CATHERINE FITCH STOUT

Neva, Tennessee

We had all kinds of apple trees, an' grape vines. We had peaches an' pears — peaches of all kinds. By th' bushels . . . couldn't gib'm away. We ewst to dry 'um an' sell 'um. We had a kiln — made a kiln — an' put a fire in it, to dry 'um.

An' we'd bust them all — had peaches that 'ud bust open. Lay 'um in that kiln, from one day, all night with heat 'under 'um: an' by mornin', they'd be about dry. They'd take 'um off that kiln an' put 'um in th' sun, out there. An' fill that kiln up ag'in.

Well, first, you'd cut 'um open an' take them seed out. An' peel 'um, ur . . . some likes th' peach peelin' left on. You busted them soft peaches, open. An' th' seed, then, hit jis' come out. That's what we called th' free-stones.

An' they was another peach that ye couldn't bust open. Us see, what did they call them? Plum-peach! Or cling-stone.

An' we dried blackberries an' razzberries an' huckleberries. An' corn. But we just dried them in th' sun. An' when you'd git 'um good an' dry, you'd sack 'um up, then, an' nothin' didn't git in 'um.

I never knowed of ennybody dryin' cherries. We never did raise cherries on this side of th' Blue Ridge. North Caroliner can, ennywhur. But we never could raise 'um on this side, too much.

And — law! — at th' punkins we did raise. We ewst to have th' fields full ov 'um. Plant 'um in th' corn.

We dried punkin, an' cooked it with meat. Most people liked it, but I never did like punkin.

An' they got to raisin' these ol' "bakes," now, an' you can keep those all year. Some calls 'um bakies, now-days. An' they're jist a reg'lar punkin — taste the same — but they're all meat, might-near't. They're good. They'll grow three foot long. But you can't leave 'um out, exposed to freezin' weather. We kept lots of 'um in th' warm house . . . till wa-a-ay in th' summer. If you've got a basement whor it's dry, you can keep 'um might-nigh all year.

Now, they's jist a certain kind of apples that ye can keep all winter, what we called winter apples. You'd put them in a box, an' put dry leaves in 'um. An' if they froze, wy, th' leaves 'ud brang th' freeze out.

Or . . . ye buried 'um. A lot of people buried thur apples in th' ground.

An' p'taters, ye'd put them in holes — we allus holed 'um — out in th' 'tater patch ur whurever ye wanted 'um. Irish p'taters.

We raised lots a' sweet p'taters, too. An' after we got 'um dried out good, we kepp 'um here in this closet. Fer lo-o-ong years. Never had no trouble. But they haff to be dried out.

HATTIE MURPHEY McDADE

Mountain City, Tennessee

We ewst to have two railroad stations here in Mount'n City. We had what we called a narrow-gauge line from Virginia, that came up from Damascus. An' that was out of th' Doe River road.

An' then, this other line here, was one that came up from Johnson City, an' down in that direction.

And both lines operated here a long time. Then they had a terrible storm. And a lot 'a people drowned, and some were covered up in th' mud till they never did find some of the bodies.

An' the railroads didn't get any help to rebuild. And they didn't rebuild. I guess it's been forty years since that happened, maybe longer. So that left us stranded.

Well, before that railroad line came from Damascus, I remember . . .

Our road goin' over toward Abingdon, that's a river road. It crossed the river, they said, twenty times in twenty-seven miles. And course, you know how water runs after a big rain.

And our family had a hack.[1] And you set way up in th' hack, an' haff t' hold.

And that's th' way I went off to school at Abingdon, in that hack. Well, I was twelve years old when I went over to Abingdon for the first time, to go to th' Martha Washington College.

An' at home in Mount'n City, we never had enny coal, we just burnt wood.

An' when I got to the edge of town, I smelt somethin' strange. It was th' burnin' coal.

I never will forget that smell.

---

[1]**hack:** a coach, or carriage.

18. Moving to the Mills

AUGUST KOHN
"Why They Go to the Mills"
1907

The advent of the Industrial Revolution in the South drew thousands of white South-erners off the land. Most of these emigrants settled in the new industrial mill villages of the Appalachians and Piedmont, where a new definition of labor and a new sense of community were taking hold. Charleston journalist August Kohn's account decidedly presents the point of view of mill owners and managers, who were at-tempting to recruit workers with promises of higher wages, better housing, and greater opportunity. Kohn was trying to refute the contention of reformers that mill

August Kohn, *The Cotton Mills of South Carolina.* Republished from *The News and Courier,* Charleston, S.C. (Spartanburg, S.C.: Reprint Company, 1975), 26–31.

workers were exploited or that they were being made to live in mill communities. Despite its bias, Kohn's account provides some insight into the considerations that prompted people to move between the farms and the mills — some of them more than once.

The people who work in the cotton mills are very much like the rest of mankind. There are more than 54,000 actual operatives on the pay rolls, and the rule seems to be to count at least two and a half times as many as being dependent upon the efforts of those who are actually in the mills — the mill population easily running to 125,000. As has been stated in my previous letter, practically all of the help now in the cotton mills has come from the farms, and mainly from those in South Carolina. It has not been very many years since farm labor was but poorly paid for. About 1897 and 1898, when the raw cotton was selling at less than the cost of production, there was a general influx to the cotton mills; and most of those who went there then still remain with the mills. The general impression among competent mill men is that not more than 10 percent of those who go to the cotton mills return to the farms. It appears that the first year in the mills is generally the hardest. The help goes into the factory absolutely without experience, and it is particularly difficult for them to withstand the confinement of the building, and to be able to stand on their feet on the wooden floor. A great many of those who for the first time go into the cotton mills have difficulty with their feet. The mill help is shortest in the summer time, and this is because of the desire of a great many operatives, particularly those living in the mountainous sections, to spend the heated months in their former mountain homes.

It appears to be an accepted fact that if the operatives remain for two years in the mills they very seldom, if ever, leave the mills for the farm. The attraction of the cotton mill, to those who are in them, in a word, is the cash money.

They do not go to the mills because they are partial to day labor, but they go there simply because they know that at the end of every two weeks, whether the crops are good or bad, whether cotton is bringing five or fifteen cents, whether the cotton mill is making money or losing money, whether the corporation is in the hands of a receiver or not, that their pay envelope is going to be handed out to them by the paymaster.

There have been frequent occasions in this State where mills have actually been running for a time at a loss to their stockholders, and the mills have continued operations in justice to the operatives and to hold the help together, because when labor is once disorganized it is difficult to reassemble.

It is not my purpose to argue whether or not it is more profitable to work on the farms or to labor in the cotton mills, but I am simply going to look into it from the standpoint of the operatives themselves. It was my purpose, wherever I went among the operatives, to inquire why they left the farms and preferred the cotton mills. I talked with men and women along these lines, and only in two or three instances did I find a marked preference for the farm, and a sincere desire, such as was expressed by Mr. Jenkins, of the Chiquola Mills, to return to the fields of Greenville. Such a desire was also expressed by an old man — Mr. Coleman Allen — who wanted to go back to the mountains of North Carolina, although he seemed very well satisfied at Pacolet.

As a general thing among those whom I interviewed, and at every place that I visited I talked along this line, there was a general disposition to remain at the cotton mills, and, as I have previously stated, the chief and convincing reason that they have for remaining is the cash consideration. In quite a number of instances the people would go over their experiences on the farms as compared with their pay in the mills, and showed me why it was preferable for them to remain at their present work. For instance, at Piedmont, I met Mr. Joe Parker, who was working in the mill at the time. He inherited a farm, about seven miles from Piedmont. He has been working in the cotton mills for about nine years and seems to be a sturdy, wide-awake young man. He is married and has one child; neither the wife nor child work in the mill. He was 27 years of age in August, and his experience is given in detail, because it may be regarded as typical of those who have gone from the farms to the mills — except that Mr. Parker owned his own place. Mr. Parker told me that he made three light bales of cotton on his place; the first of which he sold at ten cents, the second at eleven cents, the third at ten and three-quarters cents per pound. He made from thirty-five to fifty bushels of corn per acre, but this was not enough for his needs. He borrowed the money with which to buy a horse for his farm operations.

At the close of the farm year he found that he was $150 behind, and he thereupon concluded to sell his little farm, consisting of twenty-two acres, to Mr. Ja[me]s C. Sitton for $600, accepting part cash payment and part deferred payment therefor.

Mr. Parker said that on the farm he came out behind, while in the mill he made enough to live on at the rate of $1.25 per day, which was his compensation. He did not particularly fancy mill work, but he thought that it was best for himself and his family that he sell his farm and accept the certainty that he was receiving at the Piedmont Cotton Mills.

It is not at all an uncommon thing to find among the operatives' families that have left the mills, after having accumulated enough money to venture into farming operations, return and resume their work in the mills. There are some people who cannot succeed at farming as well as some people who cannot succeed in any other line of work, while a great many others fail, and this may account for the fact that so many who go from the mills to the farms fail on the farms, because mill work is very largely mechanical, and what little head work is necessary comes from others than those who have been experimenting on the farms and there failed.

There are to-day a number of owners of small farms working in the cotton mills. I should say that it would be conservative to figure that fifteen hundred farms in this State are owned by cotton mill operatives. In a great many mills there are as many as a dozen operatives who own farms, and they prefer very often to rent out these farms rather than hazard the experiment of making money on them.

The great majority of those who have gone to the cotton mills from farms belong to what is known as the tenant class; that is, they were renters upon some of the various plans of conducting small farms in vogue in this State. The systems of tenancy are not altogether the same throughout the State, but are generally on the same lines. Under the State law the landlord has the first claim upon the crop. This is, of course, altogether right, despite the arguments of the Socialists, and whether the crop is good or bad, the first claim is that of the landlord. In the Pee-Dee[1] section, for instance, the landlord furnishes the land, pays for the fertilizers, supplies the house, wood, and water, pays for the ginning and bagging and ties, and in return for this the tenant gets half of the crop. It is considered very good for a tenant to make fifteen bales of cotton. Of this amount he is entitled to seven and a half bales, which, at the rate of $50 per bale, would bring $375. If he plants eight acres of corn and makes twenty bushels to the acre, his share would be eighty bushels. Some of this corn would, of course, have to be used for his stock. Then the head of the family could hire himself out for a part of the year, if he were so inclined, to do hauling or other manual labor, and, to give him the full credit, he ought to make $150 in addition to his cotton. This would net him $525. If this family were made up of three hands; that is one plough and two hoe hands, and they went to the cotton mill, they would make on the very lowest basis $900 a year. From the figures that I expect to give later I will show exactly what such a family ought to make. Now the question is whether or not such a family would rather live on the farm, and get less cash money, or whether they would rather go to the cotton mill and "handle the coin."

In Newberry I interviewed several families — the Bouknights, Cromers, the Leopards, and others — who had gone from the mills to the farms, and who were returning to the cotton mills. Mr. Cromer's case was very interesting, because of the position that his daughters took in that they did not care to "bury themselves" on the farm, but preferred the community at the cotton mills. Mr. Bouknight had undertaken a farm, and, after losing considerable money, had decided that the mill was better than the farm.

In Spartanburg the system is very much the same as it is elsewhere — the landlord furnishes the land and stock, and gets one-half of the crop, and the tenant receives the other half; the expenses of fertilizing being shared. Various estimates have been made as to what ought to be made by a tenant farmer in the Piedmont section, but, owing to the undulating character of the farms, the average farmer does not make as much per acre as is made in the Pee-Dee section. And just here it may be very well to note that Mr. D. A. Tompkins, of Charlotte, N.C., takes the position that cotton mill help cannot be gotten from the farms where it is more profitable to work on the farm, and that on that account cotton mills will not flourish in Texas and in other sections, where the farms are exceedingly fertile and the results of farm labor are especially remunerative. . . .

As I have previously stated, a great many of the present-day operatives are coming from the mountainous sections of North Carolina. One of the mills in the

---

[1]**the Pee-Dee:** the Pee Dee River flows from the Piedmont in North Carolina, into South Carolina.

Piedmont section has distributed very freely all around Clyde, North Carolina, a hand-bill, which reads as follows:

> "Three years ago I owned a little mountain farm of two hundred acres. I had two good horses, two good cows, plenty of hogs, sheep, and several calves. I had three girls and two boys; ages run from 11 to 21. On my little farm I raised about four hundred bushels of corn, thirty to forty bushels of wheat, two hundred to three hundred dozen oats, and cut from four to eight stacks of hay during the summer. After I clothed my family, fed all my stock during the winter, I had only enough provisions and feed to carry me through making another crop, and no profit left. I sold my farm and stock, paid up all my debts, and moved my family to a cotton mill. At that time green hands had to work for nothing 'til they learned their job, about one month, but now my youngest daughter, only 14 years old, is making $6 per week, my other two are making $7.50 each per week, and my two boys are making $8 each per week and I am making $4.50 per week; a total of $166 per month. My provisions average $30, house rent $2, coal and wood $4, total $36; leaving a balance of $130, to buy clothes and deposit in the bank.
>
> "My experience is that, while you are on the farm toiling in rain and snow, feeding away what you have made during the summer and making wood to keep fires to keep your family from freezing, you could at the same time be in a cotton mill and in a good, comfortable room, making more than you can make in the summer time on the farm, and there is no stock to eat up what you make. At the mills, children over 12 years old, after they learn their job, can make more than men can make on farms. It is not every family that can do as well as the above family, but it only shows what a family can do that will try and work. Most any family can do half as well — so divide the above number of workers' wages by two and see if you would not still be doing well.
>
> "Give this matter your careful thought."

I had a talk with Mr. Morgan, who is now at Piedmont, and what he had to say is typical of hundreds of others. Mr. Morgan was born and raised at Rossman, in Transylvania County, North Carolina. He owns a farm of 100 acres, for which he paid $150, and on this he raised, until he went to the Piedmont Mills, corn, beans, potatoes, and cabbages, and with his boys skinned tan bark and sold it at the railroad station. Mr. Morgan has four girls, two of whom work in the mills. His conclusion is that it is much more profitable to work in the mill, and that the work "ain't so laborious" and "ain't so tough." A great many of these North Carolinians, as well as those from this State, are accumulating money and buying small farms not only in this State, but are considerable investors in real estate in North Carolina.

In a subsequent article it is my purpose to write of these investors to some extent.

In Rock Hill I met another North Carolinian, who came to the mill with his family and all of their earlier possessions in a one-horse wagon. When they arrived at Rock Hill Mr. Fewell very generously provided food, on which the family lived until they could work. This family now has five operatives in the mill. They have $1,000 in [the] bank. When they went to the mill there was not one member of the family who could either read or write. Now they can all read and write. When they went to the mill they had not more than a "shift" of clothing; now they are all well dressed. The head of the family, after he had been at the mill, thought that he could farm, and invested $300 in the experiment. He failed. A curious thing about this man is that every pay day he insists on having all of his money in silver.

I wish very much that some of these agitators, and particularly those who are really hunting for the facts in connection with the cotton mills, and who are willing to "dig," to learn the truth about the mill operatives as compared with their previous condition, would go to the mill villages and talk to some of the older people, and not to those who think those who go to make inquiry are hunting "sore spots." They ought to talk to an old man, like Richard Vincent, who has been connected with the Pacolet Cotton Mill for twenty-three years, to get at the real comparative conditions; and I want to emphasize the word COMPARATIVE. They can find men like Richard Vincent at almost any of the old mill communities; certainly at Pelzer, Graniteville, Piedmont, and the older of the large factories. Mr. Vincent is now 73 years of age, and he has gone through all of the "gaits." He has been a grits miller, a farmer, and a mill operative. His children have been on the farms and have worked in the cotton mills, and he is decidedly of the opinion that the best place for himself and his companions is in the cotton mills. He says that he has reached this conclusion not only on account of the money consideration, but on account of the school and church advantages, as well as because of the community of interests. Mr. Vincent has enjoyed excellent health, and is at work to-day at the age of 73. He does not believe that girls ought to work on the farms. He has money in the savings bank, was a good Confederate soldier; does not owe any one a cent, has a willing help-mate, owns a good cow, and is altogether a good citizen. Mr. Vincent is employed in the cloth room at the Pacolet Mills, where he receives $1 per day.

People can succeed at whatever they undertake, provided they stick at it and show a reasonable amount of judgment. It is the same on the farm as it is in the cotton mill, but more judgment is necessary on the farm than it is in the running of a machine that is intended to need as little executive capacity as possible.

19. The Making of the Mill Community

MARY FREDERICKSON AND BRENT GLASS
Interview with Flossie Moore Durham
1976

The mill workers who moved into the industrial villages and towns of the southern Piedmont drew on their rural traditions as they built active communities amid the new realities of the industrial work regime. The following interview, part of the University of North Carolina at Chapel Hill's Southern Oral History Program, was conducted with a worker from Bynum, a mill village in Chatham, North Carolina. The mill, founded in 1872, drew its workers from the nearby farms of the Piedmont; one of these workers was young Flossie Moore. In this interview, a much older Flossie describes her early experiences in the mill.

Mary Frederickson: When you first went to work in the mill, what was it like? Were you afraid to go, or were you excited about going?

Flossie Moore Durham: Well, I tell you, when I first went to work, it changed at one o'clock. At one o'clock in the day that morning shift would go off, and the evening shift come on, and each one had to work twelve hours.

MF: So when did the morning shift go to work, at one in the morning?

Durham: Monday morning they went to work at four o'clock. Now I've worked on every one of them shifts when I was a girl. And then Monday morning the morning shift would go to work at four o'clock, and they'd work till one in the day. The evening shift come in at one in the day, and they worked till one that night. And then the morning shift come in at one that night and worked till one the next day, and they done that all week.

MF: When you were ten years old, you did that? You would work that long?

Durham: Yes. And they didn't make anything, neither, [———] a little along them days.

MF: Do you remember what you first made when you went to work?

Durham: About twenty-five cents a day. And that was a day; that weren't an hour. That was a day.

Brent Glass: Mrs. Durham, were you going to school at the same time you were working in the mill?

Mary Frederickson and Brent Glass, *"Interview with Flossie Moore Durham, September 2, 1976, Bynum, North Carolina,"* transcribed by Jean Houston, University of North Carolina at Chapel Hill Southern Oral History Program: Piedmont Social History Project, Southern Historical Collection, Louis Round Wilson Library, University of North Carolina at Chapel Hill.

Durham: No, I didn't get to go to school anymore. Sure didn't.

MF: Had you gone to school when you lived on the farm?

Durham: Yes, we went to school when they'd have any school. We went to school when we were all living on the farm. But no, I never got to go to school anymore. I always regretted that, but I had to work to make a living. And what I picked up, I picked up for myself the best I could. . . .

BG: Do you remember your first day at work and what your job was?

Durham: At the mill?

BG: Yes.

Durham: Yes, it was spinning.

BG: At ten years old?

Durham: Yes. That's all I could have done. I weren't but ten years old. All the little ones, they'd put them to spinning, you see, or something like that. But now that weren't a bad life. We had a real good life over there on the hill. Every house was filled, and the people was all friendly and they was all nice. And Mr. Luther Bynum was looking after it, and he wouldn't have anybody over there that drank. Anybody got drinking, they left there right now. Didn't have no drinking and cutting up over there. Things was kept quiet and nice. And it was a good place over there to live.

MF: Did almost everyone on the hill go to the Methodist church?

Durham: Yes, all of them. That was all the church there was here, was the Methodist church. In other words, we'd been here five or six years. . . . Well, there was a church. We had that old schoolhouse down there; we always called it the old schoolhouse, down there in the bottom like. Well, they had school there in the week, and on Sunday they had preaching there. [——] preaching and anything in that line, and when they taught school there'd be school there for the children. So that went on that way till the church, I think, was built about 1898. I think it was just about eight years that the little church over there was built then. About 1898, just a little before I was married, and I was married in 1901.

BG: Was it a brick church?

Durham: No. Well, it's brick-veneered now. Yes, it is. And it's in good shape, but the place it's at is still bad because it's there on that hillside.

MF: Was there a preacher there all the time?

Durham: It's there every Sunday.

MF: Did he live in the town?

Durham: Yes, they live right up here in the parsonage.

MF: But I mean when the church first started, was there a preacher in Bynum all the time?

Durham: Yes. The preacher always lived here, at first. There's always been a parsonage here. And a long time the preacher had six churches. But for a long time now he just has one church.

MF: I see.

Durham: It's a young man. And they live right up there. And now they have a new parsonage, but they've been trying to get shut of the old one ever since the new one was built. And nobody don't want to fool with it, it's going to cost so much to move it. But it was built in 1894. I knew when that old parsonage was built, and it's a good old building. It's a pity to see it go down like that, but they say it would cost so much to move it, nobody won't take it. One time they tried to give it away, if anybody'd take it and get it away from there. They said, "Unh-uh." They said it would cost three or four thousand at least to get it away, and so they didn't do it.

BG: Did you play games with the little children when you lived over here in Bynum?

Durham: Oh, yes, all the children's games and all like that, yes.

BG: Do you remember any of those games?

Durham: No. [Laughter] No, I just remember that we did. The children used to get together and play games just like they would now. But there weren't nothing then. . . . Of course, there weren't no automobiles around here; there weren't no such thing as an automobile. And it was a rare thing if you ever seen a child with a bicycle or anything like that, but they'd have little wagons.

MF: Did you have much time to play, or were you really tired after you came out of the mill?

Durham: Oh, well, like I say again, didn't nobody make anything hardly then. Of course, everything you bought was cheap. And they had a pretty big country store over here that the company run. And then there was another little store around, or two. But the main store belonged to the company at that time, for a good long while. And they kept most anything you'd want.

MF: Did they pay you in cash, or did they have some kind of scrip? Did they have any kind of company money, or did they pay you in regular money?

Durham: No, because they was just ordinary, plain people. That's all I would know. I never known anything bad to happen here, especially in them days. No, I didn't, no.

MF: When you worked inside the mill, what was it like? Did you have a lot of friends who worked in the mill, too?

Durham: Oh, yes, they was all . . . one big family. A lot of people'd say, "Aw, it's just about like one big family." There weren't so many houses over here then. No. This house was here, and them over there, of course, and the parsonage. But there's a lot of these other houses was not here. . . .

BG: Were there any rules in the mill that you had to obey?

Durham: Well, of course they had some rules, but not bad.

BG: What if you were late for work? What would happen?

Durham: Of course, they had long hours, and you had to go through them long hours, and all the time.

MF: Was there any kind of whistle that blew when the shift changed?

Durham: Yes, there was. They had a bell down there. It would ring if they was leaving or coming or changing or anything. And they had a whistle. . . . Of course, it was steam het up. Down below there was a boiler room, they called it. And the mill was het up by that for a long time.

MF: Could you hear the whistle if you were in your house?

Durham: Oh, yes. We could hear the whistle or the bell either.

MF: And that's how you knew when it was time to go to work?

Durham: [——]. They'd usually ring the bell or something like that about ten minutes before changing time. Everyone knew all those things then. And the mill run regular then, night and day, all the time. But that mill burnt down. It was a real nice wooden mill, though; it weren't brick. . . .

MF: Did they ever run a shift on Sunday?

Durham: No, never did work you on Sunday.

MF: When would you quit on Saturday?

Durham: The evening shift would quit ten o'clock Saturday night. I've worked every shift they had.

MF: When did they start putting on three shifts?

Durham: They never did have three shifts here then, just two shifts. But each shift worked twelve hours and kept the mill running. They kept the mill running at that time, unless something stopped it. They started up Monday morning, and they run till ten o'clock Saturday night. They'd stay up thirty minutes at breakfast and thirty minutes at supper.

MF: Did you go home and eat breakfast and go home and eat supper?

Durham: Yes, we'd go home and eat breakfast and go home and eat supper. And that's all it stood unless it had to.

MF: Did you work all of the time except the thirty minutes? Did you get any other kind of rest time?

Durham: No. That's all. Like I say, when we moved to Bynum I was on what they called the morning shift. And at twelve-thirty at night, the watchman would come around, knock on the door and wake you up. [——] put on your skillet pan and get ready and get down there about one o'clock at night. And you worked till one the next day. And that's the way it went a long, long time. . . .

MF: Were there any boarding houses up on the hill? Did anyone run a boarding house?

Durham: Yes, they did. There was a right smart of [——] boarders here along then, because if the mill was running a lot was over there. Now they're scattered around. They come from the country and Pittsboro and all around that work down there. But at that time, everybody that worked come off the hill up there. And of course it was in good shape, and the houses were in good fix, and most of them was big families.

MF: Do you remember anyone who ran a boarding house, or did boarders tend to live with families?

Durham: There weren't no special boarding house; it was just anybody that could take another one, why, they'd take them. Girls or boys. My mother boarded several of them, her last days anyway. Not when we was all at home, no. But before she died, she had several boarders.

MF: Where would the boarders usually come from? Did they come from the country?

Durham: Anywhere, if they didn't have a family here.

MF: Were some of them young girls?

Durham: Yes, the majority was young. Didn't any old people work here then. No. . . .

BG: What did you wear to work?

Durham: We just wore dresses. We didn't wear slacks like they do now, no. No. No.

MF: What did you usually do with the money that you made?

Durham: Well, I done most everything down there. I first started off spinning, and then all my last work down there was what they call spooling.

BG: What do you do when you spool?

Durham: The bobbins would be attached onto the spinning frame there. It was run onto a big spool about so high, and it had ends about like that, too, on it, and it filled up them spools. And at that time they were going up to what they called the warp mill. That [——] downstairs. And the warp mill was a pretty big thing, and there were so many of them spools running together. Had big frames up there. It was pretty a-running, that warp mill was. And then they'd be run all down into . . . this thread. And that was baled then into big bales. That's the way they sold it.

BG: Did they have a weave mill there?

Durham: No, they never did have any looms here. No, I never did know anything about weaving.

BG: Was it mostly women working there?

Durham: The spinning was run mostly by women and girls. Didn't many women along then; the young girls would work, but now, for a good long bit, they finish high school. . . . They go to school in Pittsboro now. We used to have a real good school building here, but it got to where there weren't enough to have a high school, so they moved it all to Pittsboro. Now all the Bynum people go to Pittsboro to school. They carry them over there on a bus. By the time the girls finish high school over there now, they can get a job somewhere else, and they don't go to the mill. It's been a long time since a girl [——] go to the mill. Now they get them from the country, and they work a good many negroes down there now. A lot of them from Pittsboro.

BG: When you were working there, there were no black people working there?

Durham: No, they didn't. No. They sure didn't. Not till this company took over here. [——] Didn't get on till I say that this company leased it. They've had it about five years. No, didn't any colored. . . . You see, it's the men on the outside. They kept [——] things going on outside. Usually they had about two colored men at work on the outside. Never worked inside. No. They sure didn't, not in them days. But like I said, the young people would go to work when they got old enough. But for a long time now they didn't do that. And most of this work down there now is older people.

BG: What jobs would men do in the mill when you were young?

Durham: Men worked in the card room, mostly.

MF: And women did spinning and spooling?

Durham: Women were in the spinning and the spooling, and the boys done the doffing and. . . .

MF: When you brought your money home, did they pay you once a week?

Durham: Once a month.

MF: Once a month.

Durham: At that day and time. . . .

MF: When you were here and working in the mill, what did people do for fun? Did they ever get together and have any kind of . . .

Durham: Yes, the grown ones did. Edgar, my brother, has been to many a dance and party, things like that. . . . The dances they had then, somebody would call the figures, and they danced maybe eight or six in a [———], and they danced around and around like that. It weren't just tap dancing.

MF: Would they ever have dances in town?

Durham: No, they didn't. Them dances they had was through the country. I never went to but one or two, but I enjoyed it. And they weren't drinking or cutting up. No, they didn't do anything dirty at them dances, either. They had music.

MF: Did they ever have people get together in town and play music?

Durham: They had a band here for a good long while [———] boys that wanted to get it up. My Frank was one of them, with a guitar, and some with a fiddle, and some with a banjo, [———] and some with an organ. Just an old-fashioned organ they played. They made music here that way a lot of times. Just fun, just at somebody's house.

———

Suggestions for Further Reading

Carlton, David L. *Mill and Town in South Carolina, 1880–1920.* Baton Rouge: Louisiana State University Press, 1982.

Clark, Daniel J. *Like Night and Day: Unionization in a Southern Mill Town.* Chapel Hill: University of North Carolina Press, 1997.

Flamming, Douglas. *Creating the Modern South: Millhands and Managers in Dalton, Georgia, 1884–1984.* Chapel Hill: University of North Carolina Press, 1992.

Hall, Jacquelyn Dowd, et al. *Like a Family: The Making of a Southern Cotton Mill World.* Chapel Hill: University of North Carolina Press, 1987.

Tullos, Allen. *Habits of Industry: White Culture and the Transformation of the Carolina Piedmont.* Chapel Hill: University of North Carolina Press, 1989.

CHAPTER SIX

THE PROGRESSIVE ERA

Woman Suffrage and Progressivism in the South

The wave of reform that swept the nation beginning around 1900 proved to be a tremendous boon to the woman suffrage movement. Progressives in both national parties recognized the commonality between their political agenda — including honest government, pure food and drug legislation, and humanitarian reforms — and the traditional values, interests, and responsibilities of women — including promoting morality, nurturing children, and aiding the poor. First at the state level and then the national, Progressivism contributed to the success of suffrage campaigns: beginning with the adoption of a woman suffrage amendment in the state of Washington in 1910, the movement rolled up a long string of victories in western and midwestern states that gave new hope and energy to suffragists everywhere and strengthened support in Congress for a constitutional amendment to give women the vote.

In the South, thousands of reform-minded women and men joined the small group of pioneers who had been promoting the cause for decades. The rapid growth of industry and commerce had led to an expansion of the region's middle class, and a corresponding rise in the number of women's voluntary organizations brought more women into Progressive reform efforts. Many began to desire the vote as the traditional notion of southern womanhood's supposed influence over men seemed to count for little in effecting change. Jean Gordon, a leading Progressive and suffragist from New Orleans, observed that many Louisiana women — including wives of legislators — became suffragists after the failure of a child labor bill they strongly supported. After the defeat, "those wives realized how weak a weapon was influence, and in that moment were sown the seeds of a belief in the potency of the ballot beyond that of 'woman's influence.'" Suffragists grew weary of hearing southern legislators claim to be chivalric protectors of women and children only to reject bills that would increase support for schools, give women equal guardianship rights, or prevent the exploitation of women and children in southern industries.

Alarmed at the growth of prosuffrage sentiment in their region, southern conservatives created formal antisuffrage organizations. Together with the behind-the-scenes efforts of industries that feared women's votes (such as cotton textile mills and distilleries), they presented formidable obstacles to the enfranchisement of women. Many southern men and women were firmly committed to maintaining the traditional gender roles that consigned women to a solely domestic sphere; they believed that allowing women to vote would threaten the South's hierarchical, paternalistic political culture in which "the best men" supposedly governed in the interests of all. The antisuffragists were highly effective in exploiting southern prejudices and fears. They presented the prospect of women going to the polls as a threat to "Southern Civilization," depicting southern suffragists as ungrateful pawns of northern fanatics, foolishly endangering the South's newly reestablished white supremacy. Female "antis" claimed that they were the true representatives of southern womanhood and had no desire to be forced into politics.

On the defensive, suffragists proclaimed that voting was a natural extension of the traditional duties of southern ladies and that their moral influence was much needed in politics. But in general they shared the racial prejudices of their era: they excluded African Americans from their organizations and insisted that the disfranchisement provisions that kept black men from voting would apply to black women as well.

Aware of southern hostility to federal "intervention" and eager to be recognized as political equals by the men in their states and region, southern suffragists initially concentrated on gaining the vote by state action. They had considerable support from Progressive politicians and newspaper editors and actually won the right to vote in presidential elections in Tennessee and primaries in Texas and Arkansas. But they were defeated in every attempt to win full enfranchisement through state constitutional amendments. As one state campaign after another failed, most southern suffragists became convinced that their only hope for full political equality was through the federal suffrage amendment that was rapidly gaining support in Congress. In 1918, President Woodrow Wilson, a hero to many white Southerners who claimed the Virginia-born Democrat as one of their own, infuriated states' rights advocates by endorsing the federal amendment. The following year it was approved by both houses of Congress and submitted to the states for ratification. Wilson worked hard to persuade southern politicians to ratify in the interest of the national Democratic Party. But his efforts — together with those of the suffragists and Progressive politicians, editors, and reformers — failed to convince most southern politicians, who insisted that this amendment was just a "deadly parallel" to the Fifteenth Amendment that had enfranchised African

American men. Indeed, they insisted that ratifying it would imply southern acceptance of the Fifteenth Amendment and betray the principle of state sovereignty for which the South had fought the Civil War. In the end, four southern states — Kentucky, Texas, Arkansas, and Tennessee — broke ranks with the otherwise "Solid South" and ratified, and the Nineteenth Amendment went into effect on August 26, 1920. But of the ten states that failed to ratify, nine were south of the Mason-Dixon line.

In this chapter, articles by southern Progressives Madeline McDowell Breckenridge, Adella Hunt Logan, and S. P. Brooks make the case for woman suffrage, and two antisuffrage pamphlets demonstrate the opposition reformers faced. A 1920 article summarizes the varied positions of the southern press on the issue.

———————

As you read, look for answers to these questions: What, according to the Progressives, were the changes that had made it necessary for women to vote in order to carry out their traditional duties, and what were the reforms they sought? Why did black women, in particular, need to have the vote? What were the arguments of the antisuffragists? Why did some suffragists accuse southern politicians of insincerity when they opposed woman suffrage in the name of states' rights?

20. A Woman's Place Is In Politics

Madeline McDowell Breckenridge, Adella Hunt Logan, and S. P. Brooks
Arguments for Woman Suffrage
1912 and 1914

The following three articles take the Progressive position that woman suffrage would secure the adoption of much-needed reforms. "A Mother's 'Sphere'" was written by Madeline McDowell Breckenridge of Lexington, Kentucky, the granddaughter of Henry Clay and wife of Lexington Herald *editor Desha Breckenridge. She was one of the foremost leaders among southern Progressives and a state and national officer in the suffrage movement. Adella Hunt Logan, a faculty member at Tuskegee Institute before she married Tuskegee treasurer Warren Logan, was an active clubwoman who spoke out boldly for woman suffrage despite the reticence of Tuskegee president Booker T. Washington and the racism of the white suffragists. Though she lived next door to Washington, she published "Colored Women as Voters" and other articles in the* Crisis, *the NAACP magazine edited by Washington's rival, W. E. B. Du Bois. S. P. Brooks was president of Baylor University in Waco, Texas, when he delivered his speech, "Some Phases of Woman Suffrage" to the Waco Equal Suffrage Association.*

MADELINE McDOWELL BRECKENRIDGE

"A Mother's 'Sphere,' " c. 1912

There was a time when the children of the land were mainly taught at their mothers' knees: those mothers who could afford it supplied private governesses for their children, or sent them to private schools; the others giving their children such education as they themselves had.

This time has past. The business of teaching the children of this country has been taken over by the public schools, and though the mother herself no longer does the actual teaching of her children, it is now as much the privilege and the duty of the mother to oversee the education of her children in the public schools as ever it was to guide it in our pioneer homes.

Now the management of public schools, as of all other public business on which private life depends in civilized society, is comprehensively included in the word "politics." To realize this we must get rid of the ordinary conception of that misused word as something associated with corrupt elections, violence, graft — "dirty politics." When it has been asserted in the states not even allowing their women school suffrage that the effort to get this right for them was an effort "to get women into politics" meaning politics in its dirty sense — it was truly asserted on the other hand that on the contrary, it was an effort to get the schools out of politics. In the proper sense of the term not only is the management of the schools necessarily in politics, but it is high time that the mothers of school children were also in politics. Bernard Shaw has succinctly stated the case. "Politics," he says, "is not something apart from home and the babies. It is home and the babies."

The Strength of Natural Law. It was not originally intended that women should teach in our public schools. It was not originally intended that women should vote in our school elections, but some way and some how the women have gotten in; they are upholding the school system from within and from without. A large majority of the public school teachers in the land are women. Mothers of school children are more and more "meddling" in school affairs. They are finding out whether school houses are proper, whether school teachers are ca-

The Madeline McDowell Breckenridge Papers, Breckenridge Family Papers, Manuscript Division, Library of Congress, Washington, D.C.

pable, whether school trustees are fit persons. They are exercising the divine pre-rogative of mothers to meddle in the education of their own children. Even in the dozen and a half states where man-made laws still attempt to write women out of any share in the management of the public schools, the women have gotten in. In many of these states through the School Improvement League, women have done a tremendous work for the material improvement of the school plant. In some of them, where over seventy-five percent of the teachers are also women the anecdote of the small boy who was asked by the teacher who supported the world, seems applicable. "Atlas, m'a'm," he answered. "But who," asked the teacher, "supports Atlas?" The boy thought a moment. "I don't know, m'a'm," he said, "but I suppose it was his wife." The schools are nominally being managed and taught by men; but actually they are being supported both from the inside and the outside by the mother sex. Whom God hath joined together for the nurture and rearing of children it has proven impossible for men to put asunder.

A Mother's Right to Her Child.   Children are not the exclusive creations of men. They are not the exclusive possessions of men — at least they are not in fif-teen of our states. In six states — under the laws of a supposedly civilized people — it is still true that a mother of legitimate children has no right to them; they be-long exclusively to the father whether he be living or dead, and in fact he may will away his unborn child. In twenty-seven other states, so long as the father lives, the mother has no legal rights to her children. But even in these benighted states which have not as yet passed a co-guardianship law, no woman will acknowledge that she has not a moral right to her children, and a moral responsibility for their education and training.

Where It Leads Them.   Now it is impossible for women to fulfill this re-sponsibility without a participation in the carrying on of public business — with-out in short, being in politics. How naturally the women of the land have come to a realization of their responsibility for their children's education, and therefore, in the present day and generation for the condition of the public schools, is well shown by the recent activities of the General Federation. The education com-mittee of the Federation a few years back adopted a program of work which it rec-ommended to all the clubs scattered throughout the country. The things recom-mended were as follows:

First, more school houses — Cleaner, better ventilated and better equipped school houses.
Second, more and better equipped play grounds, with supervised play.
Third, medical inspection and school nurses.
Fourth, physical training and the teaching of personal hygiene.
Fifth, the preparation of teachers in normal schools and state universities for the teaching of personal and sex hygiene.

You will note that these mothers of the Federated Clubs did not attempt to meddle with the professional side of the teaching job. They merely decided to do for their children in the public schools that which they were doing for the children in their own homes: to provide them a clean and healthful place in which to grow up. They had come to see that it was of no avail that their own homes should be spotless, their own gardens and play grounds beautiful; that these should be fit places in which a child or a flower might grow. But that it was further necessary that the school buildings and the school yards in which these same children were to spend very many years of their growing lives should also be clean and healthful, free from contagion physical or moral.

A Mother's Sphere.   What does it profit a mother to have performed her duty within the limited sphere that used to be considered hers, within the four walls of her own home, if the child has gone out from that home into conditions to which he has succumbed? What does it profit her, when the child is brought home to her ill with diptheria or scarlet fever, or some of the many diseases to which childhood is subject — what does it profit her when he lies dead before her, or when he is brought back to her contaminated in body and soul, that she has done her duty as men saw it, or as a former generation conceived it? Does she not know then that her sphere did not end at her own front door, or her own front gate? Does she not know that it followed her child wherever her child went — into the school, into the town, into the state? And that so long as there remained in the community where his lot was cast one foul spot, one evil condition which she had done nothing to remedy, and because of this he had returned to her broken and degenerate, does she not know that she had failed to fulfill her mother's task?

No mother can fulfill her task, no father can fulfill his, who watches and guides and tries to influence the child within the home alone. In order really to protect him, in order really to influence him it is necessary that father and mother both should bear their proper part in the management of the schools, in the city housekeeping moral and physical, and in all that great public business on which, as I have said, private life in the present day absolutely depends.

The Best Tool Needed.   No mother can do this thing unless she is armed with the instrument men have found necessary in their attempts to do it, namely with the ballot. Nor will any woman lose her direct influence by gaining this direct power, any more than a man when he casts a ballot loses such influence as he has in addition as brother, father, friend, neighbor or public spirited citizen.

As the mothers of our land come to realize in the carrying out of their natural and womanly tasks, as for instance in the education and training of children, how necessary this direct influence is to enable them to carry them out properly; above all, how necessary it is when they, with the divine courage that perhaps is vouchsafed to mothers alone, are heroically facing the sex problem, the social evil as it is called, that last great dragon that stands in the way of civilization — When they fully realize these things, they will undoubtedly realize also that they must have every aid and advantage that men have had, that they must be armed with every weapon that men have found necessary with which to fight the battles of civilization. . . .

ADELLA HUNT LOGAN

"Colored Women as Voters," 1912

More and more colored women are studying public questions and civics. As they gain information and have experience in their daily vocations and in their efforts for human betterment they are convinced, as many other women have long ago been convinced, that their efforts would be more telling if women had the vote.

The fashion of saying "I do not care to meddle with politics" is disappearing among the colored woman faster than most people think, for this same woman has learned that politics meddle constantly with her and hers.

Good women try always to do good housekeeping. Building inspectors, sanitary inspectors and food inspectors owe their positions to politics. Who then is so well informed as to how well these inspectors perform their duties as the women who live in inspected districts and inspected houses, and who buy food from inspected markets?

Adequate school facilities in city, village and plantation districts greatly concern the black mother. But without a vote she has no voice in educational legislation, and no power to see that her children secure their share of public school funds.

Negro parents admit that their own children are not all angels, but they know that the environments which they are hopeless to regulate increase misdemeanor and crime. They know, too, that officers, as a rule, recognize few obligations to voteless citizens.

When colored juvenile delinquents are arraigned, few judges or juries feel bound to give them the clemency due to a neglected class. When sentence is pronounced on these mischievous youngsters, too often they are imprisoned with adult criminals and come out hardened and not helped by their punishment. When colored mothers ask for a reform school for a long time they receive no answer. They must wait while they besiege their legislature. Having no vote they need not be feared or heeded. The "right of petition" is good; but it is much better when well voted in.

Not only is the colored woman awake to reforms that may be hastened by good legislation and wise administration, but where she has the ballot she is reported as using it for the uplift of society and for the advancement of the state.

In California the colored woman bore her part creditably in the campaign for equal suffrage and also with commendable patriotism in the recent presidential nomination campaign.

The State of Washington, new with its votes-for-women law, has already had a colored woman juror. Why not? She is educated and wealthy and wants to protect the best interests in her state.

Crisis, September 1912. Reprinted in *Votes for Women! The Woman Suffrage Movement in Tennessee, the South, and the Nation*, ed. Marjorie Spruill Wheeler (Knoxville: University of Tennessee Press, 1995), 149–50.

Colorado has never had a better school than her women have made. Judge Ben Lindsey is as popular with colored women voters as he is with white women voters. The juvenile court over which he presides gives the boys a square deal regardless of color. A majority of mothers and fathers can be counted on every time to support such an official.

Wyoming, Utah and Idaho, the other full suffrage states, have few colored women, but these few are not hurt by, but are being helped by, their voting privileges.

In the states that are now conducting woman suffrage campaigns the colored woman is as interested and probably as active as conditions warrant. This is notably true of Ohio and Kansas.

A number of colored women are active members of the National [American] Woman Suffrage Association. They are well informed and are diligent in the spread of propaganda. Women who see that they need the vote see also that the vote needs them. Colored women feel keenly that they may help in civic betterment, and that their broadened interests in matters of good government may arouse the colored brother, who for various reasons has become too indifferent to his duties of citizenship.

The suffrage map shows that six states have equal political rights for women and men, and that a much larger number have granted partial suffrage to women. In all these the colored woman is taking part, not as fully as she will when the question is less of an experiment, not as heartily as she will when her horizon broadens, but she bears her part.

This much, however, is true now: the colored American believes in equal justice to all, regardless of race, color, creed, or sex, and longs for the day when the United States shall indeed have a government of the people, for the people and by the people — even including the colored people.

S. P. Brooks

"Some Phases of Woman Suffrage," 1914

Prepared by Request and Read before the Waco Equal Suffrage Association,
Waco, Texas, April 30, 1914

. . . If one asks why women want to vote we answer it by asking: Have they not come to feel the comradeship of intelligence and social responsibility of their brothers? Are they not the equals of their brothers and do they not want a square deal? Do they not know some things as well as the men and some things better than the men? The home with its food and furniture and clothes and modern mechanical contrivances is not to-day a thing apart from law and government and

S. P. Brooks, "Some Phases of Woman Suffrage," 30 April 1914, 9–12, 16–17, 20–21, S. P. Brooks Papers, The Texas Collection, Baylor University. In *Citizens at Last: The Woman Suffrage Movement in Texas*, ed. Ruth Winegarten and Judith N. McArthur (Austin: Ellen C. Temple, 1987), 138–42.

daily social activities as in the olden days. Concerning these things the women can speak at the polls. Her children not only may go to school but must go in most states. Concerning the children the women are most competent to advise the law-makers. Modern cities, with old sins exaggerated; modern tenements, with lack of normal bodily comforts for health and happiness; modern crowded thoroughfares, where no child can play — all present problems which women can help to solve.

Does anybody doubt that women want to vote when they go upon the streets of the cities and see the degradation wrought by saloons? Does anybody doubt that woman suffrage will keep alive the prohibition question as long as saloons exist and segregated vice thrives? Is there anybody that is ignorant of the fact that where woman suffrage has been adopted saloons have decreased? Wherever it has been voted upon, as recently in Michigan and Wisconsin, breweries and saloons and their paid advocates were a unit in the cry of the hurt and debasement voting would bring to the wives and mothers of our land. Women have voted only once in Illinois, and yet as a result there were immediately reported to be in that state 1,000 fewer saloons. Gamblers curse woman suffrage, as the pimps of harlots, to the shame of the race. No wonder the drink business cries out against women voting, for after Utah "in 1911 passed a statewide local option law, 110 cities went dry and only 18 went wet, and out of these 18 so-called cities, 16 were mining camps. Every county in Utah but one is now dry." This is but a sample of many in the various states where equal suffrage exists.

It is said that if women vote they are meddling in politics. Just so it is said of preachers and teachers and business men. Just so it has been said of decent conservative men from the days when ballots took the place of bullets. But time is a healer of wounds and an adjuster of many a fault. Preachers and teachers and bankers and other business men are now taking part in the politics of the country as never before. This is well. If for no other reason, it is well to effect the political dominance of the breweries, distilleries, gamblers and those who buy and sell for gold the suffrage of the ignorant, vicious men who, being males, may vote.

Some one says that politics will make women forget home, and cause them to neglect their home duties. Even so some men forget home, but they all do not. Even so some women now forget home, but they are beautiful gadabouts and not the mothers of the race. Who makes the homes of this country? Is it done altogether by the women? What after all are poetry and song and sentiment in a home without a man? What rights in the home has a woman not claimed by the man? What rights in the state may a woman not equally claim with the man? These are some questions women have asked themselves and which they now ask of us. These are some of the facts that have spurred them to action.

Again they saw criminals pardoned, lunatics cured, and all thereafter allowed to vote. They saw themselves paying taxes to uphold laws made by men, themselves tried for crimes before juries of men. They saw themselves kept back from the rewards of knowledge and on the statute books classed with imbeciles, idiots, lunatics, and criminals, all because of the accident of birth. No matter whose mothers they may be or what world problems they may have solved they are still before the makers of the law unequally yoked with their husbands.

. . . Men need not wonder that women call loudly for their rights, for observant readers of history know that as the position of women has grown so the height of a nation's civilization has grown. Under this influence and knowledge women know that employers and voters demand legislation while workers and women beg it. This they resent. Women demand to have somewhat to do with "behavior" of the community as well as its "goodness." They want outspoken virtue regardless of sex and not canned innocence. They do not want as some one has said for the men to "throw the innocence of their women-folk as a sop to God, and go about the devil's business" themselves.

. . . Some objectors of women voting speak of the baseness of it, forgetful that if the polls are indecent they ought to be cleaned up; if dangerous, made safe; if controlled by vice, overcome by the sources of virtue. Of course women [will] go to the polls like they go to the post-office, like good women, and not like wild Amazons which they are not. Men will come to honor them at the polls, on the plane of sense just as they do in the parlor, not for what they appear to be but for what they are.

. . . All my life I have had a man's appreciation of woman as mother and wife, knowing that she was and is man's equal by birth and inalienable rights. I have known, however, that she has not always had what I thought was her rights.

In the last few years my interest in the question of equal rights has been kindled above that of the historian. My interest has grown in a manner not unlike that in all public questions that vitally affect the human race. I have had much popular prejudice against it and have often wished the subject would be forgotten, but it will not [die] down. I in common with an ever-increasing number of men have come to see the justice of woman's appeal. But I have no prophet's zeal regarding it; nor will I with Don Quixotean[1] convictions attack windmills for its passage. I shall await the time with patience, conscious that those who have a zealot's passion will not have to wait long. Meantime, whenever the opportunity presents itself, in public or in private, now or hereafter, I shall cast my vote for the complete equality of suffrage of men and women.

For the courtesies of this occasion I thank you.

---

[1]**Don Quixotean:** unrealistically idealistic (a reference to the hero of Cervantes's *Don Quixote*, who misguidedly "fought off" windmills).

21. Southern Arguments against Suffrage

Antisuffrage Leaflets
1915 and c. 1919

Determined to prevent the adoption of woman suffrage, southern antisuffragists established formal organizations in several states as well as at the regional level. "Anti" men and women lobbied state legislators, spoke at public hearings on suffrage, and wrote and distributed a large body of antisuffrage literature. Editorials, such as these, first published in the Richmond Evening Journal *and the* Macon (Ga.) Daily Telegraph, *were republished as antisuffrage pamphlets and circulated throughout the region.*

TWENTY-NINE COUNTIES WILL GO UNDER NEGRO RULE
OVER SIXTY COUNTIES IN THE STATE OF GEORGIA
THE ENTIRE STATE OF MISSISSIPPI

What of Your State, Your County? Isn't It About Time for Reflecting Men and Women to Think — and Act?

THE THREATENED COUNTIES

From The Richmond Evening Journal *May 4, 1915 — Republished by Request.*

Several times *The Richmond Evening Journal* has been asked to say which counties of Virginia have more colored than white female inhabitants. The question, of course, is in connection with the somewhat noisy demands we read of in the newspapers for "votes for women." Here is the list, from the United States census of 1910:

	Colored Females.	White Females.
Amelia	2,658	1,578
Brunswick	5,549	3,843
Buckingham	3,881	3,738
Caroline	4,314	3,934
Charles City	1,817	645
Charlotte	4,267	3,599
Cumberland	2,966	1,604

Laura Clay Papers, Special Collections and Archives, Margaret I. King Library, University of Kentucky, Lexington. Originally printed in the *Richmond Evening Journal*, 4 May 1915.

Dinwiddie	4,619	2,866
Essex	2,618	1,868
Goochland	2,585	1,914
Greenesville	3,720	2,177
Halifax	10,330	9,815
Isle of Wight	3,720	3,633
King and Queen	2,635	2,069
King William	2,409	1,698
Lancaster	2,531	2,279
Lunenburg	3,338	2,856
Mecklenburg	8,280	6,160
Middlesex	2,148	2,053
Nansemond	7,847	5,602
New Kent	1,317	802
Norfolk	15,936	10,039
Northampton	4,587	3,536
Nottoway	3,715	3,016
Powhatan	1,818	1,168
Prince Edward	4,367	2,905
Prince George	2,257	1,601
Princess Anne	2,883	2,683
Southampton	8,005	5,001
Surry	2,804	1,763
Sussex	4,458	2,270
Warwick	2,053	819
Westmoreland	2,279	2,193

We may assume that the proportions of females twenty-one years of age, or over, or who have come of age since the census was taken is the same in the two races.

Assuming that the women of the two races would qualify to vote in the same proportions and that the white and colored male vote would remain as they were shown to be by the returns of the last presidential election, **the colored people would have absolute and immediate control of the counties** of Amelia, Brunswick, Caroline, Charles City, Charlotte, Cumberland, Dinwiddie, Essex, Goochland, Greenesville, King and Queen, King William, Lunenburg, Mecklenburg, Nansemond, New Kent, Norfolk, Northampton, Nottoway, Powhatan, Prince Edward, Southampton, Surry, Sussex, Warwick, and Westmoreland.

No other argument, however profound, is quite so convincing or fascinating as that word "because," accompanied by some pouting of alluring and scarlet lips — especially if there be dimples by way of re-enforcement. **But men are compelled and accustomed to face and deal with hard facts when considering important affairs in business or in politics. It is a hard fact that twenty-nine counties of Virginia would be condemned by woman suffrage to colored rule and five others would be in serious peril of it with woman suffrage.**

We do not suppose, or imagine, that the suffrage ladies would suggest resort to counting out the colored people of their own sex or to stuffing ballot boxes or padding registration lists. We wicked and inefficient and tyrannical

men who are supposed to have made such a sad mess of government in Virginia, became ashamed of such methods and alarmed by them and contrived to remove the necessity for them. Surely, we are not to be incited to return to the slimepit from which we dug ourselves.

The population and the votes are in these counties as stated. We can't get away from the figures and facts, ladies. Take twenty-nine counties and make them Republican and add them to the counties already Republican, or close, and the Democratic party and white rule in Virginia will be swinging on a mighty thin line.

In Buckingham, Halifax, Lancaster, and Princess Anne, the whites would have a fighting chance if their women vote and present white male vote combined solidly against the colored woman and present colored male vote.

It is to be remembered that the literacy test would not work in choking off the colored woman vote. The colored people are decreasing their percentage of illiteracy very fast, especially among their women and girls. The ladies of the suffrage league will hardly come forward with a property test. No safeguard would be left but the poll tax; and if colored women knew they could get votes and rule some very rich and important counties by paying $1.50 apiece, we are inclined to think most of them would be willing to go hungry, if necessary to do it.

Probably the ladies engaged in this suffrage movement are not very practical or very logical or very well informed or disposed to bother their heads with the actual facts of politics. Most of them, we surmise, hold the somewhat vague, but firmly established feminine line of reasoning that when they want something, or think they want it, they ought to have it by all principles of wisdom and justice; and are prepared always to fall back on the traditional conclusive feminine argument "because."

A SOUTHERN WOMAN SPEAKS HER MIND
"OUR MEN, GOD BLESS THEM!"

*Superbly Brave Enough to Die for Us in France, Yet
Not Good Enough to Vote for Us at Home!
Oh, the Base Ingratitude of Some Women!*

WERE YOU REPRESENTED, SUFFRAGETTE, ON FLANDERS FIELD?

Mr. James Callaway, in a column conducted by him in the *Macon (Georgia) Daily Telegraph*, prints the following letter, on November 30, from a distinguished Southern woman who sent it to him with the request that it be published.

Laura Clay Papers, Special Collections and Archives, Margaret I. King Library, University of Kentucky, Lexington. Originally printed in the *Macon Daily Telegraph*, 30 November 1915.

"Has woman suffrage, with, comparatively speaking, a little band of willful women, 'made cowards of us all'?

"Mr. McAdoo fairly spills over with 'what the women are doing for their country,' as if the loyalty of the American woman was a discovery of the present administration!

"To what 'women of the United States' does he allude when he wishes to offer the most dastardly insult written in the annals of history, that 'votes for women,' choked down the throats of 90 percent of the women of the nation, is the price of their loyalty, in the opinion of these self-appointed judges of a fitting 'reward'? Surely one may say 'thou treadest on holy ground with most unholy feet!'

"The 'solid South' elected Mr. Wilson. This eternal prating of 'women's votes' is mere stupidity, and every well-informed man and woman knows it. Today it is this same South that rises in all her outraged dignity to say, and in no uncertain tones, to any man or woman, be he or she of high or low degree, that the loyalty of her womanhood is without and beyond price!

"THE WOMEN *of the South know what war is.* They have tasted its deadly fruits of hunger, cold and privations. Drunk to its bitter depths and dregs *its fiery cup of gall! Standing upon the ashes of all save hope, we passed through our Gethsemane*[1] *over fifty years ago.*

"But we come today as one to face again, for the second time, war and all its horrors, and when hearts and souls are quivering with emotion, tears for the cruel sufferings of the past, dried but yesteryear, men dare offer this affront to us of added burdens, loathsome responsibilities, and would, with flattering, nauseous words, weigh our hearts' blood in political scale and prate of 'vote'! Are we clean gone mad? It is past belief that American manhood could fall so low!

"For every woman who stands and shrieks for the ballot there are hundreds, aye thousands, telling you *they do not wish it. Do not force their patience too far!*

"The Western States are thinly settled; if the rest of the country does not please the *dissatisfied suffragettes let them 'go West and grow up with the country!'*

"The women of the South do not come to plead, gentlemen; they demand that the sovereignty of their States be not disturbed at this most critical hour!

"Yet the Southern press sits and sucks its thumb while our very birthright is being sold for a mess of petticoats! Have our men become spineless cacti? Will they submit, as dumb, driven cattle?

" 'New York went for suffrage' we are told with bated breath. With . . . more than 70 percent foreign-born, is that surprising?

"But what is that to the South? The purest American blood in the nation flows in her veins and people. Instead of following, as sheep led astray, let us take warning from the experience of New York and stand firm in the faith of our fathers, and that ever safe rock of ages, the sovereignty of our States!

"Barter your own souls and your manhood if you must; play your cheap political games; weaken your government when its united strength is most needed, but *spare your women!*

"The Fifteenth Amendment and the force bill! How proudly they boast of

---

[1]*Gethsemane:* the garden where Jesus prayed before being arrested (i.e., a test of faith).

these two dastardly achievements in their Official History of Suffrage! To 'dear Anna Dickinson, Frederick Douglass, and Susan B. Anthony we owe them!' Suffragettes all!

"The wound is scarce healed, and some we feel that our statesmen, no matter how great the pressure, be it under the thinly buttered sop of 'war measure,' that unspeakable insult of 'reward' or any other trumped-up vaporings of political expediency, will indeed hesitate, ere they loose these upon the Southern women for the second time, and add to them that pestifrous old maid and her legacy of hell, the Susan B. Anthony amendment!

"To the naked eye it is not visible, but a careful examination of the 'inside of the suffrage cup' shows these startling words: 'Made in Germany.'[2]

"Beware, indeed, oh woman of the South, of these Greeks[3] who would bear to you this gift.

A SOUTHERN WOMAN."

[2]**Made in Germany:** the author suggests that the suffrage movement was a product of German origin intended to weaken the United States.
[3]**Greeks:** Greek soldiers infiltrated Troy hidden in a giant wooden horse presented as a gift; hence, a subterfuge to subvert from within.

22. "The Pulse of the South"

THE SOUTHERN REVIEW
"How the South Really Feels about Woman Suffrage"
1920

In May 1920, when this article was published, thirty-five states had approved the suffrage amendment to the Constitution and only one more was needed for ratification. Because many wondered if a southern state would supply the one remaining endorsement, the Southern Review *polled the leading newspapers of the region to determine the prevailing mood. The end of the article includes an excerpt from a speech by Pattie Ruffner Jacobs, the primary leader of the suffrage movement in Alabama and an officer in the National American Woman Suffrage Association (NAWSA). Her speech, "Tradition vs. Justice," was given at NAWSA's "Jubilee Convention" in Chicago in February 1920, at which suffragists celebrated a victory they*

Southern Review 4 (Asheville, N.C.) (May 1920), Laura Clay Papers, Folder 13, Special Collections and Archives, Margaret I. King Library, University of Kentucky, Lexington.

believed was now inevitable. After Madeline McDowell Breckenridge spoke for the women from states that had ratified, Jacobs spoke for the "defeated" suffragists.

No more rigorous censorship existed during the war than seems to obtain in the country at large with regard to the real sentiment of the South concerning woman suffrage. In an effort to arrive at the genuine opinion existing upon this question which presses so closely, *The Southern Review* wrote to one hundred and fifty of the leading papers in the Southern states, asking them to state their position on the suffrage question. With the exception of an occasional "anti" the Southern editors were overwhelmingly in favor of woman suffrage as a principle. Most of them believed that woman suffrage was not only a matter of simple justice but that it would prove a great national benefit. Where there was objection it was not to suffrage per se but to the method of imposing it upon the states by federal amendment. The *Richmond News-leader* takes a vigorous stand in the matter, recalling by its intensity the controversy regarding states' rights during the sixties. It exclaims:

> "This amendment was conceived in a spirit contrary to the constitution, is being urged for a purpose subversive of the constitution and will have an effect inimical to the government established under the constitution.
>
> "The federal constitution never contemplated the grant of suffrage in any form by the United States. For the best and most necessary of reasons, suffrage was left exclusively to the states. . . . The founders of the constitution knew that the unimpaired and exclusive determination of suffrage by the states was essential to the separate existence of the states and that the separate existence of the states was essential to the maintenance of the federal government. To impair to the slightest the exclusive right of the separate states to control their franchise is to weaken the dividing walls that bear a great part of the weight of the Union. Once those are removed, the whole fabric is supported only by national sentiment, by the outer walls — by whatever may be left of the constitution. And who flatters himself those walls can stand without the support of separate states? . . . The failure of the federal government to control by centralized administrative effort strikes in key industries, the high cost of living and kindred problems of reconstruction is evidence enough that the states are still needed and that without them the compounded 'common mass' will take its cast and color from the worst of its elements. From the extreme centralization of the war, America must return to the older decentralization. How can there be decentralization without separate authority, how separate authority without states, how states without control of the suffrage? To destroy the states is to destroy the Union of states.
>
> "Because the Southern states did not approve the amendments granting suffrage to negroes, they evaded those amendments until they could invalidate them. Because some of the Eastern states would not endorse the prohibition amendment, the commissioner of internal revenue has already found it necessary to announce that enforcement is hopeless without the support of the states. In case the nineteenth amendment is adopted over the opposition of Southern states, it will not have a like fate. But it should be evaded and, as respects negro

women, everyone knows that it would be evaded under the same provisions of the state constitution that keep negro men from voting as was contemplated by the fourteenth and fifteenth amendments."

In the same tenor *The Columbia State* sounds a warning against federal imposition, believing that "signs are observable in many parts of the country of the new vitality in the doctrine that the right of a state to define and limit its electorate may not be modified by any act, or concert of action, of or by other states." And it goes on to ask, "Why do not the women of South Carolina, if they crave the ballot, go about getting it, by asking for it in the manner that will certainly not be refused?" The chain of papers under the *Dallas News* stated its editorial position thus: "When the subject of suffrage via the federal route assumed importance we felt constrained to object to this, believing that it was unnecessary." *The Virginian Pilot* emphatically opposes the federal imposition and takes occasion to remark that "it is poor policy to usher in a governmental reform through the violation of a vital governmental principle," and stigmatizes enfranchisement by federal enactment as "repugnant to the states' right principle, the preservation of which is more important than the delay woman suffrage would suffer in the individual states if each were left to decide the question for itself."

In addition to objecting to suffrage imposed by federal enactment on principle, many editors feel that the amendment will aggravate the race question, and that individual states are in a better position to handle the suffrage locally for that reason. The *Bristol Herald-Courier* in this connection believes "it is quite likely that all the colored women who can qualify will exercise the elective franchise." . . . This it feels "will compel the white women to vote for the good of the state, those of them who do not wish to vote, as well as those who have fought for the ballot." The *Raleigh News and Observer* explains the opposition of the Southern states to the amendment on the ground that it would further "complicate the vexing race question." The *Chattanooga Times* is bitter, and concludes:

> "When this unholy trafficking in spineless, irresponsible congressmen and legislators has had its full fruition in giving women the vote, the only hope left for the tranquility and future maintenance of Republican principles will lie with those women upon whom the ballot is to be forced against their will and in defiance to their solemn wishes."

The *Wheeling Register* publishes a letter of despair from a business man, who asks, "What's the use in voting now that equal suffrage has been granted, when some illiterate negro woman in the southern part of the state knocks out your vote?" To which the *Clarksburg Telegram* replies: "There is no need for alarm that what illiterate votes may be brought into the ballot-boxes by reason of the enfranchisement of women will endanger good government any more than good government has been heretofore endangered by the illiterate votes deposited there by the males." The *Newport News Times-Herald* echoes the fear nevertheless that "it would admit a large number of negro women to the suffrage and open up anew a situation which was settled by the Constitutional Convention of

1901–1902." And it continues, "We stand unalterably with those who hold that the regulation of the suffrage is a matter to be determined within the several states. . . . We are still apostles of Jefferson, holding to the doctrine of local self-government and the reserved rights of the sovereign states." The *Macon Daily Telegraph* minces no words and characterizes federal enactment "as a reckless handling" not "adapted to the exigencies." With reference to the negro aspect of the question it holds:

> "There are some states where the negro problem is such that it is dangerous to upset the election procedure by any innovation. Under the circumstances the privilege of woman suffrage should be adapted to the exigencies, and worked out carefully by those who have in hand the affairs of government. It is not a matter that permits of precipitate action, or such reckless handling as will be made necessary under federal enactment. Oregon knows nothing about the difficulties of the Caucasian race in Georgia.
>
> "No one can legitimately question the importance of having the state's affairs managed by the most intelligent citizens of each state. We may say a great deal about the human being and his right to participate in the affairs of his government, but the negro is only 300 years in contact with civilization. His natural instincts lie along the lines of the lower animal. The vaccine of civilization has not thoroughly taken, and he will have to be kept in school or process of cultivation for 300 years before his moral fibre will have become sufficiently stabilized to permit his participation in government. Of course, there are a few exceptions, but these exceptions should be used to prove the possibility of consummation of the qualifications of the negro as a citizen."

On the other hand, the *Mobile Register*, though it would have preferred to have seen the suffrage handled by the states, "cannot oppose the grant because it happens to be made in another way," while *The Arkansas Gazette*, *The El Paso Herald*, and *The Republican* (Winston-Salem) approve the amendment without qualification.

As to just what influence suffrage will have on politics most papers concede that it will be appreciable and wholesome. *Holland's Magazine* (Texas) looks "for permanent cumulative benefits, not for an avalanche of improvement," while the *Fort Worth Record* assures us that woman is "opposed to the saloon," that "she believes in righteous law, is for the protection of childhood and the uplift of the race." The *Times-Picayune* predicts that "the women will go to the polls far better informed as to the political and civic questions before them than the average young man who is a maiden voter," and the *Atlanta Constitution* hopefully affirms that "in every state in which woman suffrage has been tried it has operated for the public good," and consoles those who believe women will lose their feminine charm with the assurance that "in those states it was found that after suffrage had been given a thorough test women still were women, with none of the attributes of their domestic virtues in the slightest degree impaired." The *Meridian Star* (Mississippi) anticipates considerable improvement through suffrage and thinks "women usually are blessed with good memories. They have an inherent knowledge of what is right and what is wrong. When they get the vote, as they will soon, they will exercise this gift for the good of the community in which they live, for the good of the state and the nation." The *Louisville Courier-Journal* refutes with some sarcasm the assumption that women will not vote as intelligently as men and concludes with this: "That the new voter is less well qualified than the regular voter, in so far as ability to analyze platform pledges and the issues they touch, nobody will believe who is not animated by the pretentiously but patronizingly chivalric theory that woman's intelligence is highly specialized and narrowly limited, and that she cannot acquit herself creditably save as a mother, a ministering angel, or an entertainer of men." The *News-Scimitar* reiterates, "the purifying influence of woman's presence has been felt in every activity in which she has engaged." And adds the *Nashville Tennessean*, "They are more inclined to vote for principle than for personalities. . . . It is only the poltroon, the misguided fool, and the man with a sixteenth century mind who opposes their entrance into the political arena." The *Commercial* (Memphis) *Appeal*, which has been a consistent advocate of suffrage since 1912, holds to the justice of the question and briefly declares that "In these days many of the responsibilities of life are thrown upon women. This being true, they by right must be permitted to share in all the privileges of citizenship." . . .

In a very dramatic speech which was characterized as, next to Mrs. Catt's, the most eloquent one delivered at the recent national suffrage convention at Chicago, Mrs. Solon Jacobs (Alabama) went into the suffrage situation in the South at length from the point of view of the Southern suffrage worker, painting a somewhat gloomy picture. We will quote at length from this speech, which created such a sensation:

> "If these men who invoke the doctrine of states' rights when it suits their purposes and who are still dominated by those old, unhappy, far-off memories of fifty years ago were sincere, we who live in the present might more readily forgive them. If they really wished the ballot to come to the Southern women by the state route, we would have had more referenda. The test of their sincerity has been in repeatedly declining even that medium of relief to the voteless women. They are opposed to justice, not merely to its method of attainment. It is the habitual attitude of the professional politician, until surrender is exacted by overwhelming public opinion.
>
> "There is a certain tyranny of tradition which is difficult to explain and for which it is impossible to apologize. Men seem peculiarly susceptible to its dominance. If the presiding officer of a woman's club were to terminate a meeting by merely putting on her hat, what ridicule would be meted out to her! Yet the time-honored way for the speaker of the French chamber of deputies to close a final session is to put on his hat, and when recently he neglected to perform that sacred rite, pandemonium reigned. Thus do customs handed down from age to age acquire almost the force of law.
>
> " 'Traditions in themselves have no dignity, our only interest in them is the fruitage they bear,' and while many of the traditions of the old South were gracious and kindly, beautiful and honorable, if their product is injustice they are no longer admirable.

"The old South was an aristocracy, if you will, but many years ago we began the reconstitution of an aristocracy under the democratic conditions. Now democracy is a thing of growth, by its very essence it must proceed from within and it is but natural that the democratization of the South should proceed more slowly than in other parts of the country, for we had farther to go.

"The old heritage of guardianship toward the unprivileged is not yet entirely eliminated; we are still somewhat nursing our respect for the past. We have not fully recovered from the recoil due to pressure of a democratic age.

"We are utterly weary of sectional feeling and anything which keeps it alive; we are tired of those people who think in terms of the United States and that other department of the universe south of [the] Mason-Dixon line. We know we have background and an honorable past, but we wish to occasionally be allowed to forget it, and to live in the present and build for the future. We have sickened of making constant and reiterated explanations of political blunders for which we are in no wise responsible.

"We realize we have moved beyond the period in which the practices of repression created by the exigencies of a by-gone day can longer be justified. We know, too, no state can base a present policy upon outlived conditions; and finally we know the whole body politic suffers from the disease of any of its members.

"It is acutely distasteful to Southern suffragists not to be enfranchised by Southern men, for we of all people understand the symbolism of the ballot, especially in states where its use is restricted and professedly based upon virtue and intelligence.

"And now by the thousands we have worked out our own salvation and have unshackled ourselves spiritually. We are not bound or gagged by any tradition which thwarts justice.

"Justice has become our tradition. Justice to all women, children, to the illiterates in our midst, justice to the women in industry still working unlimited hours, justice to all the hitherto unprivileged.

"It only remains for the outward and visible sign of our freedom to be put in the hands of Southern women by the generous men of other states, a situation which hurts our pride and to which we submit with deep regret but not apology."

Suggestions for Further Reading

Gilmore, Glenda Elizabeth. *Gender and Jim Crow: Women and the Politics of White Supremacy in North Carolina, 1896–1920.* Chapel Hill: University of North Carolina Press, 1996.

Grantham, Dewey W. *Southern Progressivism: The Reconciliation of Progress and Tradition.* Knoxville: University of Tennessee Press, 1983.

Green, Elna C. *Southern Strategies: Southern Women and the Woman Suffrage Question.* Chapel Hill: University of North Carolina Press, 1997.

Link, William A. *The Paradox of Southern Progressivism, 1880–1930.* Chapel Hill: University of North Carolina Press, 1992.

McArthur, Judith N. *Creating the New Woman: The Rise of Southern Women's Progressive Culture in Texas, 1893–1918*. Urbana: University of Illinois Press, 1998.

Sims, Anastatia. *The Power of Femininity in the New South: Women's Organizations and Politics in North Carolina, 1880–1930*. Columbia: University of South Carolina Press, 1997.

Terborg-Penn, Rosalyn. *African American Women in the Struggle for the Vote, 1850–1920*. Bloomington: Indiana University Press, 1998.

Turner, Elizabeth Hayes. *Women, Culture, and Community: Religion and Reform in Galveston, 1880–1920*. New York: Oxford University Press, 1997.

Wheeler, Marjorie Spruill. *New Women of the New South: The Leaders of the Woman Suffrage Movement in the Southern States*. New York: Oxford University Press, 1993.

———, ed. *Votes for Women! The Woman Suffrage Movement in Tennessee, the South, and the Nation*. Knoxville: University of Tennessee Press, 1995.

CHAPTER SEVEN

WORLD WAR I

The Debate about Intervention

For more than a century, American presidents had refused to participate in what George Washington called the "entangling alliances" of the European continent. President Woodrow Wilson's policy was no different. Soon after World War I erupted in Europe in 1914, he issued a declaration of American neutrality. Even as the war developed into a bloodletting, Americans for the most part wanted to avoid involvement. But maintaining true neutrality proved difficult. As the war unfolded, the United States did an increasing volume of business with Europe. Because the British Royal Navy controlled the high seas from the war's outset, trade quickly became directed almost exclusively toward the Allied powers, and there evolved a close — and perhaps "unneutral" — relationship. By 1917, the Allies had come to rely not only on American manufacturers and farmers, but also on American bankers to finance their purchases.

The advent of German submarine warfare further complicated the situation. Seeking to gain an advantage on the high seas, the Germans developed the U-boat to cut off the Allied — and especially British — access to imported goods and food. In May 1915, a German submarine sank the passenger liner *Lusitania* off the coast of Ireland at a great cost in lives; and in 1916, German U-boats sank several American and British freighters without warning. Many Americans saw these intermittent attacks as an affront to American dignity and a challenge to American power. President Wilson responded vigorously to the challenge. He obtained from Germany assurances that it would respect American neutrality and would neither sink unarmed passenger liners nor harm innocent civilians. But Germany reverted to unlimited submarine warfare, and Wilson declared war in April 1917.

American involvement in World War I had a powerful impact on domestic politics. Indeed, right from the outbreak of war the question of neutrality occasioned a national debate. Some Americans came to believe that intervention on the Allied side was inevitable and even desirable. Leaders such as former president Theodore Roosevelt believed that the United States had arrived as a world power and that it should behave as a responsible leader in European affairs. They saw Germany as an aggressive power whose domination of Europe — should it win the war — would be a fundamental threat to American economic and political interests; they sympathized with France and especially Great Britain, and believed that these western democracies shared our interests. On the other hand, anti-interventionists just as ardently opposed American involvement. Many were part of a pacifist movement that rejected war as a means of resolving international conflict. Others were anti-British and opposed any support to the British empire. Still others were isolationist — they believed that the physical and psychological distance between Americans and the rest of the world made active involvement abroad unnecessary.

In late 1915, President Wilson, in response to the war in Europe, proposed a major increase in military spending, to the highest level since the Civil War. In addition, he sought a major reorganization of the military. This proposed legislation, known as "preparedness," set off a debate that exposed serious divisions of opinion among Americans regarding the appropriate strength of the military, their willingness to resort to armed force to protect national interests, and the necessity of intervention in the war. In response to Wilson's proposals for a major military buildup that might presage intervention, antiwar groups held rallies around the country. Many of them invoked a traditional hostility to large military establishments, as well as America's diplomatic tradition of avoiding involvement in European affairs.

This debate held a special resonance for Southerners. Their active participation in the Spanish-American War in 1898 had helped them embrace a stronger sense of nationalism — and sectional reconciliation — than had been evident at any time since the Civil War. Many participants in the "Lost Cause" movement, which sought to glorify the Confederacy and to preserve its memory, strongly favored defending American interests during the neutrality debate; their attachment to the cause of the southern nation became a part of their devotion to the American nation. Other Southerners, fearing the consequences of intervention, remained strongly opposed.

The documents in this chapter examine the debate in the South between 1914 and 1917. From the beginning, Southerners were divided in their loyalties. A 1914 *Literary Digest* article surveys attitudes about the war, finding a majority of Americans sympathetic to the Allied cause, yet unwilling to intervene. Over the next three years, Southerners considered the wisdom of intervention. Some of them vigorously embraced the cause of preparedness. As Lilian Pike Roome's open letter to the United Daughters of the Confederacy attests, some organizations became vigorous advocates of a strong American presence on the international scene. Other advocates of preparedness, such as Mississippi Senator John Sharp Williams, argued for a strong military establishment. But even in the spring of 1917, many Americans continued to oppose intervention and many Southerners remained active anti-interventionists, as Claude Kitchin's speech, given in April of that year during congressional debate of a possible declaration of war, explains.

As you read, determine how public opinion regarded the European war in 1914 and trace the changes in opinion over the next two years. What did neutrality mean to the authors of these documents? Why did some Southerners support an expanded role in international affairs? On what grounds did others oppose it?

23. Public Opinion

LITERARY DIGEST
"American Sympathies in the War"
1914

With the outbreak of war in Europe in August 1914, Americans faced a basic question: Was it possible to remain neutral in a global war? The following article from the Literary Digest — *well known at the time as a chronicle of American public opinion — provides a comprehensive survey three months after the outbreak of world war. The survey found either neutral or pro-Allied sentiment throughout the country. For example, in responses from newspaper editors around the country, the Digest reported that of 367 editors polled, 242 were neutral, 105 favored the Allies, and only 20 favored Germany. It did not use modern polling methods — which were not then available — but conducted wide-ranging anecdotal interviews. Although the results cannot be regarded as conclusive, they do provide one measure of how Americans felt about the war. The following excerpt includes the results of the Digest's sur-*

Literary Digest, 14 November 1914, 939, 974–78.

vey for the South. It reveals a diversity of opinion about the war that reflects the divided state of national public opinion in 1914.

Much talk is heard about American sympathy in the European War, but thus far it has had no basis except hearsay or very limited personal observation. Do a majority of the American press or the American people favor the Germans or the Allies? To approach an answer to this question we have obtained statements from between 350 and 400 editors, telling their own attitudes and the feelings of their communities toward the warring nations. We need hardly say that we give the result of this inquiry entirely without partisanship, and purely for our readers' information. The replies cover the country from the Atlantic to the Pacific and from Mexico to the Canadian border. They cannot very well be woven into a connected narrative, but the reader who scans the summary presented here will find the country divided into large areas where the feeling is preponderatcly for onc side or the other, or is so mixed as to be neutral. . . .

Delaware to Texas

Making a sudden eastward shift across the country to Delaware, the first State of the South Atlantic Division, we begin to feel the contact of a general pro-Ally opinion. Dover favors the Allies "by a great majority," we hear; and from Wilmington, through neutral editors, we learn that the city is "pro-Ally, without being anti-German." Another report states that "there is much German sentiment in Wilmington, particularly among German-Americans and Hungarians. Taking the State at large, however, the sentiment is with the Allies, due largely to the English ancestry of the people."

In Maryland the press is generally neutral, although one paper avows that its "sympathy is with the Allies." The public, as we hear from the same city, is "mostly anti-German." And word comes from Cumberland that "sentiment here, even among a large number of Germans, is with the Allies and against the German Emperor and his military party. This is due to the treatment of neutral Belgium, and the belief that the Emperor and not the German people forced the war." As a straw showing the way the wind blows in Washington, D.C., we are told by an editor that his paper "in its editorial policy aims to be fair to both sides in the present European War. Public sentiment here has been distinctly in favor of the Allies, . . . a sentiment which has increased since the fall of Antwerp."

In the representative cities of Virginia the description of community feeling ranges from "practically unanimous for the Allies" to "pretty generally in favor of the Allies"; the "only exceptions," we hear from Hampton, are "among these nearly full-blooded Germans. Most of those of Pennsylvania or German descent are pro-Ally." In West Virginia, towns like Huntington and Elkins are squarely on the side of the Allies. But from Wheeling, with 28 percent of the population German, and from Morgantown, with many Germans employed in the glass-factories, we learn that public opinion is "divided." A Martinsburg neutral editor, who "deplores the biased reports of the Allies regarding German atrocities," writes that, "generally speaking, the community has recently changed from the Allies, and now favors the Germans. The Allies' censorship of the news unfavorable to them and Japan's advent at England's urging have done much to bring about this reversal of feeling, until now German successes are hailed with joy."

In North Carolina we learn that Durham is "strongly" pro-Ally, and the editor who provides this information supports the Allies in his paper, and believes what is true of Durham is "true throughout the South." At least it is said also of Winston-Salem; but we hear from Greensboro that while the Allies are looked upon as the "winning side," there are "many of German descent who favor the Germans." Four cities in South Carolina, including Columbia, the capital, report "overwhelmingly in favor of the Allies," "mainly because the general belief is that German successes mean prolongation of the war," says an Orange editor. To offset this, Newberry states that although the editor is "personally in sympathy with the Germans, his paper has not taken sides." And he adds that "the sentiment of this community, I believe, is with the Germans. I gather this from talking with the people."

The state of mind in Georgia, where the press seem divided on the question of neutral editorials, may be gathered from the following message from Atlanta: "In our opinion it is best for the welfare of this country, and that of the world in general, that the Allies should be victorious over Germany, and this expresses practically the universal sentiment of this section." So, also, in Savannah, Marion, Rome, and Gainesville, while in Athens "the general sentiment is favorable to a great degree to the Allies, outside of German residents." Completely neutral, we hear, is Jacksonville, Florida, where "the Germans are for Germany, the British, French, and Russians for the Allies." But St. Augustine, Pensacola, and Key West oppose "the militarism represented by the German Government" and support the Allies.

The interesting news comes from one editor in Louisville, Kentucky, that the city is overwhelmingly for the Allies, and from another that opinion is "divided." The latter word describes also the feeling in Covington, Paducah, and Danville, where the Germans favor the Germans and "other sentiment is for the Allies." Lexington, Owensboro, and Henderson are said to be wholly pro-Ally. In Tennessee a Greenville editor supports the Allies, and says the town is "almost unanimous in favor of the Allies," but the word comes from Memphis that the editorial policy of a certain journal is pro-German and that the opinion of the people is "about equally divided, though changing rapidly to the Germans."

Coming down into Alabama, we discover a marked pro-Ally feeling with a "divided" feeling almost as pronounced. To towns like Huntsville, Dothan, Gadsden, Evergreen, and Centre the former remark applies. But though Athens is "almost solid for the Allies," yet "a few Germans stand for the Fatherland." Of Montgomery it is said that Ally partizans are more numerous, but the German "more active." Mobile is "very much divided, with a possible shade in the Allies' favor," as it has "considerable foreign population." The original sentiment comes from Bay Minette that it is "almost unanimously with the Allies, but wouldn't object to the Germans licking the Russians."

Turning to Mississippi, we meet two Vicksburg editors who support the Allies in their papers and say that city is of the same mind; but Biloxi informs us that while the majority seems to lean toward the Allies, nevertheless opinion is "very much divided." Crossing the Mississippi River into Arkansas, we hear from an editor in Pine Bluff, whose sympathy is with the Germans although his paper is neutral, that the town favors the Allies "only for the reason that the Germans have less chance to win." He adds that his community wants the war to end. Then we hear from Fort Smith that while there "is probably a preponderance of sympathy for the Allies, still some change in the favor of the Germans has taken place since the first few weeks of the war."

Similar is the statement from Texarkana by an editor who admits that he "favors the Allies, but is fair to the Germans." He feels that the "onus of the war is on Germany," and because of that "the preponderance of public opinion in this section seems to be largely on the side of the Allies. However, the people are not partizans in the matter." Contrary is the word from Argenta, where it is said that "the German sympathizers are more aggressive in insinuating their views and making more showing," but that sympathy for the Allies "undoubtedly predominates." The same verdict comes from Little Rock, Blythesville, Harrison, and Helena.

The effect of a large German population in New Orleans, Louisiana, favoring Germany is offset, we learn, by a larger French population favoring France and a majority of American-born people of other races who incline toward the Allies. Less complicated is the situation of Baton Rouge, which is said to be wholly lined up for the Allies.

In Oklahoma ten cities stand forth unhesitatingly for the Allies, and several editors support them in their columns. From Adair we hear that public opinion is about equally divided, and that the editor of the county journal favors the Germans editorially. The opinion of Oklahoma City is that "war is wrong, and that the Powers could have settled all differences by arbitration."

Passing into Texas, we find in Dallas that the papers are neutral, while the people in general seem to favor the Allies. The Allies are said to be favored also in Palestine, Denison, and El Paso, although from the last-named city we hear that the public is "not strongly biased either way, and that the general disposition is to hear both sides." In Laredo an editor who supports the Germans says that "the community supports them," while a neutral editor in Houston writes that in this section, "outside of German influence, 90 percent are favorable to the Allies." A neutral editor in Waco says of the community feeling that "it's all according to the seasonin', as Mr. Weller was wont to say"; and we hear from Marshall, Texas, that although the majority feeling leans toward the Allies, "the disposition is to shut up about the war and talk diversification of crops. Many have quit reading war-news."

24. The Case for Preparedness

LILIAN PIKE ROOME AND JOHN SHARP WILLIAMS
Arguments for Intervention
1915 and 1916

Although many Americans vigorously opposed President Wilson's 1915 proposal to strengthen the American military, others felt it was essential to be ready to fight on short notice. The following two Southerners made a different case. Lilian Pike Roome was a Virginia leader of the United Daughters of the Confederacy (UDC), the largest organization in the South involved in the "Lost Cause." As her letter to the UDC indicates, after 1914 many Lost Cause organizations became intensely nationalistic. John Sharp Williams was a senator from Mississippi and a strong advocate of intervention, as the New York Times *report of his January 6, 1916, speech to the United States Senate shows.*

LILIAN PIKE ROOME

October 12, 1915

To the United Daughters of the Confederacy in Convention assembled:

Dear Friends,

Not being able to attend the Annual Convention and so to make my plea in person, I now make it in writing. I want my sister Daughters to join with the President General and with those members of the D. A. R. who support the various plans for an adequate national defense. I want them to urge their Representatives in Congress, as well as their Governors and State Legislators, to make the most liberal provisions for every means of defense. Let us not be led astray by the cry of "militarism," by the charge that preparing for possible war brings on war. On the contrary, to be prepared will at least postpone the evil day, if not prevent it; while unpreparedness will not only invite war, but will subject a nation to humiliation and destruction.

An attack upon any part of the United States would affect every section of the country, but the first blow will almost surely fall upon the coastal regions. The South, having two coast lines, necessarily has a double exposure: therefore, is doubly interested in coast defense. Adequate coast defense means immense quantities of artillery and ammunition, engineers and artillerymen, war vessels innumerable, aeroplanes and hydroplanes, wireless equipment of all sorts, armored

Daisy McCourin Stevens Papers, Mississippi Division of Archives and History, Jackson, Miss.

motors in abundance, an ample signal corps service and searchlights, unlimited supplies of barbed wire, and other new devices now deemed essential in modern warfare. In case of actual war, we would need an army of millions, with all the latest inventions in arms and equipments; for no human being can guarantee that we will not be forced into a war.

There is an old saying that, "When the sword must be drawn, there is no time to sharpen it"; and the Bible says: "A strong man armed keepeth his castle; but if a stronger than he come, he taketh it from him." Our forefathers and our fathers fought for freedom: some day we or our descendants will also be forced to fight to keep that freedom. If we do not prepare beforehand, we will not be able to stand against overwhelming odds, and even may be reduced to the sad plight of Belgium.[1] Let us then follow the wise counsels of the immortal Washington, of Thomas Jefferson, of Alexander Hamilton, of James Monroe, and others. Let us economise in non-essentials, but not in the means of defense: let us not expose our people to useless slaughter by stinting them of the weapons needed to ward off attack.

Let the United Daughters of the Confederacy join hands with the other patriotic organizations, and rouse the South to the necessity of helping to provide for the military needs of our reunited country, and show to the world that we are worthy descendants of American patriots. If this country should feel compelled to go to war to defend its principles, its honor or its territory, I know that the South would do its full part; there is no question of that. But no people, however brave, could defend themselves successfully against a thoroughly equipped enemy, if not prepared to the fullest extent.

President Wilson and his advisers are studying this question and will present to the incoming Congress a measure to provide for adequate national defense. We can help to secure the passage of this measure, if each of us will use her best endeavors towards that end. Our President General is leading the way, and it is my fervent hope that all the Daughters will sustain her.

For more than three years I have been working in this cause; my heart and soul are in it and always will be. If I can by this feeble effort support the plea of the President General, I shall be repaid; for I feel that it is my bounden duty to bear witness to my conviction of the greatness of this cause and give to our leaders the assurance of my earnest co-operation. May it be an incentive to some of you to do likewise. Let the motto of the Daughters of the American Revolution, "For Home and Country," inspire us also.

Your co-worker and sincere friend,
Lilian Pike Roome
(Mrs. Wm. Oscar Roome)

---

[1] **the sad plight of Belgium:** despite determined resistance, Belgian defenses were overwhelmed by superior German forces.

JOHN SHARP WILLIAMS

January 6, 1916

WASHINGTON—Senator John Sharp Williams of Mississippi, a Democratic member of the Committee on Foreign Relations, made a speech in the Senate this afternoon that was practically a warning that the United States must increase her defenses so as to resist the bullying of a victorious Germany after the war. He seemed to have no doubt as to Germany's ultimate triumph, and he argued that the Kaiser would find it difficult to lead his troops back from their career of conquest to work in ruined mills for which capital was lacking.

Mr. Williams said that he did not think this power would begin deliberately a war of conquest on the United States, but that it would start a "bullying" policy which the United States would resent, and which might bring war speedily. He said the "unwarned high-sea assassinations of American women and children"[1] were among the questions already raised by the United States with Germany, and that question was still unsettled. The right of neutrals to sell arms to belligerents, he thought, was necessary to the safety of the United States.

"The principle that neutral countries could export munitions of war to belligerents," said Mr. Williams, "was adopted by Washington himself after Jefferson had put the theory in writing. It was not founded on the desire to make money as those, whose thoughts toward the United States are treasonable, now say. This theory was maintained because it would give advantage to a country that prepared chiefly for peace, whereas the theory of the embargo gives the advantage to the country constantly preparing for war. In God's name, what chance would we have in a war at sea with Great Britain, or by land with Germany if we could not buy supplies?"

"Would not such a policy of embargoes hamstring the United States?" asked Mr. Nelson of Minnesota, a Republican.

"Not only would it hamstring us," replied Mr. Williams, "but it would hamstring us more than any country in the world. For we think the duty of a Government is the work of peace, that the Government should prepare for peace in the ordinary course."

"Does the Senator see any reason for a change in our national policy?" asked Mr. Borah of Idaho.

"There is no reason to change the national policy," replied Mr. Williams, "but there is a special reason, which it is not necessary to explain, for increasing our national defenses. When must a country prepare for trouble? When an autocratic ruler with millions of men must lead them back to work in factories which have been destroyed, and for which capital has vanished, when their victories have inclined them to follow the eagles of empire to the confines of the earth. . . .

"People say the countries of Europe will be exhausted by the war, and we need not prepare ourselves against them. But look at Bulgaria. She fought the first

[1]**high-sea assassinations of . . . women and children:** the German U-boat campaign.
New York Times, 7 January 1916.

Balkan war against Turkey and was bankrupted; she fought the second Balkan war against her allies and was bankrupted again, and now she is going into a third war with 500,000 veteran soldiers, the best soldiers in the world as far as soldiery goes. When you have these masses of victorious soldiers, you find, as the great Napoleon found it, that there comes a point when you cannot stop."

"Does the Senator really think," asked Mr. Borah, "that we will be attacked by a European country following this war, in a mere spirit of conquest?"

"I am not anticipating attack, but bullying," said Mr. Williams, "and the American people will not stand bullying. One great power believes now that we are allies of its enemies. We have raised some delicate questions with that power and they remain to be settled. The sudden unwarned high-sea assassination of our women and children on unarmed merchantmen constitutes one of these differences, and just in inverse proportion as we have a naval force as we used to have when we talked will be the height of that power's conversation with us.

"If the American people, as some one said to me the other day, have sense enough to stand this bullying it would be all right, but the American people have not that degree or that kind of sense. A man said to me that he did not want to shed the blood of any people on earth. I said that I did not either, but I did not want them to shed mine.

"I think it is a pity that these diplomatic matters could not have been left in the hands of the President with his long vision, his deep vision, and his tender vision, instead of making it the battledore and shuttlecock of politics. If Senators on the other side are planning an attack on the Administration along these lines, I will not follow them, for I will not bring so high a policy down into the dust and ruck of political combat."

25. An Opponent of War

CLAUDE KITCHIN
Speech before Congress
1917

One of the most prominent opponents of intervention was North Carolina congressman Claude Kitchin. Born in 1869, Kitchin was first elected to Congress in 1900, and there became known as one of the most eloquent debaters in the House

Alex Mathews Arnett, *Claude Kitchin and the Wilson War Policies* (Boston: Little, Brown & Co., 1937), 227–35.

of Representatives. Elected chairman of the House Ways and Means Committee in 1915, he was one of the most powerful southern Democrats in Congress during the Wilson administration and vigorously supported Wilson on most domestic issues. Indeed, Kitchin was one of several southern congressmen who embraced reform and loyally supported Wilson's legislative agenda. But he parted company with him on international issues. A strong Jacksonian, he feared international involvement and believed that the United States should follow its traditional isolationist foreign policy. The following is excerpted from Kitchin's speech to the House of Representatives, given during Congress's debate about whether to declare war. Although Kitchin voted against the declaration, he was in a small minority, and it passed handily.

April 6, 1917

Mr. Chairman, in view of the many assumptions of loyalty and patriotism on the part of some of those who favor the resolution, and insinuations by them of cowardice and disloyalty on the part of those who oppose it, offshoots, doubtless, of a passionate moment, let me at once remind the House that it takes neither moral nor physical courage to declare a war for others to fight. [Applause.] It is evidence of neither loyalty nor patriotism for one to urge others to get into a war when he knows that he himself is going to keep out.

The depth of my sorrow, the intensity of my distress in contemplating the measureless step proposed, God only knows. The right and necessity of this momentous resolution are addressed to the individual judgment of the Members of the House. Too grave is the responsibility for anyone to permit another to stand sponsor for his conscience.

Profoundly impressed with the gravity of the situation, appreciating to the fullest the penalties which a war-mad moment will impose, my conscience and judgment, after mature thought and fervent prayer for rightful guidance, have marked out clearly the path of my duty, and I have made up my mind to walk it, if I go barefooted and alone. [Applause.] I have come to the undoubting conclusion that I should vote against this resolution. [Applause.] If I had a single doubt, I would with profoundest pleasure resolve it in favor of the view of the Administration and of a large majority of my colleagues, who have so recently honored me with their confidence. I know that I shall never criticize any Member for advocating this resolution. I concede — I feel — that he casts his vote in accordance with sincere conviction. I know, too, that for my vote I shall be not only criticized, but denounced from one end of the country to the other. The whole yelping pack of defamers and revilers in the nation will at once be set upon my heels.

My friends, I cannot leave my children lands and riches — I cannot leave them fame — but I can leave them the name of an ancestor, who, mattering not the consequences to himself, never dared to hesitate to do his duty as God gave him to see it. [Applause.]

Half the civilized world is now a slaughter-house for human beings. This nation is the last hope of peace on earth, good will toward men. I am unwilling for my country by statutory command to pull up the last anchor of peace in the world and extinguish during the long night of a world-wide war the only remaining star of hope for Christendom. I am unwilling by my vote to-day for this nation to throw away the only remaining compass to which the world can look for guidance in the paths of right and truth, of justice and humanity, and to leave only force and blood to chart hereafter the path for mankind to tread.

By passage of this resolution we enter the war, and the universe becomes one vast drama of horrors and blood — one boundless stage upon which will play all the evil spirits of earth and hell. All the demons of inhumanity will be let loose for a rampage throughout the world. Whatever be the future, whatever be the rewards or penalties of this nation's step, I shall always believe that we could and ought to have kept out of this war.

Great Britain every day, every hour, for two years has violated American rights on the seas. We have persistently protested. She has denied us not only entrance into the ports of the Central Powers but has closed to us by force the ports of neutrals. She has unlawfully seized our ships and our cargoes. She has rifled our mails. She has declared a war zone sufficiently large to cover all the ports of her enemy. She made the entire North Sea a military area — strewed it with hidden mines and told the neutral nations of the world to stay out or be blown up. We protested. No American ship was sunk, no American life was destroyed, because we submitted and did not go in. We kept out of war. We sacrificed no honor. We surrendered permanently no essential rights. We knew that these acts of Great Britain, though in plain violation of international law and of our rights on the seas, were not aimed at us. They were directed at her enemy. They were inspired by military necessity. Rather than plunge this country into war, we were willing to forego, for the time, our rights. I approved that course then; I approve it now.

Germany declares a war zone sufficiently large to cover the ports of her enemy. She infests it with submarines and warns the neutral world to stay out, though in plain violation of our rights and of international law. We know that these acts are aimed not directly at us but intended to injure and cripple her enemy, with which she is in a death struggle.

We refuse to yield; we refuse to forego our rights for the time. We insist upon going in.

In my judgment, we could keep out of the war with Germany as we kept out of the war with Great Britain, by keeping our ships and our citizens out of the war zone of Germany as we did out of the war zone of Great Britain. And we would sacrifice no more honor, surrender no more rights in the one case than in the other. Or we could resort to armed neutrality, which the President recently urged and for which I voted on March 1.

But we are told that Germany has destroyed American lives while Great Britain destroyed only property. Great Britain destroyed no American lives, because this nation kept her ships and her citizens out of her war zone which she sowed with hidden mines.

But are we quite sure that the real reason for war with Germany is the destruction of lives as distinguished from property, that to avenge the killing of innocent Americans and to protect American lives war becomes a duty?

Mexican bandits raided American towns, shot to death sleeping men, women, and children in their own home. We did not go to war to avenge these deaths. We sent an armed expedition into Mexico to hunt down and punish the bandits. Away out from the American border the soldiers of Carranza, of the Mexican Government, which we had recognized, met our soldiers, shot the American flag from the hands of an American soldier, shot down to the death our soldiers, and Carranza, instead of disavowing the dastardly act, defiantly approved and ratified it. Yet we did not go to war to avenge the destruction of American lives and the insult and assault on the American flag. We were willing to forego our rights rather than plunge this country into war while half the world was in conflagration. I approved that course then; I approve it now.

Why can we not, why should we not, forego for the time being the violation of our rights by Germany, and do as we did with Great Britain, do as we did with Mexico, and thus save the universe from being wrapped in the flames of war?

I have hoped and prayed that God would forbid our country going into war with another for doing that which perhaps, under the same circumstances, we ourselves would do.

Are we quite sure that in a war with Germany or Japan, if our fleet was bottled up, helpless, and our ships of commerce had been swept from the seas, all our ports closed by the enemy's fleet, imports of fuel and food and clothing for our people and ammunition for our soldiers were denied, with our very life trembling in the balance, we would not, in the last struggle for existence, strike our enemy with the only weapon of the sea remaining, though in violation of international law? Would one contend that, under the circumstances, our submarine commanders should permit the landing at the ports of the enemy of arms and ammunition with which to shoot down our brave American boys when they had it in their power to prevent it? Would we demand of our submarine commanders that they give the benefit of the doubt to questions of international law rather than to the safety of our country and the lives of our soldiers?

War upon the part of a nation is sometimes necessary and imperative. But here no invasion is threatened. Not a foot of our territory is demanded or coveted. No essential honor is required to be sacrificed. No fundamental right is asked to be permanently yielded or suspended. No national policy is contested. No part of our sovereignty is questioned. Here the overt act, ruthless and brutal though it be, is not aimed directly at us. The purpose of the proposed enemy is not our injury, either in property or life. The whole aim and purpose and effort are directed at a powerful enemy with which she is in a life and death struggle.

The causes for which we are now asked to declare war could have been given with equal — yea, greater — force thirty days or ten days after the first step taken by the German Army in its march toward Paris. They existed then.

The House and the country should thoroughly understand that we are asked to declare war not to protect alone American lives and American rights on the high seas. We are to make the cause of Great Britain, France, and Russia, right or wrong, our cause. We are to make their quarrel, right or wrong, our quarrel. We are to fight out, with all the resources in men, money, and credit of the Government and its people a difference between the belligerents of Europe to which we were and are utter strangers. Nothing in that cause, nothing in that quarrel, has or does involve a moral or equitable or material interest in, or obligation of, our Government or our people.

To this program every impulse of patriotism, every sense of right, every feeling of humanity, every sentiment of loyalty, every obligation of duty within me combine in forbidding my consent until the Government and its people, through its rightful and constitutional voice — the Congress of the United States — have clearly spoken, in the passage of such a resolution as is now before the House. Then, and then only, will it become the patriotic duty of each Member of the House and Senate to merge his individual judgment and conviction into those so declared of his country, as it will become the duty of every American, in and out of Congress, to make the judgment and conviction of his country, thus written into statute, his judgment and conviction. [Applause.] The voice of law will command, and a patriotic duty will demand, loyal and earnest and active submission and obedience. Until then each should have and does have the inherent right, and it is his bounden duty to himself and to truth, to vote his conviction.

I can conceive of a brave, loyal, devoted son of a father who contemplates a personal difficulty with another begging and persuading him to refrain, even condemning, and protesting in vain against his proposed step, but when the final word is spoken and blows are about to be given, taking off his coat and struggling with all of his soul and might in defense of that father.

When this nation, as it doubtless will to-day, speaks the final word through the Congress, I trust I will be found in relation with my Government and my country emulating the example of that son.

Suggestions for Further Reading

Cooper, John Milton. *The Vanity of Power: American Isolationism and the First World War, 1914–1917.* Westport, Conn.: Greenwood, 1969.

Kennedy, David M. *Over Here: The First World War and American Society.* New York: Oxford University Press, 1980.

Levin, Norman Gordon. *Woodrow Wilson and World Politics: America's Response to War and Revolution.* New York: Oxford University Press, 1968.

Link, Arthur S. *Woodrow Wilson and the Progressive Era, 1910–1917.* New York: Harper and Row, 1954.

CHAPTER EIGHT

THE 1920s

Fundamentalism
and the Scopes Trial

In the decade after World War I, the United States experienced a sweeping social, economic, and cultural transformation. During the 1920s, the economy generated substantial new wealth and, for the first time, a consumer economy. New industries such as automobiles, electronics, and petrochemicals grew into prominence, and rapidly developing technologies helped American manufacturers to achieve unprecedented gains in production and productivity. The accompanying cultural changes signaled the beginning of the "modern" era. For the first time, most of the population lived in urban areas, while rural areas continued their prolonged decline as centers of social and cultural life. New forms of cultural expression emerged. The motion picture industry grew rapidly and during the 1920s became one of the foremost sources of popular amusement. Radio broadcasting — along with the development of nationally syndicated programming — introduced yet another national forum.

No group was more disturbed by these changes than were evangelical Protestants. Since the early nineteenth century, evangelicalism — effectively using the revival and a message of personal salvation — had spread throughout the nation. But it was a diverse cultural phenomenon whose northern proponents, for instance, emphasized active participation in reform movements while those in the South saw personal piety as more important. By the late nineteenth century, American evangelicalism was split by another issue: Charles Darwin's theory of evolution. First propounded during the 1850s as a way of explaining the development of plant and animal life, the theory maintained that those species that experienced mutations that provided them advantages in the struggle for survival tended to perpetuate themselves more successfully. But these ideas — popularized by a host of other writers — threatened traditional ways of viewing the cosmos. Many evangelical Protestants regarded Darwinism as a view of life that provided little room for divine direction.

During and after the 1870s, evangelicals were split among those who strongly rejected Darwinism and those who attempted to reconcile it with religious faith. Anti-Darwinism was already a powerful force among conservative evangelicals, and it received a strong boost during and after World War I by the coalescence of "fundamentalism" into a powerful national movement. Conservative evangelicals were profoundly disturbed by trends among Protestant "modernists," who in the late nineteenth century were united by a common desire to adjust Christianity to the modern world. Many of them engaged in a new view of the Bible that placed it in historical and cultural context; for the most part, new biblical scholarship came to question literal interpretations of scripture.

Common to fundamentalists was a suspicion of the emerging secular cultural and political systems. At the end of the war, in May 1918, five thousand fundamentalists organized themselves at the Philadelphia Prophetic Conference; the next year, the World's Christian Fundamentals Association came into existence; fundamentalists were now formally organized and armed with a new national magazine, *The Fundamentals*. During the 1920s, fundamentalists were united in their rejection of Darwinism and their affirmation of the explanation given in the Book of Genesis as the only proper way to understand Creation and the place of humans in it, and in their rejection of biblical modernism in favor of a new stringency in belief in inerrancy and literalism — that is, that the Bible was unquestionably and literally true.

Fundamentalists fought a prolonged cultural war on several fronts. First, within Protestant denominations, they attempted to root out biblical modernism, particularly in the seminaries that trained ministers. Second, they campaigned for new legislation that would prevent the teaching of evolution in public-supported institutions — both public schools and universities. The latter movement was especially active in the South, which became a center of fundamentalist strength. A leading figure in the anti-Darwin campaign was William Jennings Bryan, three-time Democratic presidential candidate (in 1896, 1900, and 1908), who led a national fundamentalist campaign. Beginning in 1921, he sought to purge Darwinian biology from high-school texts and curricula; there were also aftershocks that rocked the teaching of science in colleges and universities. Bryan's call to arms received support in the Middle West and particularly in the South, where it was warmly embraced by a number of fundamentalist evangelists. Between 1925 and 1927, Arkansas, Mississippi, Louisiana, and Tennessee all passed laws prohibiting the teaching of the theories of Charles Darwin in public schools.

In Tennessee, where anti-Darwinians had already scored many successes, fundamentalists in 1923 succeeded in forcing the University of Tennessee to fire a professor of genetic psychology, along with five other faculty members, for teaching evolution. Two years later, backed by Bryan and his fundamentalist allies, the legislature prohibited any instructor in the state's schools and colleges from teaching any theory that denied the biblical account of Creation or asserting that humans had evolved from a lower order of animals. In response, the American Civil Liberties Union (ACLU) offered to finance the defense of any teacher willing to challenge the law. Urged by local mining engineer George W. Rappelyea, John Thomas Scopes, a twenty-four-year-old recent college graduate and popular high-school biology teacher and coach, volunteered. Arrested on May 7, 1925, in Dayton, a small town in eastern Tennessee, Scopes was tried amid a frenzy of national publicity. Bryan joined the prosecution, under the auspices of the World's Christian Fundamentals Association; the famous defense lawyer Clarence Darrow joined Scopes's defense. Opening in July 1925, the Scopes trial, presided over by Judge John T. Raulston, attracted great crowds outside the courthouse even as more than one hundred members of the press attended the trial. Although Scopes was convicted of violating the law, the adverse publicity constituted a major setback for the cause of fundamentalism. A few days after the trial ended, William Jennings Bryan died.

The documents in this chapter examine the trial and its aftermath. An excerpt from T. T. Martin's *Hell and the High Schools* reveals the case fundamentalists made against evolution — and the intensity they invested in the cause. The trial itself contained high drama, as recounted in *Outlook*, and much of the proceedings had less to do with the law than with each side making its case before the national media. Dayton, Tennessee, became a battleground between modernism and fundamentalism: the trial, as John Porter Fort explains, involved a larger struggle raging in American culture. The death of Bryan, as H. L. Mencken observes, was emblematic of the trial as a turning point in the modernist-fundamentalist battle.

———

As you read, consider what most alarmed fundamentalists about Darwinism. What were the basic tenets of "modernism"? What were the most important differences between Bryan and Darrow in the Scopes trial? Which side — fundamentalist or modernist — ultimately triumphed in the Scopes trial?

26. The Fundamentalist Case

T. T. MARTIN
From Hell and the High Schools
1923

Among the most prominent of the evangelical fundamentalists was Thomas Theodore Martin, a Mississippi preacher who participated in the nationwide effort to uproot Darwinism from public education and from colleges and universities. Hell and the High Schools, *which became a classic in anti-evolutionist literature, attracted a wide national audience. It provides an indictment of Darwinism, identifying it as the focal point of forces undermining Protestant religious authority.*

Effects of Evolution on Students

Germany's "superman"[1] turned out to be an incarnate devil; but before that stage was reached, Evolution swept the young men and women, boys and girls of Germany from the Bible as God's word and from Jesus the Christ as Saviour and Redeemer. Some professors, as mental contortionists, by theological flimflamming, or by getting up a special brand of Evolution, kind of "home brew" for private consumption, may believe in Evolution and also in the Bible as God's word and Christ as Saviour and real Redeemer; but your open-minded student cannot. . . .

During twenty-two years as an Evangelist throughout the country, I have met with many cases, young men and women having been taught Evolution in the schools, now having only contempt and scorn for the Bible and for Jesus the Christ as Saviour and Redeemer; broken-hearted fathers and mothers weeping over the wrecked faith of their children. What care the Evolutionists for all this? They laugh and jeer, as the rapist laughs and jeers at the bitter tears of the crushed father and mother over the blighted life of their child. But the rapist laughs and jeers over the wrecked, blighted human body; the Evolutionist professors laugh and jeer over a doomed, damned human soul; and they hide behind their smoke-screen that their Evolution teaches that there is no hell. Their "culture," you know — they are the "intellectuals," you know, — teaches them that there is no hell. They'll find out — when too late. . . .

As a sample, one from many, of what is being done, here is a letter from a mother to me, dated March 24, 1922: "My son became a Christian about ten years ago. A few weeks before he graduated from ——— University (a Baptist Univer-

---

[1] **"superman"**: probably a reference to German philosopher Friedrich Nietzsche's concept of the *ubermensch*, a new race of people he believed capable of high achievement.

T. T. Martin, *Hell and the High Schools. Christ or Evolution: Which?* (Kansas City: Western Baptist Publishing Co., 1923), 147, 149–50, 151–57.

sity. — T. T. M.), they let an Evolutionist lecture there for one week (they did not "let" him, they invited him so as to be considered "broad," "liberal," "up-to-date" — T. T. M.), and my son attended the lectures; and since then he seems to have no use for the Bible and takes no interest in the Lord's cause. It almost breaks my heart." And that Baptist President of the University and those Baptist Professors sat there and let that young man's faith and life be wrecked without one word of protest, without one word explaining Evolution, for it is easily exposed; and then they will go out among the common people and talk about "loyalty to the denomination," and about "our great kingdom work" and stir the people with their eloquence and pathos about the "precious old Book" and "the blessed Saviour" and "the Cross" and "the atonement" — and then with a shrug of the shoulders and a wink of the eye, go back to their professorships with the thought, "my job, my salary, is safe for another year or two!" — when they know that no man can reconcile Evolution with the ten-times-repeated statement of Genesis that every thing brought forth "after his kind" and the Saviour endorsing Genesis as the word of God, and His Deity.

Take another example of the effects of Evolution upon students, that comes from a great denominational university:

"I really believe that God sent us up here (the writer was attending a meeting away from the University), because I needed Mr. ——'s preaching more than anything else in the world. I have been taught such terrible things in that Bible class at —— University that I was really unsettled on some things. It was taught so subtly and in such a way as to make you think that it was all to the glory of Christ, when it was not at all.

"Mr. —— has straightened me out on a good many things, and I am not going back into that Bible class. I am just going to tell the Dean that if he can't give me something to take the place of the Bible, I do not have to have my degree and can go ahead and take what I want to. But you will never know how thankful I am that I went up to ——. It absolutely saved me, because in another term of that stuff I'd be gone world without end, and no one knows it better than I do. You all can never know what I was up against. Mr. —— (professor) would sit their [*sic*] and pick out contradiction after contradiction and give the very references so we could see the faults, errors, and contradictions right before our eyes. I was not afraid to stick to what I believed, but when he stuck those things before me and asked how I could believe that the Bible was literally inspired, when I could see for myself the errors, I just did not know what to think. He told us that we could blindly go on believing the Bible was absolutely infallible and just shut our eyes to the errors, or else we could face things as they stand and have a religion that can stand all tests. With it all he was so earnest and sincere and seemed to be such a true, consecrated Christian, that he had me up in the air. I was just about gone, and Mr. —— saved me. Mr. —— gave me absolute proof of some things that Mr. —— (the professor) hooted at and said were impossible. Oh, mother and daddy, for goodness sake, don't send the boys to —— University. I was conceited enough to think that it wouldn't hurt me, and that I could sit through that stuff and come out unharmed, but oh, what a fool I was. As it is, it will take me some time to get over it. But please, oh, please, don't send the boys there. They can't stand it any more than I can. You get the same teaching in sociology, in history, in psychology, and in biology. Everything is teeming with it, and it is so subtle you can hardly detect it. I think I am all right now, and on the right road again. But if I find myself slipping like I did this last term I'm just going to quit! It's too dangerous to fool with things like this.

"Now, I know this has worried you, but don't let it too much. Only, *don't send the boys there to* —— *University*. I think I'll be able to steer clear this term. But if I don't, I'm going to quit, because, I'll tell you, I *was almost gone*. It makes me tremble now to think of how far I had gone and thinking all the time that it was Christ leading me, when it was the *devil*."

If it is this bad in a denominational school, what will it be in tax-supported schools?

The brilliant Editor of the great daily, *The Commercial Appeal* of Memphis, Tenn., says in an Editorial, "*We have found but a single young person who has returned from college in the last decade who was not an outspoken disciple of Darwin and from the discretion with which he spoke, we have grave doubts about him.*"

The President of one of our largest State Universities said, in a printed speech as quoted by Mr. [William Jennings] Bryan, "If you cannot reconcile religion with the things taught in biology, in psychology, or in other branches of study in this university, you should throw your religion away. Scientific truth is here to stay." And alas! many of them will "throw your religion away," and you are paying the taxes to have it done. . . .

Several brilliant young Baptist preachers, taught Evolution in High School and College, have recently gone into the Unitarian ministry, because they could not, as honest men, believe in Evolution and at the same time believe in the Deity of the Saviour, and hence in real redemption through his dying for our sins.

A lot more of Baptist, Episcopalian, Congregationalist, Methodist, Presbyterian, and other preachers ought to go into the Unitarian ministry — but they cannot get as good salaries as they can by masquerading in the pulpits of these Christian pulpits.

We have known quite a number of young people who have been turned into infidels or semi-infidels through the teaching of Evolution in our colleges and universities.—*The Presbyterian*, January 11, 1923

A large percentage of the boys and girls who go from Sunday School and church to college, never return to religious work. Mr. Bryan says sometimes as high as 75 percent.

Yet, fathers and mothers pay the taxes that pay the salaries of these professors to doom and damn eternally their own children, when every one of these professors can be driven from every tax-supported school, from primary to University, if the fathers and mothers will only arouse themselves and do their duty.

As another example of what is being done, read the following personal letter to a friend of mine:

May 8, 1921

"Dear Sir:
"I was the son of a Christian mother; went to college, was taught by infidel teachers, studied Evolution, New Thought, under men like ——, traveled extensively, came

home, insulted my old mother; went the primrose route, and today I am a mental, spiritual, and physical wreck. My soul is a starving skeleton; my heart a petrified rock; my mind
is poisoned and as fickle as the wind, and my faith as unstable as water. I broke the heart
of my mother, disappointed my friends, stood before my class on graduation day, delivered
the valedictory address, lauded "Darwin's Theory" to the skies, and other things I can never
recall. I have run the gauntlet, I am at the end of the rope. Oh, wretched man that I am.
There is no rest, happiness, or peace for me. I sometimes think I will jump overboard and
end it all. I wish I had never seen a college; I hope you will warn the young men of the im-
pending danger just ahead of them. I may be beyond hope, but on this glorious Mother's
Day, I wish to testify that Mother was right, and yearn for her Saviour, Jesus Christ, to be
mine. And I call upon you and your great church, who I learn, still believe in the old Bible,
and the power of prayer to save, to pray that I may be saved under the blood of Christ and
reunited with Mother in the Heavenly Kingdom.

(Signed) "A Mother's Son."

That touching tragedy of a blighted doomed soul!

The insidious, blighting curse is upon us; and our children, by wholesale, are
being swept away from God, from God's word, from the Redeemer and Saviour,
out into outer darkness, to eternal doom, and we are consenting to it, and paying
for it with our taxes.

The Only Hope

What can be done? Where is our hope? The pussyfooting apologies for the
Evolutionists will say "Don't do anything drastic. Educate the people, and the
thing will right itself." Educate the people? How can we, when Evolutionists have
us by the throat? When they have, while we were asleep, captured our tax-
supported schools from primary to University, and many of our denominational
colleges? "The Philistines be upon thee Samson!" But alas! We have been asleep
upon the lap of this Delilah and have been shorn of our strength — they have captured our schools. But "O Lord God, remember me, I pray thee, and strengthen
me, I pray thee, strengthen me only this once, O God." "And Samson took hold
of the two middle pillars upon which the house stood, and on which it was borne
up." So could we. "And he bowed himself with all his might." So can we. And the
strength of God who "created man in his own image" will come into us, and we
will slay these Philistines, the greatest curse that has come upon man since God
created him in His own image. What is a war, what is an epidemic that sweeps
people away by the hundred thousand, compared to this scourge that under the
guise of "science," when it is not science, at all, is sweeping our sons and daughters away from God, away from God's word, taking from them their Redeemer and
Saviour, to spend eternity in hell?

The two pillars are:

First, the local Board of Trustees of every public school. They are absolutely
sovereign. Even the Governor of the State, even the President of the United
States, cannot force any teacher upon any public school. It is in the hands of the

local Board of Trustees. Let the fathers and mothers see that only men and women shall be put on Boards of Trustees who will protect our children from this scourge, this "scholastic paganism." It can be done in two ways: — first, employ no teacher who believes in Evolution; second, obligate every teacher to post himself and expose the claims of Evolution every time it comes up in the text books that are being used, for many of them are poisoned with it. This can be easily done. . . .

Second, elect to the legislatures men who will cut off all support from all tax-supported schools where Evolution is taught, and require that in all tax-supported schools only teachers shall be employed who will post themselves and combat this terrible curse every time it comes up in the text books being used. Too drastic? Do you fight a scourge of small-pox with halfway measures? A scourge of small pox and yellow fever combined would be slight, as a curse, compared to this scourge that is sweeping our young men and women, boys and girls, away from God, away from God's word, away from the Redeemer-Saviour and into hell for eternity. . . .

27. The Scopes Trial

OUTLOOK
"Evolution in Tennessee"
1925

Outlook, a well-known magazine with liberal leanings and a large, mostly northern readership, was one of several national publications that covered the Scopes trial. Its account here focuses, as did many others, on the conflict between Clarence Darrow and William Jennings Bryan. The magazine's sympathies, it is clear, were with Darrow and John Scopes.

As the Scopes trial approached the verdict of guilty last week it became evident that both sides were trying the case chiefly in the newspapers.

Mr. Bryan, most conspicuous of the counsel for the prosecution of the school-teacher accused of teaching evolution contrary to law, had already argued his side of the question in public speeches outside of the court-room. He has not conducted himself with any too scrupulous regard for the proprieties. A lawyer in any case who makes public speeches about the matter at issue while his case is before the court injures the judicial system; for he makes it more difficult for that system

Outlook 140 (29 July 1925), 443–44.

to operate without bias and apart from the pressure of public passion and prejudice. Mr. Darrow, most conspicuous of the counsel for the defense, has . . . made it clear that he does not expect the real issue to be decided in Dayton, Tennessee, that he hopes by means of the publicity which the newspapers have given the case to educate the country in what he believes to be the truth of science. The effort on each side has been to make this a controversy between science and Fundamentalist theology.

The effort of Mr. Darrow to introduce the testimony of scientists as to the nature of evolution was frustrated by the ruling of the Judge. The law forbids any teacher in the public schools of the State "to teach any theory that denies the story of divine creation as taught in the Bible, and to teach instead that man has descended from a lower order of animals." Mr. Darrow sought to show by his expert witnesses that the conclusions of science concerning evolution were not inconsistent with a belief in the divine theory of creation. The Judge ruled, however, that the law specifically forbade the teaching of the theory of the animal descent of man, and that there was no need for expert testimony about evolution. The whole spirit of the case is indicated by the wholly unnecessary dictum of the Judge in his ruling that "evolutionists should at least show man the consideration to substitute the word 'ascend' for the word 'descend.' " It was in the arguments following this ruling that Mr. Darrow made remarks which later led the Judge to cite Mr. Darrow for contempt. After an apology Mr. Darrow was forgiven. Though the testimony on evolution was excluded, affidavits for possible use on appeal were admitted from various scientists giving the substance of the theory of evolution and in some instances reconciling the evolutionary theory with religious belief.

In the meantime the real question at issue, whether a legislature has the right by criminal statute to bar the free study of science from the schools, seems to have been totally forgotten.

Of all the extraordinary things in this extraordinary trial, not the least extraordinary was the calling of Mr. Bryan to the witness stand.

Though Mr. Bryan is of the counsel for the prosecution, Mr. Darrow called him as a witness for the defense. Mr. Darrow's purpose in this was to show that Mr. Bryan as an arch-Fundamentalist did not himself believe everything in the Bible literally. Instead, however, of treating Mr. Bryan as his own witness, Mr. Darrow proceeded to subject him to what amounted to cross-examination. Unjustifiable as the course of Mr. Darrow was (shown by the fact that the whole testimony was later expunged from the record), the result was a revelation of Mr. Bryan's mind. The following excerpts from the examination are merely illustrative:

Question: The Bible says Joshua commanded the sun to stand still for the purpose of lengthening the day, doesn't it, and you believe it?

Answer: I do.

Q: Do you believe at that time the entire sun went around the earth?

A: No, I believe that the earth goes around the sun.

Q: Do you believe that the men who wrote it thought that the day could be lengthened or that the sun could be stopped?

A: I don't know what they thought.

Q: You don't know?

A: I think they wrote the fact without expressing their thoughts.

Q: When was that flood?

A: I would not attempt to fix the date. The date is fixed, as suggested this morning.

Q: About 4004 B.C.?

A: That has been the estimate. I would not say it is accurate.

Q: What do you think?

A: I do not think about things that I don't think about.

Q: Do you think about things that you do think about?

A: Well, sometimes.

Q: You believe that all the various human races on the earth have come into being in the last four thousand years or four thousand two hundred years, whatever it is?

A: No. It would be more than that. . . . The flood is 2300 and something, and creation, according to the estimate there, is further back than that. . . . That is the date [referring to the Bible] given here on the first page, according to Bishop Usher, which I say I accept only because I have no reason to doubt it.

What Mr. Bryan was referring to was the list of dates prepared by Archbishop Usher (or Ussher), the Anglican Primate of Ireland who lived in the late sixteenth and early seventeenth centuries. That list of dates is described by the Encyclopaedia Britannica as "a now disproved scheme of Biblical chronology, whose dates were inserted by some unknown authority in the margin of reference editions of the Authorized Version."

Apparently Mr. Bryan has not heard of any discoveries in geology, or biology, or history, or archaeology, since 1656; otherwise, he could have hardly regarded Archbishop Usher as a final authority. It has sometimes been wondered what a person, say, of the Elizabethan period would think if suddenly brought to life and put into the midst of our twentieth-century civilization. We do not have to surmise. We have Mr. Bryan.

28. Surveying the Scene

JOHN PORTER FORT
"Behind the Scenes in Tennessee"
1925

The Scopes trial was also covered in another national journal, the Forum, *which dispatched John Porter Fort to report on it. Here Fort describes the origins of the case and how the young high-school instructor came to challenge the law, but he also attempts to provide outside audiences a social portrait of eastern Tennessee—and the social context that produced the trial.*

─────────────

Breakfast at the "Hotel Aqua" in Dayton, Tennessee, has apparently very little to do with the cause of the Fundamentalists and Modernists. Even bitter partisans must, however, sometimes cease from argument, must sometimes eat. Moreover all things must have a beginning, so let us commence with breakfast at the Aqua. (Perhaps this curious name for a hotel was earned when Tennessee first went dry, for Daytonians are both "liquor-fearing" and "God-fearing.") But *"allons a nos moutons."*[1]

Breakfast at the Aqua is no paltry affair; one is confronted with a mighty army of small dishes bearing all varieties of food that tempt man as a matutinal stimulant. It being impossible to consume everything, the obvious purpose of the array is to allow the hungry mortal to take a small bit here and there. And here, at the very threshold of the morning, the surrounding dishes are as the theories of God in His relationship to man that confront one on his entrance into this world. There is a chance for a taste of this or that, some men choosing only one and thereby acquiring indigestion and stubborness. Perhaps it is better to dine lightly from them all, — one has a better knowledge of the nature of all men's breakfasts.

On the wall of the Aqua's dining-room there are some oil paintings in brilliant blue. It is impossible to describe them with justice; the general effect is as if some stranded sign painter had done them for his unpaid bill. His only can of paint was of the one vivid color; though there is an occasional dab of red and green, like an afterthought. There on the walls of the Aqua they will cause many a sensitive soul to writhe until some day they may become priceless examples of early American art. As in arguments about God and His handiwork, a great deal depends upon the point of view of the immediate generation; so the expression of the painter's ideal was determined by the availability of his color.

─────────────

[1]*allons . . . moutons:* French for "let's return to the subject."

Forum 74 (August 1925), 258–65.

Breakfast being over, one wanders to the entrance of the Aqua fronting on the main street of Dayton. It is no different from any other "Main Street" except that immediately opposite the little hotel, there is the place of business of Dayton's "man-biting barber." In person the "man-biting barber" is to all appearances mild and not entitled to his name. It is a matter of local history, however, that in a public mass meeting, held in May in Dayton, this barber had "bitten" an argumentative opponent. How this happened is also a matter of history. A certain Mr. Rappleyea, an ardent modernist and believer in evolution, had, at the mass meeting in question, stated openly that he subscribed to the theory commonly attributed to Darwin. It was too much for the "man-biting barber." "You cannot say that my family came from monkeys," he said, and bit Mr. Rappleyea. Since that time, he has been known as the "man-biting barber."

Still considering the Modernists and the Fundamentalists, only indirectly, as they should be considered, one raises his eyes above the barber shop and there are the hills. Blue hills! Yes, in a sense Fundamental hills, not Modernist hills. Seeing them, one recalls the line of the Psalmist, "I will lift mine eyes unto the hills from whence cometh my help." "The strength of the hills is His also — and His hands formed the dry land." Encompassing Dayton are the hills, looking down on the little east Tennessee town with its courthouse, its "man-biting barber," and its argument about young Professor Thomas Scopes, on trial by a jury of his peers for teaching that God made man by slow stages instead of making him all at once in the likeness of His own image. Great rugged masses of sandstone and limestone covered with a thin carpet of trees are the background of Dayton, — inaccessible places difficult to conquer. Within five miles of its little courthouse, the wild turkeys strut in the spring-time. A few homesteaders carry their provisions up the steep mountain sides, and insist that they still have the right to make whiskey out of their corn in spite of the government's edict. The hills are the background of Dayton and its men are hill men, "southern mountaineers," they call them. One could imagine that in time of stress all the storekeepers and the bankers and, yes, even the lawyers would shed their small-town clothes, go back into those hills, and that all the enemies in the world could not dislodge them.

But Dayton is not just now having a battle of its own, and the rifle is not "speaking" from behind the boulder. Dayton is a battle ground of words. The Modernists and the Fundamentalists are in Dayton arguing about God and evolution while the hills that His hands fashioned look down on William Jennings Bryan and Clarence Darrow, in wordy argument about whether man "descended from a lower order of animals, contrary to the general interpretation of the Bible, and contrary to the statutes of Tennessee, and the peace and dignity thereof." (Just at the junction of the sandstone and limestone of which the hills are mainly formed, there is a strata of "primitive earth," as the geologists term it. It ranges in thickness from a few inches to a number of feet and underlies their mighty areas. Exposed to the light, and dried, it crumbles to the finest dust. All that is left of five million infusoria, embraced in one cubic centimeter, are scattered with a puff of wind!)

It was in the spring of 1925 that a Tennessee legislator from a county even more remote in the heart of the mountains than Dayton, a county without a railroad, introduced a bill into the State general assembly which was decidedly embarrassing to a number of persons. The bill was one of those challenging documents that make things unpleasant for lawmakers. Its author, J. W. Butler,[2] had never seen a railroad until he was twenty-one. It has since become widely known as the "Tennessee Anti-Evolution Bill." The intent of that legislative document was to the effect that from and after its passage, no teacher in any State school or university might expound the theory of evolution without being amenable to the Tennessee courts. Tennessee had a governor not averse to listening to what his constituents back home wanted. Tennessee people were for a good part rural and there was no question about the majority adhering strictly to the exact and literal interpretation of the Bible, and lining up with the Fundamentalists. Individual legislators who opposed the bill on many grounds were hesitant about offending the church people. The bill passed. After that, it was all right to think about evolution and to believe in it if you chose but not to expound it as a teacher in a State school when you were receiving the State's pay cheque. Tennessee was hoping to ban from the minds of its younger generation the thought of Modernism, even as it had hoped to prohibit from their throats the love of alcohol, long before the Federal amendment.

Quite suddenly did a young man leap into prominence from the passage of that act, and his prominence dragged into the limelight with him the little east Tennessee town, the "man-biting barber," and Bryan and Darrow, already famous, holding on to his skirts, if one may say that of a man. Down to "Main Street" with him came the Modernists and the Fundamentalists with all their panoply of high-sounding words and thunderous arguments. But the manner of their coming was in a sense curious for it sprang from one of those little events that drag in its train a mighty army of results, as did the lack of a horseshoe nail in the old poem.

Four young men were gathered around a table in a drug store on the main street of Dayton, two young lawyers just fresh from law school, a chemist, and John Thomas Scopes, instructor of biology in the county high school. They discussed nothing particular except the state of the weather, the chances of going fishing, and then a smattering of politics. The chemist, George W. Rappleyea, made mention of the passage of the Anti-Evolution Bill. This chemist was unquestionably of the argumentative turn of mind, holding with a number of a like school that the best way to find God was in the laboratory of the biologist, and the open book of the geologist. Young John Thomas Scopes, just out of college, in the main agreed with him. "I don't see," he said, "how a man can teach the theories of biology from the State text books and escape bringing in a general discussion of the theory of evolution."

In that country drug store which sold the school children their books there was a copy of *A Civic Biology* which had been adopted by the State text book commission some years previous to the passage of the act under discussion. Thereupon it was secured from the shelves, and the four young men scanned its pages. It re-

[2]**J. W. Butler:** state house representative from eastern Tennessee.

vealed quickly enough that the author had the general theory of evolution in mind when he wrote it. There were many damning paragraphs in the volume.

Questioned by Mr. Rappleyea if he followed the text, the young professor readily agreed. "Well, then you are guilty of violating the law," said the chemist, "and you ought to be arrested and tried." The four heads then bent closely together, and it was agreed that on the morrow they would swear out a warrant for the arrest of Scopes, with the two young lawyers acting as counsel for Rappleyea, as prosecutor, and the teacher as defendant. After that, the pregnant little event began to bear its fruit for Scopes was arrested, tried by committing magistrates, and later indicted. The ponderous guns of the Fundamentalists and Modernists began to creak slowly on their carriages to lay a barrage down on Main Street. Bryan stepped early into the fray, being invited to take a hand by a Fundamentalist organization in Memphis. The American Civil Liberties Union saw that the issue involved was freedom of speech and offered its aid. Fundamentalists and Modernists, looking to their weapons cast about for mighty storehouses of ammunition. H. G. Wells,[3] because he wrote a book on history that everybody knew, was sought in London. It was said that he would appear in Dayton. He spoke once ponderously from far-off England, that he had never heard of Professor Scopes, or Dayton, Tennessee. He suggested that it must be some other Wells they were speaking about, then lapsed into silence.

Clarence Darrow and Dudley Field Malone[4] volunteered their services. "If a Florida real estate man can afford to get into that case," said Darrow, "I suppose I can," and he took a hitch in his celebrated suspenders. Preachers in their pulpits and the press of the world began to comment upon the issues involved. Bryan said that it was the greatest case in American jurisprudence, and heavy salvos of legal arguments were made ready.

In the meantime Dayton, with its eighteen hundred inhabitants, preened its feathers and was proud of its new publicity. The young professor was popular and well liked; a fund was raised for his protection. As for his teaching, — that was a different matter. It was said over and over again that he had taught that "man was descended from monkey," and such heresy had no place in Dayton. And so here enters the "barber" who resented quite feelingly this scurrilous reflection upon his ancestry, claiming that he denied with might and main that his family had been "monkeys." He did not "bite" the evolutionist speaker because of the one-celled animal, but chose the higher anthropoid relationship as being a blot upon his family scutcheon.

So to the courthouse, past the shop of the barber, there to hear Bryan and the other notables; a little courthouse surrounded with trees, Daytonians *en musse*, confirmed Fundamentalists, nearly all Baptists and Methodists, with a sprinkling of Holy Rollers; young Professor John Thomas Scopes almost forgotten with the

---

[3]**H. G. Wells:** the English writer Herbert George Wells, author of such well-known works as *The Time Machine* and *The War of the Worlds*. The reference could be to Wells's *The History of Mr. Polly*.
[4]**Dudley Field Malone:** an official with the American Civil Liberties Union.

great names and the greater issues shoving him in the background. The crowding in of publicity seekers; science and religion staging a battle ground on "Main Street," in front of the Fundamentalists and the visiting Modernists; politics playing its part, for your real Tennesseeans love their politics above all things except their religion; the grinding of cameras and the clicking of telegraph instruments.

It's something of a show, this evolution trial. The shy young instructor has tried to avoid publicity saying that he wanted to test out the constitutionality of the statute for the good of the other teachers of Tennessee. "If this law stands," he says, "how can the men and women of this State who teach the fundamentals of biology know how to guard against mentioning the theory of evolution on which it is based?" Gathered around him are his advisers, men to put words in his mouth; newspaper men seeking queer events to write humorous or sarcastic things about; the Daytonians and men from the hills, standing about in groups on the streets and in the courthouse corridors, talking in low voices, as if a little awed. Then there are the lawyers with their long-winded debates, constitutional questions, and endless words. There is even a political fight in the offing, with a defeated party candidate for the governor's chair seeking to make capital out of the case and ridiculing the executive who signed such a bill, which he insists throttles all freedom of speech and thought.

And how the men from the hills love the words of the lawyers! How in the winter nights, they will sit around their firesides and recreate every syllable and gesture! Rock-ribbed in their Fundamentalism, there is no chance of all the words in the world changing their mental viewpoint one jot or tittle. But they have preserved their primitive love of oratory and cherish it in memory. (Slow of speech and gesture, only now and then there flares up a man from the mountains with an incisive wit, gift for impassioned oratory, and more than all else, an insight into the nature of his fellow men.)

And back of it all, brooding in silence are the hills that "His hands made." They have witnessed the surge of the prehistoric sea and their foundations are made from the countless remains of its lost and vanished population of teeming life. They have watched the Indian and his campfires; the first bands of intrepid settlers; the growth of towns. They have heard all of humanity seek to find in different ways the God whose strength was also theirs. They have seen men fight against each other, and brother slay brother in the name of the same God. They have heard all the foolish arguments of the men who fostered schisms, laws, and man-made rituals. "With the ancient is wisdom, and length of days is understanding."

The Commonplace, the Comedy, and the Tragedy of the unfolding scroll play their unceasing daily drama below them. The sign painter daubs again at his pictures in blue; the "man-biting barber" goes back to his trade; the trial of young Professor John Thomas Scopes drags on through the courts with only the legal issue settled after a time. Men still argue over religion and still eat of many dishes at the breakfast table, swearing only by one or else tasting of many, — never able to digest them all. And yet one last line comes to memory: "Heaven and earth shall pass away," — beyond man and his petty arguments and blind prejudices, and beyond even the mountains the "undiscovered" will still remain.

29. Fundamentalism's Legacy

H. L. Mencken
Editorial
1925

During the 1920s, there was probably no more biting social critic than H. L. Mencken. Journalist and newspaper columnist for the Baltimore Sun, *Mencken turned his pen toward an assortment of myths and conventions that prevailed in middle-brow America, and he became among the best known of the "debunkers," writers and thinkers who attacked the prudish, narrow-minded, and provincial attitudes they believed prevailed in American life. A favorite target for Mencken was the South, which he described to his readers as a cultural wasteland, what he once called a "Sahara of the Bozarts." Mencken was on hand for the Scopes trial, and in his dispatches to the* Sun *he referred to the people of Dayton as "peasants," "hillbillies," and "morons," terms he saw as generally applicable to the mass of the American people. In this piece, written for the* American Mercury *after the trial's conclusion, Mencken discusses the ultimate consequences of the Scopes trial.*

[I]

Has it been marked by historians that the late William Jennings Bryan's last secular act on this earth was to catch flies? A curious detail, and not without its sardonic overtones. He was the most sedulous flycatcher in American history, and by long odds the most successful. His quarry, of course, was not *Musca domestica* but *Homo neandertalensis*. For forty years he tracked it with snare and blunderbuss, up and down the backways of the Republic. Wherever the flambeaux of Chautauqua smoked and guttered, and the bilge of Idealism ran in the veins, and Baptist pastors dammed the brooks with the saved, and men gathered who were weary and heavy laden, and their wives who were unyieldingly multiparous . . . — there the indefatigable Jennings set up his traps and spread his bait. He knew every forlorn country town in the South and West, and he could crowd the most remote of them to suffocation by simply winding his horn. The city proletariat, transiently flustered by him in 1896, quickly penetrated his buncombe[1] and would have no more of him; the gallery jeered him at every Democratic national convention for twenty-five years. But out where the grass grows high, and the horned cattle dream away the lazy days, and men still fear the powers and principalities of the air — out there between the corn-rows he held his old puissance[2] to the end.

[1]**buncombe:** nonsense.
[2]**puissance:** strength, power.

American Mercury 6 (October 1925), 158–60.

There was no need of beaters to drive in his game. The news that he was coming was enough. For miles the flivver[3] dust would choke the roads. And when he rose at the end of the day to discharge his Message there would be such breathless attention, such a rapt and enchanted ecstasy, such a sweet rustle of amens as the world had not known since Johanan fell to Herod's headsman.

There was something peculiarly fitting in the fact that his last days were spent in a one-horse Tennessee village, and that death found him there. The man felt at home in such scenes. He liked people who sweated freely, and were not debauched by the refinements of the toilet. Making his progress up and down the Main street of little Dayton, surrounded by gaping primates from the upland valleys of the Cumberland Range, his coat laid aside, his bare arms and hairy chest shining damply, his bald head sprinkled with dust — so accoutred and on display he was obviously happy. He liked getting up early in the morning, to the tune of cocks crowing on the dunghill. He liked the heavy, greasy victuals of the farmhouse kitchen. He liked country lawyers, country pastors, all country people. I believe that this liking was sincere — perhaps the only sincere thing in the man. His nose showed no uneasiness when a hillman in faded overalls and hickory shirt accosted him on the street, and besought him for light upon some mystery of Holy Writ. The simian gabble of a country town was not gabble to him, but wisdom of an occult and superior sort. In the presence of city folks he was palpably uneasy. Their clothes, I suspect, annoyed him, and he was suspicious of their too delicate manners. He knew all the while that they were laughing at him — if not at his baroque theology, then at least at his alpaca pantaloons. But the yokels never laughed at him. To them he was not the huntsman but the prophet, and toward the end, as he gradually forsook mundane politics for purely ghostly concerns, they began to elevate him in their hierarchy. When he died he was the peer of Abraham. Another curious detail: his old enemy, Wilson, aspiring to the same white and shining robe, came down with a thump. But Bryan made the grade. His place in the Tennessee hagiocracy is secure. If the village barber saved any of his hair, then it is curing gall-stones down there today.

II

But what label will he bear in more urbane regions? One, I fear, of a far less flattering kind. Bryan lived too long, and descended too deeply into the mud, to be taken seriously hereafter by fully literate men, even of the kind who write school-books. There was a scattering of sweet words in his funeral notices, but it was no more than a response to conventional sentimentality. The best verdict the most romantic editorial writer could dredge up, save in the eloquent South, was to the general effect that his imbecilities were excused by his earnestness — that under his clowning, as under that of the juggler of Notre Dame, there was the zeal of a steadfast soul. But this was apology, not praise; precisely the same thing might

---

[3]**flivver:** a small, cheap, old automobile.

be said of Mary Baker G. Eddy,[4] the late Czar Nicholas,[5] or Czolgosz.[6] The truth is that even Bryan's sincerity will probably yield to what is called, in other fields, definitive criticism. Was he sincere when he opposed imperialism in the Philippines, or when he fed it with deserving Democrats in Santo Domingo? Was he sincere when he tried to shove the Prohibitionists under the table, or when he seized their banner and began to lead them with loud whoops? Was he sincere when he bellowed against war, or when he dreamed of himself as a tin-soldier in uniform, with a grave reserved among the generals? Was he sincere when he denounced the late John W. Davis,[7] or when he swallowed Davis? Was he sincere when he fawned over Champ Clark,[8] or when he betrayed Clark? . . .

This talk of sincerity, I confess, fatigues me. If the fellow was sincere, then so was P. T. Barnum. The word is disgraced and degraded by such uses. He was, in fact, a charlatan, a mountebank, a zany without shame or dignity. What animated him from end to end of his grotesque career was simply ambition — the ambition of a common man to get his hand upon the collar of his superiors, or, failing that, to get his thumb into their eyes. He was born with a roaring voice, and it had the trick of inflaming half-wits. His whole career was devoted to raising these half-wits against their betters, that he himself might shine. His last battle will be grossly misunderstood if it is thought of as a mere exercise in fanaticism — that is, if Bryan the Fundamentalist Pope is mistaken for one of the bucolic Fundamentalists. There was much more in it than that, as everyone knows who saw him on the field. What moved him, at bottom, was simply hatred of the city men who had laughed at him so long, and brought him at last to so tatterdemalion an estate. He lusted for revenge upon them. He yearned to lead the anthropoid rabble against them, to set *Homo neandertalensis* upon them, to punish them for the execution they had done upon him by attacking the very vitals of their civilization. He went far beyond the bounds of any merely religious frenzy, however inordinate. When he began denouncing the notion that man is a mammal even some of the hinds at Dayton were agape. And when, brought upon Darrow's cruel hook, he writhed and tossed in a very fury of malignancy, bawling against the baldest elements of sense and decency like a man frantic — when he came to that tragic climax there were snickers among the hinds as well as hosannas.

Upon that hook, in truth, Bryan committed suicide, as a legend as well as in the body. He staggered from the rustic court ready to die, and he staggered from it ready to be forgotten, save as a character in a third-rate farce, witless and in execrable taste. The chances are that history will put the peak of democracy in his time; it has been on the downward curve among us since the campaign of 1896.[9]

---

[4]**Mary Baker G. Eddy:** Massachusetts transcendentalist thinker and founder of Christian Science.
[5]**Czar Nicholas:** the last ruler of the Russian Empire.
[6]**Czolgosz:** Leon Czolgosz, the anarchist who in 1901 assassinated President William McKinley.
[7]**John W. Davis:** prominent lawyer and Democratic presidential candidate in 1924.
[8]**Champ Clark:** James "Champ" Clark, longtime Democratic Party leader and Speaker of the House of Representatives.
[9]In the campaign of 1896, Bryan ran as the Democratic and Populist candidate for the presidency. He was defeated by William McKinley, the Republican candidate.

He will be remembered, perhaps, as its supreme impostor, the *reductio ad absurdum* of its pretension. Bryan came very near being President of the United States. In 1896, it is possible, he was actually elected. He lived long enough to make patriots thank the inscrutable gods for Harding, even for Coolidge. Dullness has got into the White House, and the smell of cabbage boiling, but there is at least nothing to compare to the intolerable buffoonery that went on in Tennessee. The President of the United States doesn't believe that the earth is square, and that witches should be put to death, and that Jonah swallowed the whale. The Golden Text is not painted weekly on the White House wall, and there is no need to keep ambassadors waiting while Pastor Simpson, of Smithsville, prays for rain in the Blue Room. We have escaped something — by a narrow margin, but still safely.

III

That is, so far. The Fundamentalists continue at the wake, and sense gets a sort of reprieve. The legislature of Georgia, so the news comes, has shelved the anti-evolution bill, and turns its back upon the legislature of Tennessee. Elsewhere minorities prepare for battle — here and there with some assurance of success. But it is too early, it seems to me, to send the firemen home; the fire is still burning on many a far-flung hill, and it may begin to roar again at any moment. The evil that men do lives after them. Bryan, in his malice, started something that it will not be easy to stop. In ten thousand country towns his old heelers, the evangelical pastors, are propagating his gospel, and everywhere the yokels are ready for it. When he disappeared from the big cities, the big cities made the capital error of assuming that he was done for. If they heard of him at all, it was only as a crimp for real-estate speculators — the heroic foe of the unearned increment hauling it in with both hands. He seemed preposterous, and hence harmless. But all the while he was busy among his old lieges. . . . He did the job competently. He had vast skill at such enterprises. Heave an egg out of a Pullman window, and you will hit a Fundamentalist almost anywhere in the United States today. They swarm in the country towns, inflamed by their pastors, and with a saint, now, to venerate. They are thick in the mean streets behind the gas-works. They are everywhere that learning is too heavy a burden for mortal minds, even the vague, pathetic learning on tap in little red schoolhouses. They march with the Klan, with the Christian Endeavor Society, with the Junior Order of United American Mechanics, with the Epworth League, with all the rococo bands that poor and unhappy folk organize to bring some light of purpose into their lives. They have had a thrill, and they are ready for more.

Such is Bryan's legacy to his country. He couldn't be President, but he could at least help magnificently in the solemn business of shutting off the presidency from every intelligent and self-respecting man. The storm, perhaps, won't last long, as time goes in history. It may help, indeed, to break up the democratic delusion, now already showing weakness, and so hasten its own end. But while it lasts it will blow off some roofs and flood some sanctuaries.

Suggestions for Further Reading

Furniss, Norman F. *The Fundamentalist Controversy, 1918–1931.* New Haven: Yale University Press, 1954. Reprint, Hamden, Conn.: Archon Books, 1963.

Gatewood, Willard B. *Preachers, Pedagogues & Politicians: The Evolution Controversy in North Carolina, 1920–1927.* Chapel Hill: University of North Carolina Press, 1966.

Ginger, Ray. *Six Days or Forever?: Tennessee v. John Thomas Scopes.* New York: Oxford University Press, 1974.

Larson, Edward J. *Summer for the Gods: The Scopes Trial and America's Continuing Debate over Science and Religion.* New York: BasicBooks, 1997.

Marsden, George M. *Fundamentalism and American Culture: The Shaping of Twentieth Century Evangelicalism, 1870–1925.* New York: Oxford University Press, 1980.

CHAPTER NINE

THE GREAT DEPRESSION

The New Deal
and the New South

I n the 1930s, Americans faced the most serious economic catastrophe in their history. The stock market crash of October 1929 began a severe recession, and the collapse of international exchange in 1931 accelerated the tailspin of the economy. The financial crisis resulted in low prices and incomes for farmers, high unemployment for industrial workers, and the threat of foreclosure on thousands of homes, farms, and businesses. By 1932, the American economy was deep in depression, and Franklin D. Roosevelt was elected with the promise of providing a "New Deal" to the nation.

The New Deal transformed the nature of government—especially at the federal level. Federal agencies combated unemployment, regulated industry, rebuilt the banking system, and revived agriculture. New Deal programs experimented with unheard-of forms of governmental intervention, such as the Tennessee Valley Authority's efforts to enhance economic development through inexpensive hydroelectric power.

The largest programs were very diverse. Some, such as the Agricultural Adjustment Administration (AAA) and the National Recovery Administration (NRA), worked cooperatively with farmers and manufacturers to resuscitate the economy; others were experimental and freewheeling. The massive Works Progress Administration (WPA), created in 1935, eventually spent some $11.4 billion—in its day, an extraordinary amount—to employ scores of jobless, not only in traditional public-works projects, such as building and maintaining roads, bridges, airports, schools, and hospitals, but also as musicians, actors, artists, and historians.

As a political mechanism to confront the Great Depression, the New Deal had both supporters and detractors. Most Americans probably believed that the Roosevelt administration succeeded in limiting the adverse effects of the depression, and most retained their basic faith in democratic institutions. But others were less sanguine about the ability of the New Deal to end the nation's economic problems. Radical alternatives developed.

The depression provided an excellent opportunity for the Communist Party of America to make inroads. Their impact was limited because of their generally rigid adherence to the Soviet Union and their absolute loyalty to Soviet dictator Joseph Stalin, but they played an important role in shaping American response to the crisis. At the depth of the depression in 1932, the party had only 12,000 members. But in that year, the Communist presidential candidate, William Z. Foster, attracted 103,000 votes—a significant political presence, even if the party never succeeded in winning an election.

An especially important area of activity for Communists was the South. The region's poverty and tradition of racial oppression presented an opportunity to demonstrate the injustices of American capitalism. In the late 1920s, Communists began to organize workers in Gastonia, North Carolina, where in 1929 a major strike they led against a large textile mill ended in violence. In 1931 they led striking miners in eastern Kentucky's Harlan County and were active throughout the decade in organizing labor and in creating political coalitions with progressive southern groups.

Meanwhile, Communists became the most forthright champions on a national level of the civil rights of African Americans. When nine young blacks—the so-called Scottsboro Boys—were charged with the rape of two white women on an Alabama freight train, the International Labor Defense (ILD), a legal defense group with ties to the Communist Party, took up their cause and transformed the trial into a larger indictment of Jim Crow segregation and southern racism. The ILD also took part in the case of Angelo Herndon, an African American Communist who was convicted of insurrection in 1932 after he helped organize a march of the unemployed in Atlanta.

One of the most potent challenges to the New Deal's success came from the Populist Huey P. Long, who hailed from the Piney Woods region of northern Louisiana. He constructed a political machine in the 1920s that was based on the long-standing grievances poor people held against the state's economic elite. Addressing the needs of workers, farmers, and ordinary people, Long was elected governor in 1928 and went on to run the state government with an iron hand. Under his governorship, Louisiana built schools, hospitals, and roads. Wildly popular among ordinary folk, he was elected to the U.S. Senate in 1930 and from Washington continued to dominate state politics. Although Long was originally a strong supporter of Franklin Roosevelt, he soon drifted away from the New Deal, which he believed did not go far enough. Later Long became a serious challenger to Roosevelt's leadership of the Democratic Party.

The documents in this chapter examine different dimensions of the New Deal's impact. Two southern critics of "politics as usual" were Angelo Herndon and Huey Long. Herndon explains how he became a Communist and why he saw the party as the best means to achieve civil rights for African Americans. Huey Long describes the Share Our Wealth program and how it would redistribute income from rich to poor. And Odette Keun, writing from the point of view of European socialism, provides a defense of the New Deal in general, and the TVA in particular, as viable alternatives to the extremes of the fascist right and the Communist left.

As you read, note the differences in the way each of the authors regards the New Deal. What do they see as its most successful and unsuccessful elements? To what extent have Angelo Herndon and Huey Long lost faith in the ability of democratic institutions to solve the Great Depression and its problems? Why does Odette Keun have more faith in those institutions?

30. The Appeal of the Communist Party

ANGELO HERNDON
From You Cannot Kill the Working Class
c. 1934

One of the better-known black Communists of the 1930s was Eugene Angelo Herndon, who was born on May 6, 1913, in Wyoming, Ohio, a mining community near Cincinnati. At a young age, Angelo—like his father, Paul Herndon—worked as a coal miner in eastern Kentucky. In the late 1920s, he moved to Birmingham to seek better labor conditions in Alabama coal mines. In June 1930, aggrieved at adverse working conditions and racism against black workers, Herndon attended a Communist rally. There he heard, for the first time in his life, white leaders denouncing segregation and Jim Crow. By late 1930 Herndon had become a Communist activist among Birmingham's black workers, and in 1931 he joined the ILD's campaign to publicize the case of the Scottsboro Boys. Sometime in late 1931 or early 1932, be-

Angelo Herndon, *You Cannot Kill the Working Class* (New York, [1934?]). Reprinted in *Afro-American History: Primary Sources*, ed. Thomas R. Frazier (New York: Harcourt, Brace & World, 1970), 303, 307–18.

cause of local hostility and harassment, Herndon moved to Atlanta to organize Un-employed Councils, groups affiliated with the Communist Party, and immediately plunged himself into activism in that city.

On July 11, 1932, Atlanta police arrested Herndon. He was subsequently tried for violating an antebellum Georgia law prohibiting "insurrection," convicted, and sentenced to eighteen to twenty years in prison. The Herndon case became a cause célèbre around the country, and in 1937 the Supreme Court overturned his conviction. The following account describes Herndon's conversion to Communism, his activities as an organizer, and his confrontation with the Atlanta authorities.

My great-grandmother was ever such a tiny girl when some white plantation owners rode up to the Big House and arranged to carry her off. They bargained for a bit and then came down to the Negro quarters and grabbed her away from her mother. They could do that because my great-grandmother's folks were slaves in Virginia.

My great-grandmother lived to be very old. She often told me about those times.

There is one story of hers that keeps coming back to me. She was still a young girl, and mighty pretty, and some rich young white men decided they wanted her. She resisted, so they threw her down on the floor of the barn, and tied her up with ropes, and beat her until the blood ran. Then they sent to the house for pepper and salt to rub in the wounds.

Her daughter—my grandmother—couldn't remember much about slave days. While she was still a child, the Civil War was fought out and chattel-slavery was ended. One childhood scene, though, was scarred on her mind. It was during the Civil War. Some white men burst into her cabin. They seized her sister and strung her to a tree, and riddled her body with bullets. My grandmother herself stayed hidden, and managed to get away alive.

I remember these stories, not because they were so different from life in my own day, but for the opposite reason. They were exactly like some of the things that happened to me when I went South.

My father, Paul Herndon, and my mother, Hattie Herndon, lived for many years in Birmingham, and then came North. They settled down in Wyoming, Ohio, a little steel and mining town just outside of Cincinnati. . . .

I Begin to Question

The Jim-Crow system was in full force in the mines of the Tennessee Coal and Iron Company, and all over Birmingham. It had always burnt me up, but I didn't know how to set about fighting it. My parents and grandparents were hard-boiled Republicans, and told me very often that Lincoln had freed the slaves, and that we'd have to look to the Republican Party for everything good. I began to wonder about that. Here I was, being Jim-Crowed and cheated. Every couple of weeks

I read about a lynching somewhere in the South. Yet there sat a Republican government up in Washington, and they weren't doing a thing about it.

My people told me to have faith in God, and he would make everything come right. I read a lot of religious tracts, but I got so I didn't believe them. I figured that there was no use for a Negro to go to heaven, because if he went there it would only be to shine some white man's shoes.

I wish I could remember the exact date when I first attended a meeting of the Unemployment Council, and met up with a couple of members of the Communist Party. That date means a lot more to me than my birthday, or any other day in my life.

The workers in the South, mostly deprived of reading-matter, have developed a wonderful grapevine system for transmitting news. It was over this grapevine that we first heard that there were "reds" in town.

The foremen—when they talked about it—and the newspapers, and the big-shot Negroes in Birmingham, said that the "reds" were foreigners, and Yankees, and believed in killing people, and would get us in a lot of trouble. But out of all the talk I got a few ideas clear about the Reds. They believed in organizing and sticking together. They believed that we didn't have to have bosses on our backs. They believed that Negroes ought to have equal rights with whites. It all sounded O.K. to me. But I didn't meet any of the Reds for a long time.

I Find the Working-Class Movement

One day in June, 1930, walking home from work, I came across some handbills put out by the Unemployment Council in Birmingham. They said: "Would you rather fight—or starve?" They called on the workers to come to a mass meeting at 3 o'clock.

Somehow I never thought of missing that meeting. I said to myself over and over: "It's war! It's war! And I might as well get into it right now!" I got to the meeting while a white fellow was speaking. I didn't get everything he said, but this much hit me and stuck with me: that the workers could only get things by fighting for them, and that the Negro and white workers had to stick together to get results. The speaker described the conditions of the Negroes in Birmingham, and I kept saying to myself: "That's it." Then a Negro spoke from the same platform, and somehow I knew that this was what I'd been looking for all my life.

At the end of the meeting I went up and gave my name. From that day to this, every minute of my life has been tied up with the workers' movement.

I joined the Unemployment Council, and some weeks later the Communist Party. I read all the literature of the movement that I could get my hands on, and began to see my way more clearly.

I had some mighty funny ideas at first, but I guess that was only natural. For instance, I thought that we ought to start by getting all the big Negro leaders like DePriest and Du Bois and Walter White into the Communist Party, and then we would have all the support we needed. I didn't know then that DePriest and the rest of the leaders of that type are on the side of the bosses, and fight as hard as they can against the workers. They don't believe in fighting against the system that produces Jim-Crowism. They stand up for that system, and try to preserve it, and so they are really on the side of Jim-Crowism and inequality. I got rid of all these ideas after I heard Oscar Adams and others like him speak in Birmingham.

Misleaders in Action

That happened this way:

Birmingham had just put on a Community Chest drive. The whites gave and the Negroes gave. Some gave willingly, thinking it was really going to help feed the unemployed, and the rest had it taken out of their wages. There was mighty little relief handed out to the workers, even when they did get on the rolls. The Negroes only got about half what the whites got. Some of the workers waiting at the relief station made up a take-off on an old prison song. I remember that the first two lines of it went:

> I've counted the beans, babe,
> I've counted the greens. . . .

The Unemployment Council opened a fight for cash relief, and aid for single men, and equal relief for Negro and white. They called for a meeting in Capitol Park, and we gathered about the Confederate Monument, about five hundred of us, white and Negro, and then we marched on the Community Chest Headquarters. There were about one hundred cops there. The officials of the Community Chest spoke, and said that the best thing for the Negroes to do was to go back to the farms. They tried very hard to give the white workers there the idea that if the Negroes went back to the farms, the whites would get a lot more relief.

Of course our leaders pointed out that the small farmers and share-croppers and tenants on the cotton-lands around Birmingham were starving, and losing their land and stock, and hundreds were drifting into the city in hope of getting work.

Then Oscar Adams spoke up. He was the editor of the *Birmingham Reporter,* a Negro paper. What he said opened my eyes—but not in the way he expected. He said we shouldn't be misled by the leaders of the Unemployment Council, that we should go politely to the white bosses and officials and ask them for what they wanted, and do as they said.

Adams said: "We Negroes don't want social equality." I was furious. I said inside of myself: "Oscar Adams, we Negroes want social and every other kind of equality. There's no reason on God's green earth why we should be satisfied with anything less."

Traitors in the Ranks

That was the end of any ideas I had that the big-shots among the recognised Negro leaders would fight for us, or really put up any struggle for equal rights. I knew that Oscar Adams and the people like him were among our worst enemies, especially dangerous because they work from inside our ranks and a lot of us get the idea that they are with us and of us.

I look back over what I've written about those days since I picked up the leaflet of the Unemployment Council, and wonder if I've really said what I mean. I don't know if I can get across to you the feeling that came over me whenever I went to a meeting of the Council, or of the Communist Party, and heard their speakers and read their leaflets. All my life I'd been sweated and stepped on and Jim-Crowed. I lay on my belly in the mines for a few dollars a week, and saw my pay stolen and slashed, and my buddies killed. I lived in the worst section of town, and rode behind the "Colored" signs on streetcars, as though there was something disgusting about me. I heard myself called "nigger" and "darky," and I had to say "Yes, sir" to every white man, whether he had my respect or not.

I had always detested it, but I had never known that anything could be done about it. And here, all of a sudden, I had found organizations in which Negroes and whites sat together, and worked together, and knew no difference of race or color. Here were organizations that weren't scared to come out for equality for the Negro people, and for the rights of the workers. The Jim-Crow system, the wage-slave system, weren't everlasting after all! It was like all of a sudden turning a corner on a dirty, old street and finding yourself facing a broad, shining highway.

The bosses, and the Negro misleaders like Oscar Adams, told us that these Reds were "foreigners" and "strangers" and that the Communist program wasn't acceptable to the workers in the South. I couldn't see that at all. The leaders of the Communist Party and the Unemployment Council seemed people very much like the ones I'd always been used to. They were workers, and they talked our language. Their talk sure sounded better to me than the talk of Oscar Adams, or the President of the Tennessee Coal, Iron and Railroad Co. who addressed us every once in a while. As for the program not being acceptable to us—I felt then, and I know now, that the Communist program is the only program that the Southern workers—whites and Negroes both—can possibly accept in the long run. It's the only program that does justice to the Southern worker's ideas that everybody ought to have an equal chance, and that every man has rights that must be respected.

Work against Odds

The Communist Party and the Unemployment Council had to work under the most difficult conditions. We tried to have a little headquarters, but it was raided and closed by the police. We collected money for leaflets, penny by penny, and mimeographed them on an old, rickety hand-machine we kept in a private home. We worked very quietly, behind drawn shades, and were always on the look-out for spies and police. We put the leaflets out at night, from door-step to door-step. Some of our members who worked in factories sneaked them in there.

Sometimes we would distribute leaflets in a neighborhood, calling for a meeting in half an hour on a certain corner. We would put up just one speaker, he would give his message in the fewest possible words, we would pass out pamphlets and leaflets, and the meeting would break up before the cops could get on the scene.

The bosses got scared, and the Ku Klux Klan got busy. The Klan would parade up and down the streets, especially in the Negro neighborhoods, in full regalia, warning the Negroes to keep away from the Communists. They passed out leaflets saying: "Communism Must Be Wiped Out. Alabama Is a Good Place for Good Negroes, but a Bad Place for Negroes Who Want Social Equality."

In June, 1930, I was elected a delegate to the National Unemployment Convention in Chicago. Up to this point I had been staying with relatives in Birmingham. They were under the influence of the Negro misleaders and preachers, and they told me that if I went to the convention I need never come to their house again. The very morning I was to leave, I found a leaflet on my doorstep, put there by the Ku Klux Klan.

I went to Chicago, riding the rods[1] to get there.

A World Movement

In Chicago, I got my first broad view of the revolutionary workers' movement. I met workers from almost every state in the union, and I heard about the work of the same kind of organizations in other countries, and it first dawned on me how strong and powerful the working-class was. There wasn't only me and a few others in Birmingham. There were hundreds, thousands, millions of us!

My family had told me not to come back. What did I care? My real family was the organization. I'd found that I had brothers and sisters in every corner of the world, I knew that we were all fighting for one thing and that they'd stick by me. I never lost that feeling, in all the hard days to come, in Fulton Tower Prison with the threat of the electric chair and the chain-gang looming over me.

I went back to Birmingham and put every ounce of my strength into the work of organization. I built groups among the miners. I read and I studied. I worked in the Young Communist League under the direction of Harry Simms, the young white boy who was later, during the strike of the Kentucky miners, to give his life for the working-class.

I helped organize an Anti-Lynching Conference in Chattanooga. This conference selected delegates to the first convention of the League of Struggle for Negro Rights, held in St. Louis in 1930.

Death Penalty to the Lynchers

I myself was not a delegate to the St. Louis Conference—but the decisions of the conference impressed me. All the Negro organizations before this, and all the white liberal groups, had pussy-footed and hesitated and hemmed and hawed on the burning issue of lynching. When I read the slogan of the League of Struggle for Negro Rights—"Death Penalty to Lynchers!"—the words seemed blazed right

---

[1]**riding the rods:** probably a reference to riding railroad freight cars illegally.

across the page. The St. Louis conference called for a determined struggle for equality for the Negro people.

I had a number of experiences about this time, that taught me a great deal. I went into the Black Belt, and talked with the Negro and white share-croppers and tenants. The price of cotton had crashed, and the burden was being put on the croppers and tenants, so the landlords might go on living in style. There was practically nothing to eat in the cabins. The croppers had applied for government loans, but when the loans came the landlords, with the help of the rural postmasters, stole the money. There was as yet no Share Croppers Union, which was later to challenge the landlords' system of debt-slavery.

A Negro preacher with whom I had made contact notified a Negro secret service–man that I was about, and together they tried to terrorize me. The preacher said: "I don't know anything about the conditions of the people here. I only know that I myself am happy and comfortable." Well, the upshot of it was that the preacher called the sheriff, and [a] lynch-mob began to form, and I escaped by grabbing the first train out of town. My escape was a matter of minutes. It was a white share-cropper who supplied me with the funds to get away. . . .

Scottsboro

It was while I was in New Orleans for a few weeks as representative of the Trade Union Unity League, that I first saw the name Scottsboro. I want to go into that a bit, because the Scottsboro case marked a new stage in the life of the Negro people—and the white workers too—in the United States.

One morning I picked up a capitalist paper and saw that "nine black brutes had raped two little white girls." That was the way the paper put it. There was a dock strike on at the time in New Orleans, and the bosses would have been glad to see this issue, the Scottsboro case, used as a method of whipping up hatred of white and Negro longshoremen against each other.

I knew the South well enough to know at once that here was a vicious frame-up. I got to work right away organizing committees among the workers of New Orleans. We visited clubs, unions, churches to get support for the Scottsboro boys.

On May 31, 1931, I went as a delegate to the first All-Southern Scottsboro Conference, held in Chattanooga.

The hall where the conference was to be held was surrounded by gunmen and police, but we went through with the meeting just the same. The bosses and dicks were boiling mad because we had white and Negro meeting together—and saying plainly that the whole Scottsboro case was a rotten frame-up. I spoke at that conference.

While I was in Chattanooga that trip, I went to a meeting in a Negro church addressed by William Pickens, field secretary of the National Association for the Advancement of Colored People. Pickens made an attack on the International Labor Defense. He said we shouldn't get the governor and the courts mad. We should try to be polite to them. He said: "You people don't know how to fight. Give your money to me and to lawyers and we'll take care of this." Then he attacked the mothers of the Scottsboro boys as being a lot of ignorant fools.

Well, I was so mad I hardly knew what I was doing. I spoke up and said that the Scottsboro boys would never get out of prison until all the workers got together and brought terrific pressure on the lynchers. I said: "We've been polite to the lynchers entirely too long. As long as we O.K. what they do, as long as we crawl to them and assure them we have no wish to change their way of doing things—just so long we'll be slaves."[2]

What Scottsboro Means

Later, while I lay in jail in Atlanta, I followed the Scottsboro case as best I could. Every time I got a paper—and that wasn't too often—I looked eagerly for news of the Scottsboro boys. I was uplifted, brimming over with joy because of the splendid fight we made at the new trial in Decatur. I could hardly contain myself when I saw how the workers were making the Scottsboro case a battering-ram against Jim-Crowism and oppression. I watched the protests in the Scottsboro case swelling to a roar that echoed from one end of the world to the other. And I'd pace that cell, aching to get out and throw myself into the fight.

If you know the South as I do, you know what the Scottsboro case means. Here were the landlords in their fine plantation homes, and the big white bosses in their city mansions, and the whole brutal force of dicks and police who do their bidding. There they sat, smug and self-satisfied, and oh, so sure that nothing could ever interfere with them and their ways. For all time they would be able to sweat and cheat the Negro people, and jail and frame and lynch and shoot them, as they pleased.

And all of a sudden someone laid a hand on their arm and said: "STOP." It was a great big hand, a powerful hand, the hand of the workers. The bosses were shocked and horrified and scared. I know that. And I know also that after the fight began for the Scottsboro boys, every Negro worker in mill or mine, every Negro cropper on the Black Belt plantations, breathed a little easier and held his head a little higher.

I'm ahead of my story now, because I got carried away by the thought of Scottsboro.

I settled down for work in Birmingham, especially among the miners. Conditions in the mines had become worse than horrible. The company had gunmen patrolling the highways, watching the miners. I was arrested several times during this period, and quizzed and bullied.

[2]The Scottsboro Boys were convicted and sentenced to death, but the ILD continued to appeal their convictions until 1935. Only after they had served prison terms did the Supreme Court overturn the convictions.

During one of these arrests the police demanded that I tell them where the white organizers lived. They said: "Where's that guy Tom? We'd like to lay our hands on the son-of-a-bitch."

I said: "I haven't seen Tom for days."

All of a sudden one of the policemen struck me across the mouth. "Mr. Tom to you, you bastard!" he roared.

The Willie Peterson Frame-up

But it was during the Willie Peterson frame-up that I first got a real taste of police brutality.

There was frame-up in the air for weeks before the Peterson case started. The miners were organizing against wage-cuts; the white and Negro workers were beginning to get together and demand relief and jobs and the human rights that had been taken from them. If the bosses could engineer a frame-up against some Negro, a lot of white workers would begin to think about that instead of about bread and jobs. If they could be made to think of the Negroes they worked with as rapists and murderers, they wouldn't be so anxious to organize with them in unions and Unemployment Councils. Also, such frame-ups are always the excuse for terrorizing the Negroes.

On August 3, in Birmingham, two white girls were killed. More than 70 Negroes were lynched in the fury that was whipped up around this case! One of the papers said that the man who shot these girls was a Negro, and that he had made a "Communist speech" to them before the murder.

A dragnet was thrown out, and I was one of the first to be caught.

I was lying in bed when a large white man came to our window and put a gun in my face. At the same moment there was a crash, and some other men broke in the door. My roommate and I were forced out of bed and handcuffed. We didn't know what it was all about.

I was locked up. About an hour later, police came to my cell and dragged me down the stairs and into a car. I was carried to the woods, about twenty miles out of town. On the way one of the gun-thugs kept pointing out places where he had killed "niggers."

The car stopped and we all got out. They asked me: "Who shot Nell Williams?" I said I didn't know.

Third Degree

Two of the men pulled their coats off and slipped a rubber hose from their trousers. I was still handcuffed. They began to beat me over the head. When one man got tired, another would take the hose from him and go on with the beating. They said they knew that I had shot Nell Williams. They demanded that I point out some of the white comrades. I shut my lips tight over my teeth, and said nothing.

Next morning I couldn't get my hat on my swollen head. My ears were great raw lumps of flesh.

Willie Peterson, an unemployed coal-miner, a veteran of the World War, was framed for that murder. He is as innocent as I was.

By now I was known to every stool-pigeon and policeman in Birmingham, and my work became extremely difficult. It was decided to send me to Atlanta.

I want to describe the conditions of the Atlanta workers, because that will give some idea of why the Georgia bosses find it necessary to sentence workers' organizers to the chain-gang. I couldn't say how many workers were unemployed — the officials keep this information carefully hidden. It was admitted that 25,000 families, out of 150,000 population, were on relief. Hundreds who were jobless were kept off the relief rolls.

In the factories, the wages were little higher than the amount of relief doled out to the unemployed. The conditions of the Southern textile workers is known to be extremely bad, but Atlanta has mills that even the Southern papers talk about as "sore spots." The Fulton Bag Company was one of these. There, and in the Piedmont and other textile plants, young girls worked for $6 and even less a week, slaving long hours in ancient, unsanitary buildings.

In the spring of 1930, six organizers of the workers — two white women, two white men, and two Negro men — were arrested and indicted for "inciting to insurrection." The state was demanding that they be sent to the electric chair.

Splitting the Workers

The Black Shirts — a fascist organization — held parades quite often, demanding that all jobs be taken away from Negroes and given to whites. They said that all the Negroes should go back to Africa. I smiled the first time I heard this — it amused me to see how exactly the program of Marcus Garvey[3] fitted in with the program of the Klan.

Of course the demand of the Black Shirts to give all the jobs to the whites was an attempt to split the white workers from the Negroes and put an end to joint struggles for relief. As organizer for the Unemployment Council, I had to fight mighty hard against this poison.

From the cradle onward, the Southern white boy and girl are told that they are better than Negroes. Their birth certificates are tagged "white"; they sit in white schools, play in white parks and live on white streets. They pray in white churches, and when they die they are buried in white cemeteries. Everywhere before them are signs: "For White." "For Colored." They are taught that Negroes are thieves, and murderers, and rapists.

---

[3]**Marcus Garvey:** (1887–1940) a Jamaican-born immigrant to New York City who in 1917 founded a black nationalist back-to-Africa movement, the Universal Negro Improvement Association; the movement reached the peak of its popularity during the 1920s.

I remember especially one white worker, a carpenter, who was one of the first people I talked to in Atlanta. He was very friendly to me. He came to me one day and said that he agreed with the program, but something was holding him back from joining the Unemployment Council.

"What's that, Jim?" I asked. Really, though, I didn't have to ask. I knew the South, and I could guess.

"Well, I just don't figure that white folks and Negroes should mix together," he said. "It won't never do to organize them in one body."

I said: "Look here, Jim. You know that the carpenters and all the other workers get a darn sight less pay for the same work in the South than they do in other parts. Did you ever figure out why?"

He hadn't.

The Price of Division

"Well," I said, "I'll tell you why. It's because the bosses have got us all split up down here. We Southern workers are as good fighters as there are anywhere, and yet we haven't been able to get equal wages with the workers in other places, and we haven't got any rights to speak of. That's because we've been divided. When the whites go out on strike, the bosses call in the Negroes to scab. When the Negroes strike, the bosses call in the whites to scab.

"Did you ever figure out why the unions here are so weak? It's because the whites don't want to organize with the Negroes, and the Negroes don't trust the whites.

"We haven't got the simplest human rights down here. We're not allowed to organize and we're not allowed to hold our meetings except in secret. We can't vote—most of us—because the bosses are so anxious to keep the Negroes from voting that they make laws that take this right away from the white workers too.

"We Southern workers are like a house that's divided against itself. We're like an army that goes out to fight the enemy and stops on the way because its men are all fighting each other.

"Take this relief business, now," I said. "The commissioners tell the whites that they can't give them any more relief because they have to feed so many Negroes, and the Negroes ought to be chased back to the farms. Then they turn around and tell the Negroes that white people have to come first on the relief, so there's nothing doing for colored folks. That way they put us off, and get us scrapping with each other.

"Now suppose the white unemployed, and the Negro unemployed, all go to the commissioners together and say: 'We're all starving. We're all in need. We've decided to get together into one strong, powerful organization to make you come across with relief.'

"Don't you think that'll bring results, Jim?" I asked him. "Don't you see how foolish it is to go into the fight with half an army when we could have a whole one? Don't you think that an empty belly is a pretty punk exchange for the honor of being called a 'superior' race? And can't you realize that as long as one foot is chained to the ground the other can't travel very far?"

What Happened to Jim

Jim didn't say anything more that day. I guess he went home and thought it over. He came back about a week later and invited me to his house. It was the first time he'd ever had a Negro in the house as a friend and equal. When I got there I found two other Negro workers that Jim had brought into the Unemployment Council.

About a month later Jim beat up a rent collector who was boarding up the house of an evicted Negro worker. Then he went to work and organized a committee of whites and Negroes to see the mayor about the case. "Today it's the black worker across town; tomorrow it'll be me," Jim told the mayor.

There are a lot of Jims today, all over the South.

We organized a number of block committees of the Unemployed Councils, and got rent and relief for a large number of families. We agitated endlessly for unemployment insurance.

In the middle of June, 1932, the state closed down all the relief stations. A drive was organized to send all the jobless to the farms.

We gave out leaflets calling for a mass demonstration at the courthouse to demand that the relief be continued. About one thousand workers came, six hundred of them white. We told the commissioners we didn't intend to starve. We reminded them that $800,000 had been collected in the Community Chest drive. The commissioners said there wasn't a cent to be had.

But the very next day the commission voted $6,000 for relief to the jobless!

On the night of July 11, I went to the Post Office to get my mail. I felt myself grabbed from behind and turned to see a police officer.

I was placed in a cell, and was shown a large electric chair, and told to spill everything I knew about the movement. I refused to talk, and was held incommunicado for eleven days. Finally I smuggled out a letter through another prisoner, and the International Labor Defense got on the job.

The Insurrection Law

Assistant Solicitor John Hudson rigged up the charge against me. It was the charge of "inciting to insurrection." It was based on an old statute passed in 1861, when the Negro people were still chattel slaves, and the white masters needed a law to crush slave insurrection and kill those found giving aid to the slaves. The statute read:

> If any person be in any manner instrumental in bringing, introducing or circulating within the state any printed or written paper, pamphlet, or circular for the purpose of exciting insurrection, revolt, conspiracy or resistance on the part of slaves, Negroes or free persons of color in this state he shall be guilty of high misdemeanor which is punishable by death.

Since the days of the Civil War that law had lain, unused and almost forgotten. Now the slaves of the new order—the white and black slaves of capitalism—were organizing. In the eyes of the Georgia masters, it was a crime punishable by death.

The trial was set for January 16, 1933. The state of Georgia displayed the literature that had been taken from my room, and read passages of it to the jury. They questioned me in great detail. Did I believe that the bosses and government ought to pay insurance to unemployed workers? That Negroes should have complete equality with white people? Did I believe in the demand for the self-determination of the Black Belt—that the Negro people should be allowed to rule the Black Belt territory, kicking out the white landlords and government officials? Did I feel that the working-class could run the mills and mines and government? That it wasn't necessary to have bosses at all?

I told them I believed all of that—and more.

The courtroom was packed to suffocation. The I.L.D. attorneys, Benjamin J. Davis, Jr., and John H. Geer, two young Negroes—and I myself—fought every step of the way. We were not really talking to that judge, nor to those prosecutors, whose questions we were answering. Over their heads we talked to the white and Negro workers who sat on the benches, watching, listening, learning. And beyond them we talked to the thousands and millions of workers all over the world to whom this case was a challenge.

We demanded that Negroes be placed on jury rolls. We demanded that the insulting terms, "nigger" and "darky," be dropped in that court. We asserted the right of the workers to organize, to strike, to make their demands, to nominate candidates of their choice. We asserted the right of the Negro people to have complete equality in every field.

The state held that my membership in the Communist Party, my possession of Communist literature, was enough to send me to the electric chair. They said to the jury: "Stamp this damnable thing out now with a conviction that will automatically carry with it a penalty of electrocution."

And the hand-picked lily-white jury responded:

"We, the jury, find the defendant guilty as charged, but recommend that mercy be shown and fix his sentence at from eighteen to twenty years."

I had organized starving workers to demand bread, and I was sentenced to live out my years on the chain-gang for it. But I knew that the movement itself would not stop. I spoke to the court and said:

"They can hold this Angelo Herndon and hundreds of others, but it will never stop these demonstrations on the part of Negro and white workers who demand a decent place to live in and proper food for their kids to eat."

I said: "You may do what you will with Angelo Herndon. You may indict him. You may put him in jail. But there will come thousands of Angelo Herndons. If you really want to do anything about the case, you must go out and indict the social system. But this you will not do, for your role is to defend the system under which the toiling masses are robbed and oppressed.

"You may succeed in killing one, two, even a score of working-class organizers. But you cannot kill the working class." . . .

31. Sharing the Wealth

HUEY P. LONG
From "Every Man a King"
1934

Born on August 20, 1893, Huey P. Long traveled across the South and Middle West for four years as a door-to-door salesman before studying law at Tulane University. Admitted to the bar in 1915, he was elected three years later to Louisiana's Railroad Commission and there earned a statewide reputation for fighting the power of the out-of-state oil companies. As Louisiana's governor and U.S. senator, Long became known nationally for his inveterate support of ordinary people against the power of big business and the rich.

Long's future in national politics ran squarely into Franklin Roosevelt's New Deal. FDR regarded Long as a serious rival within the Democratic Party and Long's decision to create Share Our Wealth clubs as an effort to create a national political organization. First organized in February 1934, the Share Our Wealth clubs proposed a confiscatory tax on high incomes to dramatically redistribute wealth in the United States. Confiscated fortunes would provide each American family with a homestead worth $5,000, along with an annual income of $2,500. Long, who first outlined his plan in this radio address, enjoyed considerable national popular appeal until his career was cut short by an assassin's bullet on September 8, 1935.

February 23, 1934

Ladies and Gentlemen: —

I have only thirty minutes in which to speak to you this evening, and I, therefore, will not be able to discuss in detail so much as I can write when I have all of the time and space that is allowed me for the subjects, but I will undertake to

Huey P. Long, *Share Our Wealth* (1934). Reprint ed. Jack Frazier (Indian Hills, W. Va.: Solar Age Press, 1980), 7–17.

sketch them very briefly without manuscript or preparation, so that you can understand them so well as I can tell them to you tonight.

I contend, my friends, that we have no difficult problem to solve in America, and that is the view of nearly everyone with whom I have discussed the matter here in Washington and elsewhere throughout the United States—that we have no very difficult problem to solve.

It is not the difficulty of the problem which we have; it is the fact that the rich people of this country—and by rich people I mean the super-rich—will not allow us to solve the problems, or rather the one little problem that is afflicting this country, because in order to cure all of our woes it is necessary to scale down the big fortunes, that we may scatter the wealth to be shared by all of the people.

We have a marvelous love for this Government of ours; in fact, it is almost a religion, and it is well that it should be, because we have a splendid form of government and we have a splendid set of laws. We have everything here that we need, except that we have neglected the fundamentals upon which the American Government was principally predicated.

How many of you remember the first thing that the Declaration of Independence said? It said: "We hold these truths to be self-evident, that there are certain inalienable rights for the people, and among them are life, liberty, and the pursuit of happiness"; and it said further, "We hold the view that all men are created equal."

Now, what did they mean by that? Did they mean, my friends, to say that all men are created equal and that that meant that any one man was born to inherit $10,000,000,000 and that another child was to be born to inherit nothing?

Did that mean, my friends, that someone would come into this world without having had an opportunity, of course, to have hit one lick of work, should be born with more than it and all of its children and children's children could ever dispose of, but that another one would have to be born into a life of starvation?

That was not the meaning of the Declaration of Independence when it said that all men are created equal or "That we hold that all men are created equal."

Nor was it the meaning of the Declaration of Independence when it said that they held that there were certain rights that were inalienable—the right of life, liberty, and the pursuit of happiness.

Is that right of life, my friends, when the young children of this country are being reared into a sphere which is more owned by twelve men than it by 120,000,000 people?

Is that, my friends, giving them a fair shake of the dice or anything like the inalienable right of life, liberty, and the pursuit of happiness, or anything resembling the fact that all people are created equal; when we have today in America thousands and hundreds of thousands and millions of children on the verge of starvation in a land that is overflowing with too much to eat and too much to wear?

I do not think you will contend that, and I do not think for a moment that they will contend it.

Now let us see if we cannot return this Government to the Declaration of Independence and see if we are going to do anything regarding it. Why should we hesitate or why should we quibble or why should we quarrel with one another to find out what the difficulty is, when we know that the Lord told us what the difficulty is, and Moses wrote it out so a blind man could see it, then Jesus told us all about it, and it was later written in the Book of James, where everyone could read it? . . .

We have trouble, my friends, in the country, because we have too much money owing, the greatest indebtedness that has ever been given to civilization, where it has been shown that we are incapable of distributing the actual things that are here, because the people have not money enough to supply themselves with them, and because the greed of a few men is such that they think it is necessary that they own everything, and their pleasure consists in the starvation of the masses, and in their possessing things they cannot use, and their children cannot use, but who bask in the splendor of sunlight and wealth, casting darkness and despair and impressing it on everyone else. . . .

So, we have in America today, my friends, a condition by which about ten men dominate the means of activity in at least 85 percent of the activities that you own. They either own directly everything or they have got some kind of mortgage on it, with a very small percentage to be excepted. They own the banks, they own the steel mills, they own the railroads, they own the bonds, they own the mortgages, they own the stores, and they have chained the country from one end to the other until there is not any kind of business that a small, independent man could go into today and make a living, and there is not any kind of business that an independent man can go into and make any money to buy an automobile with; and they have finally and gradually and steadily eliminated everybody from the fields in which there is a living to be made, and still they have got little enough sense to think they ought to be able to get more business out of it anyway.

If you reduce a man to the point where he is starving to death and bleeding and dying, how do you expect that man to get hold of any money to spend with you? It is not possible.

Then, ladies and gentlemen, how do you expect people to live, when the wherewith cannot be had by the people?

In the beginning I quoted from the Scriptures. I hope you will understand that I am not quoting Scripture to you to convince you of my goodness personally, because that is a thing between me and my Maker; that is something as to how I stand with my Maker and as to how you stand with your Maker. That is not concerned with this issue, except and unless there are those of you who would be so good as to pray for the souls of some of us. But the Lord gave His law, and in the Book of James they said so, that the rich should weep and howl for the miseries that had come upon them; and, therefore, it was written that when the rich hold goods they could not use and could not consume, you will inflict punishment on them, and nothing but days of woe ahead of them.

Then we have heard of the great Greek philosopher, Socrates, and the greater Greek philosopher, Plato, and we have read the dialogue between Plato and Socrates, in which one said that great riches brought on great poverty, and would be destructive of a country. Read what they said. Read what Plato said; that you must not let any one man be too poor, and you must not let any one man be too rich; that the same mill that grinds out the extra rich is the mill that will grind out the extra poor, because, in order that the extra rich can become so affluent, they must necessarily take more of what ordinarily would belong to the average man.

It is a very simple process of mathematics that you do not have to study, and that no one is going to discuss with you.

So that was the view of Socrates and Plato. That was the view of the English statesmen. That was the view of American statesmen. That was the view of American statesmen like Daniel Webster, Thomas Jefferson, Abraham Lincoln, William Jennings Bryan, and Theodore Roosevelt, and even as late as Herbert Hoover and Franklin D. Roosevelt.

Both of these men, Mr. Hoover and Mr. Roosevelt, came out and said there had to be a decentralization of wealth, but neither one of them did anything about it. But, nevertheless, they recognized the principle. The fact that neither one of them ever did anything about it is their own problem that I am not undertaking to criticize; but had Mr. Hoover carried out what he says ought to be done, he would be retiring from the President's office, very probably, three years from now, instead of one year ago; and had Mr. Roosevelt proceeded along the lines that he stated were necessary for the decentralization of wealth, he would have gone, my friends, a long way already, and within a few months he would have probably reached a solution of all of the problems that afflict this country today.

But I wish to warn you now that nothing that has been done up to this date has taken one dime away from these big fortune-holders; they own just as much as they did, and probably a little bit more; they hold just as many of the debts of the common people as they ever held, and probably a little bit more; and unless we, my friends, are going to give the people of this country a fair shake of the dice, by which they will all get something out of the funds of this land, there is not a chance on the topside of this God's eternal earth by which we can rescue this country and rescue the people of this country.

It is necessary to save the government of the country, but is much more necessary to save the people of America. We love this country. We love this Government. It is a religion, I say. It is a kind of religion people have read of when women, in the name of religion, would take their infant babes and throw them into the burning flame, where they would be instantly devoured by the all-consuming fire, in days gone by; and there probably are some people of the world even today, who, in the name of religion, throw their own babes to destruction; but in the name of our good government, people today are seeing their own children hungry, tired, half-naked, lifting their tear-dimmed eyes into the sad faces of their fathers and mothers, who cannot give them food and clothing they both need, and which is necessary to sustain them, and that goes on day after day, and night after night, when day gets into darkness and blackness, knowing those children would arise in the morning without being fed, and probably go to bed at night without being fed.

Yet in the name of our Government, and all alone, those people undertake and strive as hard as they can to keep a good government alive, and how long they can stand that no one knows. If I were in their place tonight, the place where millions are, I hope that I would have what I might say—I cannot give you the word to express the kind of fortitude they have; that is the word—I hope that I might have the fortitude to praise and honor my Government that had allowed me here in this land, where there is too much to eat and too much to wear, to starve in order that a handful of men can have so much more than they can ever eat or they can ever wear.

Now, we have organized a society, and we call it "Share Our Wealth Society," a society with the motto "Every Man a King."

Every man a king, so there would be no such thing as a man or woman who did not have the necessities of life, who would not be dependent upon the whims and caprices and ipsi dixit of the financial barons for a living. What do we propose by this society? We propose to limit the wealth of big men in the country. There is an average of $15,000 in wealth to every family in America. That is right here today.

We do not propose to divide it up equally. We do not propose a division of wealth, but we propose to limit poverty that we will allow to be inflicted upon any man's family. We will not say we are going to try to guarantee any equality, or $15,000 to a family. No; but we do say that one third of the average is low enough for any one family to hold, that there should be a guarantee of a family wealth of around $5,000; enough for a home, an automobile, a radio, and the ordinary conveniences, and the opportunity to educate their children; a fair share of the income of this land thereafter to that family so there will be no such thing as merely the select to have those things, and so there will be no such thing as a family living in poverty and distress.

We have to limit fortunes. Our present plan is that we will allow no one man to own more that $50,000,000. We think that with that limit we will be able to carry out the balance of the program. It may be necessary that we limit it to less than $50,000,000. It may be necessary, in working out of the plans that no man's fortune would be more than $10,000,000 or $15,000,000. But be that as it may, it will still be more than any one man, or any one man and his children and their children, will be able to spend in their lifetimes; and it is not necessary or reasonable to have wealth piled up beyond that point where we cannot prevent poverty among the masses.

Another thing we propose is old-age pension of $30 a month for everyone that is sixty years old. Now, we do not give this pension to a man making $1,000 a year, and we do not give it to him if he has $10,000 in property, but outside of that we do.

We will limit hours of work. There is not any necessity of having overproduction. I think all you have got to do, ladies and gentlemen, is just limit the hours of work to such an extent as people will work only so long as it is necessary to produce enough for all of the people to have what they need. Why, ladies and gentlemen, let us say that all of these labor-saving devices reduce hours down to where you do not have to work but four hours a day: that is enough for these people, and then praise be the name of the Lord, if it gets that good. Let it be good and not a curse, and then we will have five hours a day and five days a week, or even less than that, and we might give a man a whole month off during a year, or give him two months; and we might do what other countries have seen fit to do, and what I did in Louisiana, by having schools by which adults could go back and learn the things that have been discovered since they went to school.

We will not have any trouble taking care of the agricultural situation. All you have to do is balance your production with your consumption. You simply have to abandon a particular crop that you have too much of, and all you have to do is store the surplus for the next year, and the Government will take it over. When you have good crops in the area in which the crops that have been planted are sufficient for another year, put in your public works in the particular year when you do not need to raise any more, and by that means you get everybody employed. When the Government has enough of any particular crop to take care of all of the people, that will be all that is necessary; and in order to do all of this, our taxation is going to be to take the billion-dollar fortunes and strip them down to frying size, not to exceed $50,000,000, and if it is necessary to come to $10,000,000, we will come to $10,000,000. We have worked the proposition out to guarantee a limit upon property (and no man will own less than one-third the average), and guarantee a reduction of fortunes and a reduction of hours to spread wealth throughout this country. We would care for the old people above sixty and take them away from this thriving industry and give them a chance to enjoy the necessities and live in ease, and thereby lift from the market the labor which would probably create a surplus of commodities.

Those are the things we propose to do. "Every Man a King." Every man to eat when there is something to eat; all to wear something when there is something to wear. That makes us all a sovereign.

You cannot solve these things through these various and sundry alphabetical codes. You can have the N.R.A. and P.W.A. and C.W.A.[1] and the U.U.G. and G.I.N. and any other kind of dad-gummed lettered code. You can wait until doomsday and see twenty-five more alphabets, but that is not going to solve this proposition. Why hide? Why quibble? You know what the trouble is. The man that says he does not know what the trouble is is just hiding his face to keep from seeing the sunlight.

God told you what the trouble was. The philosophers told you what the trouble was; and when you have a country where one man owns more than 100,000 people, or a million people, and when you have a country where there are four men, as in America, that have got more control over things than all the 120,000,000 people together, you know what the trouble is.

We had these great incomes in this country; but the farmer, who plowed from sunup to sundown, who labored here from sunup to sundown for six days a week, wound up at the end of the time with practically nothing.

And we ought to take care of the veterans of the wars in this program. That is a small matter. Suppose it does cost a billion dollars a year—that means that the

---

[1]**N.R.A., P.W.A., C.W.A.:** the New Deal agencies, the National Recovery Administration, the Public Works Administration, and the Civil Works Administration.

money will be scattered throughout this country. We ought to pay them a bonus. We can do it. We ought to take care of every single one of the sick and disabled veterans. I do not care whether a man got sick on the battlefield or did not; every man that wore the uniform of this country is entitled to be taken care of, and there is money enough to do it; and we need to spread the wealth of the country, which you did not do in what you call the N.R.A.

If the N.R.A. has done any good, I can put it all in my eye without having it hurt. All I can see that the N.R.A. has done is to put the little man out of business—the little merchant in his store, the little Italian that is running a fruit stand, or the Greek shoe-shining stand, who has to take hold of a code of 275 pages and study it with a spirit level and compass and looking-glass; he has to hire a Philadelphia lawyer to tell him what is in the code; and by the time he learns what the code is, he is in jail or out of business; and they have got a chain code system that has already put him out of business. The N.R.A. is not worth anything, and I said so when they put it through.

Now, my friends, we have got to hit the root with the ax. Centralized power in the hands of a few, with centralized credit in the hands of a few, is the trouble.

Get together in your community tonight or tomorrow and organize one of our Share Our Wealth Societies. If you do not understand it, write me and let me send you the platform; let me give you the proof of it. . . .

Organize your Share Our Wealth Society and get your people to meet with you, and make known your wishes to your Senators and Representatives in Congress. . . .

32. The Tennessee Valley Authority and Grass-Roots Democracy

Odette Keun
From A Foreigner Looks at the TVA
1937

Perhaps no agency better represents Franklin Roosevelt's—and American liberalism's—"middle path" than the Tennessee Valley Authority (TVA). Its origins lie in the long political struggle during the 1920s over control of the Wilson Dam at Muscle Shoals, Alabama, in which advocates of public control of hydroelectric power successfully defeated a private effort to control the project. After Roosevelt's

Odette Keun, A Foreigner Looks at the TVA (New York: Longmans, Green & Co., 1937), 78–84.

election in 1932, public-power enthusiasts saw an opportunity to expand the use of hydroelectric projects as tools for the economic development of rural areas in the South and the West. The rich water resources of the Tennessee Valley provided an ideal case in point. In April 1933, Congress established the TVA as a federal agency empowered with what Roosevelt described as the "flexibility and initiative of private enterprise"; by the 1940s the TVA dominated the utilities industry in the Tennessee Valley. As British observer Odette Keun describes in her 1937 book A Foreigner Looks at the TVA, *the authority was initiating revolutionary changes in southern life.*

———————————

. . . The TVA is wrapped heart and soul in the evolution of the mountaineers. How to transform their thinking and their agricultural customs and adapt them to present conditions; how to develop their economic life, keeping them from the servitude of factories for which they are physically and mentally unsuited (and which in any case cannot absorb them any longer), and yet increase their cash income and raise their material standards to the level of those obtaining in the flourishing portions of the Valley; how to preserve their independent spirit and their culture—the TVA calls it culture: I'd call it an obsolete form of Americanism that America needs no more than Europe needs the ideology of the Corsican or the tribal pattern of the clans of the Caucasus, to speak of peoples I know—and yet teach them responsibility to society and give them a significant and useful rôle in the community: this is the task the TVA has undertaken. It is especially for them and their brothers in the Valley that it elaborated its agricultural program, invented its fertilizer, created its Agricultural Industries Division, founded its educational and training courses. It is for them, plus the small-towner, that it is waging the fight for power against the Utilities. Its goal is to secure for them a more intelligent, dignified and assured existence, participating in the facilities our contemporary world affords but conserving the lively characteristics of the individual: a happy balance between the Jeffersonian Dream of the self-sufficing agricultural community and the mechanical advantages of the Power Age. At least, I see the goal like that, and I do not believe I have seen it awry.

The response, I must say, has been considerable. It is true, as I have mentioned before, that the TVA came upon the scene at a moment when the farmer was up against the wall; agriculture did not feed a man and his family, and despair was growing. If prices had been soaring and prospects bright, perhaps no wedge could have been driven into rural obstinacy and traditionalism. But as it was, circumstances and the wisdom and tact of the TVA's attitude pretty soon persuaded the farmers, highlanders and lowlanders alike, in spite of their caution and inveterate suspiciousness, that here was a friend intensely anxious to help them, not a "passel of Yankees" come to pour scorn on their backwardness and arrogantly tell them how to do it all. Here was real benevolence and discretion, the first manifestation, since Reconstruction, of a government's interest and care. The mere fact, which I have already cited, that in two and a half years over twelve thousand test-demonstration farms have been spontaneously laid out in a region celebrated for centuries for its ignorance and stubbornness, proves the nature of the tie between the population of the Watershed and the TVA. And if it shows the sagacity and devotion with which the TVA has handled that prickly proposition, the farmer, I concede willingly that it also shows more alertness and gratitude on the part of the farmer than one would have expected to find. Indeed, the tendency might almost become too much eagerness for aid and guidance, though that cannot be encouraged since it is inertia that must be extirpated from the composition of the human animal here.

The evil problems of the tenant farmer and the sharecropper, White and Black, the TVA has not been able to touch. These are things that can be straightened out only by Congressional legislation. You can't urge rotation of cover crops on a man who is employed by a landlord, if that landlord wants cotton on his soil; nor can you, when you are not the Government, give half the rural population a house and a field to start living like free men. Nor can you find work, however hard you try, for all the labourers who have been jerked out of their farm jobs because you had to buy up the estates of their masters for flooding purposes. All that is not your fault, though it may be your sorrow. Indirectly, however, by side-activities and industries, by part-time employment in its various projects, by free training, by diligent searching for new places, by all sorts of ingenious efforts, the TVA does what it can to enable the tenant and the sharecropper who drift within its orbit to obtain a little more security, a little more money, and perhaps even, in very fortunate cases, a little property of their own. But that aspect of the picture is not radiant with hope. It is the Government alone who can get under the skin of these very painful matters. Another tangle concerns the people who occupy the tracts of land the TVA is obliged to submerge for the reservoirs of its dams. Here human emotions are involved, as well as concrete questions. Families had to be removed so that engineering schemes of national importance might be realized, but you do not cheerfully acquiesce in the disruption of your manner of life even when national issues are at stake. The monetary compensation was very fair, as public opinion recognizes, though the value of land showed a disposition to shoot up to vertiginous heights as soon as it was learnt that "government" needed it, and every owner's estate was metamorphosed in a jiffy from farm land into dam land, the latter costing a hundred times more. The TVA had to bargain, and bargain closely, but that over, it did a lot of humane things. It explored the Valley to find farms in the vicinity of the districts to be flooded, at equivalent prices; it gave the transplanted families, whenever possible, the opportunity to choose their new homes; it worked with Federal and county institutions to facilitate their installation in unfamiliar communities, providing them with social contacts, arranging, as in the case of the shifting of whole minor villages, for educational facilities in the shape of schools and communications. Entire cemeteries had been moved at the TVA's expense when the time came for flooding, so that the people should not brood upon their dead lost irretrievably in the waters. I do not say that the process of *transvasement*[1] was never accompanied by suffering and loss: in such a gigantic enterprise every personal interest, every personal necessity, could not always be adequately satisfied, but what could be done to make the lot of the perforce-uprooted groups bearable or even to improve it, has been scrupulously tried. An interesting point is that better land or no-better land proposed, most of the people refused to leave their hills for the plains.

These traits of justice and kindness, this ideal of a common welfare, which characterize the relations the TVA established with the social groups existing in the Valley come to a peak, I think, in the Labour question, and the policies the TVA adopted in this potentially stormy field. There are more than 15,000 workers, from every rank and craft of Labour, on TVA projects in the Watershed. You can imagine what the applications were at a time when twenty million Americans were out of a job. One of the firmest rules the TVA laid down was that local labour, if it met the requirements, was to be taken on first. But it *had* to meet the requirements; patronage, favouritism and protection were out of the question, as a good many politicians and wire-pullers immediately discovered to their great disgruntlement. The major policies were three. The first related to the right of collective bargaining; the second to wages; the third to hours and working conditions—and these applied to coloured as well as to white labour, for from the outset the TVA, quietly but persistently, hired Negroes in groups until their employment percentage tallied with the population percentage in the areas concerned: about 20 percent. The Negroes received the same wages as the Whites of the same category, the same housing and the same training. Since White labour was assured that the jobs wouldn't be pulled away from under it by the ordinary trick of using cheap coloured labour, there was hardly any trouble, even when leading civic lights regretted that Negroes were being educated beyond their necessities. The TVA's answer was that neither revolt nor miscegenation was being preached, and that since the Negro was a member of the community, it was better for the community that he should be a decent citizen than an indecent one. And that was that. I should like to see the TVA do something far broader and more decisive about the Negro, and this subject is the only one in which we do not see eye to eye; but I daresay it understands its business in the South better than I. I'm afraid that if I attempted to deal with the mixture of pathological impulses and racial snobbery that is at the bottom of the attitude of the White towards the Black, I'd stir up a worse witch's brew.

The principle of collective bargaining, which recognizes and insists on the "right of employees to organize and bargain as a body through representatives of their own choosing, free from any and all restraint, interference or coercion in self-organization and designation of Labour's own representatives elected fairly by

---

[1]*transvasement*: the French word *transvaser* means, literally, to decant a liquid. In this case, Keun is referring to the process by which the TVA dammed (or "decanted") the river and submerged previously inhabited lands.

majority rule," has been observed in every detail by the TVA. It made clear to its own supervisory executives that whatever their origins or their previous philosophy were, the Authority stood unshakably for the untrammeled right of Labour to speak and act through the specific officials it voluntarily appointed. Discrimination by the supervisors because of union membership or activity resulted, in the few cases where it occurred, in changes in the staff. As regards wages, the TVA believes in keeping them high. "It's not only good social policy, but good business as well," it says. The Act provides that the Authority, in all its operations, shall pay not less than the prevailing wage, and that due attention shall be given to wages reached through collective bargaining—so that when the prevailing wage is a very low one, the TVA worker has the chance to get a raise. In the event any question crops up as to what are the prevailing rates of wages, and the matter cannot be settled by conference between the duly chosen Labour spokesmen and the Authority, it is referred to the U.S. Secretary of Labour, whose decision is final. Schedules of rates of pay, hourly and annual, are published and remain in force until revision, which takes place not more often than once a year so that there are no sudden shattering cuts and no mysteries. (By the way, the salaries of the three Directors are ten thousand dollars a year each. I just want to remark that William Green, President of the American Federation of Labour, a proletarian not a capitalistic institution, gets twenty-five thousand a year. So do some other presidents of Unions.)

As regards hours of work, they cannot exceed eight in the twenty-four hour period; overtime work is paid for at the rate of time and one-half; during the periods of marked unemployment, hours of work are still kept consistent with a reasonable minimum income. Child labour, of course, is utterly eliminated. As regards conditions of work, the Safety Committees, the admirable Division of Hygiene (health-education program, first-aid instruction, immunization against diseases, prevention of malaria, general sanitation), the housing, catering, educational and recreational facilities, the free training courses—I must mention some of them, they are so extraordinarily diversified, and show so much mental curiosity on the part of the workers as well as so much solicitude on the part of the TVA: woodworking, general metal, automotive, electrical, ground aviation, blacksmithing, welding, plumbing, wrought-iron work, blueprint reading, even foremanship—are evidence of the determination to supply Labour with chances in the future as well as in the present. Apprenticeship, a forgotten phase everywhere in the world, has been revived. Demonstration-enterprises are run for the benefit of the employees: poultry farms, communal farm gardens, dairies, stock-breeding, principles of marketing, use of farm agencies, and so forth and so on. The TVA has further created an entirely new feature, to which no parallel can be found in any other organization—a bureau for the settlement of jurisdictional disputes, and for the maintenance of proper individual and collective relations between the supervisory personnel and the supervised workers. This section investigates complaints, makes reports to the parties concerned, and adjusts differences before they reach the stage of formal grievances. It functions both for Whites and Blacks. (I assisted at a meeting where, among other points discussed, the Negroes, who gave me an impression of startling intelligence and moderation, objected to being invariably addressed as "son of a bitch" by certain foremen. The White head of this "Labor Relations Staff" instantly promised redress.) There is a Workers' Council formed by the men, who debate on problems that could not be settled within the unions and groups themselves, and which thus can champion the unorganized worker: a new departure in the history of American Labour. During its three and a half years of life there has never been a strike in the TVA personnel. There has been no bluff on the part of employer or employees. The deal has been fair and square throughout on either side; the cards have been played openly and straightly; and both Capital and Labour reveal that they can be team-mates, with good-will and co-operation in a common cause, and honesty, tolerance and patience toward problems of industrial relations.

All this seems to me exceptionally significant. When you analyze the domestic scene of a democratic country, you find that fundamentally its normal stability depends on the relations between Capital and Labour. With the exception of the Scandinavian nations where, for reasons I cannot enumerate here, admirable adjustments have been arrived at, no democratic country in Europe is a shining example of fairness; but by and large, Capital there has been bludgeoned into a modicum of wisdom. It has been frightened into compromise. It has made concessions—and a good many concessions; sometimes, even, very difficult concessions—certainly not in a spirit of magnanimity, but of self-preservation. It has perceived that the trend of the times—queerly enough, in the fascistic lands, too—is going against it; public opinion is much more readily on the side of the working-man than of the big employer; and social legislation was, until Mr. Roosevelt appeared, incomparably more developed than in the United States. No democratic European, whatever his party, can sympathize with the ear-splitting clamours of Tory Americans about measures most of us put through thirty-five or forty years ago, and which are now completely academic issues. They have become part and parcel of our social life and philosophy, and could no more be wrenched from them than the principle of religious freedom. In America, the fight for the social legislation we have already achieved is continuing, and the fight for political representation is only beginning. At first the foreign observer, especially if he lands in New York, which gives a thoroughly distorted and perverted view of American life (it throws the European entirely off his balance and is the chief source of the incredibly grotesque and false books we write about America; I have gone astray so dreadfully myself that I shall start my own study by earnestly petitioning the Federal Government to forbid inflexibly every European writer coming here for the first time to disembark in New York. The metropolis should only be visited on our way *home*) is tempted to think that the whole country is in violent social convulsions. That is not so at present, though it will happen in the future if the salient features of Capitalism are not modified. Certain spots, notably the enormous industrial and shipping centres, are in violent social convulsions, and strikes have a tendency to become horrifyingly brutal, a tendency for which I blame almost exclusively the unimaginable methods the employers use to break them, aided arbitrarily, and much too often, by the authorities and official forces of the States. The methods with which the great corporations fight the strikers are cave-man procedures, and I can find nothing approaching to an equivalent in any other democracy. But broadly speaking, Labour in America is *conservative*. It is one of the most flabbergasting discoveries I have made. This conservatism is partly due to the antiquated policies of the American Federation of Labour; to its egotistic and frequently unreliable leadership; to the splitting-up of the working classes into an aristocracy of highly protected skills and crafts and a neglected and abandoned proletariat with no attention paid to the untrained labourer and to the Negro; and to such a stupefying lack of organization that out of thirty million American workers only three and a half million are unionized. Partly, however, it is due to the temper of the American working-man himself. In general his sense of solidarity was for a very long time practically non-existent: it is not at all effective yet. He clung with intense persistence to the traditional hope of escaping one day—soon—from the ranks of the employee into the ranks of the small entrepreneur and employer, where he would be hampered by the social legislation that would have benefited him as a simple worker. Such an ambition deprived his social outlook of all universality. He was much more ignorant and unthinking than his European colleague. He read much less. In the South particularly, where unions were extremely rare, he was usually quite illiterate, and terrified to death of a system that could retaliate with literally murderous blows if he tried single-handedly to oppose it. Don't talk to me of the aggressiveness of the American worker, because it was a farce.

Today he is waking up. There is much less chance of passing into the higher strata; the activities of the Socialist and Communist parties are prodding him into the consciousness of the right to collective bargaining and to unionization which is his already in modern civilized countries; John L. Lewis, a gentleman who is not what could be termed a sentimentalist, is putting his class on a new footing, both industrially and politically. In two or three decades, perhaps sooner, Labour will really be a force that may tear the American domestic scene to pieces if Capitalism is obdurate. But the point I want to make is that at this stage, in spite of symptoms that reveal the possibility of an ultimate march instead of a stumbling about, Labour is still very ready to be conciliating. After having poked a long enquiring nose into more unions, meetings and demonstrations—pickets, too—than I can count, my unalterable conviction is that, whatever the fiery extremist groups may say or do, *the working man en bloc is still no revolutionist at all*. He still has no fanatical hatred of the capitalist. He still has no feeling that the system is essentially unjust, infamous, execrable, and must be wiped off the face of the earth. He still does not hold that he is capable of taking the lead and conducting alone his country's economics. He still is prepared to sit at the foot of Capital's table and help himself to the remains of the huge dish. The one thing he insists on with growing energy and determination is that the remains should be sufficient to satisfy his reasonable necessities.

I do not say that this attitude will be his attitude eternally. I do not say that it is the intention of Labour leaders that it should be his attitude eternally. I do not say that *any* attitude can be eternal. What I wish to drive home is the fact that it is his actual attitude. His historical and mental make-up is such that he may continue in it until the community as a whole is attuned to a basic social change, if it is met with reason and equity on the part of the employer, with co-operation on the part of Capital, and with adjustments which he himself can freely formulate and practise. If these things are denied him—well, America can count on having in time a first-class bust-up. The Labour policies of the TVA and their results prove conclusively that in a capitalistic democracy Capital need not be cannibalistic, Labour need not be revolutionary, and that the imperishable quest of man for the millennium can be pursued by evolution and adaptation instead of by blowing himself and his fellows in mud and blood to the skies. But whether autocratic Capital in this country will consent, without pressure from somebody or something more autocratic still, to take the TVA as its model, is a question on which I seem to feel a few slight doubts.

Suggestions for Further Reading

Badger, Anthony. *The New Deal: The Depression Years, 1933–1940.* New York: Noonday Press, 1989.

———. *Prosperity Road: The New Deal, Tobacco, and North Carolina.* Chapel Hill: University of North Carolina Press, 1980.

Brinkley, Alan. *Voices of Protest: Huey Long, Father Coughlin, and the Great Depression.* New York: Alfred A. Knopf, 1982.

Carter, Dan T. *Scottsboro: A Tragedy of the American South.* Baton Rouge: Louisiana State University Press, 1969.

Martin, Charles H. *The Angelo Herndon Case and Southern Justice.* Baton Rouge: Louisiana State University Press, 1976.

Reed, Linda. *Simple Decency & Common Sense: The Southern Conference Movement, 1938–1963.* Bloomington: Indiana University Press, 1991.

Sullivan, Patricia. *Days of Hope: Race and Democracy in the New Deal Era.* Chapel Hill: University of North Carolina Press, 1996.

Williams, T. Harry. *Huey Long.* New York: Alfred A. Knopf, 1969.

CHAPTER TEN

WORLD WAR II

The War That
Brought Old Dixie Down

Although people have often spoken of the Civil War as the great watershed in southern history, historians now argue that it was really World War II that "brought old Dixie down." For the four million Southerners who fought abroad and those who contributed to the war effort on the home front, it was a "modernizing" experience that led them to question traditions and to leave behind old ways of living and working. At the same time, the war planted the seeds of change that ultimately reshaped some of the defining characteristics of southern society and culture that had long set the region apart from the rest of the nation — including race relations, women's roles, and the socioeconomic structure.

Among those most affected by the war were more than one million African Americans who served in the military, the majority of them from the South. In addition to serving out of a sense of duty and patriotism, black soldiers hoped that their contributions would lead to greater fairness and opportunity. The black press and most civil rights organizations called for what the *Pittsburgh Courier* dubbed "the Double V" — victory against not only America's enemies but against American racism. Stateside and abroad, black soldiers, sailors, pilots, and nurses learned new skills and earned unprecedented salaries. Many veterans later recalled that their wartime experiences gave them a new sense of purpose, boosted their pride and confidence, and revealed alternatives to low-paying agricultural and domestic work. Encounters with white Europeans, Australians, and Filipinos — who accepted them as equals — also suggested new possibilities concerning race relations at home.

Yet there was also much to disturb black Southerners serving in the military and to make them even less willing to accept pre-war conditions in the postwar world. Black soldiers were well aware of the irony in fighting against a racist foreign enemy and for allies' self-determination when most people of their race were

not allowed to vote. They returned to the South eager to bring about change, eventually if not immediately. As Navy veteran Haywood Stepney explained to interviewer Neil McMillen,

> Having not tasted the freedom or the liberty of being or doing like other folks then
> you didn't know what it was like over across the street. So we accepted it. . . . But
> after seeing what some of the other world was doing then I realized how far be-
> hind I was. As we began to move and stir around and learn other ways then we
> had a choice—a comparison.[1]

Stepney remembered thinking, "Now it's going to be difficult to get me back in
total darkness." Recognizing that southern racial customs remained intact in the
immediate postwar world, however, most black veterans waited until the 1950s
and 1960s to press actively for improvement.

For women, World War II offered unprecedented and liberating opportunities.
Especially in the South, where the preservation of traditional gender roles had long
been a point of pride, the demands of war industry opened the door to an unimag-
ined new world. Before the war, most married women did not work outside the
home unless it was an economic necessity, and many employers would not hire
older women at all; women who held jobs were generally limited to low-paying
fields such as waitressing, farming, or domestic work. But when millions of men left
for military service, the government and the media called upon women to serve
their country. They responded in huge numbers. Many labored in defense industries; some replaced men in conventional factories; still others worked as reporters,
bus drivers, loggers, and in countless other traditionally male occupations. Between
1940 and 1945 the number of wives holding jobs doubled; by the end of the war
wives composed the majority of the female work force. Sixty percent of the women
added to the labor force were over thirty-five years of age. More than 500,000 female
workers — black and white — eagerly left menial jobs for the higher-paying war industries, which in many cases more than doubled their income. Particularly in
low-wage areas of the nation like the South, the advantage of war work was evident.

Symbolized by the ubiquitous "Rosie the Riveter," female war workers proved
incontrovertibly that women could do "men's work." Even so, traditional beliefs
about division of labor by gender persisted: they were evident in the media campaigns portraying women's war work as a temporary sacrifice; in wage discrimination and resentment of women workers; in the U.S. government's failure to
provide adequate child-care services; in the massive layoffs of women workers at
the war's end; and in the postwar glorification of domesticity. But postwar interviews and wartime correspondence also clearly indicate that working led women
to develop new confidence, attitudes, and interests. As women took on new and
unaccustomed duties, they surprised themselves as well as others. Thousands discovered that earning their own money was intensely satisfying; those who had

---

[1]Qtd. in Neil R. McMillen, *Remaking Dixie: The Impact of World War II on the American South*
(Jackson: University Press of Mississippi, 1997), 102, 103.

held "women's jobs" before the war found it difficult to return to "women's salaries." Vast numbers of women war workers who quit or were laid off at the end of the war soon rejoined the labor force — though often in "women's jobs."

In a similar vein but on a larger scale, the war seemed to drag the South out of its economic backwardness and to provide an alternative to rural life and poverty. It accelerated socioeconomic changes already underway, and its effects on rural-urban migration, the mechanization of agriculture, and infrastructures eventually altered the very basis of southern society.

A combination of the mild climate and the political clout of senior-level Democratic senators brought the South a significant proportion of the nation's training facilities and defense-industry installations, resulting in a major "war boom." During the war the federal government spent more than four billion dollars on military facilities in the South, and four billion more in contracts to privately owned military construction companies. As the number of industrial workers grew by more than fifty percent and the value added to the regional economy by industry tripled, the gap between the South's per capita income and the national average began to close.

In addition, cooperation between federal, state, and local agencies contributed to a growing tendency among southern politicians and progressive-minded business leaders to regard the federal government as an ally rather than an adversary, and to see the advantages of attracting outside industry that, even with the South's relatively low labor costs, still brought workers higher wages than had agricultural employment. The prospect of profitable employment in war-related industries increased the movement of men and women from farms and small towns to larger cities, and soon many southern cities were overflowing.

Many of the tenant farmers who left home had no desire to return to the poverty and isolation of their former lives. And there were fewer jobs to be had in agriculture: the war boom created both an increased demand for farm commodities and a rural labor shortage. Faced with a lack of agricultural workers, many landowners used their increased profits and the payments they received from the government under New Deal programs to buy farm machinery. These wartime developments paved the way for the economic prosperity of the modern South: changes in employment led to capital-intensive, mechanized agribusiness, while southern firms and military bases became an important part of the military-industrial complex.

In this chapter, letters from black soldiers and Myrlie Evers's description of Medgar Evers's transformation recount African Americans' wartime experiences at home and abroad. War correspondence and oral histories describing southern women's war work illustrate its impact on their lives. An account of the incredible "war boom" in the South reveals how it led to a massive rural-urban migration and to major changes in the region's economy and culture.

As you read, take note of how African Americans serving in America's armed forces responded when confronted by white racism. How did their experiences at home and abroad affect their attitudes? What specific experiences led to changes in outlook and ambition among southern women? In what ways did the booming economy in the South during the war years alter the socioeconomic structure of the region and make it more like that of the rest of the nation?

33. Serving in a Jim Crow Army

CHARLIE MABREY JR. AND CLARENCE E. ADAMS
Letters to the Editor
1943 and 1944

The American military was rigidly segregated in the 1940s: blacks were initially ex-cluded from the Army Air Corps and the Marine Corps, admitted to the Navy only as "messmen," and accepted in the Army only in segregated units; most served under white officers. African Americans serving in America's Jim Crow army encountered a multitude of racist practices and attitudes. In these two letters written to the edi-tors of black newspapers in Atlanta and Baltimore, black servicemen Private First Class Charlie Mabrey Jr. and Technician Fifth Grade Clarence E. Adams complain about harassment by white southern civilians as well as within the military itself. The letters demonstrate the sharp contrast between the servicemen's idealism and their experience.

The Atlanta Daily World   PFC Charlie Mabrey, Jr.
Circulation Department   226th Port Company
210 Auburn Avenue   Headquarters Command C.P.E.
Atlanta, Georgia   July 21, 1943

Dear Sirs:

I am [a] Negro soldier stationed in Charleston, South Carolina at the present. I am writing you in regard to something that occurred while I was enroute home

---

Taps for a Jim Crow Army: Letters from Black Soldiers in World War II, ed. Phillip McGuire (Santa Bar-bara, Calif.: ABC-Clio, 1983; reprint, Lexington: University Press of Kentucky, 1993), 194–95, 90–91.

on a furlough recently. On Friday, July 16, 1943 I was on my way home to La-Grange, Georgia to visit my wife and four months-old baby. I left Charleston about two-thirty o'clock and arrived in Augusta, Georgia about seven o'clock where I had a rest period of about thirty minutes. The bus driver, operator of an Atlantic Trailways bus, called all passengers to come out of the station and reclaim their seats. I got on the bus in front of a white woman who had not been a passenger on the bus but was ordered off by the driver who addressed me, "Say boy get off this bus."

I immediately got off and asked him what was wrong with my ticket. He again said for me to just get off. It was then about seven-thirty o'clock. The driver then said, "For blowing your damn top you will leave at on[e]-fifteen o'clock in the morning."

When I asked for the return of my ticket he at first refused to for some reason but finally gave it back to me. About that time two white military policemen [*sic*] walked up I asked one just why I could not ride on that particular bus. One was rather nice after I had told him of my trouble but the other one spoke up very insultingly.

He said, "You let a 'nigger' talk to you like that?" He said what if I did not like the way things were he would send me to camp foot forward and that he ought to arrest me anyway. I told him that as he had the authority to do so he could. I want you to publish this story and to also publish my name. I sent a copy of this airmail to the Pittsburgh Courier but I am sending it to you. I want everyone to know how we colored soldiers are being treated here in the South. We all have a tough time trying to visit our loved ones here in the south and if I have any more trouble of this kind I will begin to wonder just what we are fighting for. Perhaps instead of White America's fighting the Nazis and Japs they are fighting the Negroes of America. All America had better wake up to the fact that it is impossible to fight a battle abroad and at home too. I thank you in advance for your trouble.

> Yours with sincerely,
> PFC Charlie Mabrey, Jr.

T/5th Clarence E. Adams, 6,267,293
4295th QM Gasoline Supply Co.
Camp Breckinridge, Kentucky,
July 8, 1944.

Mr. Carl Murphy
Afro-American Newspapers,
Baltimore, Maryland.

Dear Mr. Murphy:

In response to your letter of this date, I am herewith closing the information that I wrote you about. It is fully understood that you are not to disclose my identity. Here is the story:

It happened on Saturday July 1, 1944. I drew a book from the Service Club Library to read. The title of the book is "Negro Poets and Their Poems," by Kerlin. I had the book with me at the motor-pool where I work (I am the dispatcher). I had finished up my work (records) for the day and was just about ready to leave when the Company Executive Officer walked in the office. My paraphenalia [*sic*] was laying on my desk including the book, so he picked up the book and began looking through it; finally he came to this poem: "Mulatto" by Langston Hughes.[1] He cursed and used all-kind of vile language about the author. He wanted to know who wrote it, where did I get the book; I told him, and this was his reply: "Take that damn book where you got it and I don't want to ever see anything like that around the company. The wrong person might get a hold of it and it might cause some trouble." I said this: "Sir, the men in the company are very intelligent and quite a few of them spend their leisure time in reading Negro works. I am certain that this book would make no difference to them." He said, "I don't care. I don't want books like that around the company, because others might not be as broadminded as you are." I said, "Yes, Sir."

I didn't take the book back as he ordered because I had not finished reading it. On Sunday I was in Company Orderly Room and I was called into his office, and again he asked me had I taken the book back to the library. I said, "No, Sir." Again I was given a direct order to take the book back. I told other members about the incident and as soon as I checked the book in at the library another member of my organization drew it out again. I don't know what the results are going to be.

This is the point, Mr. Murphy. Yes we are Negro Soldiers, giving our sweat, blood, and lives for what is known as an IDEALISTIC DEMOCRACY, and here in the midst of a world crisis we are told not to read books as that one by men of our own race. If this sort of thing happen now, what will happen when the war is over? I am sure that it will be much worse for the Negro, of which we aren't going to stand for. A few weeks ago I gave an address before a packed chapel of officers, men, and WACS. "UNDER OUR FLAG, AN AMERICAN SPEAKS." It was very militant and inspiring; so much so that I made it very uncomfortable for the white officers. Yes their faces turned all kinds of colors but there was nothing that they could do because I gave facts, dates, history, and authors. I happen to know quite a bit about the Negro, because I have and am devoting the majority of my leisure in the study of THE NEGRO.

The officer that told me to take the book back where I found it, happened to be a second lieutenant.

From time to time I will be sending you quite a bit of information of happenings here on this post; provided you want it.

Should you print this news in your paper I would appreciate a copy of it, if you will be kind enough to send me one. Whether you print it or not I still want one as they are very rare out here.

Thank you very kindly.

Respectfully Yours,
I remain,
S/T/5th Clarence E. Adams.

---

[1] "Mulatto" begins "I am your son, white man!" and discusses the sexual exploitation of black women by white southern men, producing mixed-race children the fathers then deny.

34. A Liberating Experience for African Americans

MYRLIE EVERS
On How the War Affected Medgar Evers
1967

Medgar Evers is perhaps the best-known World War II veteran to return from the war determined to challenge disfranchisement and Jim Crow. Like many black soldiers, he seized the opportunity offered by the GI Bill to gain a college education and a better life. In this excerpt from her memoir, For Us, the Living, *Myrlie Evers recalls how military service affected her husband and made him determined to bring about change in his home state of Mississippi. Medgar Evers later became an important figure in the civil rights movement and a leader of the NAACP; he was assassinated in 1963.*

. . . Medgar was sixteen and a sophomore at Newton High School when the United States entered World War II. Within a year he had quit school and followed his brother, Charles, into the Army. Eventually he wound up in a segregated port battalion that saw service in England and, after the Normandy invasion, at Le Havre, Liège, Antwerp, and Cherbourg. It was a rugged unit and a rough bunch of men, most of them considerably older than the seventeen-year-old lad from Decatur, Mississippi. Though Medgar neither smoked nor drank, his language was strongly influenced by the men around him. Obscenity must have seemed incongruous in one so young, and one day a white lieutenant took him aside.

"You're too intelligent to talk that way," the lieutenant said. "You have a good vocabulary. You can say what you want without swearing every other word. Some of these men can't. They don't know any better. You do. You can go a long way if you use the intelligence you've got."

There were other talks after that, and Medgar slowly realized that the lieutenant was right. As the war ended, the same lieutenant urged him to go back to school, to improve his mind, to finish his education, to make something of himself. He proved an important influence in Medgar's life.

Medgar had had no close friends among whites since his childhood, and I have no doubt that at first he regarded the lieutenant's interest in him with suspicion. But the whole experience of the Army was a new one, a broadening one, and it opened up new worlds to a young Negro boy from rural Mississippi. The fact that his unit was segregated, that its officers were white, would not have seemed strange to Medgar. That was the way his world had always been. But the trip by

Myrlie B. Evers, with William Peters, *For Us, the Living* (Garden City, N.Y.: Doubleday, 1967), 23–27. Reprint, Jackson, Miss.: Banner Books, 1996.

troop ship across the Atlantic was straight from a storybook, and though Medgar was seasick most of the way, the body's misery could not dampen the spirit's sense of adventure. In such an atmosphere, even a deeply ingrained suspicion of white men had to be questioned.

In France he found a whole people — all of them white — who apparently saw no difference in a man simply because of his skin color, and this was perhaps the greatest revelation of all. In time, he came to know a French family near where he was stationed, and they accepted him as one of them. A romance with a daughter developed, and nobody flinched. Before it could amount to much, the battalion was moved.

And yet even here, in France, where the French accepted both white and Negro American troops simply as American soldiers, the long arm of racism intruded. For white American soldiers brought their prejudices with them and imposed them wherever possible on the French. The white troops whispered stories about the colored troops, and more than once Medgar was asked by a naïve French girl if it were true that Negroes were some kind of monkey whose tails came out at night. There was embarrassment and shock when the lies were exposed, and there remained, for the French, wonder at what lay beneath the lies. Why should Americans hate each other? Why should they separate their troops according to color? There had to be reasons.

And so, in the end, even the openness and friendliness of the French were tainted by the presence of American racism. There was apparently no escape from it. And even the pleasant memory of Medgar's romance with the young French girl was later spoiled when, after the war, his mother pleaded with him to end his correspondence with her for fear that whites in Decatur would find out and take offense. Negroes have been lynched in Mississippi for less.

The war was liberating to Medgar in several ways. Both he and his brother, Charles, saved money from their army pay and sent it home to their parents. With some of it, Jessie and James Evers modernized their house, replacing the wood stove and bringing plumbing inside. Four rooms were added, and by the time the two boys came home, the family's living conditions were much improved.

There were many times during Medgar's army service when he felt how impossible it would be to return to Mississippi and settle down to the life he had known before the war. For if Mississippi hadn't changed, he had. He had a whole new vision of what life could be like, of the way it was lived in other places by other people. The simple fact that he had helped earn money that had done so much to improve his parent's home was an indication of the possibilities of life outside his native state.

And yet, when the war was over, back to Mississippi he went, along with Charles. Charles, who had finished high school, enrolled at Alcorn Agricultural and Mechanical College on the G.I. Bill of Rights. Medgar took a job while he decided what to do. But the changes wrought in both young men by their years outside Mississippi were not long in asserting themselves. In the summer of 1946, Medgar turned twenty-one. He and Charles rounded up four other young Negroes and went to the county clerk's office to register to vote. It was not such an innocent venture as it might seem. All of them knew that of the 900-odd voters on the rolls in Decatur none were Negroes. And all of them knew why.

A small crowd of whites gathered when the word went out that Negroes were registering. For the moment, that was all. "I never found out until later," Medgar said afterward, "that they visited my parents nightly after that. First, it was the whites, and then their Negro message-bearers. And the word was always the same: 'Tell your sons to take their names off the books. Don't show up at the courthouse voting day.' Then, the night before the election, Bilbo[1] came to town and harangued the crowd in the square. 'The best way to keep a nigger from the polls on election day,' he told them, 'is to visit him the night before.' And they visited us. My brother came from Alcorn College to vote that next day. I laid off from work. The six of us gathered at my house and we walked to the polls. I'll never forget it. Not a Negro was on the streets, and when we got to the courthouse, the clerk said he wanted to talk with us. When we got into his office, some fifteen or twenty armed white men surged in behind us, men I had grown up with, had played with. We split up and went home without voting. Around town, Negroes said we had been whipped, beaten up, and run out of town. Well, in a way we were whipped, I guess, but I made up my mind then that it would not be like that again — at least not for me." . . .

[1]**Bilbo:** U.S. Senator Theodore Bilbo, a former governor of Mississippi, known nationally for his racist rhetoric and tactics.

35. The Impact on Women

MARION STEGMAN, POLLY CROW, ERNESTINE SLADE, PEGGY TERRY, AND AUDREY WARD NORMAN
Recollections of War Jobs
1943–on

Wartime correspondence from and oral histories of southern women reveal the economic and attitudinal impact of their wartime jobs. In a letter to her mother, Marion Stegman of Athens, Georgia, describes the excitement of flying in the Women Airforce Service Pilots, a quasi-military unit that ferried aircraft across the United States, and suggests the transformative experience of succeeding in a job usually barred to women. Polly Crow brought her infant son to her mother's home in Kentucky after her husband was shipped overseas; her letters to him illustrate not only her trials and tribulations but also the thrill of earning a salary. Postwar interviews with Ernestine J. Slade, an African American woman from Georgia; Peggy Terry, a self-described "hillbilly woman" from the mountains of Tennessee; and Audrey Ward Norman, who quit high school to take a job at a converted torpedo factory in St. Louis, reveal how war jobs brought them not only better wages but also a new sense of life's possibilities, broadened horizons, and new confidence.

Marion Stegman

Sweetwater, Texas
April 24, 1943

Dearest Mother,

The gods must envy me! This is just too, *too* [good] to be true. (By now you realize I had a good day as regards flying. Nothing is such a gauge to the spirits as how well or how poorly one has flown.) Where was I? Oh, yes, I'm far too happy. The law of compensation must be waiting to catch up with me somewhere. Oh, God, how I love it! Honestly, Mother, you haven't *lived* until you get way *up* there — all alone — just you and that big, beautiful plane humming under your control. I just sit there and sing at the top of my lungs while I'm climbing up to 4,000 feet — or however high I want to go. Of course, I'm too busy to sing while in the middle of aerobatics — but you ought to hear me let loose when I'm "clearing my area" between maneuvers. (We always clear the area first to make sure there are no planes underneath or close by — safety foist!)

The only thing that I know that's going to happen that I won't like is that they are changing my instructors some day soon. Mine is going on to the B.T.'s (Basic trainers — one step ahead of primary trainers) but maybe I'll get him again when I get to the B.T.'s. Hope so! I have no idea who my new instructor will be — I hope I'll like him as much as I do this one. He'll have to be pretty good and mighty nice though, to beat Mr. Wade's time. . . .

Smackers and much love to John, Janet, Joanna, and you — M.

Sweetwater, Texas
[May 31, 1943]

Mother, Darling —

Get set! Prepare yourself! Because here comes another one of those slap-happy, nonsensical (??) ecstatic letters! OOOOOOO, Mom. I'm so happy I could die.

By now you know I've either (1) had a good day at flying or (2) passed a check ride. It just so happens that both are correct!

Honestly, mater, I was so scared when I climbed into that cockpit to take my

We're in This War Too: World War II Letters from American Women in Uniform, ed. Judy Barrett Litoff and David C. Smith (New York: Oxford University Press, 1994), 115–16.

first civilian check ride on the B.T. that I thought I'd vomit all over the controls. I had been running to the johnny for a nervous B.M. every ten minutes. One girl, seeing me dash in to the john for the fourth or fifth time (prior to my check ride) said to me, "You either are about to have a check ride or you're going on a cross country. Which is it?" It seems that it affects us gals the same way!

Anyway, I gave the check pilot a good ride and he told my instructor he might have an H.P. (hot pilot) on his hands. But since the only H.P.'s are dead pilots — proved by experience, he got his terminology mixed, but anyway, he meant it as a compliment. Happy day!

Then I went up for a ride with my instructor, and he told me to climb in the *back* seat which meant I was to do instrument (under the hood) flying — which is a very great compliment, since you aren't supposed to get instrument instruction until you are either qualified to solo or have already soloed! So he must think I'm ready to handle it alone as soon as I have the required eight hours, which makes me veddy, veddy happy indeed! I can hardly wait. He told me he thought I had the feel of the airplane now, and that I was cooking on the front burner! Also, he let me do a few slow rolls in the B.T. from the *back seat* — and he said they were *perfect*. Of course I came out from under the hood to do the slow rolls. . . .

While I was still under the hood, later, he said, "O.K. I'll take it, then you come out from under the hood when I tell you to." So he messed around awhile, then said, "All right, Come out!" So I came out from under the hood and *I was still under the hood!* He had flown right into the middle of a huge white cloud. More fun! So he flew the instruments until we were out of the cloud and could see again. . . .

So you see, your baby chile is enjoying life to the fullest. I have *everything* I want: my family loves me (and I'm sorta fond of it); I've got wonderful roommates — real *friends*; I'm doing what I love better than anything in the world; I'm so healthy and feel so good that it's revolting; and the men love me and I love the men! EEEEEEEEE, law! What a life! . . .

I love you all — M.

POLLY CROW

Pensacola, June 8, 1944

Darlin':

. . . After I get settled in Louisville I'm thinking seriously of going to work in some defense plant there on the swing shift so I can be at home during the day with Bill as he needs me — would like to know what you think of the idea, if you can write. Of course, I'd much rather have an office job but I couldn't be with Bill whereas I could if I worked at nite which I have decided is the best plan as I cain't save any thing by not working and I want to have something for us when you get

Since You Went Away: World War II Letters from American Women on the Home Front, ed. Judy Barrett Litoff and David C. Smith (New York: Oxford University Press, 1991), 146–47.

home so you can enjoy life for awhile before going back to work and Bill and I want all of your time too for awhile so's we can all three make up for lost time.

Gotta scoot as I have several more chores to do.

I love you, Darlin', Polly

Louisville, June 12, 1944

Darlin':

You are now the husband of a career woman — just call me your little Ship Yard Babe! Yeh! I made up my mind that I wanted to work from 4:00 p.m. 'till midnight so's I could have my cake and eat it too. I wanted to work but didn't want to leave Bill all day — in the first place it would be too much for Mother altho' she was perfectly willing and then Bill needs me. This way Mother will just have to feed him once and tuck him in which is no trouble at all any more as I just put him in bed and let him play quietly until he's ready to go to sleep and he drops right off. . . . I finally ended up with just what I wanted. Comptometer [calculator] job — 4:00 'till midnite — 70 cents an hour to start which amounts to $36.40 a week, $145.60 per month, increase in two months if I'm any good and I know I will be. Oh yeh! At Jeffersonville Boat and Machine Co. I'll have to go over to Jeffersonville, Ind. which will take about 45 minutes each way. Hope I can get a ride home each nite as that's the only feature I dislike but I'm not gonna be a sissy. If I can't get a ride, I'll get tags for our buggy and probably use it. . . . If I don't need it for work I may not get them but will just have to see how things work out. Want to take Bill out swimming a lot this summer so I may need it for that. . . .

Opened my little checking account too and it's a grand and a glorious feeling to write a check all your own and not have to ask for one. Any hoo, I don't want it said I charged things to 'em and didn't pay it so we don't owe anybody anything and I'm gonna start sockin' it in the savings and checking too so's we'll have something when our sweet little Daddy comes home.

Good nite, Darlin'
I love you,   Polly

ERNESTINE SLADE

Slade: I always managed somehow to work. And having [eight] children, it was necessary to work. When I started working out at Bell Aircraft, [my husband Horace Slade] was working on the day shift. . . .

Interviewer Kathryn A. Kelley: Now what kind of work did you do before you went to Bell Aircraft?

Slade: Housekeeping and laundry work. . . . What I did was, I would stretch curtains . . . putting curtains on stretchers and you would charge so much for each

Cornerstones of Georgia History: Documents That Formed the State, ed. Thomas A. Scott (Athens: University of Georgia Press, 1995), 199–201.

pair. And I would do linens because you could get a little more money for doing linens than you could for just doing a whole wash. Although I've done the family wash, too, but my specialty was washing and stretching curtains and doing the linens, the tablecloths and things like that — that's special work. . . .

Kelley: So what a big change, then, from you doing laundry and being more or less self-employed, to going to work at a big company like Bell Aircraft. Tell me about — how did that come about?

Slade: . . . It was a little difficult when Bell first came here for a person who had a regular job, a domestic worker, to get on. Because, see, like they had an understanding or had discussed or didn't want to take nobody's help away from them, especially a person who was working for, you know, a well-to-do family. If you went there, and you were working for one of these well-to-do families, you could not get on at Bell easily. And you made so much money at Bell — much more money at Bell than you could make working for a permanent family. So me and my friends, we didn't go to the employment office here in Marietta. We went into Atlanta to the employment office. And that's how I got hired. Then I came back, and I told this lady that I had been working for, they hired me that day, told me when I could start to work. So that weekend, I told her. I said, "Now I'm going to start working at the Bomber Club" — that's what we called it. Well, naturally, she didn't like it, but she didn't fuss too much about. And I said, "I'll be leaving you." And so I went on that Monday morning to work out at Bell. . . .

Kelley: Now when you went to Bell, what kinds of job openings were there and what led you to the job that you took?

Slade: I can tell you what I did. It was something like the finishing department where they sent all parts that went into the airplane, regardless of how small they were, through some kind of treatment process. We would clean those parts, and they would put it in a machine and then some kind of solution and what-have-you. I don't know whether it was strengthening or just to be sure it was clean or what. And then sometimes, after they had got a part of the plane completed, we'd go inside of that plane and clean it all in the inside. Those long parts to the plane, sometimes we'd have to take something like steel wool and rub them; and then they would put them through this process I'm telling you about. And the little, bitty pieces like that, we had in the buckets we'd drop them in. They'd put them through this process.

Kelley: Did you work Monday through Friday?

Slade: Yes, yes, I did. I went on the evening shift. We would go in around 11:00 or 11:45 and work until — now my older children had started to school. And see, I'd get here early enough to see that all was well with them and that their clothes and everything were on properly and so forth, and they could get to school without being late. . . .

Kelley: So when you came home then, some of your children were just getting up and getting ready to go to school?

Slade: Yes. I'd come in from work, do my cleaning, do my wash and my laundry work, wash the children's clothes, iron whatever needed to be done, then I would lay down and go to sleep. And when they would come in the afternoon, I'd get up and do their dinner, fix their meals for them, and have that ready for them so they could eat. Then I'd lay down again and take another little nap before going to work at night. I'd comb the girls' hair at home for the next day, and I put stocking caps over their heads so their hair would stay nice, and give them their bath and get them ready for bed and get them in the bed before I'd leave. . . .

Kelley: How much money did you make at Bell, do you remember?

Slade: Oh, Lord. It was like a million dollars, my first paycheck — it was about thirty-three or thirty-four dollars [a week]. I can't tell you the exact amount. [Before then I had been paid] seven and ten dollars a week.

Kelley: Now it sounds like a very small amount, but at the time, was that enough money for you?

Slade: It wasn't enough, but we had to manage, you know. No black woman made a whole lot of money. I remember some of our neighbors and friends used to work for five dollars a week. . . .

Kelley: Where you worked in your unit at Bell, was that all black women working together?

Slade: No, black and white worked together. . . .

Kelley: I'll bet that some jobs weren't available [for blacks].

Slade: Well, you know not, no.

Kelley: Some of the women that I've talked to that worked in secretarial services, for example, there were no black women —

Slade: That's true, that's true.

Kelley: What kinds of jobs were available for black women at Bell?

Slade: Well, just they worked in the cafeteria helping to prepare food. Some of them had a little better job than I had and a better paying job. . . .

Kelley: To sum up your experience at Bell Aircraft, do you think that that experience changed your life at all?

Slade: Well, it was a help.

Kelley: A lot of money?

Slade: Yes. Well, you know, a little more money. Yes, that was a help. Oh, Lord, it just helped in every way. I remember when I started working, I first paid off all my bills. Got my bills paid off and I was able to get some things that we needed in the home. The older girls had never had Sunday shoes — they always had shoes, you know. I bought them some nice dresses, and I bought them Sunday shoes, an extra pair of shoes. And that meant everything in the world to them and me, too. When I started working out at Bell, I never could put no money in the bank. I didn't have a million dollars, however, now, I was able to save a little bit.

PEGGY TERRY

The first work I had after the Depression was at a shell-loading plant in Viola, Kentucky. It is between Paducah and Mayfield. They were large shells: anti-aircraft, incendiaries, and tracers. We painted red on the tips of the tracers. My

Studs Terkel, *"The Good War": An Oral History of World War Two* (New York: Pantheon Books, 1984), 108–13.

mother, my sister, and myself worked there. Each of us worked a different shift because we had little ones at home. We made the fabulous sum of thirty-two dollars a week. (Laughs.) To us it was just an absolute miracle. Before that, we made nothing.

You won't believe how incredibly ignorant I was. I knew vaguely that a war had started, but I had no idea what it meant.

[Interviewer Studs Terkel:] Didn't you have a radio?

Gosh, no. That was an absolute luxury. We were just moving around, working wherever we could find work. I was eighteen. My husband was nineteen. We were living day to day. When you are involved in stayin' alive, you don't think about big things like a war. It didn't occur to us that we were making these shells to kill people. It never entered my head.

There were no women foremen where we worked. We were just a bunch of hillbilly women laughin' and talkin'. It was like a social. Now we'd have money to buy shoes and a dress and pay rent and get some food on the table. We were just happy to have work.

I worked in building number 11. I pulled a lot of gadgets on a machine. The shell slid under and powder went into it. Another lever you pulled tamped it down. Then it moved on a conveyer belt to another building where the detonator was dropped in. You did this over and over.

Tetryl was one of the ingredients and it turned us orange. Just as orange as an orange. Our hair was streaked orange. Our hands, our face, our neck just turned orange, even our eyeballs. We never questioned. None of us ever asked, What is this? Is this harmful? We simply didn't think about it. That was just one of the conditions of the job. The only thing we worried about was other women thinking we had dyed our hair. Back then it was a disgrace if you dyed your hair. We worried what people would say.

We used to laugh about it on the bus. It eventually wore off. But I seem to remember some of the women had breathing problems. The shells were painted a dark gray. When the paint didn't come out smooth, we had to take rags wet with some kind of remover and wash that paint off. The fumes from these rags — it was like breathing cleaning fluid. It burned the nose and throat. Oh, it was difficult to breathe. I remember that.

Nothing ever blew up, but I remember the building where they dropped in the detonator. These detonators are little black things about the size of a thumb. This terrible thunderstorm came and all the lights went out. Somebody knocked a box of detonators off on the floor. Here we were in the pitch dark. Somebody was screaming, "Don't move, anybody!" They were afraid you'd step on the detonator. We were down on our hands and knees crawling out of that building in the storm. (Laughs.) We were in slow motion. If we'd stepped on one . . .

Mamma was what they call terminated — fired. Mamma's mother took sick and died and Mamma asked for time off and they told her no. Mamma said, "Well, I'm gonna be with my mamma. If I have to give up my job, I will just have to." So they terminated Mamma. That's when I started gettin' nasty. I didn't take as much baloney and pushing around as I had taken. I told 'em I was gonna quit, and they told me if I quit they would blacklist me wherever I would go. They had my fingerprints and all that. I guess it was just bluff, because I did get other work.

I think of how little we knew of human rights, union rights. We knew Daddy had been a hell-raiser in the mine workers' union, but at that point it hadn't rubbed off on any of us women. Coca-Cola and Dr. Pepper were allowed in every building, but not a drop of water. You could only get a drink of water if you went to the cafeteria, which was about two city blocks away. Of course you couldn't leave your machine long enough to go get a drink. I drank Coke and Dr. Pepper and I hated 'em. I hate 'em today. We had to buy it, of course. We couldn't leave to go to the bathroom, 'cause it was way the heck over there.

We were awarded the navy E for excellence. We were just so proud of that E. It was like we were a big family, and we hugged and kissed each other. They had the navy band out there celebrating us. We were so proud of ourselves.

First time my mother ever worked at anything except in the fields — first real job Mamma ever had. It was a big break in everybody's life. Once, Mamma woke up in the middle of the night to go to the bathroom and she saw the bus going down. She said, "Oh my goodness, I've overslept." She jerked her clothes on, throwed her lunch in the bag, and was out on the corner, ready to go, when Boy Blue, our driver, said, "Honey, this is the wrong shift." Mamma wasn't supposed to be there until six in the morning. She never lived that down. She would have enjoyed telling you that. . . .

We were very patriotic and we understood that the Nazis were someone who would have to be stopped. We didn't know about concentration camps. I don't think anybody I knew did. With the Japanese, that was a whole different thing. We were just ready to wipe them out. They sure as heck didn't look like us. They were yellow little creatures that smiled when they bombed our boys. I remember someone in Paducah got up this idea of burning everything they had that was Japanese. I had this little ceramic cat and I said, "I don't care, I am not burning it." They had this big bonfire and people came and brought what they had that was made in Japan. Threw it on the bonfire. I hid my cat. It's on the shelf in my bathroom right now. (Laughs.)

In all the movies we saw, the Germans were always tall and handsome. There'd be one meanie, a little short dumpy bad Nazi. But the main characters were good-lookin' and they looked like us. The Japanese were all evil. If you can go half your life and not recognize how you're being manipulated, that is sad and kinda scary.

I do remember a nice movie, *The White Cliffs of Dover*. We all sat there with tears pouring down our face. All my life, I hated England, 'cause all my family all my life had wanted England out of Ireland. During the war, all those ill feelings just seemed to go away. It took a war.

I believe the war was the beginning of my seeing things. You just can't stay uninvolved and not knowing when such a momentous thing is happening. It's just little things that start happening and you put one piece with another. Suddenly, a puzzle begins to take shape.

My husband was a paratrooper in the war, in the 101st Airborne Division. He made twenty-six drops in France, North Africa, and Germany. I look back at the war with sadness. I wasn't smart enough to think too deeply then. We had a lotta good times and we had money and we had food on the table and the rent was paid. Which had never happened to us before. . . .

The war gave a lot of people jobs. It led them to expect more than they had before. People's expectations, financially, spiritually, were raised. There was such a beautiful dream. We were gonna reach the end of the rainbow. When the war ended, the rainbow vanished. Almost immediately we went into Korea. There was no peace, which we were promised. . . .

No bombs were ever dropped on us. I can't help but believe the cold war started because we were untouched. Except for our boys that went out of the country and were killed, we came out of that war in good shape. People with more money than they'd had in years.

No, I don't think we'd have been satisfied to go back to what we had during the Depression. To be deprived of things we got used to. Materially, we're a thousand times better off. But the war turned me against religion. I was raised in the fundamentalist faith. I was taught that I was nothing. My feeling is if God created me, if God sent his only begotten son to give his life for me, then I am something. My mother died thinking she was nothing. . . .

I was just so glad when it was over, because I wanted my husband home. I didn't understand any of the implications except that the killing was over and that's a pretty good thing to think about whether you're political or not. (Laughs.) The killing be over forever.

AUDREY WARD NORMAN

I was right in the middle of the plant. I did bookkeeping. All the machines and everything were around me. My job was to record who took out what tools, who brought them back — the tools to repair the machines.

We had no fans, no air-conditioning, and with the machinery going and all the drilling, the air was absolutely blue. All the time. The building was three stories high and with nothing but glass up around the edges of the top; it was very noisy.

One thing I remember was that because of the food shortages we were rationed on meat, and I looked forward to Tuesdays because that's the day we could have meat. The rest of the days we got scrambled eggs or something like that in the cafeteria.

Also, I don't smoke, but they rationed cigarettes, so once a week, when they sold them, I was everybody's friend because I'd get cigarettes for them.

One of the bad things I remember is that they were horsing around one day — to put out fires they had buckets of sand around — and they were horsing around near me and I could see them and they threw the sand at each other and it went into the machinery itself and that machine was shut down for several days

Nancy Baker Wise and Christy Wise, *A Mouthful of Rivets: Women at Work in World War II* (San Francisco: Jossey-Bass Publishers, 1994), 159–61.

because of that. The management came around and wanted to know if there were any eye-witnesses, and I said, "Oh, absolutely not; I never saw a thing." I didn't know what those guys might do.

It was all men. I was the only woman. Some of the men treated me as if I were a queen and some of them treated me like a whore. I mean, they said that to my face. My husband was overseas in the Navy at the time. And one man had come back from a concentration camp, and evidently his wife had been running around on him and what not, and he couldn't have a good word for me whatsoever. I think he was brain damaged because he would call me everything in the book. To my face. He would walk up to me for no rhyme or reason. Just because I was there and my husband was overseas — he thought I had no business working out there with all those men. That I was only out there for one reason.

Those four years had considerable impact on my life. I was so shy before I ever started this thing that I wouldn't even go first in the door of one of those buildings with a group of people. I'd always tail along at the back of a group. I couldn't step forward and be in front for any reason. After four years in there, I have been forward ever since. I love people. I love being around people, and I've been all over the United States.

I'm still doing volunteer work. I'm doing income tax for senior citizens, for disabled and the poor. I'm doing it for free. After I finished working for the federal government and then the state, I went into my own business as an income tax consultant and did that for thirty years.

Those four years definitely gave me everything I needed to tell myself that I could handle it, no matter what. If I could do that, I could do anything. I could handle it — bring it on. That was my attitude. Dealing with the men was what did it. The good people and the bad people both.

On top of that, at the same time I was working in the factory, I had the chance to go to night school and I was getting a higher education, which also helped my self-esteem.

I've had a wonderful life — I'm sixty-eight years old now and when I look back there's a few things I regret, but the majority of my life has been upbeat — and I really credit it to quitting school and going in and taking that job. I really don't know what I would have done otherwise, but I certainly wouldn't have been out in the public eye.

36. Structural Changes in the South

JOHN DOS PASSOS
"Gold Rush Down South"
1943

Noted American fiction writer John Dos Passos traveled extensively writing articles for magazines about the war "scene" in various parts of the nation. These articles, many of which describe the immense impact of the war on the South and its people, formed the basis of his 1943 book, State of the Nation. *The chapter excerpted here describes the old port city of Mobile, Alabama, which had been transformed into a crowded, bustling center of the defense industry.*

A Town Outgrows Itself

We are in the city now. The bus is swinging out of the traffic of the crowded main street round the low gray building of the bus-station, and comes to a stop in the middle of a milling crowd: soldiers, sailors, stout women with bundled up babies, lanky backwoodsmen with hats tipped over their brows and a cheek full of chewingtobacco, hatless young men in lightcolored sport shirts open at the neck, countrymen with creased red necks and well-washed overalls, cigarsmoking stocky men in business suits in pastel shades, girls in bright dresses with carefully curled hair piled up on their heads and highheeled shoes and bloodred fingernails, withered nutbrown old people with glasses, carrying ruptured suitcases, broadshouldered men in oilstained khaki with shiny brown helmets on their heads, negroes in flappy jackets and pegtop pants and little felt hats with turned-up brims, teenage boys in jockey caps, here and there a flustered negro woman dragging behind her a string of white-eyed children. Gradually the passengers are groping their way down the steep steps out of the bus and melting into the crowd.

Out on the streets every other man seems to be in work clothes. There are girls in twos and threes in slacks and overalls. Waiting for the light at a crossing a pink-faced youth who's dangling a welder's helmet on a strap from the crook of his arm turns laughing to the man who hailed him. "I jes' got tired an' quit." Ragged families from the hills and the piney woods stroll staring straight ahead of them along the sidewalks towing flocks of little kids with flaxen hair and dirty faces. In front of a window full of bright-colored rayon socks in erratic designs a young man with glasses meets two girls in slacks. "We missed you yesterday," they say. "I was sick. I didn't go in. Anyway, I've got me a new job . . . more money."

The mouldering old Gulf seaport with its ancient dusty elegance of tall shuttered windows under mansard roofs and iron lace overgrown with vines, and scal-

John Dos Passos, *State of the Nation* (Boston: Houghton Mifflin, 1943 and 1944), 91–95, 99–101.

ing colonnades shaded by great trees, looks trampled and battered like a city that's been taken by storm. Sidewalks are crowded. Gutters are stacked with litter that drifts back and forth in the brisk spring wind. Garbage cans are overflowing. Frame houses on treeshaded streets bulge with men in shirtsleeves who spill out onto the porches and trampled grassplots and stand in knots at the streetcorners. There's still talk of lodginghouses where they rent "hot beds." (Men work in three shifts. Why shouldn't they sleep in three shifts?) Cues[1] wait outside of movies and lunchrooms. The trailer army has filled all the open lots with its regular ranks. In cluttered backyards people camp out in tents and chickenhouses and shelters tacked together out of packingcases.

In the outskirts in every direction you find acres and acres raw with new building, open fields skinned to the bare clay, elevations gashed with muddy roads and gnawed out by the powershovels and the bulldozers. There long lines of small houses, some decently planned on the "American standard" model and some mere boxes with a square brick chimney on the center, miles of dormitories, great squares of temporary structures are knocked together from day to day by a mob of construction workers in a smell of paint and freshsawed pine lumber and tobacco juice and sweat. Along the river for miles has risen a confusion of new yards from which men, women, and boys ebb and flow three times a day. Here and there are whole city blocks piled with wreckage and junk as if ancient cranky warehouses and superannuated stores had caved in out of their own rottenness under the impact of the violence of the new effort. Over it all the Gulf mist, heavy with smoke of soft coal, hangs in streaks, and glittering the training planes endlessly circle above the airfields.

Riffraff

To be doing something towards winning the war, to be making some money, to learn a trade, men and women have been pouring into the city for more than a year now; tenants from dusty shacks set on stilts above the bare eroded earth in the midst of the cotton and the scraggly corn, small farmers and trappers from halfcultivated patches in the piney woods, millhands from the industrial towns in the northern part of the state, garage men, fillingstation attendants, storekeepers, drugclerks from crossroads settlements, longshore fishermen and oystermen, negroes off plantations who've never seen any town but the county seat on Saturday afternoon, white families who've lived all their lives off tobacco and "white meat" and cornpone in cranky cabins forgotten in the hills.

For them everything's new and wonderful. They can make more spot cash in a month than they saw before in half a year. They can buy radios, they can go to the pictures, they can go to beerparlors, bowl, shoot craps, bet on the ponies. Everywhere they rub elbows with foreigners from every state in the Union. Housekeeping in a trailer with electric light and running water is a dazzling luxury to a woman who's lived all her life in a cabin with half-inch chinks between the splin-

[1]cues: queues, lines of people.

tered boards of the floor. There are street cars and busses to take you anywhere you want to go. At night the streets are bright with electric light. Girls can go to beautyparlors, get their nails manicured, buy readymade dresses. In the backwoods a girl who's reached puberty feels she's a woman. She's never worried much about restraining her feelings when she had any. Is it any wonder that they can't stay home at dusk when the streets fill up with hungry boys in uniform? . . .

Waiting for the bus at the streetcorner in front of one of the better trailer camps that has clean white gravel spread over the ground, and neat wooden platforms beside each shiny trailer for use as a front stoop, I get to talking to a young man in a leather jacket. He's just worked four hours overtime because the other fellow didn't get there to relieve him at his machine. He's tired. You can tell by his breath that he's just had a couple or three beers. He's beefing because of the state regulations limiting the sale of whiskey and cutting out juke boxes in beer parlors. When a man's tired, he says, he needs relaxation. Works better next day. What's the use of dancing if you can't have a drink? What's the use of drinking if you can't dance? If this sort of thing keeps up he's going to pick up and move some place where things are wide open. Meanwhile several busses so jammed with soldiers from the airfield there's no more room, have passed us by. Hell, he groans, might as well go get him another beer, and he trots back into the silent "Dine and Dance" joint across the street. . . .

Twentyfive Years Behind the Times

And all the while, by every bus and train the new people, white and black, pour into the city. As fast as a new block of housing is finished, it's jampacked. As soon as a new bus is put into service, it's weighed down with passengers. The schools are too full of children. The restaurants are too full of eaters. If you try to go to see a doctor, you find the waitingroom full and a long line of people straggling down the hall. There's no room in the hospitals for the women who are going to have babies. "So far we've been lucky," the health officers say with terror in their voices, "not to have had an epidemic. But we've got our fingers crossed."

Lines of men wait outside of every conceivable office. If you go to see the mayor in the City Hall, you find him, a certain desperation under his bland exterior, desperately calling up Washington to try to pry loose some sewer pipe. The housing project has attended to the plumbing within its domain. The army has attended to these matters within its camps, but nobody has thought of how the new projects are to be linked up with the watermains and sewers of the city.

If you go to see the personnel director of one of the big yards — he used to be a football coach — you find him fuming because he can't get the old team spirit into his employees. "What can you do when workingmen are making such big wages they don't give a damn?"

If you ask a labor man why management and labor can't get together to take some action about absenteeism and labor turnover, he snaps back at you: "Management down here won't talk to labor. The men running these yards are twentyfive years behind the times."

"I try to tell the president of one of these concerns," says the Government Man, "that he ought to set up a modern labor relations department and he just gives me a kind of oily grin and says, 'Oh go 'long — you get it all out of a book.' "

The Government Man's office is under continual siege. Today two very pretty girls in overalls with magnificent hairdos and long sharp red polished nails have been waiting all morning to tell their story. Meanwhile, they tell it to a sympathetic telephone girl. They are welders. They want a release from this company so that they can go somewhere else where they can get more money. The mean old company won't see it their way. Can't the government do something about it? A group of farmboys is complaining that the local police won't let them run their cars without getting local plates. They can't get local plates until they get paid at the end of the week. Without their cars they can't get to work. Can't the government do something about it? In the hall some very black negroes are hunched in a group leaning against the white marble sheathing of the wall of the officebuilding. They are appealing to Caesar. At the personnel office they've been told that if they quit their jobs they'll have to leave town. They want Uncle Sam to say if it's true. No, it's not true, not yet.

"It's incredible," says the Government Man when his office is finally clear. "Labor turnover in this town has reached twentyfive percent a quarter. That means every man Jack of 'em changed his job in a year. It's rugged individualism, all right. What they do is come into town and get some training, then when they've qualified for the lowest rate of skilled work they go and get 'em a job somewhere else. They can say they've had experience and can get in at a higher rate. After they've worked there a while, they move to some other outfit and get taken on in a higher category still, and they don't know a damn thing about the work because they spend all their time on the bus travelling around. It's the same thing with the foremen and executives. Before any one of them has a chance to learn his work he's snatched off somewhere else. I can't keep anybody in my office. Don't know anything about organizing industry, but they all get big jobs in management. It's upgrading for fair. It's very nice, but nobody stays any place long enough to learn his job. It's a nightmare."

And still . . . the office is in a tall building. We both happen to look out the window at the same time. Across a welter of sunblackened roofs we can see in the slanting afternoon sunlight the rows of great cranes and the staging and the cradled hulls and beyond, in the brown strip of river, packed rows of new tankers, some splotched with yellow and red, some shining with the light gray of their last coat of paint. In spite of turmoil and confusion, ships are getting built, ships, ships, ships. . . .

Suggestions for Further Reading

Boles, John. *The South through Time: A History of an American Region*. Englewood Cliffs, N.J.: Prentice Hall, 1995. See especially pp. 450–56.

Daniel, Pete. "Going among Strangers: Southern Reactions to World War II." *Journal of American History* 77 (December 1990): 886–911.

Kirby, Jack Temple. *Rural Worlds Lost: The American South, 1920–1960.* Baton Rouge: Louisiana State University Press, 1987.

Litoff, Judy Barrett, and David C. Smith. *Since You Went Away: World War II Letters from American Women on the Home Front.* Lawrence: University of Kansas Press, 1991.

McMillen, Neil R. *Remaking Dixie: The Impact of World War II on the American South.* Jackson: University Press of Mississippi, 1997.

Motley, Mary Penick. *The Invisible Soldier: The Experience of the Black Soldier, World War II.* Detroit: Wayne State University Press, 1975.

Schulman, Bruce J. *From Cotton Belt to Sunbelt: Federal Policy, Economic Development, and the Transformation of the South, 1938–1980.* New York: Oxford University Press, 1991.

Thomas, Mary Martha. *Riveting and Rationing in Dixie: Alabama Women and the Second World War.* Tuscaloosa: University of Alabama Press, 1987.

CHAPTER ELEVEN

THE MCCARTHY ERA

Frank Porter Graham and the Ordeal of Southern Liberalism

In the years following World War II, the United States and the Soviet Union entered a prolonged period of competition and confrontation. The tension had started with Americans' reaction to the Russian revolution of 1917: although the creation of a worker-controlled state was a welcome event for some, others vigorously opposed it; and as the world learned more about Soviet totalitarianism, many Americans came to see Communism as a global menace to democracy. Later events, such as the spread of Soviet-style regimes in war-ravaged eastern Europe, the explosion of a Soviet nuclear device, the creation of the People's Republic of China, and North Korea's invasion of South Korea, fanned a growing unease. Americans reacted sharply to perceptions that Communists and their sympathizers were engaged in subversion and promoted Soviet interests in the United States. A full-blown anti-Communist crusade swept the country in the 1950s. Many Communist leaders were either jailed or suppressed, but equally serious was the profound effect that the crusade had on American liberalism.

Before and during World War II, Communists around the world had formed "popular front" alliances with left-liberals to defeat fascism. Though little came of these alliances, they provided a basis for subsequent charges by American conservatives of a close connection between liberalism and Communism. In Congress, anti-Communists launched a full-scale campaign that sought to link New Deal liberalism with the Communist threat. In 1938, the House Special Committee on Un-American Activities was formed to investigate alleged Communist subversion in New Deal agencies. It was reorganized in 1945 under the chairmanship of Mississippian John Rankin, renamed the House Un-American Activities Committee (HUAC), and bequeathed broad powers to investigate Communist subversion in American society. Soon, HUAC attracted considerable attention. In 1948, it led the case against Alger Hiss, an official in Franklin Roosevelt's liberal government charged with secretly giving diplomatic documents to Soviet agents. His perjury conviction and jail sentence seemed to confirm that there was a link between liberalism and Communism.

In addition, a widespread crackdown on dissent began in the late 1940s. The Truman administration inaugurated a loyalty program that scrutinized federal employees; eventually, more than twenty-two hundred of them left their jobs. The Federal Bureau of Investigation began vigorously to investigate left-wing organizations, a program that would continue for twenty-five years. The activities of Senator Joseph R. McCarthy of Wisconsin — who launched an irresponsible campaign in the early 1950s that claimed that the federal government remained thoroughly infiltrated by Communists — further encouraged suppression of dissent. Frequently, political candidates with connections to the New Deal were tarred by association as Communists. When Richard Nixon ran against Helen Gahagan Douglas for California's U.S. Senate seat, for example, he reminded voters of her associations with labor groups that had some Communist ties. Calling her the "Pink Lady," Nixon made a strong connection between liberalism and Communism.

The case of Frank Porter Graham provides another telling example of anti-Communism's impact on American liberalism. In the 1930s and 1940s, there was perhaps no better example of a southern liberal. "Dr. Frank" became president of the University of North Carolina (UNC) in 1931, and under his leadership it became the leading university in the South. Graham was well known for his participation in liberal causes. Despite the vehement hostility of many of his trustees, he supported striking textile workers. An active supporter of Franklin Roosevelt's New Deal, Graham was closely associated with Roosevelt and his advisers. At UNC's flagship campus in Chapel Hill, he promoted an environment of free enquiry and debate among students and faculty, and during the 1930s the university sponsored speakers from all over the country on a range of topics. Graham was also known as a liberal on race. Although he never openly favored desegregation — few southern liberals in the 1930s dared — he was an active participant in pioneering interracial groups.

Graham's liberal associations provided fodder for his opponents, both in North Carolina and elsewhere. Beginning soon after the war, Graham was accused of being a Communist; the charges continued through 1948 and reached a peak in 1949, the year Graham was appointed to fill a vacated seat in the U.S. Senate. When he ran for election to a full, six-year term in 1950, the attacks overwhelmed his candidacy: his opponent connected him not only with Communism, but — equally troubling to white voters — with suggestions that he favored ending segregation. Graham narrowly lost the primary and thus the Senate seat.

This chapter describes how liberalism came to be associated with Communism during 1948–49. In North Carolina, Graham had numerous political opponents, such as A. W. Black, who saw Graham's southern liberalism as a vehicle for Communist subversion. He also had many supporters, in North Carolina and nationally. In a speech delivered to the Senate, Oregon senator Wayne Morse defended Graham as a traditional New Deal liberal; others were unwilling to accept that characterization. National radio broadcaster Fulton Lewis Jr. attacked Dr. Frank's loyalty in January 1949, and although Graham immediately refuted the charges in a telegram to Lewis, the suggestion of guilt by association had been planted. The full range of accusations — most of them an extension of the guilt-by-association approach — appear in HUAC's report of February 1949.

As you read, ponder the following questions. What grounds were there for saying that Graham was a Communist? Based on the documents in this chapter, what were some of the common elements of the anti-Communism of the era? How did Graham and his supporters attempt to respond to the charges against them? Why did the anti-Communist attacks on Graham have the effects they did?

37. Dr. Frank Attacked

A. W. BLACK
"Looking at Dr. Frank Graham's Record"
1948

Frank Porter Graham's involvement with liberal causes became entangled in the broader attack on Communism. In the South, that attack was focused particularly on southern liberals active, as Graham had been, in seeking ways to loosen — though not necessarily to eliminate — the system of Jim Crow segregation. Here, a conservative newspaper columnist from Charlotte, North Carolina, lays out the basic ingredients of the attack on Graham's liberalism — and its alleged connections with Communism.

A. W. Black, "Looking at Dr. Frank Graham's Record," *Carolina Free Press* 2, no. 3 (February 1948). Frank Porter Graham Papers, University of North Carolina at Chapel Hill Library.

([*Carolina Free Press*] Editor's Note: First in a series of articles dealing with subversive and Communist front affiliations of Dr. Frank P. Graham. The data has been selected from official records, Government reports, etc.)

Substantuating affinative [*sic*] reports of Communist infiltration into educational institutions, and that like maggots in a cheese, Red fellow-travelers and liberal stooges, lend flavor and palatability to the Communist nausea, the Rapp-Coudert Committee reveals that "there are hundreds of Communists and international fellow-travelers in the school system." Correspondingly Dickson Hartwell *(Colliers Magazine)*, discloses that "there is indeed enough Communism in our colleges to supply Congress with months of oratory."

Considered in the light of intermittent reports that "the Kremlin has subtly manipulated many of our educational and political leaders, including . . . Dr. Frank P. Graham," it is appropriate that the focus of observation be directed upon the North Carolina educators long and uncomplimentary crimson record of associations with Communists, Red sponsored programs, and subversive, Soviet inspired, organizations.

Consistently following the Communist party line, and frequently the recipient of party praises, Dr. Graham has allied with the American League for Peace and Democracy (originally the American League Against War and Fascism), officially tagged as "nothing more nor less than a bold advocate of treason." American Committee for Protection of the Foreign Born, "one of the oldest auxiliaries of the Communist Party." International Labor Defense, branded by the FBI as the "legal arm of the Communist Party." American Committee for Democracy and Intellectual Freedom, "devoted to defense of Communist teachers." American Friends of Spanish Democracy, an aggregation preeminently engaged in raising funds in the United States for support of Spanish Communists. Coordinating Committee to lift the Embargo, committed to the "purpose of subverting the Congress of the United States to Communist ends."

Other Communist fronts, with which Graham was associated, include China Aid Council; China Air Council of the American League for Peace and Democracy; Committee for Boycott Against Japanese Aggression; Conference to Lift the Embargo; Medical Aid Bureau; and the North American Committee to Aid Spanish Democracy, both "Communist Party . . . so-called charity organizations."

Graham has likewise collaborated with the American Civil Liberties Union, of which "fully 90% of its activities are believed to be in behalf of Communists," and whose propaganda is "directed and dominated by Communists and Communist supporters."

Mr. Graham is a member of Vote For Freedom, a movement financed largely by Marshall Field, publisher of "the uptown edition of the *Daily Worker"*—P-M. Member of directors council of "the Communist Party line weekly — The Hour." Sponsor of a dinner held by the pro-Communist publication *Soviet Russia Today*, to celebrate the 25th Anniversary of the Red Army, and Vice-Chairman of the Citizens of Victory, "the most ambitious of the various groups engaged in the (Smear-and-Purge) campaign against Congress."

Many of these groups are regarded by official Washington as among "the most subversive organizations ever to operate in the United States," the significance of which warrants serious consideration of the reliable disclosures of the investigator Herbert Solow, who says: "Just as Hitler utilized his sympathizers in the German-American Bund and its auxiliaries to propagandize and spy for Germany, so Stalin utilizes members and hangers-on of the American Communist Party for the Kremlin espionage. . . . The American Communist Party, and its periphery of sympathizers and fellow-travelers constitute a vast reservoir of spies for the Kremlin."

And whether or not Dr. Graham surrenders to the technical status of a Communist, he is compelled to deny that this network of Stalin's confederation is indubitably an extension of the open party membership and represents the most serious single sabotage potential in America today. Neither can there be any consolation in the assumption that his political participations were confined to the "legal" end of the Communist conspiracy. The whole Stalinist system is too well integrated for such divisions.

38. Frank Graham Defended

WAYNE MORSE
"In Fairness to a Great American"
1948

Graham's participation in agencies associated with Franklin Roosevelt, such as the War Labor Board, established as a federal agency during World War II to regulate wages and labor practices in war-related industries, made him a target for anti-Communist attacks. On February 5, 1948, Senator W. Lee O'Daniel of Texas suggested to the Senate that the War Labor Board was infiltrated with Communists because of the participation of liberals such as Graham. Senator Wayne Morse of Oregon rose in his defense. Morse, formerly dean of the University of Oregon Law

Wayne Morse, "In Fairness to a Great American," *Congressional Record*, 80th Cong., 2d sess., 1948, 77570-23941.

School, was elected to the Senate in 1944 and would serve for more than a quarter century. A member of the liberal wing of the Republican Party, Morse often stood alone in the Senate. He had served with Graham on the War Labor Board, and in this speech describes his experience with Frank Graham.

February 5, 1948

MR. MORSE. Mr. President, the next thing I wish to comment on in these brief remarks is the speech made earlier this afternoon by the Senator from Texas [Mr. O'Daniel]. I wish to refer particularly to that part of the speech in which he commented upon a man who I think is one of the greatest of living Americans.

I am sure that those who read the speech of the Senator from Texas may at least infer that Dr. Frank Graham, president of the University of North Carolina, was the subject of criticism in that speech. I do not need to say anything in defense of Dr. Graham; and the remarks I now make, Mr. President, are not in defense of him, but, rather, are in fairness to him, because I think on the same day when the *Congressional Record* carries the type of remarks about Dr. Graham that were included in the speech of the Senator from Texas, a statement in support of Dr. Graham's great Americanism should also appear in the *Congressional Record.*

I served with Dr. Graham for two years on the National War Labor Board, during the war. He is the personification, let me say, Mr. President, of the idealism of Americanism. I know of no living man who is more Christlike in character than the great president of the University of North Carolina, Dr. Frank Graham. He is the son of a Confederate officer, one of the great sons of the South, a man who I think must be included in any list of the twenty-five greatest living Americans, a man who is a great inspiration to the youth of the South — not only to the youth of the South, Mr. President, but to the entire South and to the Nation as a whole. He is a man who recognizes the liberalism of the Constitution of the United States, and who fully appreciates the significance of the freedoms of its Bill of Rights, a man who recognizes that we do not answer opposition by trying to drive it underground, a man who has appeared on the platforms of America before all types of organizations in defense of constitutional government.

Mr. President, I hope we have not reached such a point in America that when one accepts an invitation to speak before any organization, he thereby becomes an endorser of the platforms or policies or principles of that organization. The fact that Dr. Graham, as was pointed out this afternoon by the Senator from Texas, has appeared on the programs of some organizations that we know to be leftist organizations, is no reflection upon his Americanism. Mr. President, as an American liberal I am perfectly willing to appear, at my convenience, before any leftist organization in America and defend the principles of Americanism for which I stand. I have done so on many occasions. I have done so, making perfectly clear my opposition to the principles for which those organizations stand.

Let me say, Mr. President, that in my opinion, the way to meet the Communist menace is to keep that menace right out in the open, beard the Communists in their dens, so to speak, go before them and their constituencies and point out to them wherein they stand for principles that cannot be reconciled with the freedoms of our Constitution. Point out to them that the principles for which they stand constitute, in the last analysis, police-state methods, and cannot be reconciled with the individual liberty guaranties of our form of government.

Frank Graham is such a liberal fighter for American principles. I wish to say that the test is not before what audiences a man speaks, but what he says before those audiences. That is the test. I am perfectly willing to let Dr. Graham's record, as set forth in his speeches, speak for itself.

I make these remarks because I think there is a danger that from the remarks made this afternoon by the Senator from Texas about Dr. Graham, president of the University of North Carolina, some persons might draw an implication reflecting upon the patriotism of Dr. Graham. I make them with this concluding statement, Mr. President, that it is my honest opinion that a more patriotic American does not live in our country than the distinguished president of the University of North Carolina, Dr. Frank Graham.

MR. WILEY[1] subsequently said: Mr. President, I was greatly moved by the statement of the Senator from Oregon. I agree 100 percent with the sentiment he expressed. I do not know the doctor to whom the Senator referred, but I do know that in these fast-moving days the thing to do is not to indulge in personalities, but to argue principles, and not so to act that nefarious forces must go underground, but if we can, argue the merits. As I have said so many times on the floor of the Senate, and as I have said in relation to Europe, we Americans have a good bill of goods to sell. The question is whether we are salesmen. The thing to do is to sell the bill of goods, and the way to counteract or to provide an antidote to communism is to expose its irrationality and lack of common sense and to expose further what communism breeds and what citizens under what form of government get. The way to do that is to show the facts, and to sell our bill of goods. So I join with the Senator in what he so ably said, only wishing that I could get on my feet and express as forcefully, as dynamically, and as clearly as he did, what I think is one of the great needs of the day, that when we disagree with a person's philosophy we present our reasons for our beliefs. It was only four or five hundred years ago that the Catholics and Protestants burned each other at the stake, thinking they were doing God's will. Each group thought they were doing God's will. We in America today know that that is not God's will; it is man's blindness. So today, we must not be so cocksure that we have arrived. America is a growing nation, and that is why we are asking for the St. Lawrence seaway.[2]

---

[1] **Mr. Wiley:** Alexander Wiley, senator from Wisconsin.
[2] **St. Lawrence seaway:** long-discussed in Congress and jointly funded by the United States and Canada, this project would eventually allow seagoing ships passage between the Great Lakes and the Atlantic Ocean, via the St. Lawrence River. With construction beginning in August 1954, the seaway opened in June 1959.

39. The Fulton Lewis Broadcast

FULTON LEWIS JR. AND FRANK PORTER GRAHAM
Accusation and Response
1949

The anti-Communist fervor against Graham culminated in early 1949, when the conservative radio broadcaster Fulton Lewis Jr. launched an all-out assault. Lewis was prompted by Graham's association with the Atomic Energy Commission (AEC), a new federal agency charged with overseeing the development of the U.S. nuclear weapons program. In October 1946, after Graham had been elected president and chairman of the board of the Oak Ridge Institute of Nuclear Studies — a consortium organized to make nuclear weapons research more widely available to southern universities — the AEC began a secret investigation of Graham's loyalty. In this broadcast, Lewis revealed that although the AEC had provided Graham with a security clearance, in fact a majority of its Security Advisory Board objected to Graham's association with liberal causes. The response among Graham's supporters was sharp. On January 13, for example, President Harry Truman vigorously defended him at a press conference. Graham himself immediately responded to Lewis's charges with a lengthy telegram that countered the accusations point by point.

FULTON LEWIS'S RADIO ADDRESS

January 13, 1949

. . . About Dr. Frank P. Graham, president of the University of North Carolina, and the action of the Atomic Energy Commission giving him complete clearance for all atomic secrets despite the fact that the security officer of the commission flatly rejected him, and the security advisory board of the commission, headed by former Supreme Court Justice Owen J. Roberts did likewise, by a unanimous five-man decision, there are further developments tonight.

President Truman was asked to comment on the matter today at his press and radio conference, and his reply was that he has complete confidence in Dr. Graham and that, in spite of the published statements to the contrary, he doubts whether there was any objection [to] Dr. Graham. On that score, with all respect to the President, I can only reiterate the disclosures I made over this microphone last night, and challenge Mr. Truman himself to call for the records from the Atomic Energy Commission, and if he does so, he will find the facts exactly as I stated them to you last night. Dr. Graham was turned down by the security offi-

Frank Porter Graham Papers, University of North Carolina at Chapel Hill Library.

cer of the commission, that officer refusing to approve him; the case went to the distinguished board of security, headed by Mr. Justice Roberts, who studied it intensively, and on last May 28 turned it down by unanimous vote, and what Mr. Truman does or does not believe cannot alter those facts in any way.

The defenders of Dr. Graham today offered the apology that during the time he joined the various subversive and Communist front organizations — organizations so listed by the Attorney General of the United States — this country was a co-belligerent with Soviet Russia, and numerous people joined such groups and causes. That argument is going to sound very thin to most American citizens, because the overwhelming majority of us would have no part of any Communist or Communist front connections at any time. But granted, for the sake of argument, that there is some justification in it, the question arises, — all right; so good for the past, but what about the present — NOW. This is the present . . . and Dr. Graham has been approved for access to all of our most secret atomic information — information on which the future security of the nation may well hinge. Is he willing NOW, for the future, to publicly resign and disavow all connections with any organizations that are listed as Communist or Communist front or subversive organizations at this, the present time?

FRANK PORTER GRAHAM'S TELEGRAM

January 13, 1949

Mr. Fulton Lewis, Jr.
Barr Building
Washington, D.C.

Returned this morning from Lake Success and New York where served as advisor on Indonesian situation and find your telegram here. In view of your questions and implications I hope you will use my statement to provide for my answers.

Know nothing of any action except decision Atomic Energy Commission.

I have always been opposed to Communism and all totalitarian dictatorships. I opposed both Nazi and Communist aggression against Czechoslovakia and the earlier Russian aggression against Finland and later Communist aggression against other countries.

I was for aid to Britain against Germany when Germany had the pact with Russia. I was a member of the William Allen White Committee and the Fight for Freedom Committee.

During the period of my active participation, the overwhelming number of members of the Southern Conference were to my knowledge anti-Communists. There were several isolationist stands of the Conference with which I disagreed.

Frank Porter Graham Papers, University of North Carolina at Chapel Hill Library.

The stands which I supported as the main business of the Conference were such as the following: Federal aid to the states for schools; abolition of freight rate discrimination against Southern commerce, agriculture, and industry; anti–poll tax bill; anti-lynching bill; equal right of qualified Negroes to vote in both primaries and general elections; the unhampered lawful right of labor to organize and bargain collectively in our region; agricultural cooperative societies; tenant farmers' union; soil conservation; the industrial development of the South; minimum wages and social security in the Southern and American tradition. It was for a number of years one Southwide organization open to all citizens of both races in which whites and Negroes could work together simply as human beings for building up the South. There has been no general meeting for about two years.

I have from the beginning been a member of Americans for Democratic Action which debars Communists from membership. I belong to the wing of the A.D.A. which supported President Truman all the way.

I have continued to support the Baruch-Acheson-Lillienthal Plan for the inspection and control of atomic energy resources and consider the Russian refusal to cooperate a major setback for whole world.

I was on Committees against Hitler, Mussolini, and France in Spain; for aid to China against Japan; against sending scrap-iron to Japan; for civil liberties and other such committees during last score or more of years. I joined with generals of the U.S. Army during the war in sponsoring a salute to the Red Army holding the gate at Stalingrad. I am still glad that the gate held and pray that the energies of Stalingrad will not be turned for further aggressions against freedom. The overwhelming majority of the people along with whom I sponsored these committees were well known as loyal Americans. If members of these committees had ulterior aims it was without our knowledge or approval. From past experience I am aware of Communist techniques of infiltration into organizations with good purposes. However, I do not now renounce any stand I made for human freedom.

I supported the major domestic and foreign policies of Woodrow Wilson and Roosevelt including such Roosevelt policies as lifting the embargo, providing the fifty destroyers to Britain and lend-lease to the Allies. I have from the beginning supported the Marshall Plan.

I support Mr. Jessup's strong statement of the American stand in the Security Council against Communist and Dutch attempts to destroy the Republic of Indonesia.

At the University of North Carolina we stand for the lawful freedom of our students to have their own political organization. The far largest number are Democrats, the next largest number are Republicans, and the third largest number are States Rights Democrats. There are a number of followers of Norman Thomas and a fewer number who are followers of Henry Wallace who include a dozen or so Communists to whom we accord and will continue to accord the lawful freedom of this community.

While personally holding that a membership in the Communist Party is not *per se* proof of an individual's crime against the government, I uphold Chancellor House in the decision to follow the ruling of the Attorney General in his interpretation of the State law to deny the use of a state building to a man under federal indictment on the grounds of being involved in a conspiracy to overthrow the government by force. . . .

Our faculty with all their intellectual freedom are conservative or liberal in the highest American tradition and will be protected in their freedom as honorable University teachers and lawful and decent American citizens.

I have been called a Communist by some sincere people. I have been called a spokesman of American capitalism by Communists and repeatedly called a tool of imperialism by the radio from Moscow. I shall simply continue to oppose Ku Kluxism, imperialism, fascism, and Communism whether in America, Indonesia, or behind the "iron curtain."

Sincerely yours,
Frank P. Graham

40. HUAC and Southern Liberalism

HOUSE UN-AMERICAN ACTIVITIES COMMITTEE
Report on Frank Graham
1949

Although Graham took great pains to refute charges of Communism, he continued to be subjected to frequent attacks by anti-Communists. Like many other liberals, he was subject to investigation by HUAC, by then the leading national anti-Communist forum. HUAC's report — most likely written in collaboration with the Federal Bureau of Investigation (FBI) under the direction of J. Edgar Hoover — restates the long-standing case against Graham, and it rests on a guilt-by-association charge: that because Graham was involved with a long list of liberal causes, many of which involved Communists, he must therefore be a Communist himself.

Frank Porter Graham Papers, University of North Carolina at Chapel Hill Library.

DATE: February 4, 1949

FOR: Honorable Charles B. Deane
SUBJECT: Frank P. Graham

A check of the files, records and publications of the Committee on Un-American Activities has revealed the following information concerning Frank P. Graham:

Letterheads dated September 22, 1939, January 17, 1940, and May 26, 1940, as well as the "Daily Worker" of March 18, 1939, . . . reveal that Frank P. Graham was a member of the American Committee for Democracy and Intellectual Freedom. This affiliation is also shown by a leaflet, "Citizens Rally," which was held by that organization on April 13, 1940, at Carnegie Hall, New York City.

The American Committee for Democracy and Intellectual Freedom was established on Lincoln's Birthday, 1939, with the announced purpose of "preservation and extension of democracy and intellectual freedom." Its establishment was featured on page 1 of the "Daily Worker." ("Daily Worker," February 13, 1939.) In Report 2277, dated June 25, 1942, the Special Committee on Un-American Activities found that "the line of the American Committee for Democracy and Intellectual Freedom has fluctuated in complete harmony with the line of the Communist Party." The organization was again cited by the Special Committee on Un-American Activities in Report 1311 of March 29, 1944, as a Communist front "which defended Communist teachers."

A letterhead of March 15, 1940, and the letterhead of the Fourth Annual Conference, Hotel Annapolis, Washington, D.C., March 2–3, 1940, list Frank P. Graham as a sponsor of the American Committee for Protection of Foreign Born. The program of the Fifth National Conference on this organization, held at the President Hotel, Atlantic City, New Jersey, March 29–30, 1941, lists Frank Porter Graham as a sponsor.

Of this organization, the Special Committee on Un-American Activities stated: "Numerous witnesses who have appeared before our committee have given testimony indicating that the American Committee for Protection of Foreign Born is a Communist-dominated front. In particular . . . the testimony of Humberto Galleani . . . that the Communist Party, of which he was once a member, assigned him to work in the American Committee for Protection of Foreign Born and that there was no doubt about the party's complete control of the organization." (Report 2277 of June 25, 1942. . . .)

The organization was again cited as "one of the oldest auxiliaries of the Communist Party in the United States" in the Committee's report of March 29, 1944. The American Committee for Protection of Foreign Born has been cited as "subversive" and "Communist" by Attorney General Clark in lists furnished by him for use of the Loyalty Review Board. (See Press Releases of the U.S. Civil Service Commission dated May 28, 1948, and September 21, 1948.)

Frank P. Graham was a member of the Committee of the American Friends of Spanish Democracy, according to a letterhead of February 21, 1938, and was one of those who signed this organization's petition to lift the arms embargo as shown by the "Daily Worker" of April 3, 1938 . . . "New Masses," January 5, 1937, . . . discloses that he was a general committee member of the American Friends of Spanish Democracy, Medical Bureau.

"In 1937–38, the Communist Party threw itself wholeheartedly into the campaign for the support of the Spanish Loyalist cause, recruiting men and organizing multifarious so-called relief organizations . . . such as . . . American Friends of Spanish Democracy." (Report 1311, Special Committee on Un-American Activities, March 29, 1944. . . .)

Frank P. Graham has been affiliated with the American League for Peace and Democracy as a signer of a statement on the International situation which that organization issued. (See "New Masses," March 15, 1938. . . .) According to a letterhead of May 18, 1938, and another of June 11, 1938, and the "Daily Worker" of April 8, 1938, . . . he was a sponsor of the Easter drive of the China Aid Council of the American League for Peace and Democracy.

The American League for Peace and Democracy has been cited as a Communist front organization in three reports of the Special Committee on Un-American Activities: Reports of January 3, 1940; June 25, 1942; and March 29, 1944. The League was "established in 1937 as successor to the American League Against War and Fascism," and was "designed to conceal Communist control, in accordance with the new tactics of the Communist International." (Attorney General Francis Biddle, "Congressional Record," September 24, 1942. . . .) The American League for Peace and Democracy has also been cited as "subversive" and "Communist" by the present Attorney General. (Press releases of the U.S. Civil Service Commission, dated May 28, 1948, and September 21, 1948, respectively.)

A folder of the Citizens' Committee to Free Earl Browder, which was issued in 1942, names Frank P. Graham as one of the prominent American educators who favored Presidential clemency for Earl Browder.

"When Earl Browder (then general secretary, Communist Party) was in Atlanta Penitentiary serving a sentence involving his fraudulent passports, the Communist Party's front which agitated for his release was known as the Citizens' Committee to Free Earl Browder . . . Elizabeth Gurley Flynn, one of the few outstanding women leaders of the Communist Party in this country, headed it." (Report 1311, Special Committee on Un-American Activities, March 29, 1944.) The Citizens' Committee to Free Earl Browder was cited as a Communist organization by Attorney General Francis Biddle. (Congressional Record, September 24, 1942. . . .)

The affiliation of Frank P. Graham with the Coordinating Committee to Lift the Embargo as a representative individual is shown by a booklet, "These Americans say." . . . The Coordinating Committee to Lift the Embargo was cited by the Special Committee on Un-American Activities as "one of a number of front organizations, set up during the Spanish Civil War by the Communist Party . . . through which the party carried on a great deal of agitation." (Report 1311, March 29, 1944. . . .)

According to "Equal Justice," publication of the International Labor Defense,

Frank P. Graham sent greetings to the National Conference of the International Labor Defense. ("Equal Justice," July 1939. . . .)

The International Labor Defense was cited by Attorney General Francis Biddle as the "legal arm of the Communist Party." (Congressional Record, September 24, 1942. . . .) The organization has been cited as a Communist front in three reports of the Special Committee on Un-American Activities: reports of January 3, 1940; June 25, 1942; and March 29, 1944. The organization has been cited as "subversive" and classified as "Communist" by the present Attorney General. (See Press Releases of the U.S. Civil Service Commission, dated May 28, 1948, and September 21, 1948.)

Frank P. Graham, according to a letterhead of July 6, 1938, was a national sponsor of the Medical Bureau and North American Committee to Aid Spanish Democracy. A letterhead of the Michigan Chapter, dated February 2, 1939, also reveals that he sponsored this organization. The Medical Bureau and North American Committee to Aid Spanish Democracy was cited as a Communist front by the Special Committee on Un-American Activities in Report 1311, dated March 29, 1944. (See paragraph [8 in] this memorandum concerning the Spanish relief organizations.)

The "Prospectus and Review" . . . of the Lawyers Committee on American Relations with Spain discloses that Frank P. Graham supported the Conference to Lift the Embargo. "When it was the policy of the Communist Party to organize much of its main propaganda around the civil war in Spain," this "Communist lawyers' front organization" supported the movement. (Report 1311, Special Committee on Un-American Activities, March 29, 1944.)

Frank P. Graham, according to "Soviet Russia Today," February 1943, . . . sponsored the Soviet Russia Today Dinner which celebrated the twenty-fifth Anniversary of the Red Army. The publication, "Soviet Russia Today," has been cited as Communist front by the Special Committee on Un-American Activities in two reports: Reports of June 25, 1942, and March 29, 1944.

A letterhead of February 7, 1946, a letterhead of June 4, 1947, an official report of the organization, and an announcement of the Third Meeting, April 19–21, 1942, at Nashville, Tennessee, reveal that Frank P. Graham was honorary President of the Southern Conference for Human Welfare. An official report of the Southern Conference for Human Welfare lists Frank P. Graham as Chairman and the program of the Conference held in Birmingham, Alabama, November 20–23, 1938, reveals that he delivered the opening address. The "Call to the Second Southern Conference for Human Welfare," Chattanooga, Tennessee, April 14–16, 1940, reveals that Frank P. Graham participated in that conference. According to a letterhead, dated August 13, 1940, Frank P. Graham sponsored the League of Young Southerners, Youth Division, Southern Conference for Human Welfare. Frank P. Graham was one of the signers of a statement issued by the Southern Conference for Human Welfare, which appeared in the "Daily Worker" of May 29, 1947. . . .

In a report on the Southern Conference for Human Welfare, dated June 16, 1947, the Committee on Un-American Activities found "the most conclusive proof of Communist domination of the Southern Conference for Human Welfare is to be found in the organization's strict and unvarying conformance to the line of the Communist Party in the field of foreign policy. It is also clear indication of the fact that the real purpose of the organization was not 'human welfare' in the South, but rather to serve as a convenient vehicle in support of the current Communist Party line" . . . . The Southern Conference for Human Welfare had previously been cited as a Communist front organization by the Special Committee on Un-American Activities in Report 1311 of March 29, 1944.

It is noted that Frank P. Graham was one of the signers of a statement issued by eighty-seven American liberals which includes an attack on the Communist Party of the United States. This statement appeared in the "Congressional Record" of May 23, 1947. . . .

Suggestions for Further Reading

Ashby, Warren. *Frank Porter Graham, a Southern Liberal.* Winston-Salem, N.C.: J. F. Blair, 1980.

Heale, M. J. *American Anticommunism: Combating the Enemy Within, 1830–1970.* Baltimore: Johns Hopkins University Press, 1990.

Kovel, Joel. *Red Hunting in the Promised Land: Anticommunism and the Making of America.* New York: BasicBooks, 1994.

Weinstein, Allen. *Perjury: The Hiss-Chambers Case.* New York: Alfred A. Knopf, 1978.

CHAPTER TWELVE

THE CIVIL RIGHTS MOVEMENT

Murder in Mississippi

B y 1964, the civil rights movement was making significant progress. Martin
Luther King Jr.'s recent March on Washington had demonstrated growing
national support, and President Lyndon Johnson was lobbying hard for
the most far-reaching bill in support of racial equality ever enacted by Congress.
Yet in the South, and particularly in Mississippi, there was tremendous opposition.
White leaders were grimly determined to continue with established racial customs
despite the demands of federal law or public opinion outside the state. Events of
the "Freedom Summer" of 1964, however, rendered that impossible by exposing
the full extent of Mississippi's denial of equal rights to its African American citizens and the violent repression of those seeking to bring about change.

In the decade following the Supreme Court's 1954 ruling against segregated
schools, Mississippi's leaders had defiantly used their power to preserve segregation and white political supremacy and to suppress dissent. They employed economic sanctions to discourage black Mississippians from participating in civil
rights activities, and like several other southern states, established an agency, the
"Sovereignty Commission," to "prevent encroachment upon the rights of this and
other states by the Federal Government." State legislators tightened segregation
laws and the already formidable voter registration requirements, and made it a
crime to advocate disobedience to state laws or "nonconformance" with "established traditions." Public schools remained segregated, and by 1964 only 6 percent
of Mississippi's black population of voting age was registered to vote.

Despite such repression, Mississippi developed one of the strongest grass-
roots civil rights movements in the South. Black Mississippians challenged every
form of discrimination despite frequent incarceration, beatings, and murders. In
1962, state civil rights groups united to form the Council of Federated Organiza-

tions (COFO), a step that greatly enhanced their effectiveness; by the winter of 1963–64, COFO leaders were making plans for Freedom Summer — a massive campaign focusing on voter registration.

Meanwhile the national gains of the civil rights movement and the failure of white leaders to suppress it within the state led to a revival of the Mississippi Ku Klux Klan (KKK). In late 1963 and the spring of 1964, "night riders" went on a rampage, burning black churches and the homes and businesses of civil rights supporters. By the summer of 1964, nearly five thousand impatient and angry whites had joined the KKK. Though state officials publicly expressed opposition to the Klan, police and elected leaders, particularly in smaller communities, often ignored or supported Klan violence; many even joined the Klan themselves. Despite warnings by the Federal Bureau of Investigation (FBI), Klan violence continued and reached a degree unmatched since Reconstruction. In the summer of 1964, there were thirty-five shooting incidents in Mississippi, and sixty-five homes and other buildings were burned or bombed, including thirty-five churches. Eighty activists were beaten and over one thousand arrested.

The violence was not unexpected. The revival of Klan activity and the blatant murders of several civil rights workers had prompted organizers to recruit volunteers from outside the state in the hope that their involvement would focus national attention on the project and provide a measure of protection against Klan violence. The volunteers, mainly white students from schools in the North or California, assembled in Ohio for orientation, where they were prepared to teach Mississippi blacks about their heritage and rights and to coach adults through the complexities of voter registration in Mississippi. The volunteers were also told about the violence they might expect in Mississippi: although Mississippi officials had hired seven hundred additional highway patrol officers and beefed up local police forces, federal officials were turning down requests for protection.

On June 20, the first group of volunteers departed for Mississippi. Twenty-year-old Andrew Goodman, a student from Queens College in New York, rode down with Congress of Racial Equality (CORE) organizers Michael "Mickey" Schwerner and James Chaney. Chaney, a twenty-one-year-old African American from Meridian, Mississippi, and Schwerner, a Cornell University graduate, were close friends. Schwerner and his wife, Rita, had set up a community center in Meridian and, with Chaney, had been making plans for freedom schools and freedom houses in the area. Within a day of their arrival, the three young civil rights workers disappeared under suspicious circumstances.

The response was a tremendous international outpouring of concern. President Johnson, alarmed about the men's fate, placed the FBI in charge of the search, sent hundreds of sailors to assist them, and dispatched former CIA director Allen Dulles to Jackson. Even FBI director J. Edgar Hoover, no friend of the civil rights movement, flew to Jackson to set up a field office and make it clear to state officials that they must crack down on Klan violence and comply with the new Civil Rights Act. A bereaved Rita Schwerner told the press it was "tragic that white Northerners have to be caught up into the machinery of injustice and indifference in the South before the American people register concern," and that if James Chaney alone had disappeared, "this case, like so many others . . . would have gone completely unnoticed."[1]

On August 4, a few days before the Democratic National Convention, the bodies of the three missing men were found: Chaney, Schwerner, and Goodman had been shot and buried beneath an earthen dam. Thousands of mourners attended services for Schwerner and Goodman in New York and Chaney's funeral in Meridian. The state did not file any murder charges but eventually seven Klansmen, including Deputy Cecil Price, were found guilty of violating the civil rights of the three murdered men and sentenced to prison. This was the first time a Mississippi jury had convicted members of the Klan for the deaths of blacks or of civil rights workers.

In the short run, the murders contributed to the growing disillusionment of black civil rights workers; many became frustrated with the idealistic, peaceful methods pursued by the interracial coalition and embraced black power and separatism. But the murders also contributed to the adoption of the Voting Rights Act of 1965 and the eventual transformation of Mississippi from a "closed society" where murders of civil rights workers went unpunished to a state where blacks participate freely in politics. By the end of 1968, 60 percent of eligible blacks were registered to vote. At the close of the twentieth century, Mississippi had more black elected officials than any other state in the nation.

In this chapter, excerpts from interviews with black and white participants in Freedom Summer explain their decision to include white volunteers and illustrate their idealism; a letter from Rita Schwerner written a few months before the murders captures the excitement and optimism of the civil rights workers. Reports on Michael and Rita Schwerner and on the murders illustrate how the Sovereignty Commission operated. Excerpts from a Philadelphia, Mississippi, resident's memoir reveal her suspicions about the close cooperation between government and law-enforcement officials and the Klan. Finally, Dave Dennis's eulogy for James Chaney shows the anger and frustration felt by many civil rights workers.

As you read, keep in mind the goals of Freedom Summer. What factors led to the decision to enlist volunteers from outside the state, including white college students? In what ways did the state's Sovereignty Commission as well as the Klan play a role in the murders? What was the response to the murders within the state, across the nation, and within the civil rights movement?

[1]Juan Williams, *Eyes on the Prize: America's Civil Rights Years, 1954–1965* (New York: Viking Penguin, 1987), 231.

41. Opening the "Closed Society"

Bob Moses, Hollis Watkins, Tom Hayden, Sandra Cason (Casey Hayden), Peter Orris, and Unita Blackwell
Interviews
1970s

The following excerpts from interviews conducted in the 1970s reveal the hopes and dreams of six organizers and participants in Freedom Summer. Bob Moses, one of the most influential non-Mississippians during Freedom Summer, grew up in Harlem and was educated at Hamilton College and Harvard University, where he earned a master's degree in philosophy. Hollis Watkins, a student at Tougaloo College and a field secretary for the Student Nonviolent Coordinating Committee (SNCC), was one of the black leaders who was reluctant to bring in whites. Tom Hayden, a white organizer from Detroit (later a California state senator) edited the student newspaper at the University of Michigan and was cofounder of Students for a Democratic Society (SDS). Sandra Cason (then married to Tom Hayden and known as Casey Hayden) was a white Texan who participated in the civil rights movement; before Freedom Summer she was in charge of correspondence with northern student volunteers. Peter Orris, a Harvard freshman, explains why it was such a "privilege" for him to participate in Freedom Summer. And Unita Blackwell, who went on to become mayor of Mayersville, Mississippi, describes the tremendous boost she and other black Mississippians received from working together with the white volunteers during Freedom Summer.

Bob Moses

There had grown a concern within SNCC[1] and the movement about the involvement of white students in the Deep South as actual organizers and workers in the field. This was first demonstrated in southwest Georgia. In 1962, Martha Prescod and Jean Wheeler, who had been working in southwest Georgia and were two young black girls, left that project and came to Mississippi because of the presence of too many white people who were working there. They mirrored a kind of concern which existed within the Mississippi staff, which was predominantly people who grew up and lived in Mississippi, were from Mississippi, had spent

---

[1]**SNCC:** Student Nonviolent Coordinating Committee.

Steve Fayer and Henry Hampton, with Sarah Flynn, *Voices of Freedom: An Oral History of the Civil Rights Movement from the 1950s through the 1980s* (New York: Bantam Books, 1990), 181–87, 191–93.

their lives under the Mississippi condition, which was strict segregation and living in this closed society, so they had very little working contact with white people and they weren't anxious to introduce them into the project, which they viewed — and rightly so — as *their* project, something which they had created out of nothing and at great risk to themselves.

They had voted down the attempt in SNCC in the beginning of 1963 to introduce white people into Mississippi as part of the Mississippi staff. Then, when the Freedom Vote[2] came and the question arose of bringing in white volunteers, they reluctantly agreed, since they were going along with the campaign, with what Aaron Henry and Ed King[3] wanted, and since they knew that it was only going to last for a couple of weeks. The volunteers from Yale and Stanford would be coming down for a couple of weeks, working with them, mobilizing the vote, and then they would be gone.

Immediately after the Freedom Vote, which was successful, there came the question of should we do this in the summer of 1964. Al Lowenstein[4] proposed that we bring down students from all across the country, from the nation's most prestigious schools. The discussion then arose within the staff as to do we want to do this or not. And we were split. We met for months over this question. You had the staff on the one hand, and the people that we were working with on the other. Mrs. Hamer[5] was an excellent case in point. She wanted the students to come back, and so we were at loggerheads. . . .

I think it was January 1964, and we were in Hattiesburg having a demonstration, picketing the courthouse. Mrs. Hamer was there and staff from all around the state, and we were taking up the question again. We got a telephone call that Louis Allen[6] had been murdered on his front lawn in Liberty. I went over there to speak to his wife, who then moved down to Baton Rouge, and in the process of helping her and thinking through this, I felt like I had to step in and make my weight felt in terms of this decision about the summer project. Because up to then I had just been letting the discussion go on. I guess what I felt was that, as we were going now, we couldn't guarantee the safety of the people we were working with. There were larger things that were happening in the country: there was the 1963 civil rights bill. Mississippi was reacting to that, and we were feeling the backlash that was growing in Mississippi against gains that were being made nationally but which were not having any immediate effect in Mississippi in terms of people

---

[2]**the Freedom Vote:** a 1963 mock election designed to demonstrate that Mississippi blacks would vote if they were given a fair opportunity to register.

[3]**Aaron Henry and Ed King:** Henry, veteran black activist and president of the Mississippi NAACP, was selected as the COFO candidate for governor in the mock election; Edwin King, white native Mississippian, supporter of the civil rights movement, and chaplain of Tougaloo College, was his running mate.

[4]**Al Lowenstein:** a white, thirty-three-year-old Yale Law School graduate and former Stanford dean, he recruited hundreds of students for civil rights work in Mississippi.

[5]**Mrs. Hamer:** Fannie Lou Hamer was a courageous and inspirational African American sharecropper who became an influential figure in the civil rights movement in the early 1960s.

[6]**Louis Allen:** a black witness to the 1961 murder of NAACP worker Herbert Lee by a member of the Mississippi state legislature. Lee had been helping Moses organize in Amite County.

being able to participate in some of those gains. But what they were feeling was the oppression, the backlash that was rising up in Mississippi — burning churches, the murder of two boys from Alcorn State occurred at that same time, Louis Allen down there in Liberty. We felt that we had to do something. And I felt that in that context that I had to step in between this loggerhead between the staff on the one hand and the people that we were working with. And so that's how the decision was made to invite the students down for the summer of 1964.

HOLLIS WATKINS

The summer project to bring students down in Mississippi was a tough issue. Some felt that it would bring out more publicity to get more whites involved, that it would serve as a deterrent to keep the whites in Mississippi from doing things. There were others of us, from Mississippi especially, that was looking at this effort in terms of a long-range project. We felt that even though it would do this, that ultimately it would destroy the grass-roots organizations that we had built and were in the process of building.

For the first time, we had local people who had begun to take the initiative themselves and do things. For the first time, we had local Mississippians who were making decisions about what moves to make next. And where the organization should be going and how the organization politically and economically would work and where it would end up. We felt that with a lot of students from the North coming in, being predominantly white, that they would come in and overshadow these grass-roots organizations, causing the organizations to go on a different course than that which had been started.

At the same time, by the local indigenous people knowing that most of the students would be more educated than themselves, they would feel, "Since they are more educated than I am, maybe I should listen to them, do it their way, do what they say." Because of that, they would become complacent, they would feel inferior and fall back into the same rut that they were in before we started the grass-roots organizations. And ultimately, when the people from the North would go back, people from Mississippi would have to start all over again, and go through that same rebuilding process. All of us knew that it is much harder to rebuild something than to keep it in motion. We wanted to keep what we had in motion rather than stand the risk of destroying it and have to rebuild.

TOM HAYDEN

I was in Mississippi when there were very few white students or northern whites there at all. I remember the thinking was that if this simply remains a black thing, where the white official violence is visited upon black sharecroppers or black civil rights workers, how will a country that is significantly prejudiced respond? What's going to make them interested? The conclusion was that for all the problems, it would be necessary to bring down the white sons and daughters of the country's middle class, from the liberal North. By the hundreds, by the thousands if possible, to experience the true nature of southern segregation. It was kind of like a political civil war. If you mobilized the North, then pressure would be put on Congress and on the administration and then they would finally do something about these strongholds of segregation in the South. I think there was some truth to that strategy.

Sandra Cason (Casey Hayden)

I had a lot of contact with northern students previous to my work in Mississippi because I'd been doing fund-raising for SNCC out of Atlanta. I was what was called northern coordinator, so I handled all the correspondence with northern college students that came into the office. And they all wanted to come to where the action was, you know? I mean, what was happening in the South was so dramatic and heroic. You've got to remember, this was the early sixties. Kids on college campuses were reading the existentialists. The black students were like heroes. They were like existentialist heroes, and people wanted to get close to this. It was beautiful, it was happening. And it drew white intellectuals. It was more real, or more profound, than most anything else happening. They wanted to get close to it.

Peter Orris

I grew up in New York City. I had been raised in a family where being Jewish was important in terms of identifying with the underdog, with people who were suffering repression and discrimination. I had come into contact with SNCC organizers the summer before, when I worked in the national office of the March on Washington for Jobs and Freedom in 1963. I was seventeen at the time, and was very impressed with the SNCC workers that were involved in that organization as well as those that I met in Washington at the time of the march.

Sometime in the spring of my freshman year at college, four of us from the civil rights coordinating committee at the college went to Atlanta for a regional meeting of SNCC and heard about what was going on. We met many people who were involved in voter registration and direct action from the southern states, and it was tremendously impressive and exciting. For me, it was a tremendous privilege to be allowed to participate in this movement for racial justice. At eighteen years old, to be able to be involved in this kind of a struggle was very important to me.

In June of 1964, I arrived in Oxford, Ohio, for the training session for the summer project. . . . We spent many hours with Bob Moses and a variety of other leaders of SNCC who had been in the South and in that area.

Additionally, it was to give us a feeling of exactly what kind of a tense atmosphere we were going into, what kind of violence we should expect, how to avoid the violence, as well as nonviolent responses to violent situations. We playacted situations where angry groups of people, mobs, would be attacking us and how we would handle ourselves in that situation where our life was threatened. The experienced SNCC workers were sure that we were going to meet situations like these during the summer, and they wanted to guarantee that we were going to respond in a nonviolent manner. Then a group of us were asked to go to Washington to make a direct appeal to the deputy attorney general, Nicholas Katzenbach, and others in the government, that they should pay special attention to what was happening in Mississippi this summer, as we felt, and the organizers felt, that our lives would certainly be at risk for engaging in this activity. . . .

[After arriving in Mississippi,] we went to a town called Mileston, which was outside of Tchula, in Holmes County. And we spent two to three weeks there, working on voter registration. What that meant was going to people's houses who we knew were not registered to vote and we would begin to talk to people about the Freedom Democratic party, about registering to vote, about the programs that were being put forward, about being ready to drive people to the courthouse, and going with them while they registered.

When we'd go to a new farmer's house, the first problem was that we were white northerners there on a mission, so to speak — all of those things were fraught with danger for the people that we were talking to. You'd get there, and the people would be sitting down and you'd shake their hands. Now, that was an unusual thing for a white person to do to a black person in Mississippi at that time. The next thing was that you would avoid a situation in which you were standing over and talking down to people — a body message about the power relationship. So we would always sit down, we'd sit on the steps, walking up to the porch. We'd either be on an equal eye level or on a lower level. We were much younger than many of the people we were speaking to, and it was necessary to establish a relationship or an understanding of the respect that we paid to them for their age and their situation. Frequently, people would respond by not looking us in the eye. At the end of every phrase there would be a "ma'am" or a "sir," depending on who was there. And they would say yes to everything we said. We'd say, "Would you like to be involved in the voter registration project? Will you go down to vote?" "Yes, sir." And we knew we were not getting across, we knew they were just waiting for us to go away because we were a danger to them, and in many ways we were. We had much less to risk than they did. This was their lives, their land, their family, and they were going to be here when we were gone.

Unita Blackwell

For black people in Mississippi, Freedom Summer was the beginning of a whole new era. People began to feel that they wasn't just helpless anymore, that they had come together. Black and white had come from the North and from the

West and even from some cities in the South. Students came and we wasn't a closed society anymore. They came to talk about that we had a right to register to vote, we had a right to stand up for our rights. That's a whole new era for us. I mean, hadn't anybody said that to us, in that open way, like what happened in 1964.

There was interaction of blacks and whites. I remember cooking some pinto beans — that's all we had — and everybody just got around the pot, you know, and that was an experience just to see white people coming around the pot and getting a bowl and putting some stuff in and then sitting around talking, sitting on the floor, sitting anywhere, 'cause you know, wasn't any great dining room tables and stuff that we had been used to working in the white people houses, where everybody would be sitting and they'd ring a bell and tap and you'd come in and bring the stuff and put it around. We was sitting on the floor and they was talking and we was sitting there laughing, and I guess they became very real and very human, we each to one another. It was an experience that will last a lifetime.

42. "Big Ambitions"

Rita Schwerner
Letter to Anne Braden
1964

Rita and Michael Schwerner arrived in Meridian, Mississippi, six months before Freedom Summer. At the time this letter was written, they were setting up a COFO headquarters as a base of operations for voter registration and other community programs. The letter was written to Anne Braden, a white civil rights activist from Louisville, Kentucky; Braden and her husband Carl were fieldworkers for the Southern Conference Education Fund (SCEF). Since the SCEF had been (falsely) accused by the House Un-American Activities Committee of being a Communist front, many white liberals shunned its participation in the movement, including Freedom Summer, fearing accusations of Communist infiltration. But the Bradens supported the work in Mississippi financially and by sending supplies.

Braden Papers, box 55, folder 15, State Historical Society of Wisconsin, Madison, Wisc.

2505½ Fifth Street
Meridian, Mississippi
January 23, 1964

Mrs. Anne Braden
Southern Conference Educational Fund, Inc.
4403 Virginia Avenue
Louisville 11, Ky.

Dear Mrs. Braden:

Your husband stopped in to see us here in Meridian this morning and we spoke about the community center which COFO is establishing in this city. I am enclosing some information about our plans with this letter, but I don't feel that statistics can adequately express our feelings about this undertaking.

My husband and myself are to be responsible for getting the center started. Before leaving New York City, I was an English teacher and Mike a social worker. I will be doing the teaching and setting up the library, while Mike's responsibilities include organizing and bringing people into the center. It is our hope that the center can eventually assume responsibility for most functions of the community. Our voter registration workers will be using the office as the center of their activities also.

In order to carry out the many facets of our program, we are desperately in need of both money and supplies. We are hoping that you will agree to run an article in the "Southern Patriot," explaining our program and appealing for aid. We have an office and one broken down typewriter. We need office equipment — typewriters, a duplicating machine, file cabinets. For our classes, (I understand that my first students are coming to visit tomorrow) we need books, as many as we can get, paper, pencils, etc. Clothing will aid us in our welfare program.

We have big ambitions and we know it, but with the help of people all over the country who believe in freedom, we know we can succeed.

Yours for freedom,
Rita Schwerner

43. The Sovereignty Commission Investigates

A. L. HOPKINS
Reports
1964

With an annual budget of $250,000, the Mississippi Sovereignty Commission, which operated between 1956 and 1973, engaged in bugging, wiretapping, and jury tampering; employed dozens of spies; intimidated white moderates; and infiltrated civil rights organizations. It also kept meticulous records of its espionage. The Commission's secret files, opened under court order in 1998, contain more than 132,000 documents on 87,000 people and hundreds of organizations.

The following reports, written by Sovereignty Commission investigator A. L. Hopkins, were found in the papers of Paul B. Johnson Jr., governor of Mississippi in 1964. During a hearing at the capitol, Betty Long, a state representative from Meridian, casually inquired of Sovereignty Commission director Erle Johnston whether or not he knew who Michael Schwerner was. Johnston had not heard of Schwerner but immediately ordered an investigation, and police in the Meridian area agreed to keep Schwerner and his wife under surveillance. When Schwerner was murdered a few months later, several local law-enforcement officers, Klan members, were involved. As the second report indicates, Hopkins was sent back to "investigate" the burning of the Mt. Zion Methodist Church in Neshoba County and Schwerner's disappearance.

March 24, 1964

Miss Betty Jane Long
House of Representatives
New Capitol

Dear Miss Long:

Enclosed is copy of a report from our investigative staff on subject you mentioned to me when I appeared before the House Committee.

This subject had not previously appeared in our files and we appreciate your calling him to our attention.

When we can be of further service, please advise.

Sincerely,
Erle Johnston, Jr.
Director

Johnson Family Papers, box 135, folder 10, McCain Library and Archives, University of Southern Mississippi, Hattiesburg, Miss.

TITLE: Investigation of Unknown White Male CORE Worker at Meridian,
            Mississippi
DATE OF INVESTIGATION: March 19 and 20, 1964
DATE OF REPORT: March 23, 1964
INVESTIGATED BY: A. L. Hopkins, Investigator
TYPED BY: Elizabeth Arnold

Investigation of above captioned subject reveals that his name is Michael Henry Schwerner, who is described as a white male, born November 6, 1939, brown hair, brown eyes, weight 175 pounds, height 5'8" who lists his occupation as social worker and his employer as CORE. His former addresses are 1017 Lynch Street, Jackson, Mississippi, and 38 Park Row, New York, New York. His present residence is 306–44th Avenue, Meridian, office address 2505½–5th Street, Meridian, telephone No. 48-34940. Ten seventeen Lynch Street is CORE headquarters in Jackson.

The subject, Michael Schwerner, drives a 1959 Volkswagen bearing Mississippi license plate issued in Hinds County January 17, 1964. This automobile is registered to Rita Schwerner and formerly had a 1963–64 New York license plate on it. The New York license was 5K213 and the present Mississippi tag number is 1964 Hinds County HA2582. Michael H. Schwerner had a minor accident in Meridian on Friday, February 21, 1964, with Mr. James A. Braisher of Quitman, Mississippi, Route 3. Neither subject received a traffic ticket.

Both Michael and Rita Schwerner are in Meridian working for CORE. Their purpose there is evidently to contact local Negroes for the purpose of encouraging them to register to vote and also to teach them how to pass the voter registration examination.

Since Michael and Rita Schwerner are married, it is presumed that they both live at 306–44th Avenue in a house that is owned by Mr. Roy Cunningham, a white male. Schwerner applied for water from the Water Department on February 4, 1964, and gave his previous address as New York City. He stated that he was employed at the Meridian Community Center, which is non-existent.

Rita Schwerner is described as a white female, born March 12, 1942, green eyes, brown hair, weight 95 pounds, height 5', occupation housewife and teacher, employer CORE. She formerly had New York State driver's license and now has Mississippi driver's license #1600175. Michael Schwerner formerly had New York State driver's license and now has Mississippi driver's license #1600177.

Rita Schwerner recently purchased a Singer sewing machine in Meridian and had it delivered to 2505½–5th Street in Meridian. This is the CORE office located in a building owned by Negroes.

These subjects do not live at the Young Hotel as previously reported and there is no record of either of these subjects at the Citizens Bank in Meridian.

There are two other CORE workers that frequently are in Meridian. They are Maureen Murphy, a white female, 21 years of age, who is usually accompanied by a young Negro man whose last name is believed to be Suarez. Suarez requested a letter from Meridian Chief of Police O. A. Booker in December 1963 authorizing him to contact and teach local Negroes to pass the voters registration examination. He was dressed in dungarees at the time and wearing a CORE button. Schwerner also dresses in dungarees and wears a CORE button.

A reproduction of a news release by Maureen Murphy which was dated December 27, 1963, and clipped from the *San Francisco Call Bulletin* is attached to this report.

Chief O. A. Booker, Detective G. L. Butler, and the sheriff's office of Lauderdale County are cooperating in this matter by keeping these subjects under surveillance and are getting information from reliable informants.

TITLE: Investigation of the disappearance of three civil rights workers after they were released from the Neshoba County jail on Sunday, June 21, 1964, at 10:30 P.M.
DATE OF INVESTIGATION: June 22, 23, 24, 25, 26, and continuing
DATE OF REPORT: June 29, 1964
INVESTIGATED BY: A. L. Hopkins, Investigator
TYPED BY: M. Curry

In compliance with orders of Director Erle Johnston, Jr., I proceeded to Philadelphia, Mississippi, on June 22, 1964, to investigate the burning of the Mt. Zion Negro Methodist Church near the Longdale Community in the eastern part of Neshoba County. This matter had not been reported to Sheriff Rainey of Neshoba County and no investigation had begun when I arrived in Philadelphia.

After discussing the matter with Sheriff Rainey, he decided to contact the Fire Marshal's office and request the assistance of one of their investigators in investigating the burning of this church in order to ascertain if it was an accident or deliberately burned. This investigation is still being conducted by the sheriff and his force, but due to the disappearance of Andrew Goodman, 20, and Michael Schwerner, 24, both white males of New York, and James Chaney, 21, Negro male of Meridian, Mississippi, all of whom are employed by CORE, has slowed down the investigation of the church burning, and the sheriff and his force are extremely busy investigating the disappearance of these subjects.

On Sunday afternoon at approximately 4:00, James Chaney, colored, male, of Meridian, was arrested by Deputy Sheriff Cecil Price[1] in Philadelphia and charged with speeding. At the time of his arrest, Chaney was accompanied by Andrew Goodman and Michael Schwerner, and they were in the area for the purpose of conducting their own investigation into the burning of the church.

After Deputy Price stopped the 1964 Chevrolet Station Wagon and arrested Chaney, he checked the registration of the automobile and found it to be registered to CORE in Hinds County, Mississippi. While Deputy Price had these subjects stopped, a tire went flat on the CORE automobile and Deputy Price assisted them in changing this tire, and Mississippi Highway Patrolmen Wiggs and

---

[1] **Deputy Sheriff Cecil Price:** Price was one of seven men convicted in 1967 for violating the civil rights of Chaney, Schwerner, and Goodman. Rainey was tried and acquitted.

Poe arrived on the scene and assisted Deputy Price in carrying these subjects in the automobile to the Neshoba County jail. Chaney was charged with speeding, only, and Goodman and Schwerner were held for investigation regarding the rumor that the Deputy had heard of the church burning.

At 10:30 P.M., Sunday, June 21, 1964, after Deputy Price had contacted Justice of the Peace Warren of Beat I, Neshoba County, and determined the amount of Chaney's bond, which was $20.00, Chaney, Schwerner, and Goodman were released from the Neshoba County jail and stated that they planned to proceed to Meridian at that time. Deputy Price observed them leaving Philadelphia on Highway 45 in the direction of Meridian and the investigation has not revealed that these subjects have been seen since.

The Chevrolet Station Wagon, which Chaney was driving, was located in the late afternoon of June 23, near the Bogue Chitto River or Creek. The vehicle had been burned and according to local officials, who discussed the matter with F.B.I. laboratory technicians, it has been determined that gasoline or some other inflammable fluid was poured in on the automobile before it was burned. There was no evidence of bullet holes, blood stains, or anything else that would indicate that the occupants had met with foul play.

On Tuesday afternoon, a party contacted Special F.B.I. Agent Procter in Meridian, Mississippi, at his office, and told him where the automobile could be found. This was either an anonymous call or Agent Procter has not seen fit to release the name of the party that gave him the information.

This automobile was parked and burned on a narrow country road that leads off of Highway 21, and dead ends in the Bogue Chitto swamp. From the position of this automobile, it appeared that the party or parties that burned it intended for it to be found soon as they could have driven this car two or three car-lengths further into the swamp and parked it to either the left or right side of the road and it probably would not have been found for weeks or even months because of the dense swamp growth. The call to Agent Procter also indicates that someone was interested in having the car found immediately.

This car has been towed to the Stokes Body Shop in Philadelphia where it has been thoroughly examined by a laboratory technician from the F.B.I. and I have been informed that it was found that the vehicle had been saturated with gasoline or some other inflammable fluid before it was burned. I was also informed that it had rained on the vehicle since it was burned and the last rain — after they were released from the Neshoba County jail, until the car was found — was on Monday afternoon, June 22, 1964, between 2:00 and 4:00 P.M.

Law enforcement agencies from Madison County, Yazoo County, Hinds County, the Highway Patrol, F.B.I., Sovereignty Commission, and others are represented in Philadelphia at this time for the purpose of assisting the sheriff in investigating this matter. The Highway Patrol, consisting of several units of uniformed patrolmen and several plainclothesmen directed by Gwin Cole, are assisting approximately 200 sailors from the Naval Air Station in Meridian in search of this area for these missing civil rights workers.

On Wednesday, June 24, 1964, John Lewis, colored, male, Chairman of the

Student Non-Violent Co-Ordinating Committee, George Raymond, Field Secretary of CORE, Dick Gregory, Comedian, and James Farmer, National Director of CORE, brought a group of approximately forty Negroes to Philadelphia for the purpose of observing the site where the vehicle was burned and the site where the church was burned and to conduct their own investigation into these matters. These four Negroes met with the city, county, district, and state officials and were advised that the investigation was being conducted by officials and that their presence in the area would only hamper or slow down the investigation. They were requested to return to Meridian or wherever they came from and let the officials conduct this investigation in the usual manner. These four Negroes did not agree to do this and insisted that they wanted to conduct their own investigation; however, they did return to Meridian and have not been seen since in Philadelphia.

There are rumors that there is a K.K.K. in Philadelphia and that some prominent citizens are members of the Klan. I have not been able to confirm this as to names of who may be members. However, Robert Shelton, National Grand Wizard of K.K.K., came to Philadelphia Thursday and stated that he was there for the purpose of conducting his own private investigation.

The people in Philadelphia are extremely upset over this matter. Most of the businessmen and good citizens still believe that this is a hoax perpetrated by the missing parties. Other citizens believed that it was a hoax to start with but are beginning to fear that these subjects have met with foul play.

There is no clue or physical evidence that indicates what might have happened to these missing people. It has been reported that all of them were seen in Alabama on Tuesday and that Goodman was later seen in Hammon[d], Louisiana. These rumors are reports that have not been confirmed.

It is not known how long the F.B.I. and state investigators plan to remain in Philadelphia and Neshoba County, but with the pressure being put on them by the President and the Justice Department, they will probably be there until these missing persons are located.

Since Deputy Sheriff Price was [the] last person known to have seen the missing persons alive, he has been questioned by the F.B.I. However, Honorable Herman Alford, the City Attorney of Philadelphia and other lawyers were present when he gave his statement.

Deputy Price has informed me when he arrested this subject on Sunday and placed [him] and the other two in jail, that there was nothing unusual about the arrest, no large crowds gathered, no one seemed to take a special interest in the arrest or the fact that these people were civil rights workers. Deputy Price states that he did not notify or tell anyone that these subjects were in jail and that there was no individual or group near the jail when he released them on Sunday night.

This investigation will continue and a report of the results will be added to this file.

44. The Response of the White Community

FLORENCE MARS
From *Witness in Philadelphia*
1977

Florence Mars was a local white woman who spoke out against the murders. She co-operated with the FBI's investigation, which made her somewhat unusual in her hometown, where rumors circulated freely but white citizens were expected to close ranks against both blacks and outsiders. In her memoir, she describes the disappearance of the three civil rights workers and her perception of the ensuing events, revealing much about the reaction of ordinary citizens to an extraordinary event.

. . . After hearing the newscast, I knew the disappearance could not be a hoax. I thought it typical harassment that Price had detained the civil rights workers for six hours, but I felt he had made a stupid and terrible mistake releasing them late at night in what he must have known was a dangerous situation.

On Tuesday morning I went to the beauty parlor and then to the drugstore and grocery. Wherever I went, the disappearance was the topic of animated conversation. The mood of the town was jovial; everyone thought it was a hoax. Although the rest of the country might fall for it, Neshoba County knew better: "COFO arranged the disappearance to make us look bad so they can raise money in other parts of the country." Besides, "Cecil Price said he and Richard Willis followed the station wagon to the edge of town and watched it disappear south, toward Meridian." That's all there was to it. Neshoba County would not be taken in by the stunt. It seemed to me the effort was forced, the conversation a little too loud, the assurance exaggerated.

That afternoon the boys' station wagon was found, abandoned and burned, twelve miles *north* of Philadelphia. The startling discovery seemed to have no impact. It was said that the burned car proved nothing: "COFO must have burned their own car to make the hoax look convincing. They are probably far out of the county laughing." Yet the mood of confidence quickly dimmed. Suddenly it was no joke; the burned station wagon opened the possibility that the boys had come to harm. Though this was not publicly acknowledged, the community began to react to the unstated possibility. Typical comments expressing the community's reaction were: "They had no business down here." "We don't think anything has happened to them, but if it has, they got what they deserved." "This wouldn't have happened if they had stayed home where they belong." . . .

When the boys' wagon was found I knew they were dead. Even if they had

Florence Mars, with the assistance of Lynn Eden, *Witness in Philadelphia* (Baton Rouge: Louisiana State University Press, 1977), 87–89, 92–95, 97–111.

wanted to stage a disappearance they would not have burned their only means of escape. I now also knew that the law enforcement of Neshoba County was involved in the "disappearance." Price must have been lying when he said the last he knew of them was when he saw them drive south toward Meridian. It was inconceivable that in Neshoba County they could have made their way from south of town to a point twelve miles north without being seen and without Price knowing their whereabouts. I now saw that the six-hour detainment and late-night release was not a matter of stupidity, but a deliberate set-up by the law to trap them and then probably release them to a mob.

There was no response from the city administration or from church groups expressing even perfunctory sympathy for the missing young men or concern for their welfare. A few days after the disappearance I went to see the mayor, an old family friend who impressed me as being a man with a strong sense of justice. I asked him why there had been no official statement, and he said he didn't know of his own knowledge what had happened and thought it would be presumptuous to assume that a crime had been committed. After that remark, there didn't seem to be anything to say.

The burning of Mt. Zion Methodist Church was considered by most to be part of the disappearance hoax. The fact that civil rights meetings were held in the Mt. Zion community negated the trust the white community had felt for Mt. Zion. Many felt betrayed, saying, "As good as we've been to them. . . ." The longstanding relationship could not now protect Mt. Zion from being seen as the enemy, capable of anything, including burning its own church. The plight of Mt. Zion evoked no sympathy.

The community grabbed at whatever evidence could be found to indicate that the church had *not* been burned by night riders. Even the leading layman of the First Methodist Church of Philadelphia, who would have been indignant over the church burning had Mt. Zion not associated itself with civil rights activity, found evidence that satisfied him that Mt. Zion had burned its own church. . . .

From the beginning a solid wall of resistance was thrown up against all outsiders. The first two newsmen to interview Sheriff Rainey and Deputy Sheriff Price on Monday, June 22, Karl Fleming of *Newsweek* and Claude Sitton of the New York *Times*, were met by four large men as they stepped out of the sheriff's office into the hall of the courthouse. The group's spokesman was Clarence Mitchell — an insurance man in his mid-thirties who was active in the First Methodist Church of Philadelphia. Fleming, at thirty-six a veteran reporter on civil rights activity, later told me that he and Sitton had been threatened with violence if they didn't get out of town. Fleming and Sitton went to a store on the square where Sitton thought he had a contact who could help them out. Sitton told the store owner the situation and said that although some men were across the street waiting for them to leave, they would like to stay on. They would appreciate it, Mr. Sitton said, if the gentleman would intervene on their behalf.

The storekeeper listened quietly and waited several seconds to make sure that Sitton had finished. Then the elderly gentleman very calmly and kindly said, "If you were a nigger and they were out there in the street beating you to death, I don't expect I'd go out and give them a hand, but they're absolutely right. If the nigger lovers and outside agitators would stay out of here and leave us alone, there wouldn't be any trouble. The best thing for you to do is what they say." . . .

Within a few days it seemed that the FBI was everywhere. They were easily recognizable in their dark pants and white shirts; also, they drove plain dark cars with high antennas, traveled in pairs, and carried briefcases. Agents began making house-to-house canvasses throughout the county; road blocks were set up at two factories, an emergency communications center was set up behind city hall, and helicopters crisscrossed the county. On Thursday one hundred naval cadets from the naval air station near Meridian began to search the Bogue Chitto swamp, where the car was found. By June 30 a contingent of four hundred sailors was working in shifts. . . .

The county felt besieged. The community felt that local and state law enforcement officers were perfectly capable of handling the case and deeply resented the federal intervention. However, newsmen, more than the FBI, bore the brunt of open hostility. By Wednesday the town was overrun with reporters. Besides state reporters, journalists from the major radio and television networks, wire services, and many large newspapers covered the story. In addition there were reporters from two London newspapers, a German paper, and the *Paris Match*. A downstairs room of the Benwalt Hotel was turned into a newsroom with teletypes and telephones. The presence of the FBI helped contain the hostility directed at newsmen; there were a few skirmishes but no serious injuries. On Thursday the car of a photographer shooting for NBC, Bill Delgado, was deliberately rammed as he backed into the street. When Delgado got out to protest he discovered about fifteen sullen-looking bystanders grouped on the edge of the sidewalk. Instead of protesting, he accepted a ticket from a city policeman for reckless driving. An "injured party" later filed suit and NBC, not wanting to risk a jury trial, settled out of court for $3,000. This was only one of several lawsuits filed against the media. The next day Delgado filmed from the safety of a low-flying helicopter and was fired on from a pickup truck. After the second incident he told the network to find someone else for the job.

The resentment of the newsmen's presence was constantly deepened by the newspaper coverage and especially by the widely viewed national evening news on television. The county thought the story was being blown out of all proportion. People mumbled that the nightly crimes of violence in every northern city didn't get this kind of treatment and thought that the disappearance was being used for publicity by national civil rights leaders who came to Philadelphia.

In addition, the coverage was considered to be very unfair. Unflattering shots of old men sitting on the courthouse steps were shown, as though they were representative of Philadelphia. Negro shacks on the edge of town were filmed, but not the nice homes in new subdivisions. The white population of Neshoba County felt that the county was being held up to ridicule and saw itself judged guilty before there was any evidence of a crime. . . .

On the Friday following the disappearance I heard that the Ku Klux Klan had murdered the boys. At my stockyard, a man I trusted told me he had talked with a farmer who was a neighbor to Mt. Zion. The farmer said he hated what had happened, but some of his relatives were involved, and there wasn't anything he could do about it if he planned to continue living in Neshoba County. . . .

Shortly after the disappearance I discovered a handful of others who also thought that a crime had been committed. My mother, though hesitant to express herself, did not believe it was a hoax. My mother's sister, Ellen, was more outspoken. Ellen Spendrup is a tall, large woman whose fiery red hair has turned white; she has never been known for espousing popular causes or for keeping her views to herself. After the disappearance she began making people uncomfortable in stores around the square saying, "Well *certainly* I think they're dead. I think you'll find their bodies over in the Mississippi River somewhere!" Ellen also had some fancy things to say about Sheriff Lawrence Rainey. She was furious that anyone in Neshoba County had pulled such a "lousy dirty trick" and was especially irritated by the silence of local leadership. G. A. "Boots" Howell, a high school classmate of mine who was from a prominent family and was in the contracting business, argued with men at the Rotary Club, including the mayor and the editor of the *Democrat*, "You know damn well our law is mixed up in this. I can't see why we have to protect them." Besides close personal friends, I discovered there were a few women who worked in businesses on the square who, in the early days especially, were outspoken in saying that a crime had been committed.

It seemed that most of the people who could see what must have happened were women, and of them, a large percentage were Catholic. Catholics generally may have been less inclined to believe in the hoax theory because they had long been a minority and had been a Klan target themselves in the 1920s. Catholic women may have felt freer to speak their minds than other women because no Catholic woman could fear that her husband was secretly a Klan member. Virtually no Negroes believed in the hoax theory. . . .

I was surprised at the federal government's determination to solve this particular crime, and grateful for the FBI's presence. I felt they were the only thing that stood between the law-abiding citizens of Neshoba County and the Ku Klux Klan. It was obvious from the first questions that the agents thought the Klan was responsible and were out to know all they could about them. I felt the agents were completely dedicated to solving the crime and to unyoking Neshoba County from the grip of the Klan. . . .

During the second week in July I went with a close friend who is a journalist, Iris Turner Kelso, to the Meridian COFO office. Iris, who grew up in Neshoba County, was covering the disappearance story for the New Orleans *States-Item*. When the lower half of a torso was found in the Mississippi River on July 12, there was speculation that it might be the body of James Chaney. I drove Iris to Meridian to cover the story. While we were at the COFO office a young Negro New Yorker of about nineteen asked me if I thought it would be safe for him to go to Neshoba County. I told him it would not. Resenting the answer, he gave me a hard look and asked, "Do you think *you* are free?" I told him I did and he said, "Well, you're not. Somebody got your name and number just as soon as you walked through the door downstairs." I didn't believe him; the idea seemed ridiculous. Before we left, Iris found out that the torso was not that of James Chaney.

A few days after the trip to Meridian a friend told me that she heard I was attending COFO meetings. I began to notice that when I went into the dry cleaners owned by a friend, a man from the store next door would cross the street to get a better view of what was going on inside the shop. The COFO worker was right; I was under surveillance. This was the first time I realized that not only outsiders were being closely watched. I was indignant.

For a while I discussed some aspect of the case almost daily with close friends. The big question for us was not who had actually committed the murders, but how high the Klan membership went in the community's structure. Through newsmen I learned that the Klan had organized quickly throughout the state in the early part of 1964 and that Neshoba County was only a small part of the organization. Of course the Klan was a secret organization and it was only possible to surmise who was in it. The main indication to us of Klan membership was participation in certain organized activities on the streets of Philadelphia. These activities included checking all out-of-county license plates, identifying every journalist and outsider and often harassing them, and generally policing the town. Many of these men worked in stores on or near the square, and we called them the "goon squad." The Klan closely watched FBI agents and kept a tight surveillance on all town activity, especially watching those whom the FBI talked to. One man who struck up a street-corner conversation with an agent, just to be friendly, discovered he was being shunned by friends. A salesman with a large family, he didn't make that mistake again.

It was particularly chilling to see klansmen get together in certain places near the square during the day, constantly watching the streets and talking with each other. . . .

My friends and I did not doubt that these men knew a murder had been committed, and that it was "theirs." Yet, they claimed as loudly as anyone that it was a hoax and probably helped convince the town that it was. At the same time, some of them made surprisingly vicious remarks such as, "I wouldn't give no more thought to killing them than wringing a cat's neck" and "I could kill them easier than I could kill Germans I didn't know."

The second indication of Klan membership was affiliation with the auxiliary police. In early 1964 the Mississippi legislature had set up machinery to form local homeguard units to assist local police in dealing with expected racial violence. Immediately after the murders an auxiliary police unit was organized at local initiative in Neshoba County. When the FBI began its investigation, the auxiliary police provided a legitimate vehicle for klansmen to get together frequently. Many men in the "goon squad" were in the auxiliary police, and though not all auxiliary policemen were members of the Klan, it was clear that a great many klansmen were members of the auxiliary police. In fact, the auxiliary was the legitimate police arm of the Ku Klux Klan. The auxiliary met openly in the National Guard Armory at night and occasionally directed traffic, sometimes having to leave work to do so. . . .

Finally, we picked up information through Negro friends and domestic help. It all added up to a large and powerful organization, one that almost certainly included the sheriff and his deputy. It was possible to be quite certain about the membership of certain individuals one might not ordinarily expect to be in the Klan because of accumulated circumstantial evidence. For example, the FBI asked repeatedly about the owner of an appliance shop, a man not associated with goon squad activities. Furthermore, the FBI virtually camped on his doorstep. We felt sure he was in the Klan; later, his maid told me that she had found a white robe in his closet.

When I began to realize the extent of Klan organization, and that it reached into the sheriff's office, I determined to do what I could to oppose Klan forces in the community. If the community was not to be a party to murder, it could not sanction the organization responsible for the murders. I knew the majority of the community saw the killings in racial terms: the COFO workers were the enemy and whatever happened to them was justified and deserved. However, I knew I would do what I could not only to assist the FBI but, if it was in my power, to help the civic leadership see the issue and act. . . .

Throughout July the FBI investigation and search for the bodies continued. Even though the FBI was piecing together what had happened that night, without the bodies there could be no crime to prosecute. Busloads of sailors went day after day to one community and then another, making their headquarters at country stores. Residents looked on the search as an affront to the good name of their communities.

As the weeks passed it began to seem less likely to many that the boys really were alive; it also seemed less likely to many that any bodies would be found in Neshoba County. However, most people continued to hang onto the hope that the disappearance was a hoax. Toward the end of July I overheard a Philadelphia matron say, in a tone she usually reserved to console the bereaved, "I believe with all my heart they are alive somewhere. We may never know it, but I believe it is so nevertheless." A proprietor in one of the stores on the square had a more realistic attitude and, at about the same time, said to me, "I just hope that if they are dead, they won't find their bodies anywhere around here." I usually didn't respond in such cases, but this time I said, "I hope they are found around here. It will be the only way to get the community to accept any responsibility for what has happened." At the time, I felt this was very important. . . .

On Tuesday, August 4, beneath fifteen feet of dirt in a newly completed earthen dam, the FBI found the bodies of Michael Schwerner, James Chaney, and Andrew Goodman. The FBI had roughly estimated from the dam construction where the bodies might be; then, an agent, on impulse, walked fifteen paces toward the center. There, directly beneath, the bodies were found, side by side. This ended one of the most extensive searches ever conducted by the FBI. The farm belonged to Olen Burrage, the owner of a Neshoba County trucking firm who lived two miles away. He said he didn't know anybody who would kill the boys and put the bodies on his property. He also said, "I want people to know I am sorry it happened. I just don't know why anybody would kill them and I don't believe in anything like that."

The discovery shattered Neshoba County's hoax rationale and was met with silence or muted conversation. A few avoided the overwhelming evidence that this was indeed no hoax by saying that the FBI had put the bodies there. This was evidenced by the fact that the FBI knew exactly where to dig. Further, it was rumored that the dirt caked to the bodies was different from the dirt in the dam.

Early in the search the FBI had widely circulated the rumor that they would pay up to $25,000 for information leading to discovery of the bodies. After the discovery the FBI claimed that its attention had been drawn to the new earthen dam during flights over the area in a helicopter. No one believed it, and there was widespread, if quiet, speculation about who had told the FBI where the bodies were. It was rumored that a preacher who was being closely interrogated by the FBI had bought an expensive new automobile. Others suspected of having told were reported to be out of town for a few days. Any evidence of new wealth was suspect. However, people generally continued to talk about the upcoming fair, trying to act as if nothing had happened.

The klansmen were unmistakably anxious over the discovery. Activity picked up again on the streets, but without the earlier swaggering self-assurance. Men scurried to the same meeting places, but with worried looks and a greater sense of urgency. Undoubtedly they were deeply concerned about who had told the FBI where the bodies were, or even more. At first, arrests were expected, but within two weeks the fear of imminent arrest waned. . . .

The following Monday, six days after the bodies were found, the Neshoba County Fair opened. As always, anticipation was great. On the weekend before families moved into the cabins that stand like a ghost town the rest of the year, and by Monday the fairgrounds were transformed into a tiny magical town.

The fair *almost* seemed the same. There were the same speakings, bands, horseraces, community exhibits, dances, sings, and carnival activities; the same crowds milled near the pavilion and sat on benches built around the oak trees, and there was the same talk about how good it was to be back. The unpleasant events of the summer were not discussed. The press, at the fair every year, was not intrusive and most fair-goers were unaware of the presence of FBI agents.

Still, there was an air of unspoken tension, greatly heightened by the bizarre presence of the auxiliary police. The full force of about fifty men patrolled the grounds wearing high boots and blue police uniforms. Their helmets rode low on their foreheads and looked like those of Nazi storm troopers. Their belts were loaded with live ammunition; a billet hung from one hip and a gun from the other. The auxiliary police made their unofficial headquarters under an oak tree by the pavilion, directly in front of our family cabin. Here they met with klansmen not in the auxiliary and together watched the crowds. Their presence was not commented on.

Just before dusk on Wednesday, a low-flying plane dropped leaflets from the White Knights of the Ku Klux Klan of Mississippi welcoming visitors to the Neshoba County Fair. The leaflet was called the Klan-Ledger and consisted largely of an interview with a Klan officer, prepared in the "public interest." Some of the questions and answers it contained were the following:

> *Q*. What is your explanation of why there have been so many National Police Agents involved in the case of the "missing civil-rights workers?"
> A. First, I must correct you on your terms. Schwerner, Chaney and Goodman

were not civil-rights workers. They [were] Communist Revolutionaries, actively working to undermine and destroy Christian Civilization. . . .

Q. But aren't all citizens, even Communists, entitled to equal protection under the law?

A. Certainly. But the Communists do not want EQUAL treatment under the law. They want FAVORED treatment under the law. . . .

Q. What persons would have a motive for killing them?

A. There are two groups which could have done it. (1) American patriots who are determined to resist Communism by every available means, and (2) The Communists themselves who will always sacrifice their own members in order to achieve a propaganda victory.

Q. Isn't it unlikely that the Communists would do that in this case? Schwerner was a valuable man?

A. Not at all. The Communists never hesitate to murder one of their own if it will benefit the Party. Communism is pure, refined, scientific Cannibalism in action. A case in point is the murdered Kennedy. Certainly, no President could have been a more willing tool to the Communists than the late and unlamented "Red Jack." . . .

Q. Was the White Knights of the KU KLUX KLAN involved in this case?

A. Only to the extent of doing everything possible to expose the truth about the Communist and political aspects of the case. We are primarily concerned with protecting the good name and integrity of the honest people of the State of Mississippi against the physical and propaganda attacks of the Communist Agitators and Press.

Q. Why is Mississippi always being attacked by Communists?

A. Mississippi is a Sovereign State in a Federal Union, and insists upon being so regarded. Communists are mongrelizers. They despise Sovereignty and Individuality. They despise local self-government, and local solution of political problems, the political factors which have made America great. . . .

There was no visible reaction to the leaflets. People just stuffed them in their pockets or walked over them. The aura of unreality was complete.

On Thursday, the biggest day of the fair, there were the political speakings in the pavilion, highlighted by the governor's speech. This year he was preceded by a Jackson leader of the John Birch Society. The Bircher gave a rabble-rousing speech advocating open defiance of the federal government and sat down amidst thunderous applause. Governor Paul Johnson followed with a moderate statement and, in repudiation of the Bircher, reaffirmed Mississippi's loyalty to the Union. He received only a sprinkling of applause at the end. As the governor moved around talking to people, I wanted to go up and speak to him, but Cecil Price never left his side. I knew that it would be just like announcing whatever I had to say at a Klan meeting. . . .

The fair officially closed on Friday. No one admitted that it had not been like always. Yet the next issue of the *Neshoba Democrat* failed to discuss what a great fair it had been, as was customary. Instead the editor was preoccupied with defending Neshoba County against the deep sting of "unjust" publicity. . . .

Two weeks later the editor lashed out in frustration and anger at the publicity focused on Neshoba County when he wrote, "Those people in Ohio who stood by and watched a fifty-two-year-old woman drown after her car left the high-way must have some sort of feeling. Can you imagine people who are supposed to be civilized standing by and listening to a drowning woman ask for help and doing nothing about it? They should have to struggle with their consciences for the rest of their lives." In this unspoken comparison with Neshoba County the editor was implying that people here were not the kind to just stand by when someone called for help, and he was right. Yet ironically he had unwittingly articulated the county's unacknowledged sense of guilt. . . .

45. "Be Sick and Tired with Me"

Dave Dennis
Eulogy for James Chaney
1964

Dave Dennis, a black civil rights leader from Louisiana, was the head of CORE's Mississippi staff and served on COFO's steering committee during Freedom Summer. Dennis went on to get a law degree and practiced law for many years until he returned to Mississippi in 1992 to serve as regional director of the Algebra Project, designed by his former associate Bob Moses to promote greater mathematical literacy among black children.

Though a young man in 1964, Dave Dennis was already a veteran civil rights worker and Schwerner's supervisor; but for a severe case of bronchitis, he would have been with the three men on the night they were killed — and he never stopped wondering if he could have done something to prevent it. Asked to deliver the eulogy for James Chaney, Dennis was urged by other civil rights leaders to keep the crowd calm; he planned to talk about the importance of nonviolent resistance. But, as Dennis later said, when he looked down on the tear-streaked face of Chaney's little brother Ben, something snapped inside him: with eyes described as "glazed, almost wild," he delivered the following address.

. . . I feel that he has got his freedom and we are still fighting for it. But what I want to talk about right now is the living dead that we have right among our midst, not only here in the state of Mississippi, but throughout the nation. Those

Juan Williams, *Eyes on the Prize: America's Civil Rights Years, 1954–1965* (New York: Viking Penguin, 1987), 238–40.

are the people who don't care. [And] those who do care but don't have the guts enough to stand up for it. And those people who are busy up in Washington and other places using my freedom and my life to play politics with. That includes the president on down to the governor of the state of Mississippi . . . as I stand here I not only blame the people who pulled the trigger or did the beating or dug the hole with the shovel. I blame the people in Washington, D.C., and on down in the state of Mississippi for what happened just as much as I blame those who pulled the trigger. Because I feel that, one hundred years ago, if the proper thing had been done by the federal government of this country . . . we wouldn't be here today mourning the death of a brave young man like James Chaney.

. . . You see, I know what is going to happen. I feel it deep in my heart — when they find the people who killed those guys in Neshoba County . . . they [will] come back to the state of Mississippi and have a jury of all their cousins and aunts and uncles. And I know what they are going to say: "Not guilty." Because no one saw them pull the trigger. I'm tired of that! . . . I look at the young kids here, that is something else I grieve about. Little Ben Chaney here and others like him. . . .

I don't grieve for James Chaney. He lived a fuller life than many of us will ever live. He's got his freedom, and we're still fighting for ours. I'm sick and tired of going to the funerals of black men who have been murdered by white men. . . .

I've got vengeance in my heart tonight, and I ask you to feel angry with me. I'm sick and tired, and I ask you to be sick and tired with me. The white men who murdered James Chaney are never going to be punished. I ask you to be sick and tired of that. I'm tired of the people of this country allowing this thing to continue to happen. . . .

I'm tired of that old suggestion that Negroes ought to go back to Africa. I'm ready to go back to Africa the day when all the Jews, the Poles, the Russians, the Germans, and the Anglo-Saxons go back where they came from. This land was taken from the Indians, and it belongs just as much to us Negroes as it does to any other group. . . .

We've got to stand up. The best way we can remember James Chaney is to demand our rights. Don't just look at me and go back and tell folks you've been to a nice service. Your work is just beginning. If you go back home and sit down and take what these white men in Mississippi are doing to us . . . if you take it and don't do something about it . . . then God damn your souls!

Stand up! Those neighbors who were too afraid to come to this service, pick them up and take them down there and register to vote! Go down there and do it! Don't ask that white man *if* you can register to vote! Just tell him: "Baby, I'm here!" Stand up! Hold your heads up! Don't bow down anymore! We want our freedom NOW!

Suggestions for Further Reading

Belfrage, Sally. *Freedom Summer.* New York: Viking Press, 1965. Reprint, Charlottesville: University Press of Virginia, 1990.

Cagin, Seth, and Philip Dray. *We Are Not Afraid: The Story of Goodman, Schwerner, and Chaney and the Civil Rights Campaign for Mississippi.* New York: Macmillan, 1988.

Dittmer, John. *Local People: The Struggle for Civil Rights in Mississippi.* Urbana: University of Illinois Press, 1994.

McAdam, Doug. *Freedom Summer.* New York: Oxford University Press, 1988.

McMillen, Neil R. *The Citizens' Council: Organized Resistance to the Second Reconstruction, 1954–1964.* Urbana: University of Illinois Press, 1971.

Mills, Kay. *This Little Light of Mine: The Life of Fannie Lou Hamer.* New York: Dutton, 1993.

Mills, Nicolaus. *Like a Holy Crusade: Mississippi 1964 — The Turning of the Civil Rights Movement in America.* Chicago: Dee, 1992.

Vollers, Maryanne. *Ghosts of Mississippi: The Murder of Medgar Evers, the Trials of Byron De La Beckwith, and the Haunting of the New South.* Boston: Little, Brown & Co., 1995.

Williams, Juan. *Eyes on the Prize: America's Civil Rights Years, 1954–1965.* New York: Viking Penguin, 1987. Also see the documentary by the same name, by Blackside Productions.

CHAPTER THIRTEEN

THE VIETNAM WAR

The South Divided

Terribly costly in terms of military expenditure and human life, the Vietnam War also generated intense social and political conflict that polarized the nation and added the "generation gap" to the list of social problems confounding Americans in the 1960s. Most Southerners strongly supported the war, even as support waned in other parts of the nation. Even so, the South, already wracked by racial tension, was further divided by the war.

A disproportionate share of those engaged in fighting the war were Southerners: President Lyndon B. Johnson, a Texan, made the fateful decision to escalate the war in 1965; General William Westmoreland of South Carolina commanded America's ground forces in Vietnam from 1964 to 1968; and, in the early 1970s, four out of five army generals were Southerners. The South also provided more than its share of enlisted personnel. Though at the time the region had only 22 percent of the nation's population, 31 percent of those who served in America's armed forces during the war, and 28 percent of those who died, were Southerners.

There were several reasons for this disproportionate participation. Many Southerners served because of the region's strong military tradition. Despite a growing national backlash against the military, the Reserve Officers' Training Corps (ROTC) continued to attract college students on southern campuses, and military academies remained popular. The relative poverty of the South was also a factor: for many, military service was a means to economic advancement. Thousands enlisted under Secretary of Defense Robert McNamara's somewhat infamous "Project 100,000" which opened up the armed services to the "marginally qualified." Poverty also left many Southerners subject to the draft; the South had a disproportionate number of poor whites and blacks who, unable to afford college, were ineligible for deferment. Blacks were twice as vulnerable to draft boards, on which few blacks served.

The war touched all classes and races of Southerners, however, particularly after college deferments ended and the draft was conducted by lottery. In fact, the very diversity of the southern contingent in Vietnam meant that the South's on-going racial problems often flared up "in country" within the most integrated army America had ever sent into combat. Though some veterans recalled that their service in Vietnam helped them overcome racial barriers, others reported serious racial tensions. Black soldiers were influenced by the antiwar positions of civil rights leaders at home, who protested the fact that so many African Americans were being sent abroad to die for a nation in which they did not enjoy equal rights. Ugly racial incidents within the military radicalized many black soldiers from the South.

Among white southern conservatives, however, support for the war remained strong. Many of them had grown up revering Confederate soldiers for fighting till the end against great odds; to them, the suggestion that the richest and most powerful nation on earth should retreat before a small, underdeveloped Asian nation and abandon the fight against Communism was unthinkable, a betrayal of national honor. In addition, southern evangelicals, including the influential Southern Baptist Convention, viewed the war as a crusade against an atheistic foe. Southerners also took pride in the fact that so many of the combat training bases — including the Special Warfare School at Fort Bragg, North Carolina, which produced the famous new military unit known as the "Green Berets" — were located in the South, bases that fed local economies and contributed to the growing prosperity of the region.

Southern supporters of the war had little patience with antiwar protesters, and southern politicians appealed to voters by attacking those who opposed it. Alabama's George Wallace denounced "pointy-headed intellectuals" who questioned U.S. involvement in Vietnam and condemned protesters as un-American. Senator Strom Thurmond of South Carolina denounced "draft dodgers" and defended Lieutenant William Calley of Florida, who was charged with responsibility for the My Lai Massacre. Senator James Eastland of Mississippi fought hard to prevent American withdrawal. And Vice President Spiro T. Agnew, former governor of Maryland, helped make Nixon's "southern strategy" a success with his alliterative denunciations of war critics, particularly those "nattering nabobs of negativism" in the media and on college campuses.

Nevertheless there was significant antiwar activity in the South. Martin Luther King Jr. denounced the war as immoral and a tragic diversion of funds from antipoverty programs. The Southern Christian Leadership Conference (SCLC) went on record against the war, and the more militant Student Nonviolent Coordinating Committee (SNCC) led by Stokely Carmichael denounced it as racist and imperialistic. Another SNCC leader, Julian Bond, elected to the

Georgia legislature in 1965, was barred from his seat for two years because of his antiwar activities.

Students staged antiwar demonstrations and protests on college and university campuses across the South, particularly after President Nixon announced the expansion of the war into Cambodia in the spring of 1970. When the National Guard fired on protesters at Kent State University in Ohio, southern students participated in the national wave of protest and mourning. At the University of Maryland, destructive students provoked the governor into sending troops on campus. At Jackson State University in Mississippi, students rallied to show sympathy with the students at Kent State; a week later, two students were killed when police fired into a crowd of protesters. Generally speaking, however, the antiwar movement on southern campuses was more moderate and less violent than elsewhere in the nation.

Though many faculty members and administrators, and a growing number of Southerners in general, were concerned about the expansion of the war and increasingly sympathetic to the students, supporters of the war bitterly resented the campus protests. Some students denounced Vietnam veterans and National Guardsmen as murderers and their nation as racist and imperialistic. Other, more moderate student protesters insisted that they hated the war, not the warriors, and supported their country but not its war policy — but it made little difference. From the other side of the generation gap came demands that students defer to the wisdom of elected officials and do their duty. To conservative southern supporters of the war, the fact that many southern intellectuals, academics, and civil rights activists now appeared to be united in opposition to a war against Communism seemed proof positive of their long-standing suspicions about southern liberals.

In the South, as in the rest of the nation, the war accentuated social tensions and created new sources of conflict. The documents in this chapter illustrate the divergent views of Southerners concerning Vietnam. Included are General William C. Westmoreland's thoughts on the war and on public opinion, and Martin Luther King Jr.'s most famous antiwar address. In several selections from oral histories, white and black veterans from the South reflect on their wartime experiences, including racial tensions within the military. Two addresses by Vice President Spiro Agnew illustrate the attitudes of those who supported the war toward those who opposed it. The chapter concludes with a letter to the editor of the *Washington (N.C.) Daily News* from antiwar students at the University of North Carolina at Chapel Hill and responses from their detractors and supporters, capturing the generation gap as it manifested itself in a small southern town.

As you read, consider the effects of the war in Vietnam on the American public. According to General Westmoreland, how did public opinion affect the war and those fighting in it? Why did Martin Luther King Jr. see the war as immoral and counter to the goals and philosophy of the civil rights movement? How did sectional and racial tensions influence southern soldiers fighting in Vietnam? How did people on the two sides of the generation gap regard one another?

46. The War and Public Opinion

WILLIAM C. WESTMORELAND
Oral History
1990

General William C. Westmoreland, the commander of American ground forces at the height of the war in Vietnam, was a South Carolinian from a prominent family with a strong military tradition. He was sometimes compared to fellow Southerner and West Point graduate Robert E. Lee — a dignified, moral, and professional soldier who cared deeply about the men fighting under his command. This excerpt from an oral history demonstrates his awareness of the importance to the war effort of public support and his concerns about the handling of the war by political leaders and its coverage in the media. Back in the United States after 1968, Westmoreland dedicated himself to trying to change public opinion on the war in order to improve the treatment of Vietnam veterans.

. . . I was not naive about the nature of the Vietnam War. I knew that the support of the American people was essential if we were to achieve success in Vietnam. I spent my first six weeks in-country traveling around and talking to hundreds of people to get a good feel for the situation. Just before I was appointed COMUSMACV,[1] I had a one-on-one meeting with Defense Secretary McNamara at the old U.S. embassy in Saigon—I think he wanted to size me up and see if I was the right man to replace General Harkins—and I told him how I felt about the war at that point.

[1]**COMUSMACV:** the military acronym for "Commander U.S. Military Assistance Command Vietnam."

James R. Wilson, *Landing Zones: Southern Veterans Remember Vietnam* (Durham, N.C.: Duke University Press, 1990), 14–15, 17, 19–21.

"Mr. Secretary," I said, "I've come to the strong conclusion that this is going to be a long war. It is a herculean task that we face and unless something is done to keep the American people aboard, we will not succeed."

McNamara listened quietly.

"The only thing that comes to mind," I continued, "is some kind of people-to-people program, maybe having American cities such as Savannah, Georgia, adopt a Vietnamese town such as Vung Tau. The American people will have to feel a sense of broad involvement."

McNamara said nothing. I later talked to one of his aides and learned that my idea had been discussed in the White House, but President Johnson by then had decided to play the war low-key. . . .

The situation in Vietnam had many sides to it, but I think we could have pulled out — gracefully in my opinion — before Ngo Dinh Diem was overthrown and killed in November of 1963. Of course, withdrawing would have generated a lot of political heat among the right-wing Republicans because Kennedy's "We'll pay any price, bear any burden in the defense of liberty" speech was still ringing in the ears of America. Still, I think he could have justified withdrawal by saying we had sent fifteen thousand troops there, the political situation was a mess, the place was paralyzed, there was nobody we could work with to pull the country together, so we're getting out. But by sanctioning Diem's overthrow, we had assumed a moral obligation to stick with our commitment.

. . . There were always problems with the Vietnamese, decisions that had to be made on the conduct of the war, and endless gratuitous advice coming from Washington. I usually palmed a lot of the advice off on my staff, giving them a little guidance in a buck slip or a short telephone call on how to respond. A lot of this how-to-win-the-war advice came from Bob McNamara's "whiz kids" in the Pentagon. Since these people usually didn't know what they were talking about, I conveniently ignored many of their cables. . . .

One of the biggest disappointments I suffered in Vietnam came from the media. I was quite disillusioned by their performance. We tried to get some visibility for the civic action and other nation-building work that was going on in the midst of the war, but that sort of thing wasn't sensational. It didn't attract readership because news, at least in the United States, tends to focus on the bizarre and the offbeat. . . .

Some of our media weren't sophisticated enough to realize they were being used by the North Vietnamese. LBJ said that when he lost the support of Walter Cronkite after the Tet Offensive, he lost mainstream America. By reporting Tet as a defeat rather than the victory it was, Cronkite was an unwitting participant in carrying out North Vietnam's very shrewd propaganda strategy. His ignorance of the war is still appalling. When CBS sent him to Hanoi to get some dirt on me during my libel suit against the network a few years ago, he quoted me as saying I could have defeated North Vietnam if I'd been given a few more troops after Tet. In the first place, I never said that. In the second place, how could I have defeated the enemy if I couldn't go after him in Cambodia, Laos, or North Vietnam?

There was no way we could win with the media, but I never really thought censorship in Vietnam was the answer to that problem. President Johnson told me a few months before he died that we should have imposed censorship. I didn't agree with him, but I didn't argue the point, either. In the first place, the Vietnamese government, as the sovereign power, would have had responsibility for censorship. . . .

When I came back to the states in 1968 and found so much misunderstanding about the war, I felt I should try to explain a little more about what we were trying to do in Vietnam. I did quite a bit of traveling as chief of staff, speaking mainly to such groups as the Association of the United States Army and other patriotic organizations. After my retirement in 1972, at a time when a lot of the troops were coming home, I felt so bad about the way they were being treated that I dedicated myself to talk to *any* group about Vietnam. I went to a number of radical campuses and received every discourtesy imaginable. . . .

I deliberately made myself a target for these people. I preferred to have them throw darts at me rather than at my troops, who were not psychologically equipped to handle that kind of abuse. . . . I believed very strongly that I had an obligation to tell the story of what the troops did and come to their public defense, although I don't like to use that term because it implies they had done something wrong. I was not, however, going to stand aside and let them be called babykillers.

. . . I've seen the American system at its best and at its worst. I had some temporary disillusionment about how well the system worked, but it hasn't lingered. The way I look back at it, that's the way the cards were stacked. I played them as they were dealt to me. . . .

47. Civil Rights and Foreign Policy

MARTIN LUTHER KING JR.
"A Time to Break Silence"
1967

In this address delivered to a gathering of Clergy and Laity Concerned about Vietnam on April 4, 1967, a year before his assassination, Martin Luther King Jr. explained the reasons he felt compelled to speak out against the war and the connection between his stance on the war and the civil rights movement. King's beliefs that

Martin Luther King Jr., "A Time to Break Silence," in *The Eyes on the Prize Civil Rights Reader: Documents, Speeches, and Firsthand Accounts from the Black Freedom Struggle, 1954–1990,* ed. Clayborne Carson et al. (New York: Penguin Books, 1991), 387–93.

many Americans supported the war because they did not fully understand the situation in Vietnam, that the South Vietnamese government was an undeserving ally, and that America was doing more harm than good for the people of Vietnam, was widely shared by those in the antiwar movement. The national reaction was intense: according to Andrew Young who was then executive vice president of the Southern Christian Leadership Conference (SCLC), the address elicited "a torrent of hate and venom."[1] Even many of those who supported King's philosophy of nonviolence when applied to the civil rights movement could not accept it in the context of solving international problems.

I come to this magnificent house of worship tonight because my conscience leaves me no other choice. I join with you in this meeting because I am in deepest agreement with the aims and work of the organization which has brought us together: Clergy and Laymen Concerned about Vietnam. The recent statement of your executive committee are the sentiments of my own heart and I found myself in full accord when I read its opening lines: "A time comes when silence is betrayal." That time has come for us in relation to Vietnam.

The truth of these words is beyond doubt but the mission to which they call us is a most difficult one. Even when pressed by the demands of inner truth, men do not easily assume the task of opposing their government's policy, especially in time of war. Nor does the human spirit move without great difficulty against all the apathy of conformist thought within one's own bosom and in the surrounding world. . . .

Over the past two years, as I have moved to break the betrayal of my own silences and to speak from the burnings of my own heart, as I have called for radical departures from the destruction of Vietnam, many persons have questioned me about the wisdom of my path. At the heart of their concerns this query has often loomed large and loud: Why are you speaking about war, Dr. King? Why are you joining the voices of dissent? Peace and civil rights don't mix, they say. Aren't you hurting the cause of your people? they ask. And when I hear them, though I often understand the source of their concern, I am nevertheless greatly saddened, for such questions mean that the inquirers have not really known me, my commitment or my calling. Indeed, their questions suggest that they do not know the world in which they live. . . .

I come to this platform tonight to make a passionate plea to my beloved nation. This speech is not addressed to Hanoi or to the National Liberation Front. It is not addressed to China or to Russia. . . .

Since I am a preacher by trade, I suppose it is not surprising that I have several reasons for bringing Vietnam into the field of my moral vision. There is at the

---

[1]Qtd. in *Voices of Freedom: An Oral History of the Civil Rights Movement from the 1950s through the 1980s*, eds. Henry Hampton and Steve Fayer (New York: Bantam Books, 1990), 344.

outset a very obvious and almost facile connection between the war in Vietnam and the struggle I, and others, have been waging in America. A few years ago there was a shining moment in that struggle. It seemed as if there was a real promise of hope for the poor — both black and white — through the Poverty Program. There were experiments, hopes, new beginnings. Then came the build-up in Vietnam and I watched the program broken and eviscerated as if it were some idle political plaything of a society gone mad on war, and I knew that America would never invest the necessary funds or energies in rehabilitation of its poor so long as adventures like Vietnam continued to draw men and skills and money like some demoniacal destructive suction tube. So I was increasingly compelled to see the war as an enemy of the poor and to attack it as such.

Perhaps the more tragic recognition of reality took place when it became clear to me that the war was doing far more than devastating the hopes of the poor at home. It was sending their sons and their brothers and their husbands to fight and to die in extraordinarily high proportions relative to the rest of the population. We were taking the black young men who had been crippled by our society and sending them 8,000 miles away to guarantee liberties in Southeast Asia which they had not found in Southwest Georgia and East Harlem. So we have been repeatedly faced with the cruel irony of watching Negro and white boys on TV screens as they kill and die together for a nation that has been unable to seat them together in the same schools. . . .

My third reason moves to an even deeper level of awareness, for it grows out of my experience in the ghettos of the North over the last three years — especially the last three summers. As I have walked among the desperate, rejected and angry young men I have told them that Molotov cocktails and rifles would not solve their problems. I have tried to offer them my deepest compassion while maintaining my convictions that social change comes most meaningfully through non-violent action. But they asked — and rightly so — what about Vietnam? They asked if our own nation wasn't using massive doses of violence to solve its problems, to bring about the changes it wanted. Their questions hit home, and I knew that I could never again raise my voice against the violence of the oppressed in the ghettos without having first spoken clearly to the greatest purveyor of violence in the world today — my own government. . . .

And as I ponder the madness of Vietnam and search within myself for ways to understand and respond in compassion my mind goes constantly to the people of that peninsula. I speak now not of the soldiers of each side, not of the junta in Saigon, but simply of the people who have been living under the curse of war for almost three continuous decades now. I think of them too because it is clear to me that there will be no meaningful solution there until some attempt is made to know them and hear their broken cries. . . .

They watch as we poison their water, as we kill a million acres of their crops. They must weep as the bulldozers roar through their areas preparing to destroy the precious trees. They wander into the hospitals, with at least twenty casualties from American firepower for one Vietcong-inflicted injury. They wander into the towns and see thousands of the children, homeless, without clothes, running in packs on the streets like animals. They see the children degraded by our soldiers as they beg for food. They see the children selling their sisters to our soldiers, soliciting for their mothers. . . .

Perhaps the more difficult but no less necessary task is to speak for those who have been designated as our enemies. What of the National Liberation Front — that strangely anonymous group we call VC or Communists? What must they think of us in America when they realize that we permitted the repression and cruelty of Diem which helped to bring them into being as a resistance group in the South? What do they think of our condoning the violence which led to their own taking up of arms? How can they believe in our integrity when now we speak of "aggression from the North" as if there were nothing more essential to the war? How can they trust us when now we charge them with violence after the murderous reign of Diem, and charge them with violence while we pour every new weapon of death into their land? Surely we must understand their feelings even if we do not condone their actions. Surely we must see that the men we supported pressed them to their violence. Surely we must see that our own computerized plans of destruction simply dwarf their greatest acts.

How do they judge us when our officials know that their membership is less than 25 percent Communist and yet insist on giving them the blanket name? What must they be thinking when they know that we are aware of their control of major sections of Vietnam and yet we appear ready to allow national elections in which this highly organized political parallel government will have no part? They ask how we can speak of free elections when the Saigon press is censored and controlled by the military junta. And they are surely right to wonder what kind of new government we plan to help form without them — the only party in real touch with the peasants. . . .

So, too, with Hanoi. In the North, where our bombs now pummel the land, and our mines endanger the waterways, we are met by a deep but understandable mistrust. To speak for them is to explain this lack of confidence in western words, and especially their distrust of American intentions now. In Hanoi are the men who led the nation to independence against the Japanese and the French, the men who sought membership in the French commonwealth and were betrayed by the weakness of Paris and the willfulness of the colonial armies. It was they who led a second struggle against French domination at tremendous costs, and then were persuaded to give up the land they controlled between the 13th and 17th parallel as a temporary measure at Geneva. After 1954 they watched us conspire with Diem to prevent elections which would have surely brought Ho Chi Minh to power over a united Vietnam, and they realized they had been betrayed again. . . .

In order to atone for our sins and errors in Vietnam, we should take the initiative in bringing a halt to this tragic war. I would like to suggest five concrete things that our Government should do immediately to begin the long and difficult process of extricating ourselves from this nightmarish conflict:

1. End all bombing in North and South Vietnam.
2. Declare a unilateral cease-fire in the hope that such action will create the atmosphere for negotiation.
3. Take immediate steps to prevent other battlegrounds in Southeast Asia by curtailing our military build-up in Thailand and our interference in Laos.

4. Realistically accept the fact that the National Liberation Front has substantial support in South Vietnam and must thereby play a role in any meaningful negotiations and in any future Vietnam government.
5. Set a date that we will remove all foreign troops from Vietnam in accordance with the 1954 Geneva Agreement.

Part of our ongoing commitment might well express itself in an offer to grant asylum to any Vietnamese who fears for his life under a new regime which included the Liberation Front. Then we must make what reparations we can for the damage we have done. We must provide the medical aid that is badly needed, making it available in this country if necessary.

Meanwhile we in the churches and synagogues have a continuing task while we urge our Government to disengage itself from a disgraceful commitment. We must continue to raise our voices if our nation persists in its perverse ways in Vietnam. We must be prepared to match actions with words by seeking out every creative means of protest possible.

48. Race Relations in the Armed Services

Douglas Anderson, Donald L. Whitfield, Don F. Browne, and Reginald Edwards
Oral Histories
1981 and 1984

In these interviews, white and black southern veterans of the Vietnam War discuss the war, its effect on the soldiers sent to fight it, the attitudes of people back home, and the tensions between blacks and whites serving in the military. Included are the recollections of two white veterans: Douglas "Doc" Anderson, a native of Tennessee who served in Vietnam in 1967 and 1968 as a medical corpsman for the marines; and Donald Whitfield, a high school dropout from a poor Alabama family, who was drafted in 1968 and served in Vietnam as an army machine gunner in 1969. Also included are two interviews with African American veterans: Don F. Browne of Washington, D.C., a career air force man who served in Vietnam in 1967 and 1968 as a security policeman; and Reginald "Malik" Edwards of Phoenix, Louisiana, who joined the Marine Corps at age seventeen to escape poverty and served as a rifleman in Vietnam in 1965 and 1966.

DOUGLAS ANDERSON

Tennessee

I was about to be drafted, so I went into the Navy Reserves. I was a hospital corpsman. At that time so many hospital corpsmen were being killed that they put the reserves on active duty. . . .

It's taken me twelve years — it'll be thirteen in March — to assimilate the gap between what I thought I would see and what I did see. First of all, I'm not a heroic type of individual. I don't believe the things I did over there. I don't believe that I got up and ran under fire as much as I did to get to people. I don't believe I made myself do those things. But I did. But what really bothered me were some of the things that I saw that were not compatible with the ideals that I'd been brought up to believe in, in terms of being a member of the military and fighting for a country that heroically helped defeat the Germans and the Japanese and was supposed to be the good guy and all of that.

I saw cruelty and brutality that I didn't expect to see from our own people against the villagers. It took me a while in country to realize why it was happening. In this type of fighting it was almost impossible to know who the enemy was at any one time. Children were suspect, women were suspect. Frequently the ARVNs[1] themselves were on two payrolls. Their army was heavily infiltrated with Viet Cong or people who were politically ambivalent, who could change sides as easily as changing clothes. . . .

I saw, strangely, American kids particularly from the South who had been brought up in religious Baptist families have a lot of trouble reconciling what they were doing, even though the communists could very well be conceived of as the anti-Christ, according to certain Baptist sects. They were having a lot of trouble killing people, basically. I saw some fairly sensitive kids begin to know themselves because of this and begin to discover contradictions in their thinking. And unfortunately this cost some of them their lives because the minute they would begin to think, they would move just a little less quickly under orders and pause just a little bit more before shooting at somebody. . . .

In my unit there were few Hispanics, there were a lot of blacks. There were two categories of blacks: Southern blacks and blacks from Chicago and Cleveland, Northern blacks. There was as much difference between the two as chalk and cheese. It was incredible. This was during the time that Muhammad Ali refused to go into the service and became a hero. The blacks in the battalion began to question why they were fighting Honky's war against other Third World people. I saw very interesting relationships happening between your quick-talking, sharp-witted Northern blacks and your kind of easygoing, laid-back Southern blacks. I began to notice certain radicalization processes going on there. Many Southern blacks changed their entire point of view by the end of their tour and went home extremely angry.

---

[1]**ARVNs:** members of Army of the Republic of Vietnam, the South Vietnamese army.

Al Santoli, *Everything We Had: An Oral History of the Vietnam War by Thirty-Three American Soldiers Who Fought It* (New York: Random House, 1981), 66, 68–69, 71–72, 203.

The black/white relationship was tense. I saw a couple of fistfights. It usually happened when somebody got mad, and the first thing that happens in an argument between a young white redneck from Louisiana or Mississippi and a black from Cleveland or Chicago is names start flying and the first word that comes out of the white man's mouth is "nigger." And the fists start flying. I saw this happen in the field, as a matter of fact. The lieutenant had a considerable amount of trouble breaking it up. When you see racial incidents developing and weapons lying around, it gets pretty tense.

Also, the VC,[2] not being dumb, were putting propaganda pamphlets along the trails that we'd find all the time, encouraging black soldiers to refuse to fight. I'm sure that the war had an incredible effect on black people. The context of this is very economic in a way because both for poor whites and poor blacks the service was one of the few alternatives to get out of an absolutely miserable, dull situation in the South.

Under fire the strangest kinds of camaraderie would develop. It had nothing whatsoever to do with patriotism. It did have a great deal to do with taking care of each other. Because when you're out there, politics notwithstanding, the basic idea is to stay alive, and in a situation where we were fighting an unconventional war, which confused most of us, the main point was to stay alive. . . .

[2]**VC:** Viet Cong, the South Vietnamese guerilla and combat forces who supported the Communist National Liberation Front (NLF).

Donald L. Whitfield

Alabama

I'm gonna be honest with you. I had heard some about Vietnam in 1968, but I was a poor fellow and I didn't keep up with it. I was working at a Standard Oil station making eight dollars a day. I pumped gas and tinkered a little with cars. I had a girl I saw every now and then, but I still spent most of my time with a car. When I got my letter from the draft lady, I appealed it on the reason it was just me and my sister at home. We were a poor family and they needed me at home, but it did no good. Once I got to Vietnam, my mother got my check; I didn't keep but ten or twenty dollars. I don't think she would have made it if I hadn't done that. . . .

My company did a lot of patrolling. We got the roughest damn deal. Shit, I thought I was going to get killed every night. I was terrified the whole time. We'd get intelligence reports about Viet Cong in the area and have to go out to find 'em. Even if we could sneak up on the sons of bitches, it was still scary. I can look back now and how some of us lived through it is beyond me. . . .

When my company came out of the bush to rest and refit, we'd go to Yellowstone National Park. That's what we called Cu Chi. We might have a movie

James R. Wilson, *Landing Zones: Southern Veterans Remember Vietnam* (Durham, N.C.: Duke University Press, 1990), 203, 204, 207, 209, 210.

and that was about it. I did go to the USO a couple of times, but I was strictly military when I went to town. I didn't mess with those women. And we didn't have no trouble with the blacks. I saw movies that said we done the blacks wrong, but it wasn't like that where I was. Let's put it like this: they make pretty good soldiers, but they're not what we are. White Americans, can't nobody whip our ass. We're the baddest son of a bitches on the face of this earth. You can take a hundred Russians and twenty-five Americans, and we'll whip their ass. I'll tell you what I hated most about going back to Cu Chi or a firebase: the shit detail. Damn, one day I had just got a haircut and was all cleaned up, and then the first sergeant, he was black, he put me on the shit detail. I had to mix it with diesel fuel and burn it.

I felt sorry for the Vietnamese people. Damn, the Cong was killin' 'em. They didn't eat much but rice and they was poverty-stricken and didn't mess with nobody. I said I was going to kick them goddamn Communists' ass to keep 'em off these civilian people. They worked so hard and had nothing to show for it except a black shirt and pants, some flip-flops, and a straw hat. . . .

I fly the Rebel flag because this is the South, Bubba. The American flag represents the whole fifty states. That flag represents the southern part. I'm a Confederate, I'm a Southerner. . . .

I feel cheated about Vietnam, I sure do. Political restrictions — we won every goddamned battle we was in, but didn't win the whole goddamn little country. It took eight years to mine a fucking harbor? It's a fucking shame! We was the sons of bitches who went over there and got into combat. No person who went into combat was the same. Before I die, the Democratic-controlled Congress of this country — and I blame it on 'em — they gonna goddamn apologize to the Vietnam veterans. All I want 'em to do is come forward and say they're sorry for not letting us win the war. I want it public. They sold us out in Vietnam, Bubba. We fought a war for ten years that we could have won in less than a year.

Don F. Browne

Washington, D.C.

. . . I was career Air Force when I got to South Vietnam in 1967. And I was rather pro-military. Vietnam, as I was told and as I read at the time, was about us trying to prevent the Domino Theory, you know, the Communists taking South Vietnam and then the Philippines and marching across the Pacific to Hawaii and then on to the shores of California.

My folks are both ministers in Washington, D.C., and they had always wanted me to go into the ministry. I started singing in the church where my mother was the pastor when I was very young. And I still sing. I've won the Air Force worldwide competition for top male vocalist four times. But I never felt the call to be a preacher.

Wallace Terry, *Bloods: An Oral History of the Vietnam War by Black Veterans* (New York: Random House, 1984), 156, 157, 158, 167, 169.

I went to Howard University on a football scholarship, and I was starting full-back right away. We were rolling along there with a three-game winning streak, and we ran up against Morgan State. And they taught us how to play football.

I didn't do anything academically that first year and flunked out. After knocking around at a job as a laborer for a period of time, I decided that maybe the service could do something for me. It was July 1959. I'd always wanted to be in the Air Force. I was just fascinated with planes. I'm in seventh heaven when I'm flying even as a passenger. I wanted to be a pilot. But I could not pass the physical because of my eyes, and, truthfully, I couldn't pass the written exam. I became a security policeman. . . .

We worked out of the Embassy basement, and the civilian who was in charge of us had an ammo cache in the back of his home in downtown Saigon that would sink half the city.

Besides escorting the VIPs to their different homes around the city, we had several side jobs. Like running escorts, training guards for the homes of the VIPs, doing background investigations on Vietnamese employees. . . .

I had one special job. To train Chinese Vietnamese or Chinese Nungs to guard these homes of the VIPs. . . .

When I heard that Martin Luther King was assassinated, my first inclination was to run out and punch the first white guy I saw. I was very hurt. All I wanted to do was to go home. I even wrote Lyndon Johnson a letter. I said that I didn't understand how I could be trying to protect foreigners in their country with the possibility of losing my life wherein in my own country people who are my hero, like Martin Luther King, can't even walk the streets in a safe manner. I didn't get an answer from the President, but I got an answer from the White House. It was a wonderful letter, wonderful in terms of the way it looked. It wanted to assure me that the President was doing everything in his power to bring about racial equality, especially in the armed forces. A typical bureaucratic answer.

A few days after the assassination, some of the white guys got a little sick and tired of seeing Dr. King's picture on the TV screen. Like a memorial. It really got to one guy. He said, "I wish they'd take that nigger's picture off." He was a fool to begin with, because there were three black guys sitting in the living room when he said it. And we commenced to give him a lesson in when to use that word and when you should not use that word. A physical lesson.

With the world focused on the King assassination and the riots that followed in the United States, the North Vietnamese, being politically astute, schooled the Viet Cong to go on a campaign of psychological warfare against the American forces.

At the time, more blacks were dying in combat than whites, proportionately, mainly because more blacks were in combat-oriented units, proportionately, than whites. To play on the sympathy of the black soldier, the Viet Cong would shoot at a white guy, then let the black guy behind him go through, then shoot at the next white guy.

It didn't take long for that kind of word to get out. And the reaction in some companies was to arrange your personnel where you had an all-black or nearly all-black unit to send out. . . .

When the North Vietnamese started taking over South Vietnam in 1974 without too many shots being fired, I felt let down. But I never had any faith in the ARVN. As long as they knew that the American platoon was two feet behind them, they would fight like cats and dogs. But if they knew that they didn't have American support real close — like right behind them — they would not fight.

When I watched on TV the cowardly, shameful way we left Saigon and left the Embassy, I felt hurt. I felt betrayed. I didn't feel very proud to be an American.

We destroyed what we couldn't carry with us. We ducked our tails and ran.

Why wait ten years and thousands upon thousands of lives later to just turn it over to the Communists? We could have done that at the very beginning. . . .

Reginald "Malik" Edwards

Louisiana

I grew up in Plaquemines Parish. My folks were poor, but I was never hungry. My stepfather worked with steel on buildings. My mother worked wherever she could. In the fields, pickin' beans. In the factories, the shrimp factories, oyster factories. And she was a housekeeper.

I was the first person in my family to finish high school. This was 1963. I knew I couldn't go to college because my folks couldn't afford it. I only weighed 117 pounds, and nobody's gonna hire me to work for them. So the only thing left to do was go into the service. I didn't want to go into the Army, 'cause everybody went into the Army. Plus the Army didn't seem like it did anything. The Navy I did not like 'cause of the uniforms. The Air Force, too. But the Marines was bad. The Marine Corps built men. Plus just before I went in, they had all these John Wayne movies on every night. Plus the Marines went to the Orient.

Everybody laughed at me. Little, skinny boy can't work in the field going in the Marine Corps. So I passed the test. My mother, she signed for me 'cause I was seventeen.

There was only two black guys in my platoon in boot camp. So I hung with the Mexicans, too, because in them days we never hang with white people. You didn't have white friends. White people was the aliens to me. This is '63. You don't have integration really in the South. You expected them to treat you bad. But somehow in the Marine Corps you hoping all that's gonna change. Of course, I found out this was not true, because the Marine Corps was the last service to integrate. And I had an Indian for a platoon commander who hated Indians. He used to call Indians blanket ass. And then we had a Southerner from Arkansas that liked to call you chocolate bunny and Brillo head. That kind of shit.

I went to jail in boot camp. What happened was I was afraid to jump this ditch on the obstacle course. Every time I would hit my shin. So a white lieutenant called me a nigger. And, of course, I jumped the ditch farther than I'd ever jumped

Wallace Terry, *Bloods: An Oral History of the Vietnam War by Black Veterans* (New York: Random House, 1984), 5–6, 7, 10–11, 12, 14.

before. Now I can't run. My leg is really messed up. I'm hoppin'. So it's pretty clear I can't do this. So I tell the drill instructor, "Man, I can't fucking go on." He said, "You said what?" I said it again. He said, "Get out." I said, "Fuck you." This to a drill instructor in 1963. I mean you just don't say that. I did seven days for disrespect. When I got out of the brig, they put me in a recon. The toughest unit. . . .

The only thing they told us about the Viet Cong was they were gooks. They were to be killed. Nobody sits around and gives you their historical and cultural background. They're the enemy. Kill, kill, kill. That's what we got in practice. Kill, kill, kill. I remember a survey they did in the mess hall where we had to say how we felt about the war. The thing was, get out of Vietnam or fight. What we were hearing was Vietnamese was killing Americans. I felt that if people were killing Americans, we should fight them. As a black person, there wasn't no problem fightin' the enemy. I knew Americans were prejudiced, were racist and all that, but, basically, I believed in America 'cause I was an American. . . .

They called me a shitbird, because I would stay in trouble. Minor shit, really. But they put me on point anyway. I spent most of my time in Vietnam runnin'. I ran through Vietnam 'cause I was always on point, and points got to run. They can't walk like everybody else. 'Specially when you hit them open areas. Nobody walked through an open area. After a while, you develop a way to handle it. You learned that the point usually survived. It was the people behind you who got killed. . . .

When I went home, they put me in supply, probably the lowest job you can have in the Marines. But they saw me drawing one day and they said, "Edwards can draw." They sent me over to the training-aids library, and I became an illustrator. I reenlisted and made sergeant.

When I went to Quantico, my being black, they gave me the black squad, the squad with most of the blacks, especially the militant blacks. And they started hippin' me. I mean I was against racism. I didn't even call it racism. I called it prejudice. They hipped me to terms like "exploitation" and "oppression." And by becoming an illustrator, it gave you more time to think. And I was around people who thought. People who read books. I would read black history where the white guys were going off on novels or playing rock music. So then one day, I just told them I was black. I didn't call them *blanco*, they didn't have to call me Negro. That's what started to get me in trouble. I became a target. Somebody to watch.

Well, there was this riot on base, and I got busted. It started over some white guys using a bunch of profanity in front of some sisters. I was found guilty of attack on an unidentified Marine. Five months in jail, five months without pay. And a suspended BCD.[1] In jail they didn't want us to read our books, draw any pictures, or do anything intellectually stimulating or what they thought is black. They would come in my cell and harass me. So one day I was just tired of them, and I hit the duty warden. I ended up with a BCD in 1970. After six years, eight months, and eight days, I was kicked out of the Corps. I don't feel it was fair. If I had been

[1]**BCD:** Bad Conduct Discharge.

white, I would never have went to jail for fighting. That would have been impossible.

With a BCD, nothing was happenin'. I took to dressin' like the Black Panthers, so even blacks wouldn't hire me. So I went to the Panther office in D.C. and joined. I felt the party was the only organization that was fighting the system.

I liked their independence. The fact that they had no fear of the police. Talking about self-determination. Trying to make Malcolm's message reality. This was the first time black people had stood up to the state since Nat Turner. I mean armed. It was obvious they wasn't gonna give us anything unless we stood up and were willing to die. They obviously didn't care anything about us, 'cause they had killed King.

. . . I had left one war and came back and got into another one. Most of the Panthers then were veterans. We figured if we had been over in Vietnam fighting for our country, which at that point wasn't serving us properly, it was only proper that we had to go out and fight for our own cause. We had already fought for the white man in Vietnam. It was clearly his war. If it wasn't, you wouldn't have seen as many Confederate flags as you saw. And the Confederate flags was an insult to any person that's of color on this planet. . . .

I used to think that I wasn't affected by Vietnam, but I been livin' with Vietnam ever since I left. You just can't get rid of it. . . .

49. Criticism of Protesters

Spiro T. Agnew
Speeches in Louisiana and Alabama
1969

Before being selected as Richard Nixon's running mate, Spiro T. Agnew served as governor of Maryland from 1966 to 1968. As vice president, he was famous for speeches that made him popular with Nixon supporters, who despised the intellectuals and students in the antiwar movement as well as war critics in the media. The first speech reprinted here was delivered in New Orleans on October 19, 1969 — just after "The Moratorium," a massive antiwar rally in Washington, D.C., that called for an immediate end to the Vietnam War. The second speech was given in Montgomery, Alabama, a month later. As Agnew reminds his audiences, it was for speeches like these that the press nicknamed him "the great polarizer."

NEW ORLEANS, LOUISIANA

October 19, 1969

Sometimes, it appears that we are reaching a time when our senses and our minds will no longer respond to moderate stimulation. We seem to be approaching an age of the gross. Persuasion through speeches and books is too often discarded for disruptive demonstrations aimed at bludgeoning the unconvinced into action.

The young — and by this I don't mean by any stretch of the imagination all the young, but I am talking about those who claim to speak for the young — at the zenith of physical power and sensitivity, overwhelm themselves with drugs and artificial stimulants. Subtlety is lost, and fine distinctions based on acute reasoning are carelessly ignored in a headlong jump to a predetermined conclusion. Life is visceral rather than intellectual, and the most visceral practitioners of life are those who characterize themselves as intellectuals.

Truth is "revealed" rather than logically proved, and the principal infatuations of today revolve around the social sciences, those subjects which can accommodate any opinion and about which the most reckless conjecture cannot be discredited.

Education is being redefined at the demand of the uneducated to suit the ideas of the uneducated. The student now goes to college to proclaim rather than to learn. The lessons of the past are ignored and obliterated in a contemporary antagonism known as the generation gap. A spirit of national masochism prevails, encouraged by an effete corps of impudent snobs who characterize themselves as intellectuals.

It is in this setting of dangerous oversimplification that the war in Vietnam achieves its greatest distortion.

The recent Vietnam Moratorium is a reflection of the confusion that exists in America today. Thousands of well-motivated young people, conditioned since childhood to respond to great emotional appeals, saw fit to demonstrate for peace. Most did not stop to consider that the leaders of the Moratorium had billed it as a massive public outpouring of sentiment against the foreign policy of the president of the United States. Most did not care to be reminded that the leaders of the Moratorium refused to disassociate themselves from the objective enunciated by the enemy in Hanoi.

If the Moratorium had any use whatever, it served as an emotional purgative for those who feel the need to cleanse themselves of their lack of ability to offer a constructive solution to the problem.

Unfortunately, we have not seen the end. The hard-core dissidents and professional anarchists within the so-called "peace movement" will continue to exacerbate the situation. November 15 is already planned — wilder, more violent, and equally barren of constructive result. . . .

Spiro T. Agnew, *Collected Speeches of Spiro Agnew* (New York: Audubon Books, 1971), 54–55. Reprinted in *Negotiating Difference: Cultural Case Studies for Composition*, ed. Patricia Bizzell and Bruce Herzberg (Boston: Bedford/St. Martin's, 1996), 882–83.

MONTGOMERY, ALABAMA

November 20, 1969

A few weeks ago here in the South I expressed my views about street and campus demonstrations. Here's how the *New York Times* responded:

"He [that's me] lambasted the nation's youth in sweeping and ignorant generalizations, when it's clear to all perceptive observers that American youth today is far more imbued with idealism, a sense of service, and a deep humanitarianism than any generation in recent history, including particularly Mr. Agnew's generation."

That's what the *New York Times* said.

Now that seems a peculiar slur on a generation that brought America out of the Great Depression without resorting to the extremes of communism or fascism. That seems a strange thing to say about an entire generation that helped to provide greater material blessings and more personal freedom — out of that depression — for more people than any other nation in history. We have not finished the task by any means — but we are still on the job.

Just as millions of young Americans in this generation have shown valor and courage and heroism fighting the longest, and least popular, war in our history, so it was the young men of my generation who went ashore at Normandy under Eisenhower, and with MacArthur into the Philippines.

Yes, my generation, like the current generation, made its own share of great mistakes and great blunders. Among other things, we put too much confidence in Stalin and not enough in Winston Churchill.

But, whatever freedom exists today in Western Europe and Japan exists because hundreds of thousands of young men of my generation are lying in graves in North Africa and France and Korea and a score of islands in the Western Pacific.

This might not be considered enough of a sense of service or a deep humanitarianism for the perceptive critics who write editorials for the *New York Times*, but it's good enough for me. And I'm content to let history be the judge.

Now, let me talk briefly about the younger generation. I have not and I do not condemn this generation of young Americans. . . . After all, they're our sons and daughters. They contain in their numbers many gifted, idealistic, and courageous young men and women.

But they also list in their numbers an arrogant few who march under the flags and portraits of dictators, who intimidate and harass university professors, who use gutter obscenities to shout down speakers with whom they disagree, who openly profess their belief in the efficacy of violence in a democratic society.

Oh, yes, the preceding generation had its own breed of losers and our generation dealt with them through our courts, our laws, and our system. The challenge is now for the new generation to put its house in order. . . .

Spiro T. Agnew, *Vital Speeches of the Day*, 134–35. Reprinted in *Negotiating Difference: Cultural Case Studies for Composition*, ed. Patricia Bizzell and Bruce Herzberg (Boston: Bedford/St. Martin's, 1996), 887–88.

For we must remember that among this generation of Americans there are hundreds who have burned their draft cards and scores who have deserted to Canada and Sweden to sit out the war. To some Americans, a small minority, these are the true young men of conscience in the coming generation.

Voices are and will continue to be raised in the Congress and beyond asking that amnesty — a favorite word — amnesty should be provided for these young and misguided American boys. And they will be coming home one day from Sweden and from Canada and from a small minority of our citizens they will get a hero's welcome.

They are not our heroes. Many of our heroes will not be coming home; some are coming back in hospital ships, without limbs or eyes, with scars they shall carry for the rest of their lives.

Having witnessed firsthand the quiet courage of wives and parents receiving posthumously for their heroes Congressional Medals of Honor, how am I to react when people say, "Stop speaking out, Mr. Agnew, stop raising your voice?"

Should I remain silent while what these heroes have done is vilified by some as "a dirty, immoral war" and criticized by others as no more than a war brought on by the chauvinistic anticommunism of Presidents Kennedy, Johnson, and Nixon?

These young men made heavy sacrifices so that a developing people on the rim of Asia might have a chance for freedom that they obviously will not have if the ruthless men who rule in Hanoi should ever rule over Saigon. What's dirty or immoral about that?

One magazine this week said that I'll go down as the "great polarizer" in American politics. Yet, when that large group of young Americans marched up Pennsylvania Avenue and Constitution Avenue last week, they sought to polarize the American people against the president's policy in Vietnam. And that was their right. And so it is my right, and my duty, to stand up and speak out for the values in which I believe. . . .

Protest and
Response

One of the largest campus protests in the South in the spring of 1970 took place at the University of North Carolina at Chapel Hill, where students went on strike and were granted "amnesty" by the faculty. On May 7, several Washington, N.C., students, calling themselves Concerned Students for Peace, wrote to the editor of their local newspaper and urged the public to write to their congressmen about the war. A few of the signees were participating in the strike; others just wanted to show their concern about the recent expansion of the war. Their letter, published on May 13, stirred up a controversy in the small town of Washington: the Daily News *was inundated with letters to the editor, a sampling of which is reprinted here. Though many of the letter writers were critical of the students, others spoke up in their defense or applauded them for stimulating discussion that might help bridge the generation gap.*

May 7, 1970

Dear Citizens of Washington and Beaufort County,

Many of us studying at the University of North Carolina are alarmed at the recent announcement of President Nixon to extend the war into Cambodia. Already many years of futile effort have resulted in the deaths of more than 40,000 American boys and countless Vietnamese. President Nixon campaigned saying that he had a plan to end the war and had announced that he was pulling troops out of Vietnam. How then can he justify pouring more troops into a country that did not even ask for our aid?

It is very difficult to know the best action to take at this time to show our opposition to a continuation of this war and most of us disagree as to what action is most effective. Yet we are all united in the opinion that something should be done. We are opposed to violence. We also do not believe that Americans should elect a President and let him make all of our decisions for four years without hearing our opinions. Many Senators and Congressmen are also alarmed at this invasion. We urge you to write to your Congressman and tell him your feelings

Washington (North Carolina) Daily News, 13–17 May 1970.

about this war so that he may act with the assurance of the support of his constituents.

If you have questions about our actions at the university or the reasons for our opinions, please write Concerned Students for Peace, 1031 James, U.N.C., Chapel Hill, N.C. 27514. We are interested in talking to people of all opinions, for free discussion of issues is what our democracy is all about.

Sincerely,
Carol Spruill, Nick Nicholson, Marjorie Spruill,
Herbert Hoell, Melinda Robinson, Harvey Elliott Jr.,
Flipper Forest, Ned Hulbert, Robin Hulbert,
Peggy Biggerstaff, Mary Day Mordecai, Andy Nassef,
Ellen Nunnelee, Larry Hamilton, Harry Ronan

May 14, 1970

Dear Members of Washington and Beaufort County,

Wednesday I read in amazement a letter to us from students of this area who are studying at the University of North Carolina at Chapel Hill. These students are your children! I am happy to say that I am not old enough to be a parent of one of these students, which I consider at present a dubious honor.

That YOU men, and some women, who fought for the preservation of freedom during World War I, II, and the Korean conflict have raised your children in such a manner as to allow them to be swayed speaks for itself.

When WE the people of these United States permit, yes, permit such things to happen, we are indeed in a sad state. We have permitted colleges, universities and perhaps even elementary and high school administrators to employ persons with leftist leanings and communist ideas or so it seems.

Americans, you fought bravely in the previous wars of our history! Now it is time to fight again. No, not with weapons, but with words. Yes, do write your Congressman and Senator. Tell them your opinions, but ask them why our government allows known communist[s] and agitators to roam freely and sway your children from the Patriotic Path which so many have trod in this country for so long.

No, I'm not against peace in Vietnam. I am all for it. For the third time, my husband is in Vietnam serving his country to help preserve freedom against the spread of communism. I pray that my husband, our friends there, and the rest of the men in Vietnam do not get killed or even worse captured.

I believe the fighting and strategy should be left to the soldiers and generals. The politicians should not try to fight or control the war from their TV armchair.

We, The People, elected the President to lead us and make our decisions for us for the next four years. NOW, let us support him. Please do write your congressman and senator telling them that you DO support our President. I am.

Mary Etta Cole
Chocowinity, N.C.

May 15, 1970

To the Editor:
. . . Many students who are demonstrating against the Cambodian extension are there just to get out of classes. Many students do not know really what is going on in Cambodia and could care less. I know the writers of the U.N.C. letter represent some radical students, but they, by no means, represent me and many other students who are glad that President Nixon is extending the war into Cambodia and who are glad that he is truly trying to hand the American people an end to the war. He is doing something that no other president has even tried to do in the past decade.

I will write my congressmen, not to scorn President Nixon's decision, but to applaud him, and tell them of my strong support as an under-thirty idealist.

Kathy Moore
Washington, N.C.

May 16, 1970

Dear Mr. Futrell,[1]
As the parent of one of the UNC students who submitted his ideas to be reviewed, discussed, criticized, and condemned, I feel that I must speak out with reference to a letter in today's issue.

These students are fine young people, who have as parents respectable people who have known fighting, war, and conflicts since 1939.

My own son I carried, nursed, and cared for; saw him through eight years of Little League baseball, through nine years of Cub and Boy Scouting, ending with an Order of the Arrow and Eagle award, plus three palms; saw him through Jr. High and High School basketball and football and honor grades, and I highly resent any reflection on his upbringing.

My advice to this young woman is: refrain from having children, or if she has already been so honored, by all means keep them behind a heavily locked door, or they will surely begin to think and form their own opinions, once they are exposed to the outside world. A parent "allows" a child to think if he wants that child to grow mentally as well as physically — when that child grows to college age, the parent has done his best, whatever that was, and the rest of the shaping is in the hands of the college personnel. To say that any of these students have "leftist" leanings is very nearly as ridiculous as it would be to say that a six year old is ready to get out and earn a living.

I, personally, am tired of all the stones being thrown at the youth of today, and think it is time we all sit down and reflect — then get up and do something rather than let the other fellow do it, and then throw some more stones if he didn't do it to suit you.

A concerned parent,
Ardis Forest

[1]**Mr. Futrell:** Ashley B. Futrell Sr., editor of the *Daily News*.

May 14, 1970

Dear Mr. Futrell:

It was with much interest that I read the recent "letter to the editor" submitted by the U.N.C. students from our area, who advocated that we join with them in petitioning our elected representatives to work toward the immediate cessation of hostilities in southeast Asia.

It would hard-press even the most conservative element to label these particular young people as the "radical-left." They are voicing their concern, and soliciting support, in a responsible manner. The paradox, unfortunately, is that their reasonable restraint will, in all probability, go unnoticed — and un-acted upon.

Most of these students were born in the years of the Korean Conflict, grew up in the Cold War era, and are striving to attain the full flower of their enlightened maturity at a time when a far-off war is literally rending asunder their own country. This causes them to ask questions, and to ponder the wisdom of seemingly endless wars. Perhaps they, through their study of history, and because of their perceptive awareness, have learned that there is no such thing as a "war to end all wars."

Perhaps they are daring to suggest to their elders that war is truly man's insensate folly, and proves nothing, settles nothing. Could it be they are saying that there must be another way to settle man's — and nation's — differences?

In a recent editorial, castigating the violence rampant among some of our college youth, (and no thinking person will take issue with you over this — although this isn't the point) you asserted that experience and maturity will serve to perhaps alter the thinking of the young. You stated that liberal views give way to conservative leanings with the passing of time. This may be true. Labels such as liberal or conservative really have no place in such matters as life or death.

But if growing older conditions one to believe that dissent is "un-American," that the losing of over 40,000 Americans' lives (almost all of them quite young), the murdering of hundreds of thousands of yellow-skinned human beings, and the slaughtering of even greater numbers of livestock is acceptable, and is the "American way," then perhaps "maturity" is not such a desirable quality.

All of us — young, old, and in-between — are deeply interested in the solution to this war, and are committed to the same goal for our nation and the world: Peace. We differ in how to achieve this objective.

You concluded the editorial I refer to by stating that someday your generation will pass on to the younger generation the "torch and the sword." Perhaps it is therein that the difference in view lies. The youth are saying that as long as the "sword" is passed, then for that long there will be war.

Why not banish the "sword" — and let the "torch" be a light of reason for all citizens of this land. . . .

Your friend,
Bartow Houston Jr.

Editor:

Let me congratulate the Chapel Hill students. They have accomplished something that no one has been able to do in Washington for fifty years. They have "cured," at least temporarily, that most horrendous disease, known as apathy. The exchange of ideas in the [*Washington Daily News*] since their letter was published attests this. Washingtonians are thinking! Right or wrong, they are thinking!

Chapel Hill students, I know you have taken much verbal abuse from your hometown "friends," but there are many of us who support you and what you are trying to do. Perhaps the ones who question your patriotism and make implications about the quality of speech you might indulge in . . . should reexamine their own definition of patriotism and be cautious, lest their own vocabulary become smudged with "vulgarity." Perhaps those "over-thirty idealists" who talk of justice should ask themselves, justice for whom? More important, perhaps all should reexamine their thinking as Christians. . . .

We should support those who ask for peace, and be proud that there are those among us who will stand up and say, "I am for peace, not necessarily victory, but peace."

Yours truly,
William R. Alligood
Washington, N.C.

Dear Mr. Futrell,

Hallelujah! We have a dialogue finally and I feel confident now that if we cannot resolve our differences, we can at least agree to disagree in a peaceful manner. I applaud the UNC students for being the ones to initiate the dialogue, and I plead with others to keep it on the high level in which they began it. It serves no purpose to accuse the students of having been duped by communists or of being so gullible as to be easily swayed. These students are among the best of the youth we have to offer for the future. They are receiving the best education any generation has ever received. They have been taught that learning is a process of individual seeking, of researching, of comparing ideas, of freely debating the issues — in short, they have been taught to question. You may consider them mistaken, immature in their thinking, short-sighted in their goals, if you will, but do not dismiss them as poorly raised children. . . .

Ours is a representative government. We choose our leaders at the ballot box. To choose them to lead and then deny them the opportunity to lead defeats the ballot box and makes it a farce. Sometimes we do not choose wisely — we have the privilege of correcting that in the next election. Sometimes our leaders make mistakes — we cannot expect infallibility. If we are overwhelmingly convinced that a leader has made an unwise choice, it is not only our privilege but our duty to let him know how we feel. Similarly, if we feel he has made a wise choice, it is our duty to so inform him. Fortunately, the mails operate most of the time.

Five hundred students burning buildings, turning over cars, blocking traffic, spitting on policemen, throwing rocks at guardsmen, baiting them with vulgarities, can do little except invite violence in return. Five hundred letters dumped on a senator's desk is a very powerful weapon. Five thousand demonstrators camped on the capitol's Ellipse can do little more than create garbage and guarantee the president a sleepless night. Five thousand volunteer workers in a political campaign strengthen our political system, make it more responsive to the people, and keep it viable.

Finally, ten thousand students professing nonviolence should do something more than stand by and watch five hundred wreck havoc on their campus. I believe disorder on the campus is a problem which must be solved by the students themselves. Solve your problem of war on the campus and when you have succeeded in that you will appreciate more fully the great difficulties involved in solving a complex problem and perhaps you will have come up with solutions which might be applicable to Vietnam and Cambodia. After that, I would suggest that you address yourselves to the developing of a world government with the authority to settle disputes between the countries without violence, and with the authority and resources to develop workable solutions to poverty, race, pollution, and population problems. But don't expect all this to be accomplished in your lifetime. Some will still be left for your children.

Sincerely,
Martha Godley

Suggestions for Further Reading

Bello, Thomas M. "The Student Strike at the University of North Carolina at Chapel Hill (May, 1970): An Eyewitness Historical Memoir." Senior Honors Essay in American History, University of North Carolina at Chapel Hill, 1971.

Gill, Gerard. "Black Soldiers' Perspectives on the War." In *The Vietnam Reader*, ed. Walter Capps. New York: Routledge, 1991.

Gilman, Owen W. Jr. *Vietnam and the Southern Imagination*. Jackson: University Press of Mississippi, 1992.

———. "Vietnam War." In *Encyclopedia of Southern Culture*, ed. Charles Reagan Wilson and William Ferris. Chapel Hill: University of North Carolina Press, 1989.

McLaurin, Melton. "Country Music and the Vietnam War." In *Perspectives on the American South*. New York: Gordon and Breach, 1985.

Scranton, William W. *The Report of the President's Commission on Campus Unrest*. Reprint, New York: Arno Press, 1970.

CHAPTER FOURTEEN

THE 1970s

The ERA and the Rise of the Pro-Family Movement

D espite its well-known traditionalism regarding women's roles, the South seemed quite receptive to the rise of modern feminism that began in the 1960s and enjoyed considerable success in the 1970s. Southerners were highly visible in this national movement, the strength of which was revealed in 1972 when Congress approved the Equal Rights Amendment (ERA) by a huge margin. Yet Southerners were at least as prominent in the organized opposition to the ERA that emerged almost immediately, blocked ratification of the amendment, and developed into the highly influential coalition of social conservatives that called itself the "pro-family movement."

As the decade began, there was considerable feminist activity in the South and little overt opposition. Newly established "women's liberation" groups as well as long-existing women's groups such as the American Association of University Women (AAUW) and the League of Women Voters (LWV) worked to end gender discrimination and open up opportunities for women. New national organizations including the National Organization for Women (NOW) and the National Women's Political Caucus (NWPC) had chapters in every southern state. Southern women, including Liz Carpenter of Texas who helped to organize the NWPC and was later cofounder of ERAmerica, played key roles in these organizations. Between 1971 and 1973 each southern state created a commission on the status of women, and Texas and Virginia adopted equal rights amendments to their state constitutions.

In 1972, when Congress gave its ringing endorsement to the ERA and sent it to the states for ratification, southern politicians were clearly on the bandwagon. Senator Sam Ervin of North Carolina fought to modify or defeat the amendment with virtually no help from his southern colleagues. Only two southern senators

(Ervin and Mississippi's John Stennis) and nine southern congressmen voted against it. Tennessee and Texas joined in the national scramble to ratify the popular amendment, approving it within two weeks. Kentucky and Maryland also ratified within the year. Prominent southern politicians, including governors Jim Hunt of North Carolina, Reuben Askew of Florida, and James B. Edwards of South Carolina, supported ratification as did the South's rising star, former governor of Georgia Jimmy Carter, who captured the presidency in 1976. Carter appointed a record number of women to office, hired Sarah Weddington (the Texas attorney who had successfully argued the 1973 *Roe v. Wade* case, liberalizing abortion laws) to direct the administration's efforts on behalf of women, and generally promoted feminist goals. Supported by First Lady Rosalynn Carter, the president vowed to do for the ERA what Lyndon Johnson had done for the Civil Rights Acts of 1964 and 1965.

The very real possibility that the ERA would be ratified awakened latent opposition and led antifeminists to mobilize, and opposition was particularly strong in the South. Phyllis Schlafly, the conservative Republican from Illinois who founded the organization STOP ERA in 1972, was embraced by southern conservatives as one of their own. She worked closely with Senator Ervin and with North Carolina's Senator Jesse Helms, first elected in 1972. Right-wing groups such as the National States Rights Party, the John Birch Society, and the Ku Klux Klan came out strongly against the amendment and the American Party denounced it as "an insidious socialistic plan to destroy the home."

Though many southern religious leaders supported the ERA, religious fundamentalists, who opposed gender equality as contrary to biblical teachings, formed a key component of the anti-ERA forces in the South. Guided by politically astute, telegenic ministers such as Virginia's Jerry Falwell, fundamentalists were inspired to new levels of political activity by this amendment which they regarded as a major threat to the traditional family. Conservative political analysts were quick to see the possibilities of adding newly politicized social conservatives to the ranks of economic conservatives, and by mid-decade "New Right" groups, including the Conservative Caucus and the National Conservative Political Action Committee, were involved in the anti-ERA movement. Through the use of sophisticated new direct-mail techniques, they mobilized hundreds of thousands of Southerners to send their legislators letters opposing ratification. Legislative support for the amendment waned.

To their dismay, ERA supporters found themselves placed on the defensive by a powerful anti-ERA coalition that blocked their progress even while public-opinion polls continued to show strong southern support for the amendment. As proponents sought the last three states needed for ratification, bitter contests developed in several southern states that pro-ERA leaders regarded as "hopeful." In North Carolina and Florida, the ERA succeeded in the House only to be narrowly defeated in the Senate. In 1977, with the support of the Carter administration, the deadline for ratification was extended to 1982, but proponents gained no new states and several, including Tennessee and Kentucky, attempted to rescind.

The fight over the ERA brought into the open deep-seated ideological and cultural divisions. ERA advocates viewed the amendment, which stated simply that "equality of rights under the law shall not be denied or abridged by the United States or by any State on account of sex," as a speedy and direct means of eliminating outmoded laws, a constitutional safeguard against future discrimination, and a long-awaited affirmation of women's equality that would guide the courts and legislatures as they enforced the amendment. Opponents, however, *wanted* the government to retain the power to make gender distinctions when crafting legislation and feared that the nonspecific amendment would undermine women's "protected" status and usher in unwanted changes. They insisted that ratification would promote abortion and gay rights. To conservative Southerners already angry about federal support for the civil rights movement, the ERA seemed to be just one more example of a radical federal government trying to force social change on the South.

As the decade drew to an end, there were clearly two strong social-reform movements in America with sharply contrasting ideologies regarding women's rights. As women's rights advocates fought to secure ratification of the ERA and to preserve and extend the victories of the modern feminist movement, antifeminists went on to form the pro-family movement through which to promote their concept of the family and oppose or repeal feminist-inspired legislation. That the pro-family movement had considerable support in the South was clear from the fact that its hero, Ronald Reagan, carried every southern state except Jimmy Carter's native Georgia in the 1980 presidential race.

The documents in this chapter include a 1977 address by President Carter affirming his support for the ERA and speeches or pamphlets by southern supporters and opponents of the amendment. The chapter ends with an excerpt from Rosalynn Carter's autobiography, written after her husband's electoral defeat, in which she reflects on their successes and failures with regard to women's rights.

As you read, consider the following questions. Why did President Carter see the ERA as an extension of the work begun by woman suffragists? What were the arguments for and against ratification? How do the proponents' statements reveal their defensiveness about supporting the ERA? What particularly southern issues or concerns are reflected in the arguments on both sides? How did the Carter administration demonstrate its concern about women's issues and why, according to Rosalynn Carter, did the ERA fail?

51. Presidential Support

Jimmy Carter
Remarks on Signing Proclamation 4515
1977

In this address, given on Women's Equality Day, 1977, President Carter affirms his and his wife's commitment to the ratification of the Equal Rights Amendment, first introduced in 1923 by National Woman's Party leader Alice Paul. Like many ERA supporters, he regarded the amendment as a way to complete the unfinished business of the women's rights movement and embraced it as part of his wider commitment to human rights. At this point in his presidency, Carter was well aware of the difficulties confronting ratificationists but still confident that the amendment would be approved.

To Dean Virginia Allan [of George Washington University] and to others who are assembled here today, I'd like to say that I appreciate the chance to be part of this effort.

My wife is sorry that she cannot be here. She's at an international conference on mental health in Canada, making a speech there about the stigma of those who suffer from mental illness. She represents me there, as she does in so many other things.

My daughter-in-law, Judy Carter, is in California today working on the equal rights amendment in the Western States.

In an hour or two, I'll be having lunch with my daughter, Amy, and I'm sure she will bring up the subject as well. [*Laughter*]

During the modern day that we observe and in which we serve, it's not dangerous, politically or otherwise, to speak out for equality of opportunity. It's not a major sacrifice. We don't have to overcome fear of persecution or even incarceration.

Standing behind me is a woman, Ms. [Hazel Hunkins] Hallinan, who in 1917 stood outside the gates of the White House when Woodrow Wilson was President, simply holding a sign in her hand that was photographed, saying, "How long will it be before women can have freedom?" She was convicted of a crime and jailed. Although we've come a long way since then, we still have a long way to go.

A recent survey by the Civil Rights Commission has shown that 3,000 governmental directives and laws have within them discriminatory concepts against

Public Papers of the Presidents of the United States: Jimmy Carter, 1977. Book II — June 25–December 31, 1977. (Washington, D.C.: United States Government Printing Office, 1978), 1502–3.

women. Today, I've issued a directive prepared by the Justice Department to all heads of agencies and departments in the Federal Government, ordering them to take the personal responsibility to examine their own attitudes, policies, directives, laws, to root out those discriminatory practices that have so long been in existence.

We've not yet been successful in having the equal rights amendment ratified by enough States. I think we will succeed. In the process, however frustrating it has been, great achievements have already been realized. Inequities and discrimination against women have been revealed.

Many actions in local, State, and Federal governments have already been taken — I have to admit, in some cases, in order to block the passage of equal rights amendment — but those actions have been taken to lessen discrimination.

And we've also seen that there has been a great educational process taking place in this country. Although we've lost the ERA vote in several States this year, those losses have been much narrower than had been the losses in the same States before. So progress has been made, even in States where we have not yet been successful.

In dozens of cases when I or my wife, Rosalynn, have talked directly and personally with State legislators, they have said, "I believe the equal rights amendment is right, I think it ought to pass, but this year I can't vote for it because of pressure from the working women in my district." I think there is a growing realization that those who have suffered most have quite often been women who have taken the least action in encouraging the passage of equal rights amendment because they've been so hard at work in their homes and in their jobs that they've not been educated or inspired, nor have they had the time to become involved. This is changing very rapidly because of the leadership of many of you assembled here today.

So my commitment is the same as yours. I believe that if we work together, we can succeed. And I believe that we are going to work together and, therefore, I believe that we will succeed.

I would now like to read and to sign a proclamation entitled "Women's Equality Day, 1977."

"August 26, 1977, is the 57th anniversary of the adoption of the 19th Amendment to the Constitution guaranteeing that the right of United States citizens to vote shall not be denied or abridged by the Federal Government or any state on account of sex.

"This was the successful culmination of the struggle of the American Women's Suffrage movement. The right to vote, to participate in the process of framing the laws under which we all live, is fundamental. But it was only the first step in achieving full equality for women. The late Dr. Alice Paul realized this, drafted the Equal Rights Amendment in 1923 and had it introduced in Congress over a period of forty-nine years, until it passed on March 22, 1972.

"Dr. Paul and other early leaders of the movement who did not live to see their work completed were reviled and imprisoned, endured hunger strikes and force-feeding in order to further their cause. Their commitment is an inspiration to women and men today who seek to finally make their dreams a reality. Equal rights for women are an inseparable part of human rights for all."

In witness whereof, I have today set my hand [*signing the proclamation*], and we are now mutually pledged to carry out the purposes of this resolution.

52. ERA Supporters Speak Out

MARIA BLISS, KATIE MORGAN, JESSIE RAE SCOTT, MARSE GRANT, AND ELIZABETH KOONTZ
Statements in Favor of Ratification
1977

When North Carolina considered the ERA in 1977, the stakes were high. Though the amendment had been defeated in 1973 and 1975, opinion polls still indicated that a majority favored ratification. Phyllis Schlafly, who conferred on strategy with state ERA opponents, feared that if North Carolina ratified, the amendment would have "a momentum we cannot match." But she also told former Senator Ervin that "if you will save North Carolina for us, I promise we can hold the other fifteen unratified states."[1]

Ratificationists in North Carolina had high hopes. Enjoying the support of President Carter and Governor Jim Hunt, they were newly reorganized as North Carolinians United for ERA (NCUERA) and led by the Reverend Maria Bliss, a Methodist minister and political activist. Senator Robert Morgan and his wife, Katie, were pro-ERA, as were several influential former governors and first ladies, including Robert and Jessie Rae Scott. In addition, many prominent religious leaders in the state were allies, including Dr. Marse Grant, editor of the Biblical Recorder *and chairman of the Baptist State Convention. Dr. Elizabeth Koontz, a prominent black North Carolinian who as head of the Women's Bureau of the U.S. Department of Labor had guided its endorsement of the ERA, lent her support.*

The following excerpts from statements by Bliss, Morgan, Scott, Grant, and Koontz represent a few of the testimonials presented by ERA proponents at a public hearing held by the North Carolina House of Representatives as it prepared to

---

[1]Qtd. in Donald G. Mathews and Jane Sherron De Hart, *Sex, Gender, and the Politics of ERA: A State and the Nation* (New York: Oxford University Press, 1990), 79–80.

ERA Proponent House Testimonials, Jane De Hart Collection, Special Collections and Rare Books Division, Walter Clinton Jackson Library, University of North Carolina at Greensboro.

consider the amendment. They were very nearly successful; the House approved the ERA 61 to 55, but the Senate defeated it 26 to 24.

Maria Bliss

NCUERA, Asheboro

Mr. Chairman, members of the Constitutional Amendments Committee, distinguished ladies and gentlemen: I thank you for giving your time to this most important issue. I am proud to say that I am president of North Carolinians United for ERA, the only organization dedicated to the equality of rights under the law. This organization is composed of thirty-two different organizations, representing hundreds of thousands of North Carolinians. It is a diverse group of people representing all races, all ages, and socio-economic groups, both political parties, many religious faiths, and a wide range of ideologies. It is appropriate that our theme for this campaign is "ERA is for everybody."

I became actively involved in the ERA campaign before the bill was passed by the Congress of the United States. The study of the issue led me to believe that I ought to do everything in my power to see justice done.

I will tell the story that I have told across the state as I have spoken to the many groups scattered from Manteo to Murphy. In 1951 I entered Woman's College, now UNC–G, as a freshman. As you know, interesting courses and good professors are recommended from one student to another. The course that was recommended to me over and over was a political science course taught by Miss Louise Alexander. . . . It was her story of the struggle to gain suffrage for women that Miss Alex passed on to each class of women students that impressed me and has pricked my conscience to this day. I can see her now, grandmotherly, hair on her head in a ball, utilitarian shoes, telling of her march down 5th Avenue in New York City, placard in hand, demanding the right to vote. . . . I have never forgotten the excitement that I felt as Miss Alex told our story. For Miss Alex working for the ratification of the 19th amendment to the Constitution of the U.S. was not only a privilege but an obligation which she assumed for the betterment of human conditions.

But Miss Alex's task and our task is not yet finished. Those of us who care about the human condition are involved in yet another struggle — the struggle to gain the ratification of the 27th amendment to the constitution of the U.S. According to Dr. William B. Aycock, Kenan Professor [of] Law and former Chancellor of the University of North Carolina at Chapel Hill, equality under the law between the sexes is an idea whose time has come. It is time for North Carolina to ratify the equal rights amendment. I believe this. Hundreds of thousands of citizens of this state believe this. Thirty-five states have ratified the proposed amendment — only three more states are needed. Three more states needed to write it into the law of this land and say to the world that the ideal of equality is a reality in our country. The outcome of the ERA will be victory. It is inevitable. We will win because we are on the side of reason, we are on the side of justice, and we are on the side of civilization. The victory will not be for women alone; it will also be a victory for men. But even more it will be a victory for democracy and the principle of equality upon which our great nation was founded. If Miss Alex were here now, if called to do so, she would come to Raleigh and plead her case before the General Assembly of this state. The ERA must be ratified — it is a necessity and it is right. [Long applause.]

KATIE MORGAN

Educator, Active in Civic Affairs, Wilmington

. . . I would thank Dr. Gamble and the members of the Constitutional Amendments Committee for the opportunity to be here in Raleigh today so that I may speak on two issues related to ERA. . . .

During the fall campaign [my husband, Senator Robert Morgan,] and I both traveled across North Carolina campaigning for Jimmy Carter and the entire Democratic ticket. One of the most important [things] Robert said and repeated during the campaign was this: "We do not want our daughters, or any of the children of our state or region, to grow up knowing that they cannot be elected president of the United States because they happened to be born in the South." With the election of our president from the deep South, we have eliminated that stigma. As you know, we are all proud of our children and grandchildren. Robert and I are also very proud of our two daughters. They are now at the ages of fourteen and sixteen looking ahead to their careers and their place in our society. Both are thinking seriously of attending law school and both are interested in law and in politics.

We said last fall that we did not believe that our children or any other children should be denied opportunity because they happened to be from the South. It would be tragic, then, if opportunity were denied them simply because they were born female. In the legal and political marketplace women clearly have not had the opportunity enjoyed by men. The membership of this General Assembly is an illustration, as is Congress. Not one woman serves with my husband in the United States Senate. . . . I do not claim that the passage of the ERA would change the situation overnight or in the two years before it is officially part of our constitution. But ratification of this amendment will signal to our children that they will have these opportunities. . . .

Much has been said and written about the effects of the ERA on Social Security laws and benefits. Opponents of the amendment have threatened us with double payment for homemakers as well as loss of benefits if the amendment becomes law. In the area of Social Security for homemakers, there has already been legislation introduced in Congress which would bring about Social Security payment for homemakers and grant them Social Security rights of their own. But whether or not it is approved, the legislation is completely independent and has nothing to do with the ERA. Opponents have also said that the passage of the ERA will deprive women of benefits. The fact is that law has been changed to equalize benefits for men and women. In this process women have not lost any benefits. In 1975 the Supreme Court ruled that a widower who had been dependent on his wife was entitled to mother's benefits. When that decision was handed down, women did not lose their rights to those benefits. An important factor differentiating between men and women is the Social Security laws that had to do with the presumption of dependency. In security benefits it was presumed that women were dependent and entitled to benefits. The presumption has not applied to men, who have been required to prove that they were dependent in order to receive benefits. There is some fear that the passage of the amendment will place the burden of proof on women as well as on men. The record shows otherwise. As sex discrimination has been removed from the Social Security laws, the burden of proof has been removed from men, not placed on women. Without citing examples or precedents, it is logical to assume that equality under the law will not force women to prove dependency. The ERA in itself will not change the Social Security laws in any way. The Social Security laws would have to be amended or revised by Congress.

I have dealt briefly with two issues this afternoon. On the first question I have been personal and positive. I do not believe that my daughters or yours should be denied the opportunity to succeed simply because they are women. On the second question I have been more general and have tried to deal with the negative fears raised in opposition to the amendment. The record and experience show these fears to be groundless and without substance. Today and in the future others will speak from different points of view. When all is said and done I hope that you will give favorable consideration to House Bill No. 43 and vote for ratification of the ERA. Again, thank you for the opportunity to appear before you here today.

JESSIE RAE SCOTT

Former First Lady of North Carolina
and Honorary Co-chair of the Board of Advisors, NCUERA

Thank you very much, Dr. Gamble, and members of the Committee, ladies, and gentlemen. I am happy to have the opportunity to speak to you today in support of the ERA amendment. I want to say at the outset that I, too, am a housewife and a mother. I have diapered babies, baked bread, and driven untold numbers of miles in carpools. Never under any circumstances have I denigrated these roles and these responsibilities. But I have also been a cotton mill worker, a waitress, a secretary, a schoolteacher, and yes, I've even poured a little tea in the elegant dining room of the governor's mansion across the way. Never under any circumstances have I denigrated those roles or responsibilities either. I say this to make the point that my life has not always been one of forty-two-room mansions or chauffeurs or domestic servants. I have, in the vernacular of my children and other young people, been in the real world; and the real world in our North Carolina and in our America encompasses years of struggle for rights and places in the sun for all our people. Thus this movement, which has been carried on for so long for equality of rights under the law by rational and dedicated men and women. I have the greatest respect for those who have expressed their opposition to this. I do not, under any circumstances, share their fears.

Many times in the past this movement for equality of rights by women, in particular, has been used as a scapegoat for some of the social ills in the country. Let me point out a few things to you and unfortunately I can't get into it too deeply.

Sometimes the movement is the fall gal for the high rate of destructions [sic] in marriage, but there are other forces which are equally significant and in [sic] this disruption. We blame it when we see a lot of women going out to join the work force, and we do see a lot today. And the fact of the matter is that we ought to be blaming recession and inflation, because a lot of women are going out to work today. I personally have friends and know women today who have worked in the last two years and supported their families because their husbands were laid off from their jobs. We blame the effort sometimes when adults and children alike are bombarded by new lifestyles in this country. In this instance consider the fact that magazines like *Hustler, Cosmopolitan, Playboy,* and *Oui* outsell what is supposedly the American woman's magazine, *Ms.,* in this country. . . . I ask you, what is responsible for the change in the lifestyle? We blame the effort sometimes when we should really be blaming our individual selves if our children fail. We blame it sometimes when women by choice want to go out and work in the world. I do not share the feelings either of those who think that this is going to be a unisex world. I somehow have a feeling that, when the final curtain goes down on you men and women here, that the men are still going to grunt and groan to prove their machismo and we women are going to hem and haw to prove our femininity. So let me say to you here (and I'm not going to finish all that I have to say), I hope that those of you who are on this committee and in the legislature [will] think rationally and be dedicated to the things that proud citizens of North Carolina are dedicated to [and] will see fit to pass this amendment. . . .

Marse Grant

Editor of the Biblical Recorder *and Chairman of the Baptist State Convention of North Carolina, Raleigh*

. . . I'm glad to speak in favor of this human rights amendment. Actually, in my opinion it's misnamed. It should be a human rights amendment. It also should have been passed . . . long, long ago. Recently I received a letter in which the writer told me to pick up my Bible. . . . ("The authorized King James version" — little did he realize that King James put to death Sir Walter Raleigh. That made no difference to this letter writer.) He told me to read what God would have me do about ERA. I told him that this is exactly what I had done. And from my Bible I learned long ago that God loves all His children. That He gave them talents and abilities, and that in Him there is no male or female. That I cannot and will not have any part in denying full citizenship to more than half the people of this country. That perhaps some day the entire world would hear His message of love and this archaic and un-Christian discrimination will end.

The New Testament reveals countless ways in which women are an integral part of Jesus' ministry. He gave them new respect and dignity. He forsook the old traditions of his day — He talked to women in public — He visited in their homes — and it's little wonder, and not just accidentally, in my opinion, that women were the last ones at the cross. They were the first ones at the Resurrection, too. How anyone can distort the teachings of Christ and try to say that Christ was against equality and freedom for all people is hard for me to understand. . . .

Scare stories [of those] opposing ERA try to give a picture of a massive conspiracy by the U.S. Congress, the U.S. Supreme Court, the state legislatures, and other institutions on which our country depends for freedom and justice. It's hard to fathom this lack of confidence, this lack of faith in our democracy. . . . [It's hard to understand] those who would try to paint a picture of the Jimmy Carters, the Gerald Fords, . . . the Bob Scotts as being some sort of oddball-type people bent on the destruction of our country — these people love America, they love this state, and they want to do what is right.

It is unfortunate that I am here to apologize today that some here in the church oppose this amendment, but some in the church also opposed the Civil Rights Act in 1964. Some in the church defended slavery and quoted scripture to try to prove it. Some opposed the right of women to vote using many of the fallacious arguments that they are now using against ERA, but they were wrong. Dead wrong. I have great faith in this government, in this General Assembly, and in the five and a half million citizens of this state, black and white, male and female. I believe this General Assembly is ready to grant women the full opportunities and human dignity that is due all people. I hope that, when historians look back on this era, they'll be able to say that — in this spot here in 1977 — that the church and this General Assembly stood for that which is right and just and I believe you will.

Elizabeth Duncan Koontz

Assistant State Superintendent for Public Instruction and Former President of the National Education Association, Salisbury

Members of the committee, members of the legislature, ladies and gentlemen. A short time ago I had the misfortune to break my foot. Today I could have told you that it will rain tonight. But the pain of having broken my foot and the inconvenience of that did not hurt me as much as when I went into the emergency room and the young woman upon asking me my name, the nature of my ailment, then asked me for my husband's social security number and his hospitalization number. I asked her what did that have to do with my emergency? And she said, "We have to be sure of who is going to pay your bill." I said, "Suppose I'm not married, then." And she said, "Then give me your father's name."

I did not go through that twenty years ago when I was denied the use of that emergency room because of my color. I went through that because there is an underlying assumption that all women in our society are both protected, dependent, cared for by somebody who's got a social security number and hospitalization insurance. Never once did she assume that I might be a woman who might be caring for my husband, instead of by him, because of some illness. She did not take into account the fact that one out of almost eight women heading families in poverty today [is] in the same condition as men in families and poverty. It did not even cross her imagination that there could be such a thing as a woman who carried an insurance policy that includes family. But you see, that really is not the greatest concern. She did not understand.

My greater concern is that there are so many women today who do not know their rights and limitations under the present law, who today oppose the passage of the ERA very sincerely and, with all due respect to those of us who are for it, they tell you without batting an eye, "I don't want to see women treated that way." And I speak up, "What way is that?" And I provide for them the facts that were available to me as director of this nation's bureau designated to look at the cause of women and their rights, the Women's Bureau of the U.S. Dept. of Labor, [and] they say, "Why didn't somebody tell us?" And I must say to them that maybe the reason that nobody told them is that very few women have money in their own names, to finance the kind of distribution that would be required so that all women would know these facts.

But I also must say that there is another reason and that is that women themselves have been a bit misguided. We have mistaken present practice for law, and women have not assumed too many times that their present conditions of being protected cannot change. The rate of divorce, the rate of desertion, the rate of separation, and the rate of death of male supporters is enough for us to say: "Let us remove all legal barriers to women and girls making their choices — this state cannot afford it." [*Applause.*]

53. Southern Conservatives Fight the ERA

SAM ERVIN JR., STOP ERA, AND JERRY FALWELL
Statements against Ratification
1971, 1975, and 1980

Senator Sam Ervin, an opponent of civil rights legislation during his long career in the U.S. Senate, became nationally famous in the 1970s as a staunch defender of the Constitution while he was chairman of the Senate Watergate Committee. He also gained national attention for his strong stand against the ERA during his last years in the Senate. STOP ERA capitalized upon Ervin's reputation as a legal expert, often reprinting his statements to the Senate for broad national circulation. The first excerpt, from his statement to the House Judiciary Committee on March 23, 1971, drew on legal arguments as well as on Ervin's own traditional attitudes to make a case for opposing the ERA as the wrong way to aid American women. The case against the ERA also appears here in excerpts from "You Can't Fool Mother Nature," a STOP ERA pamphlet distributed in North Carolina in 1975, and an excerpt from conservative minister Jerry Falwell's book Listen America, *in which he states the fundamentalist position on the ERA.*

SAM ERVIN JR.

March 23, 1971

Let us consider for a moment whether there be a rational basis for reasonable distinctions between men and women in any of the relationships or undertakings of life.

When He created them, God made physiological and functional differences between men and women. These differences confer upon men a greater capacity to perform arduous and hazardous physical tasks. Some wise people even profess the belief that there may be psychological differences between men and women. To justify their belief, they assert that women possess an intuitive power to distinguish between wisdom and folly, good and evil.

To say these things is not to imply that either sex is superior to the other. It is simply to state the all important truth that men and women complement each other in the relationships and undertakings on which the existence and development of the race depend.

The physiological and functional differences between men and women empower men to beget and women to bear children, who enter life in a state of utter helplessness and ignorance, and who must receive nurture, care, and training at the hands of adults throughout their early years if they and the race are to survive, and if they are to grow mentally and spiritually. From time whereof the memory of mankind runneth not to the contrary, custom and law have imposed upon men the primary responsibility for providing a habitation and a livelihood for their wives and children to enable their wives to make the habitations homes, and to furnish nurture, care, and training to their children during their early years.

In this respect, custom and law reflect the wisdom embodied in the ancient Yiddish proverb that God could not be everywhere, so he made mothers. The physiological and functional differences between men and women constitute the most important reality. Without them human life could not exist.

For this reason, any country which ignores these differences when it fashions its institutions and makes its laws is woefully lacking in rationality.

Congressional Record, 15 February 1972. Reprinted in *The American Experience: A Writer's Sourcebook* by Laurence Behrens and Annabel Nelson (Boston: Allyn and Bacon, 1992), 641–44.

Our country has not thus far committed this grievous error. As a consequence, it has established by law the institutions of marriage, the home, and the family, and has adopted some laws making some rational distinctions between the respective rights and responsibilities of men and women to make these institutions contribute to the existence and advancement of the race.

It may be that times are changing and more and more women will leave the home to compete in the business and professional community. However, I would like to call the Committee's attention to the remarks of Professor Phil Kurland of the University of Chicago Law School on this point. He said:

> Times have changed in such a way that it may well be possible for the generation of women now coming to maturity, who had all the opportunities for education afforded to their male peers and who had an expectation of opportunities to put education to the same use as their male peers, to succeed in a competitive society in which all differences in legal rights between men and women were wiped out. There remains a very large part of the female population on whom the imposition of such a constitutional standard would be disastrous. There is no doubt that society permitted these women to come to maturity not as competitors with males but rather as the bearers and raisers of their children and the keepers of their homes. There are a multitude of women who still find fulfillment in this role. In the eyes of some, this may be unfortunate, but it is true. It can boast no label of equality now to treat the older generations as if they were their own children or grandchildren. Certainly the desire to open opportunities to some need not be bought at the price of removal of legal protections from others.

The Destructive Potentiality of the House-Passed Equal Rights Amendment. Time and space preclude me from an attempt to picture in detail the constitutional and legal chaos which would prevail in our country if the Supreme Court should feel itself compelled to place upon the Equal Rights Amendment the devastating interpretation feared by these legal scholars.

For this reason, I must content myself with merely suggesting some of the terrifying consequences of such an interpretation.

The Congress and the legislatures of the various states have enacted certain laws based upon the conviction that the physiological and functional differences between men and women make it advisable to exempt or exclude women from certain arduous and hazardous activities in order to protect their health and safety.

Among federal laws of this nature are the Selective Service Act, which confines compulsory military service to men; the acts of Congress governing the voluntary enlistments in the armed forces of the nation which restrict the right to enlist for combat service to men; and the acts establishing and governing the various service academies which provide for the admission and training of men only.

Among the state laws of this kind are laws which limit hours during which women can work, and bar them from engaging in occupations particularly arduous and hazardous such as mining.

If the Equal Rights Amendment should be interpreted by the Supreme Court to forbid any legal distinctions between men and women, all existing and future laws of this nature would be nullified.

The common law and statutory law of the various states recognize the reality that many women are homemakers and mothers, and by reason of the duties imposed upon them in these capacities, are largely precluded from pursuing gainful occupations or making any provision for their financial security during their declining years. To enable women to do these things and thereby make the existence and development of the race possible, these state laws impose upon husbands the primary responsibility to provide homes and livelihoods for their wives and children, and make them criminally responsible to society and civilly responsible to their wives if they fail to perform this primary responsibility. Moreover, these state laws secure to wives dower and other rights in the property left by their husbands in the event their husbands predecease them in order that they may have some means of support in their declining years.

If the Equal Rights Amendment should be interpreted by the Supreme Court to forbid any legal distinctions between men and women, it would nullify all existing and all future laws of this kind.

There are laws in many states which undertake to better the economic position of women. I shall cite only one class of them, namely, the laws which secure to women minimum wages in many employments in many states which have no minimum wage laws for men, and no other laws relating to the earnings of women.

If the Equal Rights Amendment should be interpreted by the Supreme Court to prohibit any legal distinctions between men and women, it would nullify all existing and future laws of this kind.

In addition there are federal and State laws and regulations which are designed to protect the privacy of males and females. Among these laws are laws requiring separate restrooms for men and women in public buildings, laws requiring separate restrooms for boys and girls in public schools, and laws requiring the segregation of male and female prisoners in jails and penal institutions.

Moreover, there are some state laws which provide that specified institutions of learning shall be operated for men and other institutions of learning shall be operated for women.

If the Equal Rights Amendment should be interpreted by the Supreme Court to forbid legal distinctions between men and women, it would annul all existing laws of this nature, and rob Congress and the states of the constitutional power to enact any similar laws at any time in the future. . . .

STOP ERA

"You Can't Fool Mother Nature," 1975

ERA WILL HURT THE FAMILY:

ERA will invalidate all state laws which require a husband to support his wife. ERA will impose on women the equal (50%) financial obligation to support their spouses (under criminal penalties, just like husbands).

Pamphlet distributed in North Carolina by STOP ERA, 1975.

ERA will impose on mothers the equal (50%) financial obligation for the financial support of their infant and minor children.

ERA will deprive senior women, who have spent many years in the home as wife and mother, of their present right to be supported by their husbands, and to be provided with a home.

ERA will eliminate the present right of a wife to draw Social Security benefits based on her husband's earnings. For a homemaker to receive benefits, her husband would be forced to pay *double* Social Security taxes on the *assumed* value of her services in the home.

ERA will compel the states to set up taxpayer-financed child-care centers for *all* children regardless of need. (See Ohio Task Force Report)

ERA will deprive state legislatures of all power to stop or regulate abortions at any time during pregnancy. ERA will give women a "constitutional" right to abortion on demand.

ERA will legalize homosexual "marriages" and permit such "couples" to adopt children and to get tax and homestead benefits now given to husbands and wives.

THE MISCHIEF OF ERA:

ERA is a big power-grab by the Federal Government. It will transfer jurisdiction over marriage, property rights, divorce, alimony, child custody, and inheritance rights out of the hands of the individual states and into the Federal bureaucrats and the Federal courts.

ERA will make women subject to the draft on an equal basis with men in all our future wars. ERA will make women and mothers subject to military combat and warship duty.

ERA will eliminate all-girls' and all-boys' schools and colleges. ERA will eliminate single-sex fraternities and sororities in high schools and on college campuses.

ERA may give the Federal Government the power to force the admission of women to seminaries equally with men, and possibly force the churches to ordain women.

ERA will deprive women in industry of their legal protections against being involuntarily assigned to heavy-lifting, strenuous, and dangerous men's jobs, and compulsory overtime.

ERA will require police departments to eliminate physical tests and to pass over qualified men so that women will be hired and assigned on a one-to-one basis.

ERA will eliminate present lower life insurance and automobile accident insurance rates for women.

WHAT ERA WILL NOT DO!

ERA will **not** give women "equal pay for equal work," better-paying jobs, promotions, or better working conditions. ERA can add nothing whatsoever to the Equal Employment Opportunity Act of 1972.

ERA will **not** help women in the field of credit. This has already been mandated by the Equal Credit Opportunity Act of 1974. On the other hand, ERA will take away from wives their present right to get credit in their husband's name.

ERA will **not** give women better educational opportunities. This has already been mandated by the Education Amendments of 1972.

ERA will **not** help women in athletics, but will require sex-integrated coed nonsense such as the recent order by the Pennsylvania courts that all high schools must permit girls and boys to compete and practice together in all sports including football and wrestling.

ERA will **not** protect privacy, but instead will prohibit privacy based on sex in public school restrooms, hospitals, public accommodations, prisons, and reform schools.

With so much to lose and nothing to gain, why take a chance?
ERA is a fraud. It pretends to improve the status of women but actually is a big takeaway of the rights women now possess.

Jerry Falwell

1980

I believe that at the foundation of the women's liberation movement there is a minority core of women who were once bored with life, whose real problems are spiritual problems. Many women have never accepted their God-given roles. They live in disobedience to God's laws and have promoted their godless philosophy throughout our society. God Almighty created men and women biologically different and with differing needs and roles. He made men and women to complement each other and to love each other. Not all the women involved in the feminist movement are radicals. Some are misinformed, and some are lonely women who like being housewives and helpmeets and mothers, but whose husbands spend little time at home and who take no interest in their wives and children. Sometimes the full load of rearing a family becomes a great burden to a woman who is not supported by a man. Women who work should be respected and accorded dignity and equal rewards for equal work. But this is not what the present feminist movement and equal rights movement are all about.

The Equal Rights Amendment is a delusion. I believe that women deserve more than equal rights. And, in families and in nations where the Bible is believed, Christian women are honored above men. Only in places where the Bible is believed and practiced do women receive more than equal rights. Men and women have differing strengths. The Equal Rights Amendment can never do for women what needs to be done for them. Women need to know Jesus Christ as their Lord and Savior and be under His Lordship. They need a man who knows Jesus Christ

Jerry Falwell, *Listen America* (New York: Doubleday, 1980, 150–51). Reprinted in *Major Problems in American Women's History*, 2d ed., ed. Mary Beth Norton and Ruth M. Alexander (Lexington, Mass.: D. C. Heath and Co., 1996), 491–92.

as his Lord and Savior, and they need to be part of a home where their husband is a godly leader and where there is a Christian family.

The Equal Rights Amendment strikes at the foundation of our entire social structure. If passed, this amendment would accomplish exactly the opposite of its outward claims. By mandating an absolute equality under the law, it will actually take away many of the special rights women now enjoy. ERA is not merely a political issue, but a moral issue as well. A definite violation of holy Scripture, ERA defies the mandate that "the husband is the head of the wife, even as Christ is the head of the church" (Ep. 5:23). In 1 Peter 3:7 we read that husbands are to give their wives honor as unto the weaker vessel, that they are both heirs together of the grace of life. Because a woman is weaker does not mean that she is less important.

54. Failures and Successes

Rosalynn Carter
Reflections on the Carter Administration's Record on Women's Rights
1984

After the defeat of the ERA, some proponents suggested that Rosalynn Carter, being (in her own words) "a relatively traditional person," was not a strong enough advocate for the amendment. This excerpt from her 1984 memoir, First Lady from Plains, *however, indicates her conviction that she and her husband did all they could have done. She also affirms her great disappointment at the ERA's failure and admits to a strong sense of frustration that their best efforts were not enough to overcome the doubts created by the amendment's opponents.*

———————

My greatest disappointment in all the projects I worked on during the White House years was the failure of the Equal Rights Amendment to be ratified. Jimmy and I made dozens of calls to state legislators as individual states considered the

Rosalynn Carter, *First Lady from Plains* (Boston: Houghton Mifflin, 1984), 286–92.

issue, and it was very close at one time, so close that if only thirteen legislators — two in Florida, two in North Carolina, and nine in Nevada — had voted yea instead of nay we would have made it. The ERA would have been over the top . . . but it was not to be.

My files are full of speeches about the ERA; they are full of the phone calls I made to legislators in various states. They are full of letters written and invitations to fund-raisers and other meetings I attended, including the Houston Conference celebrating the International Women's Year in the fall of 1977, where Lady Bird Johnson, Betty Ford, and I appeared together. I held many events and meetings at the White House and did just about anything I could think of for the cause. I remember when my staff was wondering if it would be appropriate for a First Lady to be auctioned off at a dance for the ERA. Jimmy said, "Well, it's better than being a wallflower!" And so I danced for the ERA.

Our one victory came during the fall of 1978, when Jimmy and Fritz Mondale worked to turn seven congressional no votes into yes votes to pass legislation extending the ratification deadline. It was even more disappointing to see the deadline for the extension go by in 1982 with the ERA still not ratified.

Why have we had such a hard time trying to get the amendment ratified? After all, it is a simple twenty-four-word declaration: "Equality of rights under the law shall not be denied or abridged by the United States or by any state on account of sex."

Most people think it says much more than this. I have had women tell me that if I would send them a copy they would pay the postage, as though it were volumes. And Erma Bombeck has described it as the most misunderstood few words since "one size fits all."

The Equal Rights Amendment says nothing about men having to give up their places as head of the household or about women being drafted or forced to go to work, leaving their children at home. It says nothing about unisex bathrooms, homosexual marriages, or about personal family relationships, and it would not force any changes in them. What it would do is guarantee women the legal protection that should be rightfully theirs under the Constitution.

The U.S. Constitution is the most basic concept of what this nation stands for: freedom and equality for all. Yet today the only right the Constitution guarantees women is the right to vote. It contains no clause granting women legal status as persons or guaranteeing equal protection for them. Some argue that women's rights are guaranteed under the Fourteenth Amendment, passed to protect slaves. However, the Supreme Court in case after case has not extended this amendment to include women, although it has repeatedly been urged to do so.

One of the problems is the fervor and organization of the opposition. It is so vocal and so powerful at the polls that local legislators, who are the ones who must vote for ratification, are reluctant to do so. I have talked with many who have told me that they couldn't afford to go against this opposition. Also, due to the many erroneous and often wild contentions by the opposition, people are confused by what the ERA really is and what it would do to their lives.

The image of the ERA has been a serious problem. Attention has often centered on those supporters who have appeared to be demanding and strident man haters — mostly urban, professional women. "Nice" women, as my daughter-in-law Judy says, have been reluctant to be identified with such a group, though they support the ERA itself. In fact, I learned that a majority of people do support the ERA when they know the facts.

During the campaign for the ratification of the ERA, I talked with one state senator who had always been opposed to the amendment until he had gone with his wife to make a will. He told me he had found out that under the laws of their state, his wife would have no control over what he owned. If he died without a will, the business that he and his wife had developed together would go to his blood relatives, not to his wife. Furthermore, if he changed the ownership of his property and put half in his wife's name, they would have to pay a gift tax on the half he gave her. He told me he had changed his mind and was going to support the ERA. I wish a few more legislators had confronted the issue in such a personal way.

In years past, many laws were written with different provisions for men and women. In some states, women could marry at an earlier age than men. Men could drink at an earlier age than women. In Alabama, girls had to be seventeen before they could be newspaper carriers; boys only had to be ten! In some instances, women were required to have their husbands' consent to sell property. Everyone agrees that today these laws are outdated. But society at the time thought that women were different and should be protected; staying at home with the family, teaching school and working with children, or being a secretary helping a man were the kinds of things that women really wanted to do and could do well.

The movement for equal rights for women began with the simple reasoning that while women are biologically different from men, they have the same ability to serve as doctors or lawyers or do other things that had traditionally been viewed as men's jobs, and that society should take advantage of these talents.

I am grateful that because of the women's movement, there are not as many discriminatory laws as there once were. The lieutenant governor of Louisiana, Bobby Freeman, told me of one celebrated case in his state where a woman worked and bought her home. Her husband was disabled and did not contribute to the purchase, but later he placed a second mortgage on the house without her knowledge. The lender foreclosed and took the home. Under Louisiana's law at the time, the wife had no right to protect her house from her husband's mortgage or even to know about it, even though she had paid for it. Since then, the law has been changed.

An Equal Rights Amendment to the Constitution would protect women's gains and ensure that future laws would not discriminate against them. But great progress comes slowly, and someday, a day I hope to see in my lifetime, we will look back on this struggle as we look back now on the long but successful struggle for women's suffrage and wonder why. Why all the controversy and why such difficulty in giving women the protection of the Constitution that should have been theirs long ago?

While Jimmy was President, I understood clearly that times were changing in our country and that women everywhere were undergoing a period of adjustment. Many were forced to work outside the home to help supplement the family income or to support a family as a single parent; many were pursuing careers for their own fulfillment; and many others chose to remain at home and care for their families.

I felt very fortunate to identify with women in all these categories. I am a relatively traditional person and enjoy my roles as wife and mother, but it has also been natural and essential for me to expand my life and to participate outside the home as a partner and businesswoman and in public service as First Lady.

Jimmy has always supported women's causes, but he didn't have much choice, surrounded by active women as he was: his mother, me, and Amy. It was interesting how the pattern in our family reversed. I had been surrounded by men, Jimmy and the three boys, for years. Then, after our sons were grown, Amy came along, Miss Lillian moved back home to Plains, and Jimmy was surrounded by women.

Before his inauguration, Jimmy asked me to work with his staff and our women's campaign committee to develop a list of women who would be likely prospects for available positions in the federal government. Keeping an up-to-date list of qualified women in every job category, ready to submit for consideration as appointments became available, was very helpful. Some statistics:

Only six women had ever been appointed Cabinet secretaries in the history of our country; Jimmy appointed three of them.

Only five women had ever been appointed as undersecretaries in the history of our country; Jimmy appointed three of them.

He appointed 80 percent of all women ever to hold the post of assistant secretary.

He was the first President to name women as general counsels and inspectors general.

Of the forty-six women serving as federal judges at the end of his term, forty-one had been appointed by Jimmy. We knew a number of women who would have been good Supreme Court justices, and it was always understood between us that a woman would be appointed if a vacancy occurred. That didn't happen, but the appointment of many women judges helped to compensate for their not having a voice on the Supreme Court and ensured a permanent and powerful voice for women in interpreting the laws of our land.

In previous administrations, a total of twenty-five women had held ambassadorial posts. Jimmy appointed sixteen women as ambassadors.

And more women were serving on federal boards and commissions and on delegations representing the United States at conferences throughout the world.

In addition to receiving presidential appointments, women need to be elected to positions at all levels of government. When we were in Washington, there had been only fourteen women senators and ninety women in the House of Representatives in our history. I agree wholeheartedly with the well-known slogan: "A woman's place is in the house . . . and the Senate."

We also included women in all activities at the White House, taking care to invite representatives from women's groups to participate in all events — government consultations and briefings on such issues as SALT II,[1] inflation and energy,

[1] **SALT II**: the second round of the Strategic Arms Limitations Treaty with the Soviet Union.

education, Middle East peace, and on the progress of women's issues. Every year we held receptions and briefings for congressional wives, women in business, women legislators, rural women, Jewish women, black women, Mexican-American women, Democratic women, educators, and many more, and I learned a lot from these discussions.

From my own experience, I remembered how the long hours at Carter's Warehouse had to be coordinated with my duties as a mother and housewife, and supported flexitime schedules for working mothers in the federal government, our nation's largest employer. And I was pleased when expanded day-care centers became one of Jimmy's priorities. When my mother had to work full-time while we were children, she was lucky to have friends and relatives in Plains who could care for us. Most working women today are not so fortunate.

I had learned about small business management also by working alongside Jimmy at the warehouse, and now I wondered what I would have done if it had been necessary to organize my own business. Women were given some help in the Carter years: The Small Business Administration offered entrepreneurial training workshops for them and significantly increased loans available to businesses owned by women; the Farm Home Administration sponsored workshops and made it a priority to inform rural women of loans available for their businesses; HUD had seminars to teach women about housing finances and their rights to mortgage credit, removing barriers to women who wanted to own homes.

The President's Advisory Committee for Women came to realize that women nominees for federal judgeships were being penalized because they had had relatively little experience as judges in the lower courts or because they had taken several years away from their careers to have children. We discussed this with Jimmy and the attorney general, and they both agreed to be careful not to discriminate against women in the appointment process because they were mothers or because they had not been treated fairly when previous appointments had been made.

Other steps were taken to tackle the issue of discrimination, including: the amendment of the Civil Rights Act of 1964 to protect working women from occupational discrimination based on pregnancy; the consolidation of nineteen separate enforcement units in the federal government under one agency to handle discrimination complaints more efficiently; and the development of an interagency task force to eliminate sex discrimination from laws and policies and to focus government resources on increasing opportunities for women.

In most cases, the executives responsible for carrying out these decisions were women, often the "first" in their positions, which further strengthened the effectiveness of the programs.

The need for advice about the special concerns and problems of women in our country has been recognized by every President from John Kennedy through Jimmy Carter, all of whom appointed a women's advisory group. My daughter-in-law Judy served as honorary chair of this group, working closely with Kathy Cade in my office and Sarah Weddington in Jimmy's and with Chairpersons Bella Abzug, Carmen Delgado Votaw, and Lynda Robb. Unfortunately, there has been no such opportunity for American women to present their views to President Reagan, perhaps another cause of the highly publicized "gender gap" that affects his administration. . . .

Suggestions for Further Reading

Berry, Mary Frances. *Why ERA Failed: Politics, Women's Rights, and the Amending Process of the Constitution.* Bloomington: Indiana University Press, 1986.

Boles, Janet K. *The Politics of the Equal Rights Amendment: Conflict and the Decision Process.* New York: Longman, 1979.

Brady, David W., and Kent L. Tedin. "Ladies in Pink: Religion and Political Ideology in the Anti-ERA Movement." *Social Science Quarterly* 36 (March 1976): 564–75.

Felsenthal, Carol. *The Sweetheart of the Silent Majority: The Biography of Phyllis Schlafly.* Garden City, N.Y.: Doubleday, 1981.

Mansbridge, Jane J. *Why We Lost the ERA.* Chicago: University of Chicago Press, 1986.

Mathews, Donald G., and Jane Sherron De Hart. *Sex, Gender, and the Politics of ERA: A State and the Nation.* New York: Oxford University Press, 1990.

Steiner, Gilbert Yale. *Constitutional Inequality: The Political Fortunes of the Equal Rights Amendment.* Washington, D.C.: Brookings Institution, 1985.

CHAPTER FIFTEEN

Contemporary America

The New Immigration in South Florida

In the last third of the twentieth century, the pattern of immigration to the United States changed significantly. For much of the nineteenth and twentieth centuries, most immigrants had come from Europe. When the traditional open-door policy ended after World War I, it was replaced by a strict quota system that restricted immigration to a trickle and favored immigrants from northern and western Europe. Then, with the passage of the 1965 Immigration Act, immigration law no longer gave any national group an advantage. From the 1960s to 1990s, more and more immigrants originated in Asia and Latin America, and a declining proportion in Europe.

One center of this "new" influx was South Florida, which has attracted political and economic refugees from the Caribbean basin. Among them were Cubans leaving in the wake of the Communist revolution and other Caribbeans— especially Haitians—facing political turbulence and economic distress, as well as Central Americans fleeing political revolutions and economic upheaval. In addition, waves of retirees from other parts of the country have joined an existing population of white and African American "native" Floridians. In this mix, divergent Anglo, black, Cuban, and Caribbean cultures came into close proximity. South Florida has become a new sort of "melting pot," and what has happened there reflects national, American trends.

In the late nineteenth century, South Florida had become a safe haven for Cuban nationalists, and in the twentieth century it remained a popular vacation spot for upper-class Cuban tourists. During the Cuban Revolution, in which Fidel Castro in 1959 overthrew the regime of Fulgencio Batista and gradually established a Communist regime, a stream of refugees fled to the Miami area. Between January 1959 and April 1961, about 135,000 Cubans emigrated to South

Florida. Four years later, in 1965, nearly 210,000 lived there. As a result of an understanding between Cuba and the United States, the flow continued—despite outright hostility between the two countries and an embargo imposed by the United States—and between 1965 and 1973 another 340,000 refugees migrated to the Miami area. In response to the concerns of Floridians, some Cubans were resettled outside the state, but many of them eventually returned to the Miami area. By 1979, about four-fifths of all Cubans in the United States lived there; Miami possessed the largest Cuban population of any city but Havana.

Miami's Cuban community was supplemented with additional waves of immigrants during the 1980s and 1990s. In April 1980, Castro declared the port of Mariel to be open and permitted anyone wishing to leave the country to do so. He further urged Cuban exiles in the United States to transport their relatives and friends across to Florida. The result was a massive flotilla of boats that eventually transported some 125,000 new immigrants to American shores. Still more Cubans migrated in 1994, when refugees congregated at the American naval base at Guantanamo, but this time the flotilla was stopped by vigorous enforcement—and Cuban–United States cooperation—to stem the flow.

South Florida was the destination of other ethnic and racial groups as well. Beginning in the late 1970s, substantial numbers of Haitians sought to flee their country's oppressive political system and their desperately poor economy. The numbers grew, from over 56,000 legal immigrants in the 1970s to over 185,000 in the 1980s. Although the primary destination of Haitian emigrants remained New York City—which counted more than 400,000 Haitians during the 1990s—many others began to move to South Florida. Migrants from Haiti arrived in the United States by the perilous means of crossing in small craft over often dangerous waters. The result was an influx of so-called boat people that lasted into the 1990s. During the 1970s and 1980s, Miami attracted substantial numbers of Nicaraguans seeking relief from revolution and economic distress. Although at first many of them were upper- or middle-class refugees from the Sandinista regime, by the 1980s more and more were poor, unskilled laborers who came to Florida in search of a better life.

By the 1990s, South Florida had become an unusual mélange of divergent racial and ethnic groups. Each had a strong identity and its own ethnic enclave. In Miami, Cubans were a major component of the city's economy, culture, and politics. With "Little Havana" as a center for Cuban American life, Cubans in Miami had become a successful part of South Florida's life, and Nicaraguans and Haitians had established similar enclaves. Sometimes the ethnic mixture was volatile. In May 1980, for example, African Americans in Miami rioted after police on trial for the beating death of a local black insurance agent, Arthur McDuffie, were acquitted of all charges. Much of the racial tension was, however, between blacks and Cubans. In the African American enclave of Liberty City, nearly $80 million of property damage resulted from the boiling over of resentments by blacks toward the ethnic fragmentation of the city.

The documents in this chapter examine different dimensions of the new immigration in South Florida—and their implications for late-twentieth-century society—with particular attention on the experiences of two of the largest groups of recent arrivals: Cubans and Haitians. Two articles from *Business Week* focus on how Cubans sought and found economic success with remarkable speed, but how their incorporation into American society was accompanied by ethnic and cultural conflict. Alex Stepick and Jake C. Miller examine the very different experience of Haitians, most of whom arrived in South Florida in extreme poverty—and without any official sanction as political refugees. The last document, looking at immigration from another perspective, examines the extent to which new immigrants have assimilated into American society.

As you read, try to differentiate between the characteristics that are common to the new immigrants to South Florida and those that set them apart. To what extent do the different cultures and races conflict with each other? What forms has this conflict taken?

55. The Cuban Experience

BUSINESS WEEK
"How the Immigrants Made It in Miami" and "South Florida's Melting Pot Is About to Boil"
1971 and 1985

By the 1970s, Cubans composed a significant part of the economic and political power structure of South Florida. Because many of the immigrants were middle-class refugees from Castro's revolution, they arrived in Florida equipped with strong family structure and an educational background that enabled many of them to achieve relatively quick prosperity—in many cases, within a decade or less of their arrival. The national press quickly took notice. In a 1971 article, Business Week described in some detail how many in Florida's Cuban American community had achieved economic success by the early 1970s. At the same time, as an article from the same magazine fourteen years later illustrates, the entrance of large numbers of immigrants engendered ethnic and cultural conflict that became apparent early on.

"How the Immigrants Made It in Miami"

May 1, 1971

It seems to me remarkable that when you consider that these refugees arrived here with nothing but their skills and abilities, that 83 percent are fully self-supporting and only 17 percent require federal assistance.

—Howard H. Palmatier,
Director, Cuban Refugee Program,
Health, Education & Welfare Dept.

In the ten years since Cubans began fleeing to the United States from Castro, they have made faster progress in their adopted country than has any other group of immigrants in this century. Almost overnight they have emerged from the deprived, refugee state and moved into the middle class, skipping lightly over— or never even touching—the lowest rung of the economic ladder that was a necessary first step for the Irish, the Jews, the Italians, and others. Today there are colonies of hardworking, prospering Cubans in the suburbs of New York and as deep into the Midwest as Chicago. Nowhere, though, has their imprint been felt more than in Miami, the original port of call for most of them.

Indeed, in the past decade, Miami has become a Latinized city. Of nearly 600,000 Cuban refugees believed to have entered the United States from 1960 to 1970 (about 410,000 are known to have arrived), more than 300,000 have settled in Dade County. The rapid staccato of Spanish is now commonplace in much of the City of Miami and is heard increasingly in Miami Beach. In many sections, signs printed in English have become the exception rather than the rule.

Cubans have avoided some usual immigrant problems. True, friction exists between Cubans and mainland whites and blacks. But the small percentage of Cubans receiving federal aid consists mostly of the young and elderly. The Cubans' crime rate is low; the rate at which they have learned to speak English is high. What is more, even their harshest critics acknowledge that the immigrants are resourceful, aggressive, and energetic. In fact, the Cubans have enjoyed an economic success that is spectacular.

Rags to Riches.   Cubans operate 60 percent of all service stations in Miami, and companies that they own are putting up about 30 percent of all construction now underway in the city, including a $35-million, forty-story office building that will be the tallest in Florida when completed. Three presidents, 21 vice presidents, and 200 officers of Cuban origin are in banking. Cubans operate 20 cigar manufacturers, 30 furniture factories, 10 garment plants, 45 bakeries, 12 private schools, 230 restaurants, 10 record-making plants, 3 radio stations, at least a dozen "giveaway" shopping guides printed in Spanish, and a daily newspaper, *Diarios Las Américas*, with 60,000 circulation.

There have been, of course, innumerable rags-to-riches stories. Probably the best known is that of David Egozi and Eugene Ramos, who parlayed $40,000 smuggled out of Cuba and $30,000 in borrowed capital into Suave Shoe Co., which makes low-priced, private-label leisure footwear and had sales of $42.6 million last year.

Such enterprise has benefited Miami's entire Cuban population. First Research Co., which periodically surveys the Cuban community, estimates that the total annual income of Cubans in Dade County as of last September 30 was nearly $588 million, an increase of $246 million since mid-1968. And the median income of Cuban families rose from $5,244 in 1967 to $7,200 last year, a 37 percent increase and well above the national average. In addition, nearly 90 percent of all Cuban families own more than one automobile.

To accomplish all this, the Cubans have borrowed liberally from neighborhood banks. Riverside Bank, for example, now has 18,000 Latin accounts worth $14 million, or 30 percent of total deposits. Current loans made by Cubans amount to $5½ million, or 19 percent of the bank's total.

"Their repayment record has been good," says Riverside President Tully F. Dunlap. "We find them industrious, conscientious, a definite asset to the bank." Tom Butler, district director of the Small Business Administration, reports that Dade County Cubans made 118 loans totaling $2.2 million in fiscal 1969, 75 loans totaling $1.1 million in fiscal 1970, and 147 loans totaling $2.1 million in the first eight months of fiscal 1971.

Assimilation.   Because of the Cubans' economic success, a number of their leaders believe that the next five years will be more trying for the refugee population than were the last ten. Carlos Arboleya, president of Fidelity National Bank and a refugee himself, believes that the immigrants have done perhaps too well for themselves in too short a time. "The large majority of people in Miami used to look upon us as the 'poor Cuban refugee,' " he explains. "Now, suddenly, they don't see us as being so poor any longer. They see that we are a decisive force in the community socially, economically, and politically." As a result, he says, there is some envy, resentment, and jealousy on the part of the general public.

Many Miamians also see the Cubans as too clannish. Arboleya acknowledges that Cubans do stick together, especially while there is a language barrier. But he says: "I don't think this is true on the whole. The Cubans are a part of the community, from membership in the PTA to the Lions Club and other groups." And assimilation is moving forward. "I've had an opportunity to speak with civic leaders, with church leaders," says Palmatier, "and by and large they have only good things to say about the refugees—that they are ambitious, have strong family ties, and do not show up as a crime statistic, something of which we are especially proud."

Miami Police Chief Bernard Garmire confirms this last point. Cubans, he says, account for only 5 percent to 6 percent of the crime in the city while making up 30 percent of the population. Says Wilson Purdy, chief of the metropolitan Dade County police: "I think Cubans have made excellent citizens. While there has been some increases in narcotics violations among people with Spanish names, we can't say that it's a Cuban problem, but a problem of the community in general."

Both police departments have been actively recruiting Cubans, particularly because they need bilingual policemen. But they have had only limited success. "I think it has to do with their background," says Garmire. "Too many remember the police state in Cuba and don't want any part of police work."

Education.   The Cubans, many of them highly skilled or with university degrees, have taken a more-than-usual interest in the schools, however. Thus, their children have not had the adjustment problem that some foresaw in the early 1960s. Says Paul W. Bell, executive director of the Dade County school system's division of instruction: "By and large, Cuban kids have had more of a positive than a negative impact. The concerns of many that academic standards would drop drastically because the Cubans didn't speak English and that they would drain resources from American pupils never materialized."

Bell believes that the vast majority of Cuban children adjusted well because they:

—Immediately began learning English as a second language (taught by American teachers with the assistance of Cuban aides).
—Attended classes with their American counterparts from the moment they entered school, and were concurrently taught the same subjects in their native language.

Because of this, the children have not fallen behind in their studies and take 1½ years, on average, to become proficient enough in English to end special instruction. "Keeping them with American students gave them maximum opportunity to learn English and use it on the outside while, at the same time, learning in their native tongue," says Bell. "There's no telling how long it might have taken had we kept the children apart—but it certainly would have been a lot longer."

Nationalization.   Though the youngsters adjusted swiftly in school, their parents have not, to any degree, become involved in the American political system. Latest figures from the U.S. Immigration & Naturalization Service show that, while the number of exiles becoming citizens doubled to almost 21,000 between fiscal 1969 and fiscal 1970 (ending last June 30), less than 60,000 of the approximately 600,000 that have come to the United States since 1962 have become citizens. Fewer still have registered to vote, and Miami political experts doubt that as many as 10,000 cast ballots in last November's election.

Their involvement in Miami politics is just as lethargic. Miami Mayor David Kennedy offers this assessment: "They're more worried now about survival, reestablishing themselves socially and economically. The political adjustment comes last, but I believe we're seeing some signs of it."

Manual Suarez, who polled 8,141 to run fifth in the Dade County mayoralty race, points out: "When they do vote, as the figures show, they tend to vote in a bloc, but they're more interested now in Castro than in pollution."

Friction.   Probably the biggest complaint against the refugees is that they are taking jobs that might otherwise go to native-born Americans, primarily blacks.

Palmatier doubts that this occurs, except in isolated instances. Instead, he contends, Cubans created their own job opportunities as they expanded into a myriad of enterprises in retailing, wholesaling, and manufacturing. A good example, he says, would be Suave Shoe. Nonexistent before Egori and Ramos came to the United States it currently employs 1,900, more than 99 percent of them Cuban refugees.

Robert Sims, Dade County's community relations director and himself a black, argues the Cuban influx has hurt Negroes. He believes that when the Cubans began swarming into Miami in the early 1960s, members of his race were on the threshold of being "upgraded" into semiskilled clerical positions in department stores and offices.

"No," says Sims, "they didn't take away jobs. Instead, the jobs that were just about to go to blacks went to Latins, many of whom had the expertise, the know how, the drive to get going, and, in some cases, a willingness to work for less money." Then, says Sims, when the Cubans began creating jobs of their own, they gave them to later-arriving Cubans because of clannishness and language ties.

Sims describes Negro-Cuban relations as tense. "There is friction," he says, "not because they are Cubans but because they are recipients of favor from whites. The black community is not unlike an underdeveloped nation. There are tremendous problems, and it is looking to the developed nation, in this instance, white people, for help. And the blacks are upset because the Cubans have received a greater response." Dade County Mayor Steve Clark, who thinks the Cuban vote in the last election helped to beat his opponent, contends that "certain elements" are trying to create difficulty between blacks and Cubans. "If there was to be trouble," he says, "it should have happened eight years ago, when they first came to Miami."

Sims does not agree. He believes that, because of their growing numbers and their aggressiveness, Cubans will eventually become a major concern of the whites. "Suddenly, they're going to look around," he says, "and discover that Latins have taken over Miami, lock, stock, and barrel."

"South Florida's Melting Pot Is About to Boil"

February 4, 1985

Miguel Pérez is used to waiting. He spent fifteen years waiting to get out of Fidel Castro's Cuba, three of them in jail for trying to escape the island. Even after he got his wish—leaving Cuba for Miami with 125,000 other *Marielitos* in the 1980 boat lift from the Cuban port of Mariel—the slender meat cutter has had to wait. This time he is waiting for approval from Washington to apply for U.S. citizenship and for the right to send for his twin eleven-year-old sons and the elderly parents he left behind.

Business Week, 4 February 1985, 86–87.

Pérez's waiting days may finally be over. In November the Immigration & Naturalization Service announced that more than 120,000 Mariel refugees without criminal records could begin applying for legal residency in the United States. Former political prisoners such as Pérez are likely to be included under the edict. Some could become eligible for citizenship as early as this summer. And Pérez may soon be able to send for his family. He will try to bring his father to the United States first. "He is old," says Pérez, "and he wants to die free."

Pérez's private dream, multiplied by the thousands of transplanted Cubans who share it, is viewed by some non-Latin Floridians as a potential nightmare. As a result, the ethnic and political pots are boiling in South Florida. Key to the tensions is a recent U.S.–Cuban agreement under which nearly 3,000 Mariel criminals and mental patients now held in U.S. prisons will be shipped back to Cuba. As part of the deal, normal immigration between Cuba and the United States will be restored. This means that once the *Marielitos* who remain in Florida are sworn in as citizens, they will have the right to send for an unrestricted number of husbands, wives, parents, and minor children — and the Castro government says it will not stand in the way.

Some South Florida residents fear the region cannot absorb tens of thousands — perhaps hundreds of thousands — more Cuban refugees. They warn that the state lacks the jobs, schools, and social services to cope with them. In the past, black leaders, edgy about outbreaks of racial violence in Miami's teeming slums, worried that blacks would be shoved aside by waves of Cuban immigrants. Now some whites are also concerned.

The charge that South Florida is already too Latinized — Latins constitute 44 percent of Dade County's population — is raising ugly passions. State and local politicians are treading a fine line between their Anglo constituents' fears and the reality of growing Latin political muscle. Some Republicans, encouraged by the predominantly pro-GOP sentiment among Cubans in Florida, see a new influx as a potential boon to their party. Democrats, sensing a threat to their dominance in the heavily Democratic state, are raising the specter of a GOP plot to tip the political balance.

Fueling Fears. Charges are flying that South Florida could be deluged with up to 300,000 Cuban newcomers. INS officials in Washington, however, sharply dispute these estimates — although they admit they don't yet know how many will immigrate. INS Commissioner Alan C. Nelson maintains that Florida leaders have "overreacted." He says: "It will not be 300,000, and it will not be tomorrow." In particular he points out: "Many of the people who came in 1980 came to be reunited with relatives. They're already here."

Nonetheless, in living rooms and political gatherings all over South Florida, anxious talk of another Mariel invasion is topic A. The public debate is being fueled by several Miami radio talk-show hosts who are conducting a campaign aimed at fanning resentment to large-scale Cuban immigration. Anxious listeners are jamming the stations' phone lines. Their biggest worry: being displaced by Cuban newcomers.

"The idea that these people are being assimilated is ridiculous. They are absorbing us, and not the other way around," talk-show host Al Rantel charged on a WNWS broadcast. Most of his callers agreed, pouring out their resentment over not finding a job or even being able to shop for groceries in Miami unless they speak Spanish. "It's like we're the foreigners here," complained one caller from South Miami.

Working with other radio personalities, Rantel has organized a write-in campaign to persuade Washington to reverse its decision on the *Marielitos*. The campaign, called Save Our South Florida, or S.O.S., has raised some $10,000 and mailed thousands of postcards protesting the INS policy to politicians in Tallahassee and Washington.

R. Ray Goode, president of the Babcock Co., a major Miami developer and homebuilder, says that more than just "the lunatic fringe" is concerned. He is particularly worried about who will pay. "The federal government must recognize that this is by no means a local problem," he declares. "It came about as the result of federal policies—or nonpolicies—and they [Washington] must subsidize the cost."

Governor Bob Graham agrees. He says he was not consulted on the deal with Castro or the decision to legalize the *Marielitos*, even though 80 percent of them have settled in South Florida. He claims Washington still owes state and local governments more than $150 million for services provided in the wake of the 1980 boat lift. "Immigration policy is a federal responsibility," Graham declares. "Washington must pay the cost." To which White House assistant Lee Verstanding counters: "Southwest states are facing the same problems [from other refugees]. We can't just single out one state."

Florida political observers suspect that Graham, a Democrat, has more than money on his mind. GOP sources admit that the addition of Cuban immigrants to voter rolls could dramatically boost Republicans' political power in Florida. And there is speculation that in 1986 Graham may challenge Republican Senator Paula Hawkins, a popular figure in the Cuban community. That challenge could be in jeopardy if the Cubans are registered en masse by the GOP.

Soul-searching.   Currently there is a ten-month wait in Miami between eligibility for citizenship and naturalization, but the Reagan Administration could shorten the waiting time if it chooses to. "President Ford's people sent ten [federal immigration] lawyers down to Miami to speed things up before the 1976 elections," says an INS source. "The Reagan people did the same before last year's election. All they would have to do is put the Cubans in the Orange Bowl and swear 'em in."

While the politicians examine the angles, soul-searching over the new immigrants has extended to the heart of Miami's Cuban enclaves, where some established Cubans also worry about the cost of another wave. "We are not against people coming over from Cuba," insists Sergio Pereira, Dade County's assistant administrator and a Cuban refugee himself. "As a Cuban, I can tell you what will happen. The people come over [to Florida] on a Wednesday. Their families take off Thursday and Friday, and on Saturday they roast a pig. But by the time Monday comes around, they have to go back to work, and uncle needs a driver's license, and mother needs to go to a doctor. That," says Pereira, "is when they'll turn to us."

56. Haitian Boat People

ALEX STEPICK AND JAKE C. MILLER
Accounts of Haitian Refugees
1982 and 1984

The following documents examine the experiences of Haitians in South Florida as immigration began to accelerate in the early and mid-1980s. As both accounts suggest, Haitians arriving in Florida met a hostile atmosphere. Unlike Cuban refugees, they were not welcomed on political grounds. Most Floridians greeted their arrival with alarm; African Americans saw them as threatening their economic status. In a report to the Minority Rights Group, Ltd., a British international watchdog organization, Alex Stepick, a professor of anthropology and sociology and the director of Florida International University's Immigration and Ethnicity Institute, reports on the status of Haitians' human rights. Similarly, Jake C. Miller describes the experience of Haitians in a hostile American environment in a chapter from his 1984 book, The Plight of Haitian Refugees.

ALEX STEPICK

Report to the Minority Rights Group
1982

Since 1972 an increasing number of Haitians have preferred to risk the . . . sea journey to the United States.

In 1981 there were fifty to sixty boats just in the area between Port-de-Paix and Cap-Haitian, each capable of carrying one hundred or more people each trip.

Alex Stepick, with the assistance of Dale Frederick Swartz, *Haitian Refugees in the U.S.* (London: Minority Rights Group, 1982), 11.

Making a trip every twenty-two days, carrying 6,000 people a month, the captains charge two, three, and even four times what cruise ships charge, but for much worse accommodations. It is now a big business.

In Port-au-Prince there is an employment agency which apparently fronts for refugee smuggling. The agency advertises over the radio and sends agents out to the countryside claiming to have many jobs in a country where most are unemployed. People pour into the agency, sleeping on the floor and outside in the corridors. They are counseled that they can buy or trade their way to the United States. Many literally sell everything they have, including land that has been in the family since the revolution.[1] They leave from Port-de-Paix, Cap-Haitian, or Jeremie with hopes of making it to the United States.

Recurringly Haitian officials attempt to control the flow. In May 1980, the military commander for the Northwest called together all of the area's pastors to inform them that the government wanted to stop the flow. They asked the religious community for their assistance. Indeed, the flow was stopped for about a week. But the first boat to leave after the embargo departed from directly below the headquarters of the military commander. Residents claim that the real reason for stopping the flow was to allow the military commander to obtain a monopoly on kickbacks. Rumors are rife within and outside Haiti, that government involvement reaches right into the Presidential Palace. The Haitian and civilian authorities claim they are powerless to stop the flow while most Haitians state that they simply find it in their economic self-interest to maintain and control the flow.

When the Haitians first began arriving back in the early and mid-1970s, reaction was mixed. Some were struck by the desperation and courage motivating a seven-hundred-mile sea journey in overcrowded, barely seaworthy boats. Others believed that the Haitians were a disruptive force, destroying the community and draining public resources. While Miami's economy may have been rejuvenated by Cubans, the black Haitians without skills or capital were viewed as an unwanted burden. The subsequent 1980 riots revealed the frustration of American blacks in Miami and the lack of integration and opportunity for some in the midst of an economic boom based on tourism, international banking, and illegal drugs.

As with other migrant flows of low-wage labor, the workers are frequently competitive and sometimes complementary to domestic sources. In some cases, they will take jobs that natives no longer want; jobs that might disappear, go undone, or migrate abroad if there were no migrants. In other cases, employers exploit their cheap labor to depress wages artificially. In both cases, the migrants' impact is often exaggerated. It becomes easy to blame them for conditions created for, but not by, them.

Certainly, they have an impact. In Miami there is only a 15 percent vacancy rate in housing and Haitians are forced to double, triple up, and even worse. In some cases there are twelve to a room and they must take turns sleeping. On average, there are six people per household, four of whom are nonworking adults.

[1] **the revolution:** reference to Haiti's war of independence during the 1790s and 1800s.

Many Haitians carry diseases with them from Haiti, particularly tuberculosis and typhoid. But a Dade County Health Department study indicates that the most severe health problem among the Haitian community is malnutrition and starvation. The largest strain on public services, however, is in the maternity wards. In 1980, at Jackson Memorial Hospital, Miami's county hospital, 11 percent of the births were Haitians.

The Haitians, just as any other resident, pay for these services. They pay sales taxes; those working have income and social security taxes withheld which they most likely will never claim. Those who own property, of course, pay property taxes. Those who rent pay property taxes indirectly, as does any other rentor.

Nevertheless, they receive proportionately far fewer services than any other subset of the community. Virtually all Haitians, but especially those in the United States illegally, are afraid of government organizations. They would rather bear their suffering individually or turn to their friends and relatives. Less than 50 percent of those eligible for benefits actually apply for them.

If they do turn to public agencies, they find little help. The agencies already feel overtaxed, underfunded, and reluctant to open up to more clients. There are some Haitian community organizations who make a notable and valiant effort to fulfill their community's needs. But their resources are far too few.

But given the high levels of unemployment, together with the low wage and spending levels of those who are employed among the Haitians in Miami, there must be some drain on the economy, however temporary. Nevertheless, the mayor of Miami, Maurice Ferre, was quoted in the *New York Times* on May 27, 1980, as saying: "I think we can absorb another 25,000." This was before the full impact of the Mariel exodus was felt in Miami.

Over the past several decades, three major streams of migrant labor—legal and illegal—have developed through the United States. One flows up and down the West Coast, from Southern California to Oregon and Washington state. Another flows out of southern Texas to the Midwest. The third has gone from South Florida to the Eastern Seaboard. All three streams are fed by tributaries from the others. For the past ten to fifteen years, the Florida flow has been divided into the American Blacks, the Chicanos, and a body of Jamaicans (contract migrants who fly into South Florida each November to harvest sugarcane and are allowed to come legally because the cane producers and the Department of Labor certify that there is a "shortage" of domestic labor).

Now, a Haitian stream is evolving. In Immokalee, 1,500 Haitians have found work. In Belle Glade, where a year-round population of 17,000 swells to 25,000 during the harvest, more than 3,000 have come to cut sugarcane. In Dade County, some 1,000 Haitians have found their way into the fields.

At peak harvest there are more than 15,000 farm workers and their families competing for about 9,500 jobs in the fields of Collier and West Henry Counties. American farmers, saddled with spiraling production costs, have always been eager to employ workers whose illegal status circumvents numerous state and federal work forms and who don't complain about wages.

The increased labor pool helps farmers, but not all workers. "We have worked about two months, it is very difficult to find work, but sometimes we can work part time. Those of us who work help those of us who can't. It is very off-and-on. Some weeks we work three days, some weeks not at all."

There is also growing resentment among Immokalee's blacks and Mexicans toward Haitians. "The Mexicans here tease our people too much. They don't make us feel good. They make it hard for us," says Elites Pierre, Immokalee's only licensed Haitian crew leader. Mexican crew leaders won't hire Haitians or American blacks. Mexican crew leaders hire only Mexicans.

As resentment grows, flares, and smolders, the Department of Labor and the cane producers continue to claim that there is not enough locally available labor and Jamaicans must be certified to come and cut the cane.

Jake C. Miller

"A Home with Walls and Fences"
1984

When Haitians arrived in Pompano Beach, Florida, in 1972 and rejoiced over having reached the land of freedom, they did not know that hours later they would be confronted with an imprisonment similar to that which many of them had known previously in Haiti. Their detention, however, was short-lived and they were released on their own recognizance to Church World Service (CWS). In spite of their legal struggle to obtain asylum here in the United States, they were later deported to Haiti. Since then city jails, county stockades, and federal prisons throughout South Florida have been the initial American homes for many of the arriving Haitians who sought their first taste of freedom in the United States.

City Jails and County Stockades. Within the walls of U.S. jails and prisons have occurred many bizarre and dehumanizing experiences for Haitians, including the imprisonment of Roselene Dorsainvil, an eight-year-old girl, in a West Palm Beach jail. The child, who was found in a jail cell by a Haitian priest and a nun, had been there for about three weeks, along with other refugees who had come ashore in November 1978. Roselene reported that her mother was dead and that her father, whom she had accompanied to the United States, was in another cell of the jail. After officials were questioned concerning her detention, she was released, and later her father was freed as a humanitarian gesture.

In another striking case, Marie Amy Bastien, one of fifteen refugees who came ashore at North Palm Beach marina on November 10, 1978, was held in the jail as a material witness, while her children were being cared for in a shelter home by the State Division of Youth Services. Her forty-two-day stay in the West Palm Beach jail came to an end after the Immigration and Naturalization Service (INS) granted a request by the Florida Rural Legal Service that she be released as a hu-

Jake C. Miller, *The Plight of Haitian Refugees* (New York: Praeger, 1984), 123–26.

manitarian Christmas gesture. At first, Richard Gullage of the INS rejected the appeal, insisting that she post a $2,500 bond, but later he reconsidered, attributing his change of heart to his "humanitarian and compassionate nature." Not only did such imprisonment raise questions concerning the wisdom of separating a mother from her three children, especially when she posed no threat to society, but it also raised questions relative to the INS need for so many material witnesses. The *Palm Beach Post*, which was very critical of the holding of Haitian refugees in jail while allowing the man who was accused of bringing them here to go free on bail, also questioned the need for so many material witnesses. It observed, "the answers are as obvious as the color of the Haitians' skin. And they reflect poorly on the nation that is supposed to lift its lamp beside the golden door."

The *Palm Beach Post* was also critical of Assistant Deportation Director John Eldred's announced policy of attempting to discourage illegal immigration from Haiti by giving refugees the choice of staying in jail until deportation hearings or returning immediately to Haiti.

Because of numerous criticisms of the situation in the West Palm Beach jail, a group of blacks, including elected city commissioners, sought permission to inspect the facilities, but were denied. Two days later, in a sudden move, officials transferred the Haitian inmates to other jails in South Florida. Not only did the *Post* criticize the INS for the imprisonment of the Haitians—some of whom had been there for more than sixty days—but also the police chief, who had denied the two city commissioners access to the jail. In assessing the Haitian plight the *Post*, while conceding that Haitians are illegal aliens, questioned the logic of filling the local jails with them, thus "crowding out the muggers and thugs who pose a more imminent danger to the local populace." Instead of imprisoning these Haitians, the *Post* suggested that it would be both humane and practical to convert a nearby vacant migrant housing project into a refugee processing center.

The plight of Haitian detainees can best be assessed by considering the experiences of Haitians who arrived in Boca Raton on August 30, 1978, as passengers on the sailboat *Au Nom Dieu*. The description of the experiences of one of them in four Florida jails during a six-month period provides a vivid picture of the use of detention as a weapon to force Haitians to accept deportation to their homeland. According to the affidavit filed in the *HRC v. Civiletti* case, the refugees were placed, initially, in the jail at West Palm Beach, where they were detained during the period of processing. From this jail they were periodically taken to Miami to be questioned by INS officials. At the outset, all of the Haitians in the group were told the advantages of returning voluntarily to Haiti, and after encouraging them to do so, the officers asked those who wanted to return voluntarily to step aside. A majority of the Haitians in the party did so, but twelve (eleven males and one female) refused the offer. During the hearings the judge asked if the twelve Haitians would be able to secure a lawyer, but according to the affidavit, he did not advise them that a lawyer could be provided through legal services or other means. The eleven males remained in the West Palm Beach jail until November 3, 1978, when they were transferred to the Collier County Stockade in Immokalee, Florida. The Haitians found conditions in the stockade to be worse than in the West Palm Beach jail, with unsanitary conditions, poor food, inadequate medical services, and no access to telephone and mail services. Because of the deplorable conditions, the Haitians requested the prison guard to call INS officials who, upon their arrival, made empty promises of anticipated improvements. Later, the INS officials were summoned for the second time and were informed by the dissatisfied Haitian inmates that they did not want to remain in the prison, that they wanted either their freedom or to be sent to Cuba. In order to force their demands to be met, on November 23 the Haitians began a hunger strike, which once again brought INS officials to the stockade. On this trip, the officials were accompanied by a Haitian, referred to as "Tony," who instructed the inmates that they were going to be transferred to another prison in groups of twos. When they objected to this procedure, insisting that they should be allowed to go as one group, Tony advised them that if orders were not followed they would be beaten. Later that afternoon, when the process of transferring the inmates to Belle Glade was begun, prison guards felt compelled to use force.

In Belle Glade the Haitians found the conditions to be better than in Immokalee, especially the food and telephone and mail services. The inmates ate in their small cells and were able to use showers and toilets in their cells. By mid-February they still had not been told how long they would be held in jail, and expressed their frustration by initiating another hunger strike, which lasted for three days. In order to calm the situation they were told that they would have their freedom in two weeks, but once again, they vowed not to eat until they were free. One inmate remarked, "We had not left Haiti to be imprisoned once more. We thought the U.S. government would treat us differently than it has."

After a disturbance on the evening of February 23, which was designed to gain the attention of the guards so as to force them to call in INS officials, force was once again used as the Haitians were transferred to a jail in Fort Pierce—their fourth confinement. According to the Haitians, the conditions in the jail were deplorable, with dirty unflushed toilets and garbage on the floor. When the Haitians protested the conditions by making noise, the guards came in, closed the windows, and sprayed the cells with tear gas. Because of the hunger strike, the spraying of the tear gas, and the general unsanitary conditions of the jail, four of the five Haitians had to be hospitalized prior to their return to Immokalee, where they were released on March 1, 1979. According to one of the Haitian inmates, he was wearing the same clothes he wore on the day he arrived in the United States. He was never given additional clothes by the prisons or by the INS.

When questioned about the treatment of prisoners, John Eldred, an INS official, denied knowledge of "beating or gassing," but James Lester, the warden at the jail in Immokalee, admitted that his men and the immigration officers had beaten the Haitians, insisting that "they didn't want to move when we told them to move." He continued, "We had lots of fun for a few minutes. There was some bloodshed and we cracked some heads."

Jack Cassidy of the Christian Community Service Agency of Miami had earlier criticized conditions at the facility at Immokalee. During a visit to the stockade in 1975, when Haitian inmates were conducting a hunger strike there, he found eighty-two Haitian men housed in two cells, each measuring 35' × 45'. According to Cassidy, prison officials admitted that they were understaffed, they could not provide daily opportunities for the inmates to go outside the cell, except to the adjoining room for meals. As a result of the hunger strike at that time, the INS was ordered to remove the Haitians immediately, which it did—sending forty-four of them to the INS facility in Port Isabel, Texas, a more spacious facility, which officials believed would provide "better overall detention conditions, including fresh air and exercise."

Because of the lack of federal facilities in the South Florida area, the INS has, from time to time, leased space in local jails, including the Collier County Stockade in Immokalee, which it was leasing in 1977 for $8 per prisoner per day. The capacity at the stockade was 132 inmates, and approximately three-quarters of the space has been filled regularly by Haitian refugees since 1974. According to Warden James T. Lester, the county took in more than $140,000 during 1976. As late as December 1981, the leasing of facilities in local jails was still in practice, with Haitians being housed as far away as Leesburg, Florida, including twenty-five young Haitians who were accused of attempting escape from the Krome Detention Center. Sgt. Pete Peterson, a jailer, considered the inmates to be ideal prisoners, never tearing up things and always taking care of each other. The jailer offered this description: "I'll come back here and if one is down and crying, they all are crying. Then other times they'll sing—and what beautiful voices, all three cells harmonizing."

57. Assimilation and Conflict

Mireya Navarro
"Black and Cuban American: Bias in Two Worlds"
1997

In the 1980s and 1990s, immigration had clearly remade the face of South Florida. The changing cultural, ethnic, and racial characteristics of that immigration created new conflicts. Many of those conflicts were among the very diverse immigrants themselves. In this article, the New York Times *bureau chief for Miami explores the racial tensions that exist among Cuban Americans and African Americans.*

Mireya Navarro, "Black and Cuban American: Bias in Two Worlds," *New York Times,* 13 September 1997.

When black and Hispanic residents in this racially polarized city fought over a vacant City Commission seat, Henry Crespo stepped in and offered himself as the solution.

Being both black and Cuban, and a Spanish-speaker who lives in a black neighborhood, Mr. Crespo said he could bridge their worlds. But blacks said they would only accept a "black American" and Cubans regarded him as an oddity with questionable allure.

Mr. Crespo was not appointed to the commission; the seat went to an African American woman.

"I'm as black as you can get but I'm Cuban," Mr. Crespo, thirty-three, said recently, while on his job as housing director of the small city of Opa-Locka, near Miami, where he lives. "I have to be myself, understanding that I can't please everybody."

As black and Hispanic, Mr. Crespo is part of two worlds he says he relishes equally. But as African Americans and Hispanic Americans wrestle for political influence here and the Hispanic majority increases, what Mr. Crespo sees as an advantage, indeed a rich example of multiculturalism, can also be a liability.

Black Cuban Americans find themselves in a bind. As Cubans they belong to an immigrant group that has enjoyed tremendous economic and political success. But as blacks they have experienced the discrimination and hardships of African Americans.

And they remain virtually invisible in the Miami power structure—there are no black Cuban American elected officials, no leaders of a major exile group, and no major academic studies documenting their migration—even though they are more representative of an island where half or more of the population is now estimated to be black and mulatto.

"People think I'm Dominican," said Alexis Barcelay, twenty-five, a black boxer who left Cuba by going to the American naval base on Guantánamo Bay three years ago. "I have to tell them that there are blacks in Cuba, too."

Part of their invisibility is the result of their small numbers. The 1990 census found that fewer than 30,000 of nearly one million Hispanic residents in Dade County, or 3 percent, were black, most of them Cubans, with some Dominicans and Puerto Ricans. Nationwide, black Hispanic residents were also 3 percent of all Hispanic residents, the census showed.

Sociologists here say one reason that whites have overwhelmingly predominated in the exodus from revolutionary Cuba in the last thirty-eight years is that the first waves of immigrants consisted mainly of the white elite who then sponsored relatives into the United States. And many blacks stayed behind longer because they had supported a revolution that provided social gains, opening educational and professional opportunities previously denied them, even if it had not extended equally to leadership positions in government.

But black Cubans say Cuba's government has also hampered their migration through propaganda that paints the United States' society as violently racist and by portraying those who want to leave as not only traitors but ingrates.

Cuba's dismal economic problems have compelled more blacks to leave in recent years, experts on Cuban affairs say, although information on the demographics of the most recent waves of immigrants is scarce. The Immigration and Naturalization Service, for instance, says it keeps no racial breakdown of the estimated 20,000 Cubans allowed to immigrate legally into this country each year.

But even more crucial than numbers in determining influence for black Cubans here has been their inability to fully integrate into either the black or Hispanic worlds, which requires them to overcome cultural and linguistic barriers among blacks and racism among white Hispanic residents.

Studies by a geography professor at the University of Miami, Thomas D. Boswell, show that the median income of black Hispanic residents of Dade County lagged behind that of white Hispanic residents—$8,000 to $11,100—although the disparity was less than that between non-Hispanic whites and blacks. And his analysis of the 1990 census found the largest concentrations of black Hispanic Miamians in neighborhoods like Allapattah, sandwiched between Hispanic Little Havana and black Liberty City.

The predicament afflicts parents like Emmanuel and Luz Mery Angarica, a black Cuban and a white Colombian, who say they are rearing their six-year-old son as "American," with no racial or ethnic labels, after two older sons suffered confusion and harassment from schoolmates over choosing an ethnic identity. "We never said anything but there was pressure from the other children to join their band," Mrs. Angarica, forty-seven, said. "One of them came home from school and told me, 'Mommy, I am red.' Now we're going to be more careful."

The two older brothers chose black because African Americans were in the majority at their school.

Black Cubans like Carlos Moore, fifty-three, are not torn about their ethnic identity. In 1986, when Mr. Moore was a professor at Florida International University, he came under harsh attack on Spanish-language radio and received death threats for focusing on racial issues and portraying revered white Cuban patriots as racists in a course at the university. He said the harassment forced him to leave Miami in 1987.

Mr. Moore, now a professor of international relations at the University of the West Indies in Trinidad, said his experiences here convinced him that those like him should come out "against racism" and ally themselves with other blacks, both Hispanic and African American.

The substantial number of blacks in Cuba are descendants of slaves brought to the island from Africa to work the sugar plantations, and blacks from other Caribbean islands who came after slavery to do the same work.

"I have everything in common with the American black," Mr. Moore said, "the history, slavery, being kicked by whites."

For Rosa Reed, forty-three, a manager for a pharmaceutical company who moved to the United States from Cuba when she was five, a watershed moment came in 1990, when she said she was dismissed from a Cuban American organization when she assumed the role of spokeswoman for one of its programs.

"I was told that when Americans saw a black person they saw crime and poverty and that for the benefit of the organization I couldn't be a spokesperson," Ms. Reed said. "It was so shocking."

Ms. Reed now writes a current affairs column for a black newspaper, the *Miami Times*, is engaged to an African American, and belongs to a group of black Cuban Americans that is holding talks with the National Association for the Advancement of Colored People intended to start a nationwide black Hispanic section. The group is rallying around domestic issues like sensitizing white Hispanic Americans to racial discrimination in employment and other forms of racism suffered by black Hispanic Americans.

But the group of black Cuban Americans says it is also concerned about supporting blacks in Cuba, who they say suffer the island's economic hardships more acutely than whites because fewer can count on relatives here to send them money and basic necessities.

A poll of Cuban Americans in Dade County this year by Florida International University and the *Miami Herald* indeed showed marked differences between black and white Cubans in attitudes toward Cuba, with more blacks favoring a dialogue with the Cuban government to help bring about democracy and opposing continuing the American embargo of Cuba or military action to overthrow President Fidel Castro.

Because Hispanic populations are the product of different racial influences, for instance, racial self-definitions go beyond black and white. A Cuban regarded as black by American standards could be *moro*, *indian*, or *jabao* in Cuba, depending on skin color and hair texture, with the gradations making racial classifications more ambiguous.

Cubans like Manuel Elizondo, thirty-eight, a trainer on the Cuban Olympic boxing team who defected in 1994, said they find racism to be worse in this country.

"In Cuba, racism dictates who is a leader and who is not," Mr. Elizondo said. "Here, because private property is allowed, the racism is determined by money. There are more class differences."

But ethnicity has a stronger pull than race in his new country, which has forced two new identities on him: black (in Cuba he was considered mulatto or Indian) and Hispanic.

"I'm Cuban and I speak Spanish," Mr. Elizondo said. "I am who I am, and I live in my own world."

But those with political aspirations like Mr. Crespo, a Manhattan native, have no such luxury. The sharpest criticism against Mr. Crespo when he sought a City Commission seat vacated by a Hispanic lawyer facing criminal charges, who himself had replaced a black commissioner who is in prison on a bribery conviction, came from black civic and political leaders. The loss of the commission's only black left the panel with four Hispanic members and one white one.

"It worked against him by the fact that he tossed the word Cuban out there," said one of the critics, the Rev. Willie E. Sims Jr., assistant director of the Dade

County office of black affairs. "When things get hot, people go back to those they're comfortable with."

Mr. Crespo, in a response in the *Miami Times* to his critics, insisted on claiming ownership of two cultures.

"What may I ask you authenticates one's blackness?" he wrote in a letter to the editor. "Is it that tired age-old debate of skin color? If so, I'm chocolate brown. Is it if one's ancestors were slaves? If so, my great-grandfather was born a slave. Is it if one's family knows the suffering and humiliation of segregation? If so, my mother was forced off the bus in 1959.

"But really, is not this whole discussion silly?"

Suggestions for Further Reading

Garcia, Maria Cristina. *Havana USA: Cuban Exiles and Cuban Americans in South Florida, 1959–1994.* Berkeley and Los Angeles: University of California Press, 1996.

Masud-Piloto, Felix Roberto. *From Welcomed Exiles to Illegal Immigrants: Cuban Migration to the U.S., 1959–1995.* Lanham, Md.: Rowman & Littlefield, 1996.

Portes, Alejandro, and Alex Stepick. *City on the Edge: The Transformation of Miami.* Berkeley and Los Angeles: University of California Press, 1993.

Zephir, Flore. *Haitian Immigrants in Black America: A Sociological and Sociolinguistic Portrait.* Westport, Conn.: Bergin & Garvey, 1996.

pany, 1967). Copyright © 1967 by Myrlie B. Evers. Reprinted with the permission of Curtis Brown, Ltd.

Marion Stegman, "Recollections of War Jobs" (letters dated 24 April 1943 and 31 May 1943), from *We're in This War Too: World War II Letters from American Women in Uniform*, edited by Judy Barrett Litoff and David C. Smith. Copyright © 1994 by Judy Barrett Litoff and David Clayton Smith. Reprinted with the permission of Oxford University Press, Inc.

Polly Crow, "Recollections of War Jobs" (letters dated 8 June 1944 and 12 June 1944), from *Since You Went Away: World War II Letters from American Women on the Home Front*, edited by Judy Barrett Litoff and David C. Smith. Copyright © 1991 by Judy Barrett Litoff and David C. Smith. Reprinted with the permission of Oxford University Press, Inc.

Ernestine J. Slade, "Recollections of War Jobs" ("A Black Female Employee at Bell Bomber"), from *Cornerstones of Georgia History: Documents That Formed the State*, edited by Thomas A. Scott (Athens: The University of Georgia Press, 1995). Reprinted with the permission of The Oral History Project, Department of History and Philosophy, Kennesaw State College, Marietta, Georgia.

Peggy Terry, "Recollections of War Jobs," interview excerpted from *The Good War: An Oral History of World War II*, by Studs Terkel. Copyright © 1994 by Studs Terkel. Reprinted with the permission of Pantheon Books, a division of Random House, Inc.

Audrey Ward Norman, "Recollections of War Jobs," interview from *A Mouthful of Rivets: Women at Work in World War II*, by Nancy Baker Wise and Christy Wise. Copyright © 1994 by Jossey-Bass, Inc. Reprinted with the permission of the publishers.

John Dos Passos, "Gold Rush Down South," excerpted from *State of the Nation*, by John Dos Passos (Boston: Houghton Mifflin, 1943). Copyright © 1943 by John Dos Passos. Reprinted with the permission of Lucy Dos Passos Coggin and the Estate of Mrs. Elizabeth Dos Passos, c/o Mr. W. Taylor Murphy Jr., Smith, Murphy & Taliaferro, Warsaw, Virginia.

CHAPTER ELEVEN: FRANK PORTER GRAHAM AND
THE ORDEAL OF SOUTHERN LIBERALISM

Fulton Lewis Jr., "Accusation" (radio address, 13 January 1949), and Frank Porter Graham, "Response" (telegram, 13 January 1949), from the Frank Porter Graham Papers, Southern Collection, Wilson Library, University of North Carolina at Chapel Hill, #1819.

CHAPTER TWELVE: MURDER IN MISSISSIPPI

Bob Moses, Hollis Watkins, Tom Hayden, Sandra Cason (Casey Hayden), Peter Orris, and Unita Blackwell, "Interviews," excerpted from *Voices of Freedom: An Oral History of the Civil Rights Movement from the 1950s through the 1980s*, edited by Steve Fayer and Henry Hampton, with Sarah Flynn. Copyright © 1990 by Blackside, Inc. All reprinted with the permission of Bantam Books, a division of the Bantam Doubleday Dell Publishing Group, Inc.

Rita Schwerner, "Letter to Mrs. Anne Braden" (23 January 1964), from the Braden papers. Reprinted with the permission of the State Historical Society of Wisconsin.

A. L. Hopkins, "Reports" ("Investigation of Unknown White Male CORE Worker at Meridian, Mississippi" [23 March 1964] and "Investigation of the disappearance of three civil rights workers after they were released from the Neshoba County Jail on Sunday, June 21, 1964, at 10:30 p.m." [29 June 1964])," from the Johnson Family Papers. Reprinted with the permission of the McCain Library and Archives, The University of Southern Mississippi.

Florence Mars, "From *Witness in Philadelphia*,"excerpted from *Witness in Philadelphia*, by Florence Mars. Copyright © 1977. Reprinted with the permission of Louisiana State University Press.

Dave Dennis, "Be Sick and Tired with Me" ("Eulogy for James Chaney"), from *Eyes on the Prize: America's Civil Rights Years, 1954–1965*, by Juan Williams. Copyright © 1991 by Blackside, Inc. Reprinted with the permission of Viking Penguin, a division of Penguin Putnam, Inc.

CHAPTER THIRTEEN: THE SOUTH DIVIDED

William C. Westmoreland, "Oral History," excerpted from *Landing Zones: Southern Veterans Remember Vietnam*, by James R. Wilson. Copyright © 1990 by Duke University Press. Reprinted with the permission of the publishers.

Martin Luther King Jr., "A Time to Break Silence" (4 April 1967). Copyright © 1967 by Martin Luther King Jr. Reprinted with the permission of the Writers House, Inc., for the Estate of Martin Luther King Jr.

Douglas Anderson, "Oral History," excerpted from *Everything We Had: An Oral History of the Vietnam War by Thirty-three American Soldiers Who Fought It*, by Al Santoli. Copyright © 1981 by Albert Santoli and the Vietnam Veterans of America. Reprinted with the permission of Random House, Inc.

Donald L. Whitfield, "Oral History," excerpted from *Landing Zones: Southern Veterans Remember Vietnam*, by James R. Wilson. Copyright © 1990 by Duke University Press. Reprinted with the permission of the publishers.

Don F. Browne, "Oral History," excerpted from *Bloods: An Oral History of the Vietnam War by Black Veterans*, by Wallace Terry. Copyright © 1984 by Wallace Terry. Reprinted with the permission of Random House, Inc.

Reginald "Malik" Edwards, "Oral History," excerpted from *Bloods: An Oral History of the Vietnam War by Black Veterans*, by Wallace Terry. Copyright © 1984 by Wallace Terry. Reprinted with the permission of Random House, Inc.

Concerned Students for Peace et al., "Letter to the Editor" (of the *Washington [North Carolina] Daily News*) and responses from local citizens (May 1970). All reprinted with the permission of the authors.

CHAPTER FOURTEEN: THE ERA AND THE RISE
OF THE PRO-FAMILY MOVEMENT

Jerry Falwell, "Statements against Ratification" ("Jerry Falwell Condemns the ERA"), excerpted from *Listen America!* by Jerry Falwell. Copyright © 1980 by Jerry Falwell.

CHAPTER FIFTEEN: THE NEW IMMIGRATION
IN SOUTH FLORIDA